THE GRAIL LEGEND

To Tim

On your ordination
2nd July 2016

with best wishes,

Vivienne Tufnell

THE GRAIL LEGEND

by

EMMA JUNG

and

MARIE-LOUISE VON FRANZ

Second Edition

Translated by
ANDREA DYKES

SIGO PRESS
Boston

COVENTURE
London

Published 1986.

SIGO PRESS, 77 North Washington Street, #201
Boston, Massachusetts, 02114

Publisher and General Editor: Sisa Sternback
Associate Editor: Kevin Gaines

COVENTURE LTD., 23 Chesham Street
London, SW1

Library of Congress Catalog Card Number: 86-10797

Originally published in 1960 as *Die Graalslegend in psychologischer Sicht,* Zurich and Stutgart, in the series Studiem aus dem C.G. Jung-Institut Zurich, XII.

Printed in the United States of America.

Contents

Illustrations

Key to sources

1 Bibliothèque Nationale, Paris
2 K. Richstätter, *Die Herz-Jesu-Verehrung des deutschen Mittelalters*, Kösel-Verlag, Regensburg
3 Dr Jacob Hirsch, Adolph Hess AG, Lucerne
4 Hessisches Landesmuseum, Kassel
5 Kropp, *Ausgewählte koptische Zaubertexte*, Edition de la Fondation Egyptologique Reine Elisabeth, Brussels
6 British Museum, London
7 Musaeum Heremeticum, Frankfort
8 Victoria and Albert Museum, London
9 Nationalmuseet, Copenhagen

Foreword

IT WAS NOT the intention of Emma Jung, in this work, to examine the Grail legend from a historical or literary point of view, but to rely, in these respects, on the numerous and distinguished achievements of other scholars. Rather, the material provided by the Grail stories will be considered here from the standpoint of C. G. Jung's depth psychology. Like alchemy and its curious symbolic productions, these poetic fantasy creations and their symbolism are also illustrative of deep-seated, unconscious psychic processes that are still of the greatest significance, for they prepare the way to, and anticipate, the religious problem of modern man. The connections between the Grail legend and alchemy are so abundant and so profound[1] that it may well be asked why Professor Jung did not include them in his researches into the psychology of alchemy. The reason was that Mrs. Jung had been engaged on the Grail legend for thirty years and was planning an extensive publication on the subject. Her labours were cut short by her death in 1955 when, in response to Professor Jung's wish, I undertook to bring her work to a conclusion. In order that the completed work might be as homogeneous as possible, I have continued the interpretation from the point at which it was interrupted, and I have based my work, in the first instance, on the material collected and sifted by Mrs. Jung. For the same reason I have also inserted a few short passages which are intended to serve as

[1] This was already known to R. Palgen, *Der Stein der Weisen: Quellenstudien zum Parzival*. Cf. also J. Evola, *Il Mistero del Graal* and Fanni Bogdanow, *The Romance of the Grail*. Cf. also "Les romans du Graal," in *La Littérature des XII et XIII Siècle*.

transitions to those parts that had already been completed.[2]

A serious problem invariably remains in all such interpretations, however, and that is the question of the completeness of the elucidation. In order to satisfy the scientific prerequisites of an interpretation along the lines of Jungian psychology, and so as to describe these comprehensibly to a wider public which is not familiar with its concepts, it would have been necessary to give extensive information on the history of symbols and of religion, with historical digressions in connection with each symbolic motif, as well as practical psychological examples. Considering the enormous profusion of motifs in the Grail legend—and nearly all of them are of prime importance—this would have produced a work of monstrous proportions, through which even the most industrious of readers would scarcely have been able to thread his way. There remains no other alternative, therefore, but to presume an acquaintance with Jung's work and especially with his book *Aion*, which throws light on basic problems of our Christian aeon. This has kept the individual explanations relatively short, in the hope that in those instances where the evidence could be only briefly indicated, the "solution" might, within the framework of a meaningful context, also prove convincing to the reader.

I wish to take this opportunity to extend my warmest thanks to Miss Andrea Dykes, whose great zeal, devotion and arduous labour have alone produced this speedily completed, yet exact and excellent translation, and also to Fraulein Dr. E. Rüf who most self-sacrificingly relieved me of the labours of work in the public library. I wish, further, to thank Professor Max Wehrli for his constructive criticism and for some literary references.[3]

M.-L. VON F.

[2] Under the circumstances it has not been possible to include all of the newer literature. The authors have limited themselves, on the whole, to psychological interpretations. The literature can be found in the *Bibliographical Bulletin of the International Arthurian Society of Paris*; in A. C. L. Brown, *Bibliography of Critical Arthurian Literature*; and in the *Modern Language Quarterly*.

[3] Prof. Wehrli has himself written a paper along the lines of a psychological interpretation of Wolfram's *Parzival*, to which frequent reference will be made.

CHAPTER I

Introduction

THE GRAIL LEGEND is an especially stimulating subject for psychological consideration because it contains so many features that are also to be found in myths and fairy-tales. Moreover, it has lost far less of its fascination for contemporary men and women than have the latter, which may indicate that it still embodies a living myth.

The story is known to everyone, at least in its general outlines. A mysterious, life-preserving and sustenance-dispensing object or vessel is guarded by a King in a castle that is difficult to find. The King is either lame or sick and the surrounding country is devastated. The King can only be restored to health if a knight of conspicuous excellence finds the castle and at the first sight of what he sees there asks a certain question. Should he neglect to put this question, then everything will remain as before, the castle will vanish and the knight will have to set out once more upon the search. Should he finally succeed, after much wandering and many adventures, in finding the Grail Castle again, and should he then ask the question, the King will be restored to health, the land will begin to grow green, and the hero will become the guardian of the Grail from that time on.

So runs the story in its barest outline. It is one of those fairy-tales of which there are many, in which the search for a "treasure hard to attain" and deliverance from a magic spell form the principal themes. What is of special interest about the Grail story, however, is that the fairy-tale is interwoven with a Christian legend, and the treasure that must be sought for is thought to be the vessel in which Joseph of Arimathea received the blood of Christ at the Descent from the Cross. This remarkable blend of fairy-tale and legend gives the Grail stories their peculiar character, for through these stories the "eternal" fairy-tale enters, as it were, the realm of the temporal drama of the Christian aeon and thus reflects not only fundamental human problems but also the dramatic psychic events which form the background of our Christian culture. The present presentation of these happenings will be based on C. G. Jung's *Aion*, to which repeated reference will be made.

We are indebted to the poet of northern France, Chrétien de Troyes, for one of the oldest literary compilations known to us today,[1] which he may have begun about 1180. He says in the introduction that he is trying

> To put into rhyme (at the Count's command)
> The best of tales
> That are told in royal court:
> This is the story of the Grail.[2]

The "best of tales" that are told at the courts of kings must therefore be the Grail legend, and Chrétien has, as he says, rendered it into verse from a book which his patron, Count Philip of Flanders, has loaned him for the purpose. It is certainly true that even if other stories from the same cycle, such as those of Lancelot, Tristan, Erec and Yvain, and others enjoyed an equal popularity in those days, yet none of them stirs the feelings as deeply and as lastingly or has been so much elaborated as the story of the Grail.

As if a subterranean watercourse had been tapped at the end of the twelfth and the beginning of the thirteenth centuries, a great number of different adaptations of the same material was produced in quick succession, not only in French but in

[1] Some scholars, for instance B. A. Birch-Hirschfeld, *Die Sage vom Graal*, and more recently Bodo Mergell, *Der Gral in Wolframs Parsifal*, p. 118, consider that Robert de Boron's trilogy, "Josef d'Arimathie," "Merlin," "Perceval," is somewhat older than Chrétien's poem, but this is not proved with any certainty. The oldest of the manuscripts preserved is one of Chrétien's *Contes del Graal* from the early thirteenth century. Cf. J. D. Bruce, *The Evolution of Arthurian Romance*.

[2] Quoted from *Der Percevalroman*, a 1936 German translation of Chrétien's *Li Contes del Graal*, verses 65*ff*.

German, English, Welsh, Spanish and the northern languages. Many of these are certainly based on Chrétien, although they deviate from him in numerous, often important, features, thereby implying other sources. None of the stories strike us as being new or essentially original productions; they all convey the impression that a more or less well-known narrative is being retold and elaborated, as if they expressly referred to a theme that was already very familiar.

After the first two decades of the thirteenth century, scarcely any new versions of note were produced,[3] but rather a mass of transcripts, translations and, at a later date, printings[4] which prove that the story did not cease to exercise its magic, spellbinding influence down through the centuries.

Owing to the fundamentally new and different orientation which the Renaissance brought, the old stories fell more and more into oblivion, but they were again brought to light in the second half of the eighteenth century. It was a native of Zurich, J. J. Bodmer, who was the first to rediscover Wolfram von Eschenbach's *Parzival* and to publish it in translation under the title, *Parzival, a poem after the style of thought of Wolfram von Eschenbach, a poet of the time of the Emperor Henry VI, Zurich, Anno Domini 1753*. It was another Zuricher, Heinrich Myller, a grammar school teacher in Berlin, who, at the suggestion of Bodmer and with his assistance, published the *Parzival* together with the *Nibelungenlied* and other Middle High German poems in 1784. He appears, however, to have met with no special appreciation, as is indicated by a letter of Frederick the Great to whom a copy of the book was presented. This letter is preserved in the Zurich Central Library.[5] Dated

[3] Except perhaps for Albrecht von Scharfenberg's *Titurel*. Cf. R. Nelli, *Lumière du Graal*, p. 231.

[4] A French prose edition of 1530 may be specially mentioned, as well as Sir Thomas Malory's *Le Morte d'Arthur* which, among numerous stories from the Arthurian cycle, contains one about the Grail. In England the popularity of these stories is maintained to this day. A new edition in three volumes, edited by Eugene Vinaver, was published in 1947.

[5] E. Wechssler, *Die Sage vom heiligen Gral*, p. 85. Dr. Forrer, Director of the Zurich Library, provided the information concerning this letter which is available in the Library under Catalogue No. RP8.

February 22, 1784, it is addressed to the publisher and reads as follows:

> Very Learned, Esteemed, Faithful,
>
> You judge far too favourably of those poems of the 12th, 13th and 14th centuries, the printing of which you have promoted. . . . In my opinion they are not worth one shot of powder and do not merit being hauled out of the dust of oblivion. At any rate I would not tolerate such wretched rubbish in my collection of books but would fling it out. The copy sent to me may accordingly await its fate in the large library. Such things do not, however, give promise of many inquiries.
>
> Your otherwise, Gracious Sovereign,
>
> Frch.

In spite of this royal lack of understanding the old poems did not fall into oblivion a second time, since a fresh interest in folk- and fairy-tales developed in the following Age of the Romantics. (We are reminded of the fairy-tale collection of the Brothers Grimm.) New critical editions appeared and later, as was to be expected in the scientifically oriented nineteenth and twentieth centuries, a vast amount of historical criticism on the subject was produced. Finally, in the nineteenth century, there was an artistic reshaping of the material. Wagner's *Parsifal* is an extremely gifted revival of the Grail legend, of a pronouncedly psychological character. That Wagner was able to express in this guise the problems of the nineteenth century, whether transiently nationalistic or personally conditioned, is proof of the genuinely symbolic nature of the legend, which is so real that even after Wagner's time research into the subject has not lost its fascination.

It is not only art and science which have concerned themselves with the Grail legend but also certain spiritual movements of our time, such as the secret orders, anthroposophy and other fellowships of a similar nature, which take the Grail and the Grail quest as subjects of meditation or of initiation ceremonies.[6] From its place of concealment the Grail still calls seekers to the quest and knights still set out upon the way to the castle that is difficult to find, where the treasure is preserved.

Naturally the Grail Castle cannot be localized in reality, and this is certainly in accord with its essential nature and therefore in no way remarkable. The origin of the legend, however, has also remained untraceable until now. Of the various theories concerning its beginnings, only a few of the most important will be mentioned here. According to one, the story can be traced back to pre-Christian, western European and especially to Celtic legends or myths.[7] Other authorities derive it from Eastern Christian sources[8] or else from Persian or pre-Christian cult practices,[9] while a third view is that it originated in

[6] W. J. Stein, a follower of Rudolf Steiner, asserts in his book, *Weltgeschichte im Lichte des Heiligen Graal*, that in the eighth and ninth centuries "Grail experiences suddenly came to the fore" in Charlemagne's entourage, which then continued as esoteric mystery teachings concurrently with the teachings of the Church until they were made generally known about 1180 (at the time of the Grail poems). His assertions, however, are not sufficiently precise and not always convincingly proved, since they are based in part on nothing beyond Steiner's own intuitive conjectures. In *The Holy Grail; Its Legends and Symbolism* A. E. Waite offers a comprehensive survey of the entire field, as well as a critical assessment of the various interpretations. For him, too, the Grail is a mystery, and the search for it, known as the Quest, is a way of initiation, as it was probably imagined in the mystery teachings of all ages. His views, though somewhat coloured by the "occult," are certainly the nearest to a psychological interpretation.

[7] To name only a few representatives of the various schools of thought, cf. A. T. Nutt, *Studies on the Legend of the Holy Grail*, and *The Legends of the Holy Grail* by the same author; Dorothy Kempe, *The Legend of the Holy Grail*; A. C. L. Brown, *The Origin of the Grail Legend*; J. Pokorny, *Der Graal in Irland und die mythischen Grundlagen der Graalsage*, pp. 340*ff*; Roger Sherman Loomis, *Arthurian Tradition and Chrétien de Troyes*, *Arthurian Literature in the Middle Ages* and *The Grail in the Perceval Saga*; and St. Hofer, *Chrétien von Troyes Leben und Werk*.

[8] L. E. Iselin, *Der morgenländische Ursprung der Graalslegende*; W. Staerk, *Über den Ursprung der Graalslegende*; A. von Wesselofsky, "Zur Frage über die Heimat der Legende vom heiligen Graal," E. Faral in Beolies-Hazard, *Littérature française*; and Urban T. Holmes and Amelia Klenke, *Chrétien, Troyes, and the Grail*, p. 171.

[9] Jessie L. Weston, *From Ritual to Romance*; W. A. Nitze, "The Fisher King in the Grail Romances."

Christian ritual,[10] especially in that of the Byzantine Mass.[11]

In *From Ritual to Romance*,[12] a book based on Frazer's researches[13] (which appeared in 1920), Jessie L. Weston, an outstanding authority on the Arthurian romances, considers the Grail legend as a Christianized, no longer understood, relic of an old Near Eastern Phoenician or Syrian vegetation ritual. That the legend originates, at least in part, in the East is indisputable and may be discerned from the texts themselves. L. E. Iselin provides ample evidence for this in his excellent article, "Der morgenländische Ursprung der Grallegende" ("The Oriental Origin of the Grail Legend"). His theory was to a great extent taken up again by L. J. Ringbom in *Graltempel und Paradies*. Ringbom attempts to establish the core of the legend as stemming from a Persian tradition and he has also compiled some very interesting material concerning the mandala form of the Grail temple.[14] According to him the followers of Genghis Khan in Iran were the transmitters of many of the motifs appearing in the Grail legend.[15] F. von Suhtschek had already prepared the ground along those lines.[16] Side by side

[10] Cf. Holmes and Klenke, *op. cit.*; Amelia Klenke, "Liturgy and Allegory in Chrétien's Perceval." Cf. also D. de Séchelles, *L'Origine du Gral*, p. 51. Against these theses, cf. Jean Marx, *Medium Aevum*, XXIII, p. 132.

[11] K. Burdach, "Der Graal", pp. 450–52; E. Anitchkof, "Le Graal et les Rites Eucharistiques," and Mario Roques, *Le Graal de Chrétien et la Demoiselle du Graal*. J. D. Bruce gives an outstanding and comprehensive description of the whole field in *The Evolution of Arthurian Romance*.

[12] See also J. L. Weston, *The Quest of the Holy Grail*.

[13] Sir James Frazer, *The Golden Bough*, especially "The Dying God" and "Adonis, Attis, Osiris". Similarly, Flavia Anderson, *The Ancient Secret*.

[14] Published in Stockholm in 1951.

[15] L. von Schroeder, "Die Wurzeln der Sage vom heiligen Graal," pp. 8*ff*, locates the first home of the Grail in India and cites parallels and examples from the Vedas where the sun and moon are spoken of as miraculous vessels on the inaccessible mountains of Heaven. There they may be approached only by gods, demi-gods and the blessed dead, and von Schroeder compares the Grail with these wonder vessels.

[16] "Die iranischen Quellen in Wolframs Parsifal." Also "Herrn W. von Eschenbachs Reimbereitung oder Pârsîwalnâma," in which the author tries to trace Wolfram's *Parzival* back to an Iranian national epic, *Barzû-Namê*, and equates Monsalvatsch, for instance, with *sal-wadsche*, a famous Parsee holy place. The legend of Anfortas was supposed to have taken place in Bundeheš. Cf. his "Wolfram von Eschenbachs Pârsîwalnâma-Übersetzung,"

with its Oriental origins, an undoubtedly Celtic influence can also be discerned; according to most of the texts the Grail Castle is to be sought for in Britain where King Arthur and his knights, among whom Perceval is numbered, are thought to live and whither, according to some versions, the Grail was supposed to have been brought by Joseph of Arimathea or his descendants. Glastonbury is said to be the spot where he landed and, although this is pure legend, the place is still today linked in many ways with the story of the Grail.

According to a view very widely held in those countries, the Grail Castle is situated in France or Spain.[17] This idea has its source in Wolfram's poems *Parzival* and *Titurel*, as well as in the work known as the *Jüngere Titurel* (*The Younger Titurel*) by Albrecht von Scharfenberg. The latter first appeared in the second half of the thirteenth century and, following Wolfram's poem, includes an introductory story according to which the family of the Grail King had come to Spain from the Orient and introduced Christianity there and in the south of France. Wolfram says that his authority, Kyot, found the story, written in a heathen script, in Toledo and that through the study of various chronicles he had come to the conclusion that the House of Anjou should be regarded as the guardian of the Grail.[18] The remaining versions, nearly all of which are older than Wolfram's, do not anywhere give occasion for this view, which has none the less maintained itself very tenaciously. O. Rahn's book *Kreuzzug gegen den Graal*, for example, which appeared in 1933,[19] attempts to prove that the Grail was a relic or cult object of the Albigenses, the sect of the Catharists which, on the grounds of heresy, was persecuted and exterminated in

p. 139. Prof. Emil Abegg is of the opinion that Gahmuret, the name of Perceval's father, could possibly be related to the Persian Gayomard, whereas the previous assertions of F. von Suhtschek are not proved unequivocally. Cf. also, A. U. Pope, "Persia and the Holy Grail," pp. 57*ff*.

[17] Montserrat (Monsalvat) in the Pyrenees has only subsequently been identified with Mon Salvàsche (Mont Sauvage).

[18] An effort has been made to identify Wolfram's Anschouwe with Antschau, a place in Styria, with which Wolfram had certain connections, though this hardly seems likely.

[19] In Fribourg.

the south of France in the thirteenth century.[20] He believes that contents of a Catharistic nature which, on account of the risk of detection, were clothed in poetical and romantic language are concealed behind the texts of the Grail poems, and he even appears to believe that the Grail itself, the cult object, is still lying hidden in some Pyrenean cave. This view is shared by a group of French people living in that neighbourhood and is set forth in a book, *Le Graal pyrénéen*. The Grail stories do in fact contain very unorthodox features, and the fellowship of the Grail knights—Templeise, as Wolfram calls them—might perhaps be compared to the followers of the Albigensian sect, as they were equally thought to be connected with the Templars. In spite of all the controversies associated with the subject, the possibility that the Templars were spiritually influenced by certain movements in Islam, especially esoteric Gnostic ones, cannot be dismissed out of hand. In his stimulating book *L'Islam et le Graal*,[21] P. Ponsoye has investigated these influences, but the extent of the influence of Islamic mysticism which he asserts seems questionable. The problem is further complicated, when viewed from the psychological angle, because a parallelism of symbols can be engendered by certain archetypal unconscious psychic conditions (instead of a historical-causal connection) and thus also comes into consideration as an explanation.

Attention may here be drawn to a stimulating, profound and wide-ranging study of Grail symbolism by Helen Adolf.[22] The writer seeks, in the first place, to establish a relation between the symbolism of the Grail and the historical events of the time of the Crusades. Connections of that nature could indeed have played some part in the ideas of the poets, but they do not seem as important as Mrs. Adolf assumes. On the other hand, in the second part of her book the author enlarges on the archetypal element in the Grail events and in modern literature, in a

[20] The crusade against the Albigenses lasted from 1207 to 1229. Among others, cf. B. Luc, "Le Graal pyrénéen".

[21] Paris, 1957.

[22] *Visio Pacis, Holy City and Grail.*

highly stimulating manner which in many respects approaches our psychological interpretation. Mrs. Adolf presumes a close connection between Wolfram's poem and the Templars that does seem significant, since the subsidiary influence of the various movements of the age certainly played a part, although it is probably incorrect to look for the *whole* elucidation of the Grail symbolism in any one of them.

In his important book *Ideal und Wirklichkeit in der höfischen Epik*,[23] Erich Köhler has thrown a penetrating light on the conscious conflicts and problems of that age and especially on that of the knight's personal attitude to Eros. His statements could serve the reader as a description of the collective conscious ideals that evoked the compensatory production of symbols by the unconscious, which is the focal point of our exposition.

In an interesting work on Joachim of Floris[24] E. Anitchkof tries to establish connections between the views expressed in individual versions of the Grail poems and the doctrines of Joachim and those of the Neo-Manicheans or Catharists, widely distributed throughout France in the twelfth century. A kindred idea is evoked by J. Evola;[25] indeed, he goes even further when he points out similarities between the ideas advanced in the Grail poems and those of the Fedeli d'Amore and Hermetic tradition.[26] Further comment on these con-

[23] See also *Trobador Lyrik und Höfischer Roman* by the same author.

[24] *Joachim de Flore et les Milieux courtois.*

[25] *Il mistero del Graal.* Cf. also Harry F. Wilson, "Apocryphal Gospels and the Arthurian Romance," p. 124. P. Wapnewski, *Wolframs Parzival*, defends Wolfram's orthodoxy.

[26] The fact that the Grail was considered to be a real object engendered the very widely held belief that it was identical with the vessel known as the *Sacro Catino*, a bowl, ostensibly of emerald, brought back as plunder and payment by the Genoese after the siege of Caesarea in 1101. A sixteenth-century Genoese chronicle in the Library at Berne says that this exceedingly precious bowl was called the Saint Graal and that according to some it was a platter Christ had used at the Last Supper with his disciples, but that others held that it was the vessel from which King Arthur ate, very devoutly (*religieusement*), at important ceremonies with the Companions of the Round Table. Napoleon took it to Paris, where under expert examination it was found not to be emerald at all but simply moulded glass. Cf. J. R. von Sinner, "Catalogus Codicum MSS. Bibliothecae Bernensis."

nections will be made in due course, for it might well be more a question of a psychological than of a historical relation. As Jung has explained in *Aion*, Christian symbolism not only emerged from a psychic problem of opposites but this problem also characterizes its further development, as is already implied in Christ's reference to the coming of an "Antichrist". This problem of the opposites is emphasized by the synchronistic fact that the Christian aeon is distinguished astrologically by two fishes in opposition to each other. Corresponding to this coincidence, numerous spiritual movements of historic importance, which in part run contrary to the Christian outlook and could be subsumed under the idea of an apparently heathen regression, began to come to the surface in the age of the second fish of this sign. To these movements belong certain rituals of the Templars, the sexual libertinism of some of the neo-Manichean sects and the adoption of meditation exercises and magical practices from the culture of Islam. On the other hand, there were also movements, such as alchemy or certain Holy Ghost movements within the Church, which were endeavouring rather to *reconcile* the problem of the opposites of Christ and Antichrist. To these also belong much that is in the Grail poems, for which reason the latter in part appear to reactivate heathen elements to some extent, though, as we shall hope to prove, they equally appear to be striving towards a further development of the Christian symbol.[27] The extent to which the historical connections with the Templars, with Persia, with Islam and with Celtic-Germanic heathendom and pagan antiquity play a part has already been noted by many. For the most part, however, these connections have been exalted into a single, exaggerated causal principle of explanation of the Grail legend, whereas it is actually more a question of a psychologically based parallelism which does also lead to various contemporary references to, and borrowings from, the above-mentioned spiritual and intellectual manifestations. In

[27] Cf. also Holmes and Klenke, *op. cit.*, pp. 165–67. In *Ideal und Wirklichkeit* Erich Köhler also tries to prove that Chrétien is concerned with spiritual problems.

other words the Grail poems probably had their origin in a twofold psychic need, on the one hand to elaborate further the central symbol of the Christian religion and on the other to develop in a creative way certain still unsolved problems, such as those of sexuality, the shadow and the unconscious in general. It is with reason, therefore, that Max Wehrli[28] emphasizes that the symbolism of the Grail stories probably stems from the most divergent sources: from the Christian doctrine of redemption and from fairy-tales; from the symbols of worldly and spiritual ceremonial; from alchemy, dreams and legends; and from ancient Celtic and Oriental sources.[29]

Before we turn to a psychological consideration of the legend, however, let us look more closely at the ground from which it grew. The story of the Grail belongs to the series known as the *Contes bretons* and especially to the *Romans de la Table ronde*, that cycle of stories which is centred round the semi-historical, semi-legendary figure of King Arthur of Britain and which recounts the deeds of his knights. Arthur's Round Table is described in these tales as a kind of school of knightly training.[30]

Through the centuries these stories have served as an embodiment of the code of knightly virtue and conduct. Of course, the deportment depicted therein represents, and even then represented an unattainable ideal, as may easily be seen by comparing it with the actual circumstances and events of the age. It is a standard of perfection at which we might smile, as

[28] "Wolfram v. Eschenbach: Erzählstil und Sinn seines 'Parzival,'" pp. 17*ff.* Wehrli says: "Besides concerning themselves with the science of symbols in depth psychology, without being competent to do so, the literary historians also venture to make use of its fundamental trends. This occurs all the more since the possibility undoubtedly exists that a powerful admixture of an alchemistic knowledge of the soul is concealed in the mythology of the Grail. Thus, since the speculations of alchemy do not offer any chemico-technical methods but rather a knowledge of the soul projected on to external matter and objectified in 'chemistry,' so too the symbolism of the Grail may be related to the psychic processes of the hero (as an explanation, for example, of the fact that the Grail Kingdom became stricken in the person of Anfortas and would itself be redeemed only through Parzival's own redemption)."

[29] *Ibid.*, p. 31.

[30] CF. *Der Percevalroman* (*Li contes del Graal*), verses 1634*f.*

we would at something childishly naïve; but our own time, which fancies itself as being exalted so far above the so-called Dark Ages, could nevertheless learn much of value from it.

Our stories belong to what is known as the *Matière de Bretagne*, probably so named because they were circulated by Breton and British (Welsh) and Anglo-Norman singers and storytellers who, at the courts of France and England, recited the living legends and fairy tales of their homelands. The stories stemmed partly from Celtic origins but also from sources in the East and in antiquity.[31] This literature became the fashion in the twelfth century, enjoying great popularity on account of its new and curious character. E. Faral, an outstanding authority in this field, has described this character as follows:

> Without disdaining either sublimity or grace, the Arthurian romances produce a sense of wonderment through a feeling of strangeness; this is their style. They break of set purpose with reality, they carry the reader off into a world of the supernatural where human destiny is liberated from the laws of this world. Strange characters, adventures which get tangled and disentangled in a fog of mystery, obscure magical powers which electrify or else paralyse the will, this is the spectacle usually offered by these stories, a scene where things take on an enigmatic quality and where the magic of the setting adds to the intoxication of the psychological love-philtre.[32]

We see therefore that these are stories of a different type from those in the *Chansons de Geste*, stories known as the *Matière de France* which grew up around Charlemagne and his circle and in which more real or at least more possible deeds and happenings were sung. That this new genre should have become the fashion at this particular time is explained on various grounds; above all, the contact with the East, brought about by the Crusades, had caused a tremendous activation of the world of fantasy.

[31] Cf. E. Faral, *Recherches sur les sources latines des Contes et Romans Courtois du moyen-âge.*

[32] *La Légende Arthurienne*, Preface, pp. i–ii.

Since the Conquest of England (1066) the English throne had been occupied by the Dukes of Normandy. Henry II of England had married the celebrated Eleanor of Aquitaine who had previously been the wife of Louis VII of France.[33] (One of the Grail stories is dedicated to Henry II and in his reign the reputed grave of King Arthur and his spouse was discovered at Glastonbury. Also, according to Wolfram, Perceval was descended from the House of Anjou.) Out of these close ties between England and France, which began with the conquest of England by William of Normandy, arose a new culture and a new style, the Anglo-Norman, which found expression in the *Contes bretons*.

This, however, was not the only reason for the new fashion. A further and more important one of a more psychological nature may be sought in another phenomenon of the age, that is, in the service of woman, then at the peak of its development. Eleanor of Aquitaine and her daughter, Marie de Champagne, are said to have presided at one of those Courts of Love which instituted a code of behaviour in affairs of love, much as did Arthur's Round Table in matters of knightly virtue.

Although it is to be doubted that the Courts of Love were serious institutions[34] and that the rules laid down in writing by one Andreas Cappellanus,[35] in the service of Marie de Champagne, were very strictly adhered to, it is none the less an established fact that woman in that age exercised an extraordinarily powerful influence on manners and culture and that the formation and validity of the courtly ideal is to be attributed largely to this influence.[36] It is obvious that where woman plays such a considerable role, this must also find expression in the literature of the age.[37] For the poets of that time, especially, woman means much more than simply a

[33] A granddaughter of Guillaume IX de Poitou, the first troubadour.

[34] Cf. J. D. Bruce, second edition, pp. 105–7.

[35] *De amore libri tres*. English version by J. Parry, *The Art of Courtly Love.*

[36] Cf. R. Bezzola, *Les origines et la fonction de la littérature courtoise en Occident.*

[37] It is known that Chrétien obtained the material for his *Roman de la Charrette* from Marie de Champagne.

patroness, listener or reader; through her the poet is inspired, to her he turns, by her he desires to be admired and loved, and it is his wish to understand her.[38] This had its most perfect form in the *Minne* poetry, then in its golden age, which had as its subject matter the emotions, the sorrows and joys of the lover, and love itself, whether as a simple human emotion or as a mystical experience.

The *Contes bretons* have another form, although they too contain an element with which woman is particularly intimate and which suits her well. This is the sphere of the irrational, the world of fantasy. This material therefore appeals quite particularly to women and is favoured by them. It is not a matter of chance that it was a woman, Marie de France,[39] who first took down, or herself wrote, a series of stories ("*des contes dont les Bretons firent leur lais,*" as she herself said) which are preserved under the title of *Les lais de Marie de France.*[40] Whether the content of the lays is actually of Breton origin in every case cannot always be proved. But they do indisputably exhibit that quality which Faral describes in the quotation cited above, the "charm of faerie," "the charm of wild and delicate fancy," as J. D. Bruce puts it, which exactly characterizes the work known as the *Matière de Bretagne.*

The predominance of the irrational, or the taste for it, distinguishes the feminine as well as the Celtic mentality, to which not only fairy stories, legends and myths bear witness but also ideas, traditions and customs which have survived in part

[38] In a very interesting study, "Guillaume IX et les Origines de l'amour courtois," R. Bezzola describes the remarkable phenomenon of woman, almost without warning, suddenly appearing in quite a new light to the poets—as their sovereign lady. This was the beginning of the attitude known as the Service of Woman and the Service of Love (the *Minnedienst*).

[39] Nothing is known of Marie de France but her name and her writings and that she probably lived in England in the twelfth century. According to J. D. Bruce, *op. cit.*, p. 104, the King to whom she dedicated her poems was probably Henry II of England. In "Marie de France," pp. 103*ff*, J. C. Fox has identified her as a half-sister of Henry II, who was Abbess of Shaftsbury in 1181 and was still living in 1215. For further details see Holmes and Klenke, *Chrétien, Troyes, and the Grail*, pp. 17–59.

[40] There are editions edited by M. Warnke and Jeanne Lods.

into the present day.[41] An extremely prominent feature of the Celtic world of fantasy is the belief in a Beyond which is not so much a dwelling place of the departed as a "land of the living," as it is also called, a kind of Elysium inhabited by immortals.[42] It was a land without sickness or death, where men with god-like natures lived in everlasting youth, enjoying delicious food and drink and listening to sweet music, to which, however, since it had been lost to mankind, only a few of the elect could find the way. The heroes of the Breton stories were also numbered among these elect. Without expecting to, they crossed over into that land and back again "on lightly built bridges", in the words of Hölderlin. It is precisely this traffic to and fro between this world and that which constitutes the quite peculiar magic of the stories.

British national traditions and tribal history, into which the fairy-tale motifs are interwoven like an iridescent thread, provide a further source for the *Contes bretons*. The tales are set against the historico-legendary background of King Arthur's Court. The first mention of Arthur in literature is in a *Historia Britonum*, attributed to one Nennius, which very likely appeared towards the end of the ninth century.[43] In this work Arthur is referred to not as king but as *dux bellorum*, commander-in-chief, who, as leader of the Britons, vanquished the invading Saxons in twelve battles, the last of which took place in A.D. 516.[44] The battles with the Saxons, who invaded Britain in the fifth and sixth centuries and drove the indigenous inhabitants further and further west into mountainous and inaccessible Wales and even as far as Brittany, together with a geographical description and a few legends and genealogies, comprise the main content of the *Historia*.

[41] Cf. John Rhys, *The Arthurian Legend*.

[42] J. A. McCulloch, *The Religion of the Ancient Celts*, pp. 362 *ff*.

[43] Cf. E. Windisch, "Das keltische Britannien bis zu König Arthur." According to other authorities this history is thought to have been written as early as 796. Cf. Rhys, *Sir Thomas Malory's "Le morte d'Arthur,"* Vol. 1, p. xi; and Loomis, *Arthurian Literature in the Middle Ages*, pp. 1*ff*; and Richard L. Breugle, *King Arthur of Britain*.

[44] Cf. Marx, *La Légende Arthurienne et le Graal*.

In the first half of the twelfth century, around 1135, a cleric, Geoffrey of Monmouth, wrote a history of the British kings of Britain, the *Historia regum Britanniae*,[45] in the course of which he delved into the older, anonymous *Historia* of Nennius besides making use of other, oral traditions and, indeed, allowing his own fantasy considerable rein as well. He states that he took his material from a book which Walter of Oxford brought over from Brittany and which he, Geoffrey, translated.[46] This history won great approval and shortly after its appearance was translated into French by a Norman called Wace and published by him under the title of *Brut*. (According to Geoffrey, a descendant of the Royal House of Troy, by name of Brutus, was said to have been the ancestor of the Britons, who derived their name from him.)[47] The translators Wace and Layamon, who rendered *Brut* into Anglo-Norman, added all sorts of features not included by Geoffrey. Wace, for instance, mentions Arthur's Round Table for the first time ("*la table dont les Bretons disent maintes fables*"), which was round so that no disputes as to precedence should arise among those privileged to sit at it. Stories about Arthur must therefore already have been popular at that time, even though the historical accounts of him are extremely meagre. As conqueror of the foreign invaders and saviour of Britain he became a national hero and attained an almost mythical importance. This is expressed by the belief, among others, that he did not perish in his last battle but was thought to be spending his time on the fairy Isle of Avalon,[48] from whence at some future date he would return to take up his leadership once again. His battles actually brought no lasting success, for not long afterwards the Saxons were able to establish themselves permanently in Britain. This, however, in no way diminished Arthur's fame as a hero; on the contrary, it may have helped to raise his image to the level of the mythical and

[45] Ed. Jacob Hammer or Acton Griscom.

[46] Cf. Loomis, *Arthurian Literature*, p. 72.

[47] For philological details see R. A. Caldwell, *Wace's Roman de Brut*, and the variant version of Geoffrey of Monmouth's *Historia regum Britanniae* in *Speculum*, 1956, p. 675*sq*.

[48] Cf. Holmes and Klenke, *op. cit.*, pp. 32*ff*.

the mystical.[49] According to Bruce[50] and other scholars, it has not been proved that stories of Arthur were circulating in Britain before Geoffrey of Monmouth's time or that a tradition connected with him existed, more particularly in Wales. It is considered far more likely that these stories originated in Armorica (Brittany).

The symbolism of the Arthurian myth has been amplified and interpreted in an excellent psychological essay by R. F. Hobson,[51] who concentrates for the most part on the returning motif.

There is no mention of a grail in Geoffrey's pseudo-historical account, however, although it must have greatly excited the fantasy of the poets, for only a few years after its appearance a whole body of literature was produced that, inspired by his chronicles, singled out characters and events and then transformed and elaborated them into the British stories, to the general benefit of the educated world of the time.

In each of these elements—the propensity for the irrational, the prominence of the feminine element, the assimilation of the Oriental fantasy material and, most clearly of all, in the ever more prevalent symbolism of a magical Beyond and land of the dead—there is a psychological expression of an extraordinary stirring of the unconscious, such as does happen from time to time, especially in periods when the religious values of a culture are beginning to change.

In spite of the stress laid on these collective psychological foundations, the achievement of the creative personalities who knew how to draw the hidden treasures of the psychic tendencies lying below the threshold up into the light of day should not be

[49] Cf. McCulloch, *op. cit.*, pp. 24, 120. Some scholars are of the opinion that Arthur was raised to the status of a national hero and honoured as such, especially by those Britons who were living as exiles in Brittany. Others like to trace him back to an ancient Gallic god. Cf. Rhys, *Arthurian Legend*, p. 31. According to Bruce, *op. cit.*, pp. 4*f*, and others the name stems from Arturius, the designation of a Roman *gens*. Cf. also Marx, *Le Légende Arthurienne*, pp. 48*ff*, and pp. 63*ff*; also Loomis, *Arthurian Literature*, p. 2.

[50] *Op. cit.*, pp. 72–74.

[51] "The King Who Will Return."

minimized, since in so doing they invested them with a symbolic form. To Chrétien de Troyes belongs the special merit of having been the first to work this material—*Erec*, *Yvain*, *Le Chevalier au Lion*, *Le Roman de la Charrette*, etc.—into individual literary compositions. To these stories may be ascribed the fact that the Breton heroes achieved popularity and esteem, as well as becoming known, important or beloved personalities with whose characters and fate everyone was conversant. (In German literature this could be compared roughly to *Faust*.) *Li Contes del Graal*, Chrétien's last work, remains incomplete; it breaks off at verse 9,034,[52] owing to his death, according to the statement of one of his continuators.[53] Other poets carried on his work and in round numbers completed sixty thousand verses in approximately thirty years. The first was an anonymous writer known as Pseudo-Wauchier or Pseudo-Gautier, followed by Wauchier de Denain who wrote between 1190 and 1212, and finally by Gerbert and Manessier. Each of the three Continuations is longer than Chrétien's original, but they form a long succession of adventures rather than a completed whole.[54]

It might well be objected that it was an infringement of Chrétien's rights for other poets to continue and complete his

[52] It closes in the middle of the account of the arrival of Gauvain's messenger at Orcanie, inviting Arthur to be present at the duel with Guiromelanz at Roche des Champguins (Bearoche).

[53] For the date see Rita Lejeune, "La date du Graal de Chrétien de Troyes," p. 51*sq*.

[54] Chrétien's first anonymous continuator, known as Pseudo-Wauchier, takes up the thread where it breaks off in Chrétien, at the impending contest between Gauvain and Guiromelanz. This Continuation is made up of Gauvain's further adventures. The writer of the second Continuation, a certain Wauchier de Denain (between 1190 and 1212), turns back to Perceval again and recounts his further deeds but without bringing the story to a definite conclusion. Manessier, who wrote the third Continuation about 1230, finally brought the story to a close but changed it radically, for he quoted freely from the prose versions that appeared in the first quarter of the thirteenth century. In most of the MSS. the Continuations join directly on to Chrétien's *Perceval*, but in two of them another Continuation is interpolated into the works of Wauchier de Denain and Manessier. Compare details in *The Continuations of the Old French Perceval of Chrétien de Troyes*, ed. W. Roach. Cf. also Loomis, *Arthurian Literature*, pp. 214*ff*.

unfinished work. But since the "Grail" and the "Grail quest" are ideas of such an archetypal and, consequently, universally human nature, it is interesting to see precisely how the fantasy of the different authors reacted to the same material, as if to a problem that was clearly felt to be peculiarly important just then, even if from a literary point of view the poem appears to have suffered in the process. Thanks to this "united effort", different aspects of the material are illuminated and a more profound and comprehensive understanding is made possible than if the poem had remained the work of a single author.

Chrétien's poem, also called the *Romanz de Perceval* in many manuscripts,[55] has a fairy-tale quality, and at its centre is the hero Perceval and his quest for the Grail. Almost contemporaneously with Chrétien's *Contes del Graal* (according to Bruce, between 1180 and 1199), another version of the story appeared in metrical form, the *Roman de l'Estoire dou Graal* by Robert de Boron, which had more of the nature of a Christian legend. The first part of Robert's version, "Joseph of Arimathea," is preserved in its entirety, although only a fragment of the second, entitled "Merlin," is extant. In addition, there is a prose adaptation of the work that corresponds exactly to the poem, and which also includes a third section called "Perceval,"[56] so that it forms a trilogy[57] which is also known as the *Petit Saint Graal*. Part One treats exclusively the previous history of the Grail. In Part Two, "Merlin," the connection with the Breton cycle of legends is established through Merlin, counsellor to

[55] Cf. Alexandre Micha, *La Tradition Manuscrite des Romans de Chrétien de Troyes*; and J. Fourquet, *Wolfram d'Eschenbach et le conte del Graal*.

[56] As well as an abridged version of the *Mort Artu*.

[57] The metrical version was edited by F. Michel under the title, *Le Roman du Saint Graal*; by Frederic J. Furnivall, *Seynt Graal or the Sank Ryal*; and more recently by Nitze, *Le Roman de l'Estoire dou Graal*.

E. Hucher's prose version, entitled *Le Saint Graal ou le Josef d'Arimathie: Première Branche des Romans de la Table Ronde*, contains "Josef d'Arimathie" according to both the Cangé (1250) and the Didot (1301) MSS. the latter draft also including the "Perceval." The "Perceval" was also edited by Weston in 1909 from a manuscript in Modena, in the first volume of *The Legend of Sir Perceval*. We owe an outstanding new edition of the *Didot-Perceval* to William Roach: *The Didot-Perceval, According to the Manuscripts of Modena and Paris*.

King Arthur and his father; while Part Three, "Perceval," comprises the quest.[58]

As mentioned, it cannot be established with any certainty whether Robert de Boron was the first to combine the legendary material with the fairy-tale, or whether this had happened earlier. Although a prototype is alluded to in some of the texts,[59] none has been discovered so far, thus allowing free reign to the widest range of conjecture. A hint that the Grail legend is older than the surviving forms appears in a passage from the Chronicle of Helinandus, a monk of Froidmont. The Chronicle was concluded in 1204 and written therefore during the golden age of the Grail poems.[60] In it we read:

> *Hoc tempore (717–719) in Britannia cuidam heremitae demonstrata est mirabilis quaedam visio per angelum de sancto Joseph decurione, qui corpus domini deposuit de cruce et de catino illo vel paropside, in quo dominus coenavit cum discipulis suis, de quo ab eodem heremita descripta est historia quae dicitur de gradali. Gradalis autem sive Gradale gallice dicitur scutella lata et aliquantulum profunda, in qua preciosae dapes cum suo jure divitibus solent apponi gradatim, unus morsellus post alium in diversis ordinibus. Dicitur et vulgare nomine graalz quia grata et acceptabilis est in ea comedenti, tum propter continens, quia forte argentea est vel de alia preciosa materia, tum propter contentum, i.e. ordinem multiplicem preciosarum dapum. Hanc historiam latine scriptam invenire non potui sed tantum gallice scripta habetur a quibusdam proceribus, nec facile ut aiunt, tota inveniri potest.*[61]

[58] With this work Robert de Boron may be said to have created an entirely new form of the romances of chivalry. Cf. E. Brugger, "L'Enserrement Merlin;" Bruce, *The Evolution of Arthurian Romance from the Beginnings down to the Year 1300*; and Roach, *The Didot-Perceval*, pp. 15*ff.* Also Loomis, *Arthurian Literature*, pp. 251*ff.* See also K. Sandkühler, *Die Geschichte des hl. Graal.*

[59] Cf. Brugger, *op. cit.*, Chrétien, as well as Robert de Boron, Wolfram von Eschenbach and others, all refer to a book from which they claim to have taken the story. In the opinion of some scholars traces of such a prototype may be discerned in the works themselves, but since nothing is known of any such work we are forced to fall back on conjecture. Cf. Weston, *The Legend of Sir Perceval*, Vol. 1, Ch. XV.

[60] From 1211 to 1223. Cf. Nitze, *Perlesvaus*, p. 71.

[61] J. P. Migne, *Patrologia Latina*, Vol. CCXII, col. 814/15.

At this time (717–719) a hermit in Britain was shown a wonderful vision by an angel, a vision of Joseph, the noble decurion who took the body of Christ down from the cross, and of that bowl which the Lord had used at the Last Supper with his disciples. The hermit himself wrote a description of these visions, which account was called after the *gradale*. *Gradalis* or *gradale* is the French for a wide and somewhat hollowed-out vessel in which delicious food is served to the rich, the single pieces being arranged in various rows. In popular parlance it is also called a *greal*, because it is agreeable and good to eat from, partly on account of the vessel itself, which is perhaps of silver or else of some other precious metal, and in part because of the contents, the arrangement of a multitude of delicious foods. I could not find this story written in Latin but it can be found, in French only, in the possession of a few nobles, and it is said not to be easy to find it in complete form.

This account gives us an explanation of the derivation of *grail* from *gradale*, which is universally accepted as valid. We shall return to the subject later.

A further suggestion is to be found in J. Bale's *Illustrium maioris Britanniae scriptorum summarium*, first printed in Ipswich in 1548.[62] Referring to Vincent de Beauvais' *Speculum historiale*, Bale gives the following account:

Eremita quidam Britannus, cuius ignoratur nomen, inter Cambros natus, et ab ipsa infantia nutritus, post prima literarum studia astrorum scientiam una cum historia Bardorum illius regionis more per omnem aetatem coluit. De rebus in sua patria insigniter gestis ille multa collegit, ac non parvo labore literis mandavit: praecipue de illustrissimo Britannorum rege Arthuro, atque ejus mensa rotunda. De Lanceloto etiam, Morgano, Percevallo, Galyvano, Bertramo et aliis fortissimis hominibus multa tradidit; sed famam ipse suam vehementer laesit, quod seriis inepta et veris fabulosa nonulla admiscuerit; et ut recitat in Historiali Speculo Vincentius, "De

[62] In Le Roux de Lincy, *Essai sur l'Abbaye de Fécamp*, and Weston, *The Legend of Sir Perceval*, Vol. 1, p. 292.

Josepho Arimathensi" ad Vualwanum quendam pleraque scripsit. Opus vocant ignoto mihi sermone—Sanctum Graal, lib. I. Et eius operis fragmenta quaedam vidi. Claruit iuxta Vincentium, anno ab Christi nativitate, 720, regnante Ina Visisaxorum rege.

A British hermit of unknown name, born in Wales and living there, who after the manner of the bards of that region had devoted his entire life to the study of the science of the stars and of history, assembled the notable events that had taken place in his fatherland and wrote them down with no mean labour. He wrote chiefly of the famous British King Arthur and his Round Table. He also had much to tell of Lancelot, Morgan, Perceval, Gauvain, Bertram and other valiant men. But he spoiled his own reputation through mixing serious matters with absurdities and truth with fable, and, as Vincentius relates in the *Speculum Historiale*, he dedicated most of his work about "Joseph of Arimathea" to a certain Vualwanus.[63] The work is known in a language unknown to me. *The Holy Grail, Book I.*[64] I have seen fragments of the work. According to Vincent it was famous in the time of Ina, King of the West Saxons, somewhere around 720.[65]

According to Jessie L. Weston[66] this statement of Bale's cannot actually be traced in Vincent de Beauvais,[67] so that Bale

[63] De Lincy, *op. cit.*, translates this as follows: "*Mais il a fait un grand tort à sa réputation en mêlent beaucoup de fables à ces récits et en nous racontant de Gauvain, ce que dit Vincent de Bauvais à propos de Josef d'Arimathie.*" This does not accord exactly with the Latin text, which is not quite clear either. It could perhaps best be expressed as "and because he connected Joseph of Arimathea with a certain Gauvain."

[64] This is missing in de Lincy.

[65] Ina was King of Wessex from 688 to 728, extending its frontiers as far as Somersetshire. His name is associated with the origins of Christianity in England and with the subsequently famous see of Wells, which is only a few miles from Glastonbury, the place so closely associated with the Grail legend. Ina tried to be just towards the Britons in the conquered regions and issued edicts along those lines. It would not be altogether beyond the bounds of possibility therefore to suggest that a legend about the Grail might have played some part during his reign.

[66] *The Legend of Sir Perceval*, p. 292.

[67] Nor could it be found in the 1624 edition of the *Speculum historiale*, but since the author frequently quotes Helinandus—for instance in Book 20,

might be confused as to his sources, and indeed Vincent must have read this passage in Helinandus, whom he knew. On the other hand his account recalls the introduction to the work known as *The Lancelot Grail*, in which we read:[68]

> On the eve of Good Friday of the year 717 after the Passion of Jesus Christ, the writer lay in his hut in one of the wildest regions of Britain (White Britain), plagued by doubts about the Trinity. Then Christ appeared to him and gave him a small book, no bigger than the palm of his hand, which would resolve all his doubts. He, Christ, had written it himself, and only he who was purified by confession and fasting might read it. On the following morning the writer opened the book, the sections of which were superscribed as follows:
>
> 1. This is the book of thy descent.
> 2. Here begins the Book of the Holy Grail.
> 3. Here begin the terrors.
> 4. Here begin the marvels.[69]

After a further account of how he was drawn up into the Third Heaven and of what adventures he had to undergo until the book—which in the meantime had disappeared—should be found again, the story of Joseph of Arimathea begins.

According to this evidence the Grail legend was already in existence in the eighth century, which is not impossible, even if no certain proofs have as yet been adduced. Quite possibly the single elements of the story go back to an earlier time while their inclusion in a unified, creative work was reserved for a later age.

Apart from the works already referred to—Chrétien de Troyes' *Li Contes del Graal* and Robert de Boron's *Le Roman de*

Chapter 56; Book 21, Chapter 74; Book 23, Chapter 174 and many other places—he must have been acquainted with his work.

[68] This introductory story reminds us of Robert de Boron's account of the origins of the Grail.

[69] The complete text is quoted on pp. 319–20.

l'Estoire dou Graal—the following adaptations of the material remain to be mentioned:[70]

The so-called *Lancelot Grail*, also known as the *Cycle de Walter Map* or *Vulgate Cycle* because in the Middle Ages it was the most popular rendering of the romance, very nearly supplanted the others. This long cycle, produced around 1200 to 1210, consists of five romances: *L'Estoire del Saint Graal*,[71] which conforms to Robert de Boron as to content; *L'Estoire de Merlin*, a prose rendering of de Boron's "Merlin" with a sequel; *Li Livres de Lancelot; La Queste del Saint Graal*; and *La Mort Artu.*[72] This cycle is the basis of Thomas Mallory's *Morte d'Arthur.*

The *Queste del Saint Graal*,[73] probably written about 1200, is a well-rounded story with a pronouncedly religious bias. A. Pauphilet, who edited the work, and E. Gilson see it as a product of the Cistercian type of mind. In any event, it is attributed to Walter Map, who, as the text says, translated a book extant in Salisbury from Latin into French for his master, Henry II. This *Queste*, in which it is no longer Perceval but the superhumanly spiritual Galahad who is the hero, comprises the same basic story as the *Estoire del Saint Graal.* The mystical element is very much to the fore here, coupled with allegories.

A very singular work is the prose romance *Perlesvaus*, written, according to W. A. Nitze, to whom we owe an excellent new edition, between 1191 and 1212.[74] A story departing radically from all the others, written as the text tells us for a cleric,

[70] Only a few of the most important of these can be cited here, for it would overstep the limits of this book to enter into the particulars of all the different works and their variants.

[71] Formerly known as the *Grand Saint Graal*, now also called the *Lancelot Grail.* Published by E. Hucher, 1875–78, in the above-mentioned work.

[72] The complete work is published by H. O. Sommer, *The Vulgate Version of the Arthurian Romances.* The last three parts of the cycle are erroneously ascribed to Walter Map, an influential cleric at the court of Henry II of England.

[73] This story is retold by Sir Thomas Malory in *Le Morte d'Arthur.* A somewhat divergent edition is preserved in a Welsh translation, *Y Saint Graal*, edited by R. Williams.

[74] *Le haut livre du Graal, Perlesvaus*, particularly pp. 58*ff.*

Monseigneur de Nesle, and written, or else translated from Latin into French, by a cleric "*dans une Maison de religion dans l'île d'Avalon*" meaning the cloister at Glastonbury. Here too the Grail is the vessel of Joseph of Arimathea, and the lance is that of Longinus. The story has an extremely allegorical or even symbolical style, to which adventurousness is added, and it gives such an impression of spontaneity that S. Evans,[75] who has translated it into English, thinks that it is on the whole the original version—which, however, cannot be the case.

An English *Sir Percyvelle,*[76] which in its simplicity may be closely connected with the original form, agrees in essentials with Chrétien's account of Perceval's youth, although it does not mention the Grail.

The Welsh *Mabinogion* of Peredur[77] is based on Chrétien but is clearly interwoven with Welsh motifs of an earlier date that impart a very archaic character to the work. In place of the Grail, a dish is carried in bearing a severed head which calls for revenge of the murdered victim.

Diû Krône by Heinrich von dem Thuerlin[78] is a somewhat confused story but with interesting and informative features. For the most part it reminds us slightly of Chrétien's continuator, Wauchier de Denain, and has Gauvain as the Grail hero. The Grail is described as a reliquary casket in which there is a piece of bread. One third of the bread is broken off by the woman who is carrying it, to give to the Lord of the Grail Castle. Apart from the casket and in addition to the usual objects, the lance and sword, that accompany the Grail, a *toblier*[79] which contains three drops of blood is also mentioned; here we have an unmistakable allusion to the Eucharist.

Finally there is the work best known to us, Wolfram von Eschenbach's *Parzival,* written between the years 1200 and 1207

75 *The High History of the Holy Grail.*

76 *Sir Perceval of Gales,* in *Alt- und Mittelenglische Texte,* Vol. 5. This work was probably produced around 1370. Cf. also R. H. Griffith, *Sir Perceval of Galles.*

77 Cf. also Loomis, *Arthurian Literature,* pp. 199*ff*.

78 *Diû Krône* appeared about 1220.

79 *Toblier* is usually rendered as "cloth," "tablecloth."

and therefore almost twenty years later than Chrétien's *Contes del Graal*, which it follows closely as to content, although Wolfram claims that the story stems from a Provençal by the name of Kyot (=Guyot)[80] and reproaches Chrétien that "he wronged the tale." Wolfram's story is distinguished above all others by its compactness, its depth of thought and feeling, and its psychological subtleties, which often sound quite modern. As mentioned, it conforms largely and often in detail to Chrétien's *Perceval*, apart from the introductory story and the ending which are both lacking in Chrétien and which follow a different course in his continuators. Wolfram's *Parzival* clearly betrays Oriental influences. He also declares that a heathen Jewish astronomer called Flegetanis had read about the Grail in the stars and had then recorded his discovery in a heathen language (probably Arabic). On one point, however, Wolfram differs quite essentially from Chrétien, for according to Wolfram the Grail is not a vessel but a *stone*. Through this, and also through several other details, Wolfram connects the Grail with the psychologically important *realm of alchemical symbolism*. As Jung has pointed out,[81] this latter formed something like an undercurrent to the Christianity which ruled the surface layers, and it endeavoured to fill in those lacunae which the tension of the opposites in Christianity had left wide open. It will be shown in the course of this work how important alchemy is for an understanding of the symbolism of the Grail. Of all the Grail poets, it is Wolfram to whom belongs the merit of having especially strengthened this connection with alchemy.

[80] Many scholars maintain that Kyot never existed but was invented by Wolfram in conformity with the habit of the age in which reference to an authority was made in order to lend greater credibility to the matters expounded. Others think that he is the poet Guyot de Provins, some of whose works are preserved, although these contain no poems about Perceval. Others think of a poet, Guyot, who wrote about miracles. Kyot could be a source that goes back to Thabit ibn Qurrah (cf. H. and R. Kahane, "Proto-Perceval and Proto-Parzival"). Thabit ibn Qurrah also translated a book of Hermes Trismegistus into Syrian. A new interpretation of the Kyot problem is to be found in Herbert Kolb, *Munsalvaesche: Studien zum Kyotproblem.*

[81] Cf. particularly *Psychology and Alchemy*, pars. 25*ff*.

The *Jüngere Titurel* of Albrecht von Scharfenberg[82] gives an early history of the Grail and of its first guardians who came to Spain from the East and introduced Christianity there.

The rise of so many different versions, and the refashioning which the material has undergone, are proof that there is a peculiar vitality inherent in it. Refusing to be confined to any particular form but displaying now this now that aspect, it has been transformed from the popular fairy-tale of the simpleton into a mystical religious quest. Psychologically it also points to the fact that it revolves around a difficult and apparently insoluble problem.

We may close this introduction with just such a fairy-tale which, if it is really authentic (and this is not quite certain since it was only transcribed for the first time in 1845), could serve as the original popular form of the Perceval story. It is the Breton fairy-tale of Peronik.

> Peronik, a poor youth, hears from a passing knight that two magic objects, a golden goblet and a diamond lance, are to be found in the Castle of Ker Glas. A drink from the goblet heals all ills and the lance destroys everything it strikes. These things belong to the magician Rogear who lives at Ker Glas. To reach the castle, so the knight has learned from a hermit, one must first pass through the forest of illusion, pluck an apple from a tree guarded by a corrigan [dwarf] with a fiery sword and find the laughing flower guarded by a snake-maned lion. Then, passing through the Sea of Dragons and the Valley of Joy, the hero will reach a river, at the only ford of which a black-clad woman awaits him. He must take her up on to his horse, so, that she may show him the way. Every knight who has previously sought the castle has perished in doing so but this does not deter Peronik. He sets out upon the way and succeeds in safely undergoing all the adventures and in reaching Ker Glas. The magician dies after he has taken one bite from the apple and been touched by the woman, who is revealed to be the plague. In an underground

[82] The authorship is disputed.

chamber Peronik finds the goblet and the lance, "*la lance qui tue et le bassin qui vivifie*".

The castle vanishes in a clap of thunder and Peronik finds himself in the forest. After dressing himself in fine clothes he goes to the court of the king, who loads him with gifts and makes him commander of his soldiers. So the foundling child becomes a great and mighty lord.[83]

Vessel and lance are here a death-dealing and life-giving pair of opposites, a clear and obvious interpretation. However, it is far too simple to cast much light on the Grail stories. None the less, the tale is psychologically significant in so far as it points to the universally human basis of the Grail poems, for which reason such simple folklore motifs are of particular interest, since they can be considered as products of the creative fantasy and as direct expressions of the soul, as portrayals, that is, of psychic contents, processes and connections, quite similar to those that are presented in dreams. But unlike dreams these are not predominantly subjective manifestations; on the contrary, they possess a generally human, that is, an archetypal character. In the tale of Peronik we see something like the representation of the most universal archetypal basis of the Grail legend, while the legend itself in its specific forms is nearer to consciousness and therefore richer in nuance, but also more transitory.

By *archetype*, Jung, who introduced this term into psychology, understands a "preconscious psychic disposition that enables a (man) to react in a human manner."[84] Jung compares these dispositions or dominant structures in the psyche to the invisible potential existence of the crystalline structure in a saturated solution.[85] They first take on a specific form when they emerge into consciousness in the shape of images; it is therefore necessary to differentiate between the unapprehendable

[83] Recorded by E. Souvestre in *Le Foyer Breton*. Recorded here from *Légendes bretonnes*. Cf. V. Junk, "Graalsage und Graalsdichtung des Mittelalters," pp. 19*ff*. Junk considers this fairy-tale to be the direct source of the Grail poems.

[84] Jung, *Archetypes and the Collective Unconscious*, par. 152.

[85] *Ibid.*, par. 155. Also Jung, *Psychology and Religion*, par. 222, note 2.

archetype, the unconscious, pre-existent disposition, and the archetypal images. As inborn possibilities of forms of behaviour and comprehension, the archetypes are connected with the instincts, with which they have a reciprocal relation. They are human nature in the universal sense, in that they lead to the production of similar and ever-recurring archetypal images.

Myths and fairy-tales are also characterized by this universal validity which differentiates them from ordinary dreams. There are also of course dreams of a predominantly archetypal character, but these also contain a subjective element since they usually occur at moments of real significance for the dreamer, such as important turning-points in life, or in critical situations which require a fresh orientation or adaptation and for which the present attitude which dominates consciousness does not suffice. The appearance of an archetypal image will draw the individual's attention to its general human quality or to the idea underlying it.[86] He will become aware of new, previously unrecognized possibilities and through them will experience a fresh influx of energy; for the archetypes possess a numinous quality and function as a hidden source of energy. When a myth is enacted in a ritual performance or, in more general, simpler and profaner fashion, when a fairy-tale is told, the healing factor within it acts on whoever has taken an interest in it and allowed himself to be moved by it in such a way that through this participation he will be brought into connection with an archetypal form of the situation and by this means enabled to put himself "into order". Archetypal dreams can have the same effect. Equally, this putting oneself "into order" or "becoming one with a higher will" is the content of religious experience.

The fascination and vitality of myths and fairy-tales lie precisely in the fact that they depict basic forms of human experience. For this very reason the same motifs are found the world over, not only as the result of migration but also because the human psyche which produces them is everywhere the same.

[86] *The Archetypes and the Collective Unconscious*, pars. 148*ff*.

In its rudiments the Grail legend is of a similar type. However, it is distinguished from an ordinary fairy-tale by the fact that it is not anonymous—at least not in the form in which it has come down to us—but has been shaped by specific poets. It therefore contains archetypal features in the foregoing sense of the word, but it is also the product of a particular age and attitude of the mind. For this reason it allows us a glimpse into the specific mentality of the Middle Ages and thus touches upon problems of the Christian aeon which are psychologically important for the present day.

CHAPTER II

Perceval's Early History according to Chrétien de Troyes[1]

THE STORY OF the young Perceval belongs to the world-wide fairy-tale theme of the simpleton,[2] in which it is precisely the youngest or most stupid brother who invariably accomplishes the great deed or gains the treasure hard to attain.

Like so many fairy-tale heroes, Perceval grows up in a forest. With its plant and animal life, its twilight and its restricted horizon, the forest aptly illustrates the as yet barely conscious condition of the child,[3] close to nature as he is. This primitive state is emphasized by the fact that Perceval is fatherless and knows only his mother, who brings him up in loneliness, far from the world.

Understood as protecting and nourishing nature, the forest also represents the all-embracing quality of the mother, so that the original condition of any life lived within the orbit of the mother is here described in a two-fold manner. The important role played by the figure of the mother in our tale will be illustrated in the following:

[1] Preference is given here to Chrétien's version because it conveys a more spontaneous effect than the admittedly better known and more important work of Wolfram, who shaped the material according to a conscious idea and thus interpreted it to a certain extent. Nevertheless we shall refer frequently to Wolfram's version in this interpretation.

[2] Cf. "The Lay of the Great Fool," in J. F. Campbell's *Popular Tales of the West Highlands*.

[3] In many fairy-tales and poems the forest is the starting point for the journeyings and deeds of the hero. This represents the emergence from a relatively unconscious situation into a far more conscious one. Cf. Jung, *Alchemical Studies*, par. 241.

To have chosen such an out-of-the-way dwelling place proves that Perceval's mother wished to protect her son from the perils of the world and especially from those of chivalry to which both his father and his brothers had fallen victim. Behind this rationalizing explanation, however, something far deeper lies hidden: the problem of mother and child which is as basic as it is universal and which is already present in the original situation. This problem is inherent in everyone from the beginning of life and is of such weight and significance that man everywhere and in all ages appears to have felt the need to concern himself with it, not only outwardly in concrete reality but also by describing its various aspects in myth and fairy-tale.

Modern psychology has also recognized the fundamental importance of this problem for modern man and has studied its effects upon him, to which the works of Sigmund Freud, C. G. Jung and their pupils bear witness. In his *Symbols of Transformation*[4] Jung gives a far-reaching and illuminating description of the whole problem, not only in its personal-human but also in its general and transpersonal aspects. The numerous parallels from mythology and the history of religion there quoted show clearly that they do not simply refer to something subject to personal limitations but to quite universally inherited archetypal situations and modes of behaviour.[5]

First, however, we will turn our attention to the personal aspect, which is best suited for throwing light on the problem. Perceval's mother wished to keep him under her wing, far from all the influences of the world, and to preserve him from dangers and hardships. This attitude corresponds to a fundamental instinct which is also present in animals and which is referred to as the instinct for nest-protection of the young. This is very important so long as the child is helpless and dependent on maternal protection. But when, as often happens, the mother maintains this attitude longer than is necessary, the

[4] First published in English as *Psychology of the Unconscious*, 1916.

[5] Cf. Jung, "Psychological Aspects of the Mother Archetype," in *Archetypes and the Collective Unconscious*, pars. 148–98; and Erich Neumann, *The Origins and History of Consciousness* and *The Great Mother*, *passim*.

development of the child may be impaired or even obstructed. The result is particularly unfortunate when the child of such a mother is of a timorous and fearful nature, so that instead of venturing out into life he prefers to remain within the security of the maternal circle.

Such ties to the mother play an important part in certain neurotic states. Freud saw unconsciousness or repressed "incest wishes" behind such conditions, and these, according to his view, engendered the so-called Oedipus complex, to which he assigned a central significance.

Incestuous images or situations, which appear to confirm Freud's view, do in fact sometimes appear in dreams. But Jung has explained in *Symbols of Transformation* that the "longing for the mother" can also be understood in another way. He sees it not only as an infantile neurotic-regressive craving but points to the abundance of symbolic material which indicates a concealed urge to rebirth and transformation of the personality.

This leads us to a consideration of the transpersonal significance of the mother. From this angle she is not so much a particular person as she is the absolutely universal giver and preserver of life, and as such she may be compared to the unconscious which is the source and origin of all psychic life.

Like the personal, the transpersonal mother-image also has a negative aspect which expresses a desire to hold the child back. In myths and fairy-tales this is often depicted as the killing or devouring of the child. Jung therefore speaks of the "terrible or devouring mother". In mythology this figure is portrayed as a gruesome and destructive goddess, the Indian Kali for instance, and in fairy-tales as the cruel stepmother or the witch, expressing the death-aspect of mother nature who kills her offspring from time to time and takes them back into herself. The unconscious exerts a corresponding influence in that it sets up a definite opposition to the development of consciousness or else it threatens to dim or even to extinguish the painfully achieved consciousness.

Actually, the archetypal images are already present in the

psyche as structural forms of the instinct[6] before any individual consciousness arises. For this reason the child's world consists more of archetypal forms and images than of ordinary people and objects. The child lives in a fairy-tale world. This is understandable when one reflects that the archetype is defined as an inborn pattern or form of perception and behaviour.[7] It may therefore be assumed that there are entelechies existent in the psyche which serve as models for the correct understanding of, and behaviour in, the outer world. Any kind of situation can animate such a *typos*, that is to say, it will be immediately and automatically understood or related to accordingly. It associates and assimilates the *a priori* pattern with a present situation, whereby the innate inner image appears outside in the given object. The next step in the process of becoming conscious consists in learning to differentiate between the outer, so-called "real" world, with its real people and solid objects, and the primordial world of the archetypes into which man is born, so to speak. The archetypal world exercises an uncanny fascination, indeed it has a numinous effect. It is a world full of wonders; it not only shelters terrible mothers and other monstrosities but is also, like the Celtic "Land of the Living" or Paradise, an abode of bliss. The necessity for giving up this world of wonder often excites the most violent resistance, for that which will be received in exchange is mostly far less attractive. The magic of this world is one of the reasons why the state of childhood is greatly loved and worth striving for and why the step into "life" and reality is so difficult. For the same reason so many myths tell of the origin of human existence in Paradise, or of a golden age that was lost and replaced by a far less perfect world.

The yearning for the mother can therefore also be understood, in non-mythological language, as the attraction exerted by the unconscious, a constant occurrence that is comparable to the

[6] Jung, "On the Nature of the Psyche," in *The Structure and Dynamics of the Psyche*, pars. 377*f* and particularly pars. 397*ff*.

[7] Jung, "Instinct and the Unconscious," in *The Structure and Dynamics of the Psyche*, par. 280. For the role of the archetype in the child's development, cf. Michael Fordham, *Children as Individuals*.

effect of the law of gravity. The development and preservation of ego consciousness is, for that very reason, often represented by the hero myth, for it is an achievement that can be compared to a fight with an overwhelming monster and which calls for almost superhuman strength.

Consciousness is an accomplishment which requires energy. It can only maintain itself for limited periods, after which a state of unconsciousness—sleep—is again necessary in order to renew the used-up energy.

The emergence of consciousness appears almost like a miracle or a supernatural phenomenon and the sinking back into the original condition occurs therefore all too easily. In this sense—in so far as unconsciousness is a primary state, the overcoming of which requires great effort—nature or the unconscious can be compared to a mother who holds her children fast in the initial situation or who wants to draw them back into it. The seduction of sinking back into unconsciousness is a widely-known human experience which has found expression most particularly in folklore and fairy-tales. So, for instance, the numerous and widespread legends of nymphs and nixies who, with their irresistible song, entice men into their element aptly describe the attraction which comes up from the depths, from the unconscious.

The wish to hold the child fast and possess it, manifested on the human and personal level as a power drive, is based in reality on these patterns inherited from mother nature herself and, in the last analysis, on the inertia of matter. It is precisely the circumstance that it is based upon such primitive, fundamental facts which gives to the corresponding human attitude that power of suggestion and effectiveness that characterizes it. It is natural archetypal behaviour, from which one can extricate oneself only through a higher state of consciousness which makes it possible to overcome pure nature.[8]

[8] When on the other hand a woman identifies with the role of the mother at the cost of her individual personality, she thereby becomes a collective figure and her influence is increased accordingly. This is very seldom fortunate and all too often directly catastrophic in its effect. Such a state of

Thus the archetypal figure of the Great Mother is always to be found behind the personal mother as, unnoticed, she permeates the individual human with the far larger archetypal image.

This portrayal illustrates only one side of the mother-child problem, however. For just as nature desires not only inertia, sleep and death but also life, growth and fruitfulness, so equally this latter trend is present in the mother as well as in the child. A woman does not wish to bear children simply in order to devour them. She also desires that they should flourish and be happy and successful.

This tendency when followed one-sidedly, however, also conceals dangers. Maternal ambition may possibly force the development of the child and lead it along the wrong paths. The only attitude that can be described as maternal, in the true sense of serving life, is one that arises out of the conflict as well as out of the cooperation between the opposing tendencies of holding back and encouraging. Only then will the child escape the mother's orbit and the childhood Paradise. Normally he also feels an urge to be off into the world, which appears to him as attractive, interesting and full of possibilities. Not least of the reasons for this is the fact that the archetypal images of the inner world appear outwardly; in other words, they are projected on to the outer world, which they then invest with a

affairs has led to the concept or designation of the "devouring mother," a well-known theme in myth and fairy-tale, portraying the reverse side of the alluring façade. This aspect is depicted in terrible mother goddesses such as Astarte and Cybele in Asia Minor, the Ishtar of the Gilgamesh epic, the Irish Scatach who at the same time is a goddess of war, and Kali, still venerated in India today. Such figures exist in most mythological systems and this ubiquity expresses a universal and typical conception. The most important action of the heroes of myths and fairy-tales often consists in overcoming the monster which is the terrible mother, for instance the overpowering of the primal water dragon Tiamat by the culture hero Marduk, or the fairy-tale of "Hansel and Gretel," in which the witch who plans to devour the children is thrown into the oven and burned up. In the study of such myths the "overcoming of the mother" describes an indispensable step towards the achievement of consciousness, in connection with which the mother appears as the negative devouring aspect of the unconscious. Cf. Neumann, *The Great Mother*, *passim.*

heightened power of attraction.[9] The urge towards life and action thus excited also fills our hero Perceval, draws him away from the mother and sets him off upon the search for the "treasure hard to attain", the "quest" of the Grail. That which most allures him is the very thing against which his mother seeks to warn him.

Before we follow him on his way, one more characteristic feature of the original situation needs to be discussed: the fact that *Perceval is fatherless.* The various accounts differ to some extent on this point. In the Chrétien de Troyes version,[10] it is said that Perceval's father was wounded in both thighs in battle and lamed. As a result of unfortunate events and social upheavals which took place after the king's death, he lost his possessions and was himself compelled to flee. Together with his family he was carried in great haste, on a litter, to a forest which belonged to him and in which there was a house where no one could find him. He died of grief over the death of two of his sons, killed in battle on the same day, when Perceval was two years old. It should be noted how similar the situation of Perceval's father is to that of the sick Grail King. In other versions his father is already dead at the time of Perceval's birth.[11]

To be fatherless appears to some extent to be one of the attributes of the mythological hero, as may be observed in so many myths and fairy-tales. This same feature is met in the dreams and fantasies of modern men and not least in life itself. How may it be explained? Perhaps it is that with a fatherless boy all those conditions that dispose him to become a hero are strengthened and intensified because he has to make his own way and is compelled to develop independence and feelings of responsibility, while a boy who lives under the guidance of a father who offers him support will be less impelled towards such

[9] Cf. Jung, "General Aspects of Dream Psychology," in *Structure and Dynamics*, par. 507.

[10] Verses 435*ff*.

[11] As for instance in Wolfram von Eschenbach's *Parzival*, or in the *Peredur*.

achievements. While for the latter the father represents the figure of the "successful man" outwardly, this image falls back upon the fatherless boy himself, so to speak, and drives him on to its realization. On the other hand, it is possible that as a result of the father's absence—whether he be dead or simply not fulfilling his role as father and masculine example—there is engendered in the son the feeling or attitude that all possibilities and provinces of masculine achievement are open to him who can anticipate nothing from the father. There is the disadvantage, however, that such a son is in danger of overreaching himself in some direction. A further factor seems to be connected with the mother. A woman without a husband will naturally be inclined to transfer what she would have expected of him—that he be a hero, for instance—on to the son, in the hope that he will fulfill what the father was unable to achieve. The following curious fact also plays a part. In the dreams and fantasies of even happily married women, a mysteriously fascinating masculine figure often appears, a demonic or divine dream or shadow lover to which Jung has given the name of *animus*. Not uncommonly, the woman cherishes a more or less conscious secret idea that one of her children, preferably the eldest or youngest, was fathered by this psychic lover.[12] Superhuman powers will readily be attributed to such a child. The figure of the ghostly lover is not only personal but, to the extent that it seems transpersonal and demonic, it is a matter of the archetype. It is not, that is to say, simply the influence of the parents which produces the image of the hero; it is a question of a kind of inherent primal phenomenon. For the hero figure is one of those eternal, archetypal images which slumber in the depths of every soul and which determine human life and destiny in unsuspected measure.

If to be fatherless is one of the characteristic features of the hero, it must be made clear that he is considered to be descended from either a superhuman or a nonhuman father

[12] See also Esther Harding, *The Way of All Women*, where this figure is called the Ghostly Lover; and Emma Jung, "On the Nature of the Animus," in *Animus and Anima*; also C. G. Jung, *Aion*, *passim*.

instead of an ordinary human father. In the religions of many primitive peoples an animal or plant, or more seldom an object, is regarded as the ancestor of the race and honoured accordingly.[13] Numerous examples of this are to be found in myth, folklore and fairy-tale. The stories in Greek mythology of a god, often in animal form, uniting with a human woman—Zeus, for instance, as a bull with Europa or as a swan with Leda—are universally known. Demigods and heroes result from such unions. It is also well known that children frequently have the idea that they are not the offspring of their parents, but were substituted or adopted by them; such a child feels that in reality he or she is probably either a prince or a princess. Such fantasies, even when not conscious, can have an influence on the behaviour of a child and may be the basic cause of an estrangement from reality and a lack of adaptation. These can, of course, be set aside simply as wish-fulfillment fantasies—which on the one hand they undoubtedly are; on the other, however, they possess a certain value. They serve to inspire courage in a young person who, face to face with the world, naturally feels small, weak, helpless and in its power; they help him to master his fear and uncertainty. Correctly understood, this means that in the prototype of the hero, an ideal is personified, which is an invaluable spur and an effective support in life.

In this way the archetype proves helpful, in that it indicates the basis or the pattern for behaviour in specific situations and reminds the individual of these patterns time and again. It has been observed that archetypal dreams occur in critical life-situations, at those turning-points which call for a new orientation or adaptation. The appearance of an archetype at such a moment can provide the individual with that encouragement and confidence which he needs in order to master the problem before him. Therein lies the so-called therapeutic value of myths and fairy-tales. They depict an archetypal event, a basic pattern of human behaviour, by which one may find one's bearings or which can serve as a model. The action of the

[13] Cf. J. Hastings, *Encyclopaedia of Religion and Ethics*, under "Totemism."

archetypes can also be negative, of course, often leading to a complete denial of life or even to a psychosis when, for instance, the individual identifies with the hero-image and misuses it solely for the glorification of the ego. This does not mean that he *thinks* he is a hero, but that he will conduct himself like one if the occasion arises. On a higher level than the mythological or the childish the same idea is expressed when the unknown father is considered as being a spiritual, divine being or principle. This idea is particularly clearly expressed in Christ, the son of God and man. It is evident that this concept means a great deal more than just a support in life or an infantile fantasy. It expresses in itself the fundamental and ineradicable feeling that something dwells in man which is more than purely human or animal, namely an immortal soul, a divine spark—or whatever one prefers to call it.

We will now return to our story.

As "the young son of the widow" ("*le filz à la veve dame de la gaste forest soutaine*") rides through the forest one fine morning he hears the clash of arms and the trampling of horses which, he thinks, proceed from devils. He is not afraid, however, but considers how best he may fight against the strongest of them. But when he sees five knights in shining armour come riding out of the forest he is so overwhelmed by the splendid sight that he no longer takes them for devils but for angels. His mother has told him that angels are the most beautiful of beings, apart from God, so he asks one of the knights, who has made some inquiry of him, whether he be God, and learns that the dazzling apparitions are called knights. Without listening to the knight's questions he inquires endlessly about his weapons and armour. The knight remarks to his companions that there is nothing to be gained from this Welshman who asks only about what is under his eyes, what it is called or of what use it may be. Whereupon they shout to Perceval:

"Sir, know full well
That the Welsh are by nature made
More stupid than the beasts at pasture.

This one too is like a beast;
Foolish is he who with him tarries."[14]

That Perceval should be expressly designated as Welsh[15] has far less to do with the question of his nationality than with the fact that the hero of the story is described as an uncouth bumpkin. *Welshman* was obviously synonymous with a primitive, uncultivated, somewhat inferior man.

In the account of Perceval's meeting with the knights this rather crude behaviour is clearly illustrated. It is, however, also fully apparent that it in no way reflects his nature, for when the knight replies that he received his armour from King Arthur, Perceval unhesitatingly decides to seek out the King and entreat a similar suit for himself; he is determined to become a knight. This knowledge and this intention are the first expression of a budding awareness of himself which plainly reveals—although in the form of a childish wish to begin with—what will prove to be his ultimate goal and true vocation. Suddenly a way opens out before him, which is in a deeper

14 *Sire, sachiez bien antreset*
Que Galois sont fuit per nature
Plus fol que bestes an pasture;
Cist est aussi comme une bestie
Fos est qui delez lui s'arreste.

15 Concerning the designation of *Galois* (Welsh), Geoffrey of Monmouth says: "When the foreigners, i.e. the Saxons, invaded the country, the Britons were no longer known by that name, but were called the *Guallenses*, which derives from Guallo, one of their chiefs, or else from the word for foreigner" (*Hist. Reg. Brit.*, Chs. 206–8). In his *History of England* G. M. Trevelyan says, page 40: "The name of 'Welsh,' for the indigenous inhabitants who were driven into Wales, Strathclyde and the Devon peninsula was bestowed on them by the Saxons. It is a Saxon word for 'foreigner'." According to F. Kluge, *Etymologisches Wörterbuch der deutschen Sprache*, under "*welsch*," the Anglo-Saxon word *Wealh* denotes the Celts and also slaves. The use of *welsch* for "foreign" is still to be found in the German-Swiss designation of *Welschland* for French Switzerland. Italy also was thus referred to at an earlier date, on account of the language, which was foreign to German speakers. At the time of the compilation of the Grail stories the Norman Plantagenet kings, Henry I and II, were trying to subdue Wales, whose still more or less barbaric and unruly population was offering a powerful resistance which may have contributed to the above-mentioned reputation of the Welsh.

sense the way to himself and from which he allows neither the suffering of his mother[16] nor anything else to divert him. It often happens that such an intense experience in childhood or early youth is decisive for an individual's entire later life. At such a moment something appears outwardly—that is to say, in projection—that is essentially real for the individual, so that he is moved and stirred by it to his very depths. It is a fact frequently observed that the archetypal images of the inner world project themselves on to the outer world and there become manifest. In so far as they excite and attract the attention of the individual they enable or enforce his turning towards the outer world. This is certainly one of the meaningful functions of the mechanism of projection. Its purpose is not only to keep painful insights at a distance, while their contents are ascribed to others, but also to serve the opposite purpose of making things consciously perceptible and distinguishable, for they confront the ego with the non-ego.[17]

For Perceval the encounter with the knights is of this nature and therefore brings about the separation from his mother and his emergence into the world. When he tells his mother of the meeting she characteristically falls into a swoon and by this behaviour forfeits her power over the boy. Consciousness recovered, she tells him about his father, how, like herself, he was of the highest descent, how he was wounded in both thighs in battle and crippled as a result, how he then undeservedly lost his property and finally retired into exile in the forest. Chivalry, no less than the world, played him a dirty trick, for not only was he himself incurably wounded but both his elder sons also fell victims of their profession and suffered death in battle. Their father died of grief over this, reason enough for the mother to wish to preserve herself and her only surviving son far away from the world. Perceval, however, evinces not the slightest interest in any of this information. He merely remarks, "I do not understand what you are telling me. Give me rather

[16] Cf. Jung, *Aion*, especially pars. 20*ff*.

[17] Cf. also Jung, *Psychological Types*, especially pp. 582*ff*, for definition of "projection."

something to eat. I wish to go to that king who makes knights, and go I will, cost what it may."

We see here with what determination the boy expresses himself. For him the mother simply betokens food; what she says or feels is unimportant to him compared with the urgency of his desire to become a knight.

When the mother sees that her doubts make no impression on him, she resigns herself to the inevitable, fits him out with riding clothes and makes him a garment in the Welsh style, an imaginatively uncouth costume, so that at court he will cut the figure of a gawky, boorish fool.

After his mother has imparted all kinds of good advice and precepts,[18] Perceval takes his departure and sets out upon his way. He looks back once after he has gone some distance and sees his mother lying on the bridge as if dead, but he spurs his horse and continues on his way without a moment's concern. No trace of hesitation checks the impetus of his instinctively impelled departure, which indicates that the vision he has seen —the knights—possesses a power beside which everything else fades into the background.

[18] She tells him that whenever he comes to a church, which is a beautiful house with holy relics where God is worshipped and where the body of Christ of the Holy Prophet [*sic*] was offered up, he should go in and pray. He should honour women and succour those in distress, and should he have an opportunity to obtain a ring from a maiden he should take it.

CHAPTER III

The Defeat of the Red Knight and the Meeting with Blancheflor

PERCEVAL UNDOUBTEDLY behaves in a reckless and boorish manner after setting out on his journey. On the following day when he comes to a splendid tent, which he mistakes for a church, he surprises a young woman asleep inside, kisses her by force and robs her of her ring,[1] with the explanation that he has been instructed to do so by his mother. Then, following the directions of a charcoal-burner, he arrives at Carduel, King Arthur's residence. As he rides up to the castle a knight armed in red and carrying a golden goblet in his right hand approaches through the gates. The knight has stolen the cup from Arthur's table and he orders Perceval to carry his challenge to the King; he is disputing Arthur's title to his lands.

Perceval rides into the castle, straight into the great hall where King Arthur is sitting at a table so deeply immersed in thought that he does not notice the newcomer. Reluctantly Perceval turns to depart; in so doing his horse butts against the King, who is consequently roused from his reverie. Arthur apologizes to his guest for not returning his salutation; his preoccupation he attributes to his rage over the insult that has befallen him. His arch-enemy, the Red Knight, has audaciously robbed him of the golden goblet and in doing so has spilt its contents over the Queen, who has withdrawn in anger to her apartments.

[1] The returning owner, l'Orguelleus de la Lande, is enraged at what has happened and makes the lady, whom he accuses of infidelity, pay heavily for it.

Perceval requests the King to knight him on the spot, for he wishes to set out at once to win for himself the Red Knight's armour, which has taken his fancy. Keu, the court seneschal, ever ready with ridicule, advises Perceval to go ahead and get it. Perceval does not wait to be told a second time. Returning to the Red Knight, he abruptly demands the surrender of his armour and weapons, whereupon the knight, taking him for an insolent youth, deals him a blow with the shaft of his lance. Perceval retaliates by hurling his spear, piercing the knight through the eye so that he falls dead to the ground. Assisted by one of Arthur's squires, Perceval strips the armour from the slain man and puts it on over his Welsh garment, from which he does not wish to be parted. He takes the weapons and the horse of the dead knight for himself, hands his old nag over to the squire and gives him the stolen cup to return to the King.

This first appearance of Perceval at Arthur's court introduces, in an accidental and an even more uncommitted manner, the motif which is later to become one of the leitmotifs of the legend. He arrives to find the court in a somewhat disorderly state; the King has suffered a wrong, the Queen has been insulted and both, as a result, are out of countenance.

The first indication of the disturbed and unredeemed state of the Land of the Grail is noted here in the disrupted condition of the King's court. It is like a presentiment of the future, a kind of prefiguration, an idea with which the medieval mind was well acquainted. In many religious writings, for instance, the events of the Old Testament were explained as prefigurations of the life of Christ. In this connection special attention should be paid to the work of Joachim of Floris who consistently pointed out how, down through the ages, the idea of the Kingdom of God is ever more clearly and purely expressed. He described three succeeding realms: the first corresponding to the Old Testament, the Kingdom of God the Father; the second to the New Testament, the Kingdom of the Son; and finally, as the third Kingdom, that of the Holy Spirit, which many people believed would dawn in their lifetime.[2]

[2] Cf. Jung, *Aion*, pars. 137*ff*.

Ideas of this type also play an important part in the Grail legends. They belong to those concepts deeply rooted in the soul, to those archetypal images which lend direction and meaning to human life. "For now we see through a glass, darkly; but then face to face."[3] Or, as Meister Eckhart says, "The meaning of all corn is wheat, and of all metals gold, and of all births that of man."[4] The idea behind this remark is that that which now is, is a first incomplete expression of that which is to come.

The same thing can be observed in ordinary life where, subject to variation, certain situations repeat themselves again and again. At first perhaps, they appear to be accidental and meaningless, like this exploit of Perceval's. Should one's attention be aroused, however, by the frequent recurrence of such coincidences, and if these are more carefully observed, it will be noted that for the most part they are modified expressions of a significant natural tendency characteristic of the particular individual, until their meaning is finally grasped and their purpose accomplished.

The "deeds of the hero," which play such an important part in myths and fairy-tales, should also be understood in this sense. Under continually renewed exertion and often under more than human strain, undeterred by failure or danger, the hero is impelled to strive for the highest values; this need, as a presentiment and a task, is laid with him in his cradle.

The story of Perceval is a particularly fine example of this endeavour. As we have seen, to be a knight was no more to him at first than the realization of a covetousness; only slowly, through many mistakes, did he develop into what he was intended to be, namely that foremost knight who alone could win the Grail.

In the literary works with which we are concerned, the knight embodies the image of the higher man as it was conceived in that age. For instance, only selected knights might join Arthur's Round Table, those who were masters not only of

[3] I Cor. 13:12.

[4] *Schriften*, p. 37: "Von der Erfüllung," Sermon on Luke 1 : 26.

the knightly *arts*, such as the handling of arms, riding and hunting, but who also possessed the knightly *virtues* of fortitude, valour, fearlessness, love of battle, thirst for adventure, and above all of constancy and loyalty in the highest degree. Faithfulness to friends and vassals and loyalty even towards the enemy himself were looked upon as the highest of these virtues and whoever violated them forfeited his knightly honour. In addition to engaging in contests and embarking on adventures for the honour and glory of chivalry, the functions of Arthur's knights were to create order in the land, to prevent wrongdoing and acts of violence, and above all to succour women and maidens in distress. Through the centuries, these knights of Arthur's embodied an ideal by which, in this case, even Perceval was deeply moved. Thinking was not one of the knightly arts; the only intellectual activity mentioned in the stories is an occasional game of chess. Thinking was the concern of the clerics.[5] In Arthur's circle, however, the function of thinking was performed for the others by Merlin who, by reason of his two-fold descent—his father was a devil, his mother a pure maiden—knew the secrets of both past and future and therefore to some extent possessed both Promethean and Epimethean thinking.

The figure of the king exhibits, to a greater extent even than that of the knights, a superimposed ruling principle of consciousness, as can clearly be recognized from fairy-tales and dreams.[6] Arthur, the Lord of the Round Table, should therefore figure here as the dominant collective idea of Christian knighthood. To some extent the king embodies in himself the *Anthropos*—a visible and collectively conscious aspect of human totality—now become visible. In this sense Arthur represents the idea of wholeness as it was conceived in the first millennium of the Christian era, his Round Table and twelve knights clearly connecting him with Christ. This King—Perceval's

[5] From about the twelfth century chivalry began to be more interested in intellectual matters, to which the stories written in French and therefore called *romans* bear witness, as do also the *Minne* poems.

[6] Cf. Jung, *Psychology and Alchemy*, pars. 434*ff*, and *Mysterium Coniunctionis*, *passim*.

future master—therefore represents for Perceval the concept of wholeness which is comprehensible to him, the ideal which he serves. In addition to Arthur, another king, the wounded Grail King, will at a later date also play a central role in Perceval's life. Perceval's father, ailing like the Grail King, portrays the human and personal authority of the father; King Arthur is a higher and more far-reaching authority, the idea of totality in Christian chivalry; while finally the Grail King exhibits this conception in a yet more developed form.

The question of the exact psychological meaning of the Red Knight is also relevant. In many ways he appears to be similar to Perceval in that he too does not know how to behave at the King's court; when he steals the goblet and spills its contents over the Queen, he is committing an offence against the feminine principle, as Perceval also will similarly offend in the course of the story. He could therefore be interpreted as Perceval's double or *shadow*. Psychologically the term "shadow" denotes the inferior and for the most part, darker or poorer character traits of a person which, though not much noticed by the conscious ego, coexist with it. Most often it is made up of traits of an emotional nature which possess a certain autonomy and which occasionally overrun consciousness.[7] These contents are partly of a personal nature and could, with moral effort, be observed in the light of self-knowledge. They are only relatively evil, since they often indicate vitality and a nearness to the instincts, which also possess a positive value. But on the other side, the shadow is connected with the collective darkness which crystallizes into the archetypal image of a destructive deity and faces mankind with terrifying problems. The motif of the Red Knight will in the end lead Perceval into the threatening abysses of the problem of evil. For the moment, however, he can be taken as Perceval's personal shadow, as the sum of emotion and barbaric thoughtlessness which Perceval must overcome before he can become a Christian knight.

In numerous, still living Northern folk tales there is a character called Ritter Rot who acts the role of the envious

[7] Cf. *Aion*, pars. 13*ff.*

slanderer of the hero.[8] In ancient Ireland the otherworldly fairy realm from time to time sent out red warriors (the Siths) against the heroes of this world, and the Red Knight also has just such an otherworldly background.[9] He slanders the hero to the King, attempting thereby to cause his death, but such an action, on the contrary, usually leads to the hero's advancement. The knight therefore fulfills the role of a dangerous shadow element. In mythology the colour red is frequently associated on the one hand with blood, fire, love and life, and on the other with war and death.[10] From the two-fold meaning of the colour it may be perceived that this shadow figure is consequently not only destructive, but that it is also able to work in the interest of life when it has been integrated into consciousness. In the symbolic speech of the alchemists, a "red man" appears as the personification of the *prima materia* of the philosopher's stone. It was said that he should be gently treated and not feared, since he was helpful in spite of his terrifying appearance. In a special sense, therefore, the Red Knight is the first manifestation of Perceval's future inner wholeness.[11]

Perceval, however, strikes him dead with a thoughtless brutality which does nothing to commend him. Nonetheless the Red Knight had insulted Arthur and was merely being paid back in his own coin. Psychologically this killing of the red shadow-knight corresponds to a violent repression of Perceval's own individual affects and emotions as a first step towards building up a conscious personality. Every young person who grows up in a social milieu and develops into a responsible personality must go through this phase of a merciless subjugation of individual inner primitive emotionality before he can develop further. In this instance, however, it happens quite

[8] Cf. J. Bolte and G. Polivka, *Anmerkungen zu den Kinder- und Hausmärchen der Brüder Grimm*, Vol. III, p. 18.

[9] Cf. Marx, *Légende Arthurienne*, p. 102, and A. C. L. Brown, "The Bleeding Lance," p. 19.

[10] Cf. Eva Wunderlich, "Die Bedeutung der roten Farbe im Kultus der Griechen und Römer."

[11] Cf. Jung, *Alchemical Studies*, par. 124. Concerning the tendency of the content that later appears as the "Self" to present itself first in the form of an enemy to be overcome, cf. *ibid.*, par. 428.

without reflection, as a result of Perceval's wish to become a knight and thus to be received into Arthur's court.

After Perceval has stripped the armour from his enemy and is wearing it himself, he too will be spoken of as the "Red Knight".[12] Because he has overcome the emotions assailing him from within, the vitality and energy that it contained will now be at the disposal of the ego, which is thereby enhanced in strength and significance. At the same time, it is to be expected that Perceval will himself now display a streak of ruthless masculinity which will entangle him in difficulties. It is a further characteristic of his youthful and foolish attitude that he did not fight the Red Knight in order to win the cup back for Arthur but simply killed him with his spear because the red armour excited his covetousness. The cup is no more than a side-show to him. He sends it back to Arthur by one of his squires, without troubling to go himself and without having any presentiment that the motif which will later become the main motif—the vessel, the Grail—is by chance, as it were, here hinted at for the first time. The cup is a familiar object in legends and fairy-tales and often plays a fateful role, either because of the drink it contains, as in the story of Tristan and Isolde, or because it is closely connected with the life of its owner or the life of someone who has drunk from it.[13] At this stage of his development Perceval is obviously unaware of the significance of the cup.

A further important factor is the *armour* which Perceval has stripped from the slain knight and taken for himself. The mode of seizure is far from chivalrous, so that a measure of guilt attaches to it. It is noteworthy that Perceval puts the armour on over his coarse Welsh undergarment, from which he will not be parted. On the one hand this means that he feels the armour is

[12] Wolfram makes the Red Knight a relative of Parzival.

[13] In the "Glück von Edenhall," for instance. Comparison may also be made to the vessel known as "the cup of Anacreon" and to Joseph's cup (Genesis 44:2–5). Of the former the Naassenes said: "My tankard tells me/ Speaking in mute silence/What I must become." Cf. Jung, *Psychology and Alchemy*, par. 550. Cf. also the motif of the cup in Celtic legend, Marx *Légende Arthurienne*, pp. 102–3 and p. 118. Also the Oriental legend of Solomon in F. Kampers, *Das Lichtland der Seelen und der heilige Gral*, pp. 72*ff*.

essentially a part of him, on the other that basically he is not yet a knight, as he would wish to be, but only exhibits a knightly exterior. This corresponds to the concept that analytical psychology designates as the *persona* (mask).[14] The term "mask" indicates that it is not the essential nature of an individual that is concealed behind the exterior and that a certain impression is the result when seen from the outside. To some extent, therefore, the persona forms a façade and is usually so constituted as to be suitable to the society in which the individual lives; for this reason Jung considers it a segment of the collective psyche.[15] This means that the individual appears merely as a member of a race, clan, professional class, etc., and not as a human being with his own unique characteristics. Such a persona comes into existence more or less automatically, since the human being belongs to a particular nation and a particular family or class whose traits of character and way of life he shares. The original psychic condition of children is one of just such participation or identity with the surroundings, and differentiation from the environment only comes about through increasing consciousness. At first he has simply to accept the role which falls to him as his share of the family or society to which he belongs. Consequently one is the child, the son, the daughter, the young man, the marriageable girl, the father of a family, the wife, the mother, the representative of a particular profession and so on. It is accordingly significant that Perceval does not know his own name, knows himself only as *cher filz*, *beau filz* or *beau sire*—the words his mother used in addressing him.

On the other hand, it is frequently observed that children in the first four to six years of life often show a distinct and individual peculiarity and originality which later, on going to school for instance, they lose because they have then to adapt themselves to the collective pattern. This might appear regrettable, but such a collective affiliation is essential. One cannot face the world as a child of nature or as mother's little son. For this reason the persona is not to be understood as nothing

[14] Cf. Jung, *Two Essays on Analytical Psychology*, pars. 245*ff*.
[15] *Ibid.*, par. 243.

but a mask, as a wish to simulate something before the world; it is also an important and necessary mode of adaptation. It is not possible to live together in human society unless the requisite forms are observed, as can be seen in even the most primitive social groups, in totemistic customs or in tabus, marriage rituals, etc. The development of social forms is a very practical phenomenon of culture, but it does not come about without the sacrifice of something of the natural primitive attitude which is manifested by the Red Knight. It is for this reason that puberty initiations, through which a boy becomes a viable member of the tribe, are frequently combined with extremely severe and painful rites. The persona deteriorates into a mere mask when it no longer fulfills its purpose but only conceals a void or worse, therefore falsifying the essential nature of the individual. At the same time the persona-like clothing offers a defence against the world without which the individual would be all too vulnerable. It also often represents, in a way, a prototype or ideal of what is to be achieved, of what one hopes to realize. Thus it can serve as a valuable guideline. But when the ideal is wrongly chosen, when it is unattainable or unsuited to the individual nature, then striving towards it can often lead one into error.

To become a knight is just such an ideal for the youthful Perceval. However, he is not one yet; he only possesses the armour, which is the outer appearance and into which he still has to grow. The knight, as embodiment of a higher type of man, enjoyed universal esteem and respect in that age and, owing to the development of the feudal system, gave that world its characteristic stamp. From the eleventh to the fourteenth centuries especially, chivalry played an impressive part. The knights were the energetic representatives of worldly power, while the clerics represented spiritual values and cultivated spiritual power (which also soon became a worldly one, to be sure). *Clergé* and *Chevalerie* formed the two higher ranks, over against the burghers and peasants.[16]

[16] Cf. Erich Köhler's exposition in *Ideal und Wirklichkeit in der höfischen Epik* and *Trobadorlyrik und höfischer Roman.*

The knight represents—at least as a concept—a higher, more differentiated form of the warrior, even though the individual knight might in fact have been undifferentiated enough. What the ideal of chivalry meant to that age has been given expression by poets through the figures of King Arthur and his knights of the Round Table. It is clear that a higher, nobler and more disciplined human being was indicated by the term knight. The virtues demanded of him—strength and skill in arms, valour, courage and loyalty, to the feudal lord in particular but also to the friend and even *vis-à-vis* the foe—were no small requirements. In the profoundest sense a religious idea was concealed behind all this. *Arthur's Round Table might therefore be looked upon as a symbol in which is mirrored the developing consciousness of Christian man in the first millennium.* In those days the spread of Christianity was linked with the great civilizing task of subduing the aboriginal brutality and unconsciousness of the heathen peoples. This lent a higher meaning to the Christian knight's aggressive masculinity, which was put to the service of a nobler ideal and a higher state of consciousness.

Since the Christian Church had reached its most perfect flowering in the twelfth century, it might perhaps be objected that the conquest of the heathen, barbarian elements could be considered as having long since been fully achieved. Christianity, however, was the prevailing religion, or at least that of the wielders of power, and its acceptance did not have to spring from a deep, unqualified inner conviction, as it did in earlier times when its followers were persecuted. It was often the case, for instance, that when a king or a powerful man was baptized, his followers and vassals went through the same ceremony as a matter of course.[17] The reasons which led to a conversion were more often of a practical than of a religious nature, such as hoping that the new god might prove stronger and more helpful in a difficult situation than the old gods had been.[18] This was the case in the conversion of King Clovis I (A.D. 496). In a

[17] Cf. Wace, *Le Roman de Brut*, verses 5212*ff*, and Ordericus Vitalis, *Histoire de la Normandie*, Vols. II, LIV, III.

[18] Cf. E. H. Meyer, *Die Mythologie der Germanen*, Ch. I.

discourse on the causes of conversion, the German monk Caesarius von Heisterbach[19] says that many are converted by a divine summons, others by exhortation or pious example, while yet others are incited by evil spirits or by a particular indiscretion. Countless people are driven to join an order by some painful circumstance or other, such as sickness, poverty, captivity, shame over past lapses, danger to life, fear of the pains of hell or a longing for the heavenly land. It should also be taken into account that while the Anglo-Saxons were already Christianized in the sixth and seventh centuries, this was not true of the Normans. Rollo, first duke of Normandy, was baptized in 912, according to Ordericus Vitalis' history of Normandy,[20] and at his burial sacrifices were still to be made to the old gods. This was not much more than a century and a half before the conquest of Britain by William the Conqueror and two and a half centuries before the time our story was being written. In the twelfth and thirteenth centuries, therefore, the Anglo-Norman world was still quite close to heathendom.

A religion as spiritual as Christianity could not be assimilated immediately by a mentality as primitive as that of the Western and Northern peoples of the era. This was already clear to Gregory the Great when he entrusted Augustine with the mission to the Anglo-Saxons; he advised Augustine not to proceed abruptly and not to destroy the old shrines but to revere them so that the people should congregate in the accustomed places, though now for the worship of the true God. "For it is obvious that it is not possible to cut everything off all at once from a rough and uncultured spirit, just as someone who is preparing to scale the heights is able to do so only step by step or a stage at a time and is not able to achieve it by leaps and bounds."[21] Viewed from this angle, the great spiritual

[19] *Dialogus Miraculorum*, Vol. I, Dist. I, Ch. V. The author lived between 1180 and 1240.

[20] *Op cit.*

[21] "*Nam duris mentibus simul omnia abscindere impossibile esse non dubium est, quia is, qui locum summum ascendere nititur, necesse est ut gradibus vel passibus, non autem saltibus elevatur.*"—The Venerable Bede, *Historia ecclesiae Anglorum*, Book I, Ch. XXX.

task of helping to realize the Christian ideal still fell to Christian chivalry.

Perceval's journey now leads him to a teacher, Gornemant de Goort (Gurnemanz, according to Wolfram), who instructs him in the art of arms and the knightly virtues and who tells him he is now too old to be tied to his mother's apronstrings. He also impresses upon the youth that *he should not ask too many questions*—advice that will have fateful consequences later on. In this way Perceval is given to understand that he has now outgrown childish things and should conduct himself accordingly. After this instruction, Gornemant confers the accolade:[22]

Et dit que donee li a
La plus haute ordre avuec l'espee
Que Deus et feite et commandee
C'est l'ordre de chevalerie,
Qui doit estre sanz vilenie.

And said that he had given him
The highest order with the sword
That God has made and ordained.
This is the order of chivalry
That must be without stain.

Having achieved his first aim—that of becoming a knight—Perceval now prepares to leave his patron Gornemant, who represents a father figure and who would willingly have kept the boy with him. But Perceval chooses to proceed further on his way out into the world, with the intention of looking after his mother, for he now remembers that on his departure she had fallen down on the bridge. This is a subtle psychological point which Chrétien inserts here and which is missing in Wolfram.

However, he does not return to his mother's house but arrives instead at the castle of Belrepeire, where he immediately finds occasion for chivalrous deeds. The chatelaine of the castle, the beautiful Blancheflor (Condwiramurs in Wolfram), is in distress, for an unacceptable suitor is besieging the castle and has

[22] Verses 1635*ff*.

almost starved it out. On this stage of his journey, Perceval therefore meets not the mother but the woman, and in the form—so exceedingly attractive and almost irresistible to masculine sentiment—of the "damsel in distress," the oppressed beauty in need of deliverance. In a charmingly naïve way she comes to his bed at night to lament her troubles. Perceval's lust for battle is aroused, he fights passionately on her behalf and succeeds in overcoming the enemy and freeing the castle. Blancheflor repays him with her love; thus he becomes conscious of his manhood in a dual capacity. To pledge himself for a woman and to succour her was not only one of the virtues required of Arthur's knights; his mother had also recommended that he do so. This appears to be a characteristic feature of that age, in which the service of women played such an important role. Perceval's action can be understood as a compensation for the overevaluation of the masculine. The *Minnedienst* (homage of love) is an expression of the fact that the principle of relatedness, of Eros, was making itself more noticeable and was requiring greater consideration. The literature of the period clearly illustrates what an important part this homage played—in the songs of the troubadors as well as in other poems, but above all in the *Romans de la Table ronde*.

It may at first have been a matter of giving more consideration to the real woman, of establishing with her a relationship which was more than merely the sensual drive of nature. But hand in hand with this went a regard for the feminine in general and especially for the man's own individual femininity, the *anima*. By "anima" Jung understands a personification of the unconscious in the man, which appears as a woman or a goddess in dreams, visions and creative fantasies. She portrays his "Lady Soul," as Carl Spitteler has called her.[23] This figure would seem to be a derivative of the mother-imago,[24] and it is as if it encompassed within itself both the man's own inherent femininity and his actual experience with the real woman. At the same time, this image is prior to all his exper-

[23] Cf. *Aion*, pars. 25*ff* in particular.
[24] *Ibid.*, par. 26.

Knight on the Quest, illuminated manuscript, 1380–1400

King Arthur, a twelfth-century gate fragment from Modena

The Heart of Jesus

iences with woman, since in so far as the anima manifests herself as a goddess,[25] she is an archetype and consequently has a real, though invisible, existence transcending all actual experiences.[26]

When the anima is not projected on to a woman but remains in her own place in the soul, she is for the man a mediatrix of the contents of the unconscious.[27] The Grail Bearer, whom Perceval is to meet later, can be considered as such a figure. On the whole there are many feminine characters in the Grail literature who bear the stamp of the anima and are to be understood less as real women than as anima figures endowed with superhuman qualities and archetypal traits.

However, the figure of Blancheflor in our story does seem to emphasize the real woman rather than the anima, since the latter is still entirely projected. It accords with Perceval's development that having left his mother in order to go out into the world and after having been made a knight, he should then meet the objective woman, who at this stage is still indistinguishably entwined with the problem of the anima.

Even though a privileged position beckons him to Blancheflor's side at Belrepeire, Perceval is too manly to be able to rest content with the love of his lady and the agreeable and respected existence of the ruler of a castle. For this reason, after a short rest at Belrepeire, he sets forth in search of fresh adventures.

[25] *Ibid.*, par. 41.

[26] Cf. Emma Jung, *Animus and Anima*.

[27] Cf. Jung, *Two Essays*, par. 296, and *The Practice of Psychotherapy*, pars. 421*ff*.

CHAPTER IV

Perceval's First Visit to the Grail Castle

IN THOSE DAYS it was considered effeminate and unworthy of a true knight to indulge too long in homage to women; such indulgence was known as *accidie* according to many contemporary poets, for instance Chrétien in *Erec and Enide* and the *Chevalier au Lion.*[1] Perceval therefore does not tarry at Belrepeire. In this instance his urge to action is further coloured by his desire to seek out his mother and bring her to Blancheflor. But his yearning has even deeper roots than that; let us see where they lead him.

Riding along at random he comes to a deep river. He supposes that his mother's house must be somewhere on the far bank, but there is no crossing visible, and the road he is on leads no further. As if in answer to a prayer that God enable him to find what he is seeking, he sees a fisherman who shows him the way to the Grail Castle. He does not, it is true, find his mother there, but he does come to that other world which corresponds to the mother, that land which "can only be come upon unawares," as Wolfram puts it, that realm of dreams and visions—the unconscious.

That our hero is about to set foot into an otherworldly domain is indicated by the change in atmosphere which, in contrast to that of the previous events, now becomes magical. We have already seen that this other world plays a very important part in the Breton *contes* and in the Celtic world of fantasy. Significantly, the Gauls or Celts, as reported by Caesar,[2] looked upon Dispater, the god of the underworld, as their forefather. He must originally have been an earth god who had replaced a still

[1] Cf. R. Bezzola, *Le sens de l'Aventure et de l'Amour.* [2] *De Bello Gallico,* VI, 18.

older mother deity.[3] According to Irish and Welsh accounts, this other world was sometimes imagined as being under the earth. It was thought that the mythical inhabitants of Ireland, the *Tuatha De Danann*, "the people of the goddess Danu," had withdrawn into the hills (meaning the burial mounds) and lived there in everlasting youth and beauty, in magnificent palaces called *sidh*. Additional Irish names for the other world were *Mag Mor* (the Great Plain) and *Mag Mell* (the Pleasant Plain, also the Other World, the Land of Youth, the Land of the Living and, under Christian influence no doubt, the Land of Promise). This locality is also often thought of as lying under water and is then known as "The Land beneath the Waves" or as "The Green Isle in the West," "The Land beyond the Sea." It is also frequently called "Island of Women," because it or at any rate some such island, may only be inhabited by women.[4] Or else—and as such it is known to all of us—it is to be found in the midst of the everyday world but concealed by a magic haze, and it only becomes visible under special conditions and to particular people. Such a situation has now arisen in our story. Perceval, arriving at a place where the road leads no further,[5] sees a fisherman who directs him to the castle. The castle then suddenly appears before his eyes, after he has thought that the fisherman has played a trick on him; he finds the gate open, as if he were expected, and the Fisher King, now the suffering Lord of the Castle, is seated in the great hall waiting to receive him. All of this has a dream-like character, just as subsequent events will also have. Perceval therefore has suddenly arrived unawares, as if in a dream, at this central place which is an archetypal image, a fact that explains the numinous atmosphere of the Grail Castle.

[3] Cf. J. A. McCulloch, *The Religion of the Ancient Celts*, p. 44.

[4] Cf. E. Faral, *La Légende Arthurienne*, Vol. I, p. 133.

[5] It is a frequently observed fact that dreams of an exceptional, i.e. an archetypal, nature usually appear when the individual finds himself in a critical situation to which he can see no solution. Perceval is in such a situation when he arrives at the river bank. Cf. Jung and Kerenyi, *An Introduction to a Science of Mythology* (English title), *Essays on a Science of Mythology* (U.S. title), especially pp. 86*ff*.

The peculiar otherworldly quality of the Grail precincts has occasioned the view that the castle domain refers to the underworld. A. Pauphilet,[6] for instance, connects it with the legend of the Ville d'Ys, a submerged Breton town which is visible from time to time. A. C. L. Brown and other scholars are of the same opinion.[7] It seems obviously more appropriate, though, to interpret the Grail Castle as the region of the unconscious which can, it is true, be looked on as a sort of underworld in the sense that it is the realm of the immortal images. Turning back to the unconscious and paying attention to its contents is often depicted in dreams and fantasies as a descent into the underworld, and this motif also frequently recurs as one of the typical deeds or tasks of a hero.[8] But inasmuch as the unconscious also contains life and the future—that is, growth and development—within itself, it is more than merely the realm of the dead or an accumulation of the departed. The Grail Castle is therefore suitably compared with the unconscious, since anyone who penetrates to it can also, in contrast to the situation in the underworld, return from it.

After greeting the newcomer and excusing himself for not rising on account of his infirmity, the Lord of the Castle, grey-haired and arrayed in costly robes and a sable cap, bids Perceval be seated near him and asks him whence he has come. On learning that his guest left Belrepeire that morning, he can scarcely believe that he has achieved such a great distance in only one day. That it is a distance of a peculiar kind is explained by a reference in Wagner's *Parsifal*. On the way to the Grail Castle, Parsifal says:

> I scarcely move,—
> Yet swiftly seem to run.

To which his companion replies:

[6] "Au Sujet du Graal."

[7] In *The Origin of the Grail Legend*. Cf. also F. Kampers, *op. cit.*, pp. 42*ff.*

[8] Odysseus, for instance, in "Nekyia," the eleventh book of the *Odyssey*, or Aeneas in the sixth book of the *Aeneid*, Gilgamesh's descent to the underworld, or Faust's journey to the Mothers.

My son, thou seest
Here Space and Time are one.

It is thus a timeless dimension, of the kind we often experience in dreams.

Owing to the curious nature of the events which now befall Perceval, it seems legitimate to treat the whole episode as a dream or as a descent into the collective unconscious. It is a well-known fact that "big dreams," which are a determining factor in the later life of the young person, often occur at puberty,[9] so that it is not misleading to interpret this experience of Perceval's in a similar manner.

After the King and Perceval have conversed a while, a page enters with a sword which he presents to the "rich man," as the Lord of the Castle is here called, with the comment: "The blonde damsel, a niece, sends thee this; thou mayest bestow it on whom thou wilt." There are only three such swords in existence and the smith who forged them will die, so that he will be unable to make any more. The damsel hopes that the recipient will know how to value this one adequately. On the blade it is written that the sword is made of such true steel that it will not break except under perilous circumstances known only to the man who forged it. His host presents the sword to Perceval with the remark that it is an outstandingly rare and precious weapon and that it is destined for him in particular.

In Wolfram the sword is missing; in place of it the King's niece lends her cloak to Parzival. In most of the other versions,[10] the sword is broken to pieces and it is expected of the knight destined to guard the Grail that he should be able to restore it to wholeness.

After contemplating the sword for some time Perceval lays it

[9] An example may be found in *Black Elk Speaks*. Black Elk is a recently deceased medicine man of the Ogalala (Sioux) Indians, who recounts his visions and his life story.

[10] In Robert de Boron, for instance. For further examples, cf. Weston, *Legend of Sir Perceval*, Vol. I, pp. 138*f*.

aside with his other weapons. There follows the description of the true Grail vision which, because of its extreme importance, we will consider in detail.

Large candles, similar to those on altars, illuminate the chamber. While the Fisher King is conversing with Perceval, a page carrying a white lance enters from an adjoining apartment and crosses over between the fire and the two men sitting on the couch. From the iron a drop of blood drips on to the tip of the white shaft and flows down the shaft on to the page's hand. Like the others present, Perceval notices this, but mindful of his teacher's admonition not to ask too many questions, he does not trust himself to say anything about it. Two more pages enter carrying many-branched golden candelabra with lighted candles. Between them walks a maiden, gracious and beautifully adorned; in her hands she bears a grail of pure gold and richly set with precious stones, from which streams such a brilliant light that the lustre of the candles is dimmed. Another damsel follows the Grail Bearer carrying a silver carving platter. Like the page with the lance, the two maidens pass by the couch as they go from one apartment into another. Still Perceval does not dare say anything. The master now orders washing water to be brought and the table prepared for the meal. A broad ivory table is set up on two ebony supports in front of the couch and covered with a snow-white cloth. For the first course hind with pepper sauce is served and delicious wine is poured into the golden goblets. Meanwhile the Grail again passes before them—and Perceval observes that with every dish it circulates "*trestot découvert*" ("quite uncovered"). But however much he marvels over it he cannot find the courage to ask what it all means. He decides, however, to inquire the next morning of one of the servants. After the meal the host converses yet a while with his guest, then all manner of fruit and drinks, such as are taken before going to bed, are handed round. The Lord of the Castle says goodnight and has himself carried out by four serving men. Perceval retires to the bed prepared for him in the great hall and sleeps until morning. On waking he finds his armour and weapons lying ready beside him, but no one is present to help him arm, so he has to do it unaided. The doors giving on to the hall, with the exception of the one by which he entered, are all closed, and no one answers his knocking and calling. In the courtyard his horse is waiting, saddled, the gate is open, the drawbridge lowered, and Perceval prepares to depart from the deserted castle. The bridge is raised while he is still on it so that his horse is only just able to jump across. He turns around and challenges whoever has raised the bridge to show himself because he wishes to ask him something, but no one proffers a reply and nothing remains for him but to be on his way.

In Wolfram, the episode of the Grail Castle runs much the same course. Since, however, it does show variations in places, we shall also quote it in detail.

Parzifal leaves Belrapeire and his wife Condwiramurs in order to go out into the world and win more fame as a knight. The psychologically important point of his wishing to seek his mother is lacking here. Instead of coming, like Perceval, to a river, Parzifal arrives at a lake where he too finds a fisherman who directs him to the castle.

The events in the Grail Castle, and particularly the Grail procession, are far more elaborately and magnificently described in Wolfram. There are also features that are lacking in Chrétien, which permit us to infer another source. It is emphasized, for instance, that at the sight of the bleeding lance, those present break into loud lamentations. In Chrétien the company is not specifically mentioned; it is simply noted that a good five hundred knights could have taken their places around the gigantic hearth. Wolfram, on the other hand, describes in detail the arrangement of the hundred tables and the seats occupied by the four hundred knights who partake of the banquet. The Grail Bearer (Repanse de Schoye) is escorted by a train of twenty-four damsels in many-coloured robes, some of whom carry candelabra while others bear a precious table-top of "garnet hyacinth" and the ivory legs belonging to it, as well as two silver knives, concerning the use of which we shall hear in due course. The Grail itself is carried in on a "deep green achmardi," a piece of green silk material, and it is not a vessel but a *stone*.

The solemn, gorgeously coloured procession forcefully calls to mind the accounts of the mystery festivals of antiquity[11] in which holy objects were carried in procession. In the last book of *The Golden Ass*,[12] Apuleius presents a picture of a procession in honour of Isis, in which Henry and Renée Kohane go so far as to see the actual model for the Grail procession in Chrétien.[13] Apuleius describes how the hero, as the mystagogue, is attired in a cloak on which are depicted griffins and dragons, to identify him with the sun god. This signified the conclusion of his consecration into the service of Isis. The sight of the Grail Bearer reminds Parzival that he is wearing the cloak she gave him on his arrival at the Castle. The abundant meal, served on valuable dishes, is described in loving detail, and it is stressed that each person receives the food that he desires, "all by the power of the Grail."[14]

When everything has been tidied away after the meal and the procession of maidens has withdrawn again to the chamber from which it emerged, Parzival glimpses through the open door "the most beautiful old man he had ever beheld," with hair as white as snow. He is the same old king to whom, in Chrétien, the Host is brought in the Grail. Having gazed on all these things, Parzival, mindful of the admonition of his teacher whom he follows all too literally, forbears to put the questions which force themselves upon him. His host bids him good-night and he is led to a chamber where a luxurious bed has been prepared for him. Young pages undress him and four damsels bring "mulberry juice, wine, and claret, and . . . on a white cloth, fruits of the kind which grow in Paradise." After the damsels have retired, Parzival lies down to rest, but

[11] Cf. V. Magnien, *Les Mystères d'Eleusis*, pp. 1–36. Cf. also Mary Williams, "Some Aspects of the Grail Procession." For Celtic sources see Marx, "Le Cortège du Château des Merveilles."

[12] Apuleius, *The Metamorphoses or the Golden Ass*, Book XI.

[13] Henry and Renée Kahane, "Proto-Perceval und Proto-Parzival."

[14] Cf. verses 410*ff*.

his sleep is disturbed, for "*gesellecliche unz an den Tac, was bî im strengiu arbeit, ir boten künftigiu leit, sanden ime in slâfe dar,*" [15] which means that, like his mother, he is plagued by bad dreams.

As in Chrétien he finds on waking that the castle is empty and quiet, and he departs without catching sight of anyone whom he might have questioned concerning the state of affairs in the place.

Perceval has seen the mysterious castle, the sick King, the bleeding lance and the Grail, but as he did not ask what they meant they vanished without his having discovered anything about them. For this reason the whole incident has the effect of a dream, of an initiation dream, one might say.

When Perceval wishes to return to his mother, he arrives instead at the castle which is difficult to find—it is in the unconscious, which means in the "realm of the mothers." To be sure it is not described as such here; but it is so described when it appears in a later context, in that fantastic castle, the *Chastel merveilleux* (Castle of Marvels), also called the *Château aux pucelles* (Castle of the Maidens), which is freed by Perceval's double, Gauvain, from the enchantment under which it is burdened. Real mothers are living in that castle, Arthur's aged mother and Gauvain's own mother, together with many other women and girls. We are reminded that the Celtic other world is often called the "Island of Women," which does suggest that by these magical castles precisely that other world, the unconscious, is to be understood.

At any rate, Perceval does not find a world of mothers in the Grail Castle. On the contrary, he finds a world of "fathers," who, however, belong on the distaff side. The Rich Fisher, as the master of the Grail Castle is called, is a cousin of Perceval, according to Chrétien, while the mysterious old king to whom the Host is brought in the Grail is his uncle, *a brother of his mother*, to whom the meaning of a "spiritual father" is frequently given in primitive societies. According to Wolfram, Anfortas, the Grail King, is a brother of Parzival's mother, and Repanse

[15] Cf. verses 632*ff*.

de Schoye is his aunt.[16] We recall that before his departure Perceval's mother had told him about his father and his brothers and their fate, and that he had shown not the slightest interest, being wholly intent on his own enterprises. It would seem, however, that the mother's story has produced an after-effect in the unconscious of the youth and has there aroused the images of the paternal figures, which he then meets in the Grail Castle. This is a reaction which can often be observed in real life: An experience to which no importance is attached in consciousness will activate unconscious contents; in their turn these contents will then give rise to the appropriate dreams. This is an example of the frequently remarkable psychological subtleties in Chrétien, which cannot but provoke amazement.

It is also significant that (in Wolfram) the guardian of the Grail is Parzival's mother's brother, or else his grandfather or forebear on the mother's side.[17] Quite possibly, this is connected with the prominence accorded the feminine element which, in that age, was expressed by the "service of women." Matrilineal features, which might perhaps refer to an older order of society and might be connected with Celtic influences, are found rather

[16] Cf. also Nelli, "Le Graal dans l'Ethnographie." As stated in Wolfram Kyot was supposed to have been the first to discover in some old chronicles that the House of Anschouwe (Anjou) had been chosen as the Guardians of the Grail, obviously through the union of Gahmuret, the "Anschewin," and Herzeloyde, daughter or granddaughter of the Grail King, Frimurtel or Titurel, and sister of Anfortas, and Queen of Wales and Norgal; which brings us back to Britain once more, where an "Anschewin," Henry II, was king during the period of the composition of these poems.

[17] According to Wolfram's first book, Parzival's descent was as follows: A Gahmuret, the younger son of Gandin, King of Anschouwe (Anjou), entered the service of Baruch of Baldak (Bagdad), the mightiest monarch of his day, and fought in the East. He had a love affair with the dark-skinned Belakane, whom he secretly abandoned in order to pursue fresh adventures. He made the excuse that he could not marry her on account of her colour and her different religion. She bore him the piebald Feirefiz. Gahmuret's father was himself a son of Addanz, a cousin of Uther Pendragon. The two brothers, fathers respectively of Uther Pendragon and Addanz, were called Lazaliez and Prinkus. Their father was Mazadan who was abducted to Feimurgen (Fata Morgana) by a fairy. Gahmuret's family was descended from this Mazadan and his fairy.

generally dispersed throughout this literature. More probably, however, it is due to a predominance of the unconscious, which in the man is distinguished by feminine elements.

Whether it is a question now of maternal or paternal forebears,[18] it is always—with the exception of the Grail Bearer, who may be taken as an anima figure—father figures whom the hero meets in the Grail Castle.

The ancestors or spirits of the ancestors also play an important part in the initiation dreams and ceremonies of so-called primitive peoples. The establishment of the relation to the ancestors belongs to the very essence of the rites of initiation.[19] Only thus can the youth become a fully adequate member of the tribe. In like manner Perceval is initiated in the Grail Castle, for while he was made a member of a brotherhood by the accolade bestowed on him by his teacher, Gornemant, he here becomes acquainted with his spiritual forebears, so to speak. For him, the fatherless "son of the widow," this is doubly important, for through the connection with the male members of the family he does, in a way, acquire a father. The emphasis on the masculine element which results from this turns the youth into a true man for the first time. The importance for our story of this kinship motif is indicated by its appearance in all the versions, and in some of them it is expressly stated that he who wins the Grail must not only prove himself to be the greatest hero, but at the same time to be either a descendant or a relative of the Grail King.

In primitive initiation rites the novice is instructed and initiated into the tribal mysteries by the ancestors or the ancestral spirits. In the same way the treasures guarded by the Grail King are brought out for Perceval, rather as if they were the holy relics of the tribe. Before we investigate these relics more closely, however, the question arises as to the kind of family

[18] In those versions that connect the Grail with Joseph of Arimathea it is the ancestors of the father's side who are the Guardians of the Grail and it is Perceval's duty to seek out his grandfather or uncle and take over his office.

[19] Cf. Hastings, *Encyclopedia*, Vol. VII, under "Initiation."

into which Perceval is to be admitted.[20] In this context the masculine obviously does not refer to the actual physical father or to ordinary masculinity but rather to that masculine spirit which corresponds to the world of the father and which should here be understood as *a higher state of consciousness.* This has heretofore been lacking in the young Perceval, who has been driven solely by his instincts. His mother had already told him that she came of a very noble family indeed, and from the hermit Trevrizent he later learns that she was the sister of the hermit and of the old Grail King. In this stressing of a matrilineal and especially of a *spiritual* pedigree, a hint may be discerned that it is not a question of a physical/worldly but rather of a psychic/spiritual relationship. His mother's two brothers, Perceval's uncles, are both characterized as being very unworldly; the hermit lives on bread and grapes brought to him daily by an angel, and of the old Grail King (the father of the Rich Fisher) it is said that

il est si esperitans,
qu'a sa vie plus ne convient
que l'oiste qui el graal vient.

he is so spiritual
that for his life nothing here is required
than the Host that is brought in the Grail.

If Perceval belongs to this family it must refer more especially to the spiritual Perceval, the higher man within.

In those versions which connect the Grail with Joseph of Arimathea, the descent of the Grail King is traced either from Joseph or from Nicodemus, and he who wins the Grail must show that he is descended from this family. Thus he is brought

[20] Membership in a society, tribe, nation, church or other group is of the utmost importance, since it represents support and protection without which the single individual can only manage with difficulty, if at all. It should also be mentioned here that in those nations to which Perceval, Arthur and the others belonged, the clan wielded a quite exceptional power. But it is a question of more than that in the present case, for what Chrétien's poem described is not so much Perceval's social as his psychic development.

into close connection with Christ, which confirms the hypothesis that by the "Grail hero" the higher man, in the religious sense of the word, is indicated. Here two different aspects, which we can trace right through the whole work, are introduced. On the one hand, the events described can be understood as symbolic representations of the archetypal development of the hero, as already explained;[21] on the other hand, they possess a dimension in depth which points quite specifically to the problem of the Christian era. Seen in this connection, *the figure of Perceval is set within the framework of the problem of the psychological development of the Christian age, within which he appears to be destined for a specific saviour role.* As Christ was himself prefigured by a long line of ancestors, divided into three groups of fourteen each,[22] so Perceval is here related back to the lifetime of Christ, so that there is at least a hint that *he appears to be set up as a parallel to Christ.* Perceval's role as a Christ-like redeemer figure will be made still clearer later on from the context.

We come now to the description of the Grail procession in which feminine figures also appear. One of these, the Bearer of the Grail, a niece or daughter of the Grail King (in Chrétien she is the sister of the Rich Fisher and Perceval's aunt), is particularly clearly portrayed. As mentioned, we may take her as an anima figure, a personification, that is, of the inner psychic realities, since she is at home in the dream world in which these events are played out. It is one of the anima's functions to bring to view a vision of the contents of this dream world, the images of the unconscious as Perceval here experiences it. That this role belongs to the anima is indicated, among other things, by the fact that the perception or seeing of inner images requires an attitude of feminine receptivity, whereas the ability to grasp and understand what has been seen is made possible by the masculine mind. To this may be added that the man's

[21] Max Wehrli considers that as a "universal ego" Perceval is a figure of objective significance, for which reason the romance of his self-development is also a romantic analogy to the story of humanity's redemption. In other words, Perceval is an inner figure.

[22] Corresponding to the fourteen ka's of the Egyptian Pharaohs.

individual anima, his own feminine aspect, is for the most part very largely unconscious to him; so for this reason too the functions corresponding to this aspect will also take the lead in the unconscious. There will be a more exhaustive discussion of this anima figure in due course, for she seems to stand in a compensatory relationship to Blancheflor. This is illustrated by the functions of both these feminine figures. But first let us turn our attention to those things which Perceval is permitted to see in addition to the Guardian of the Grail and the archetypal anima figure. These are the sword, the lance, the Grail, the table, the carving platter and—in Wolfram—two knives.[23] In these objects some of the essential meaning of the Grail legend appears to be symbolically represented.

[23] They are carried in instead of the platter, and it is stated that they serve to scrape away the poison that forms in Anfortas' wound. It may, however, be assumed that Wolfram's faulty knowledge of French caused him to understand *tailleoir* (plate) as "knife," from *tailler* (to carve). But it seems worth noting that in the Légende de Fécamp, which has the Holy Blood for its subject, two knives used by Joseph of Arimathea to remove the blood from Christ's wounds are also mentioned.

CHAPTER V

The Sword and the Lance

THE FIRST OBJECT shown to Perceval in the Grail procession is the sword which will never break except under dangerous circumstances known only to the smith who forged it. Perceval merely looks at it and lays it aside.

As a masculine weapon the sword denotes strength, power and, in that age more particularly, chivalry; it is an implement which serves to overcome hostile powers.[1] As the weapon especially characteristic of heroes or knights, the sword is often very closely connected with its owner, as if it were a part of him, and sometimes it has a name and a personality of its own. Arthur's sword is called Excalibur or Caliburnus, Roland's is named Durandel. Before Arthur departs by boat to Avalon, an arm reaches up out of the water and carries Excalibur down into the depths. The sword is therefore a symbol or representative, so to speak, of its owner, and since the knight has the task of coming to terms with the outer world and overcoming it, the sword can be compared with certain functions of the ego personality to whom this task belongs. It might seem paradoxical that Perceval finds the father, the masculine, the incentive to become conscious, in the "motherly" realm of the unconscious, of which the Grail Castle forms a part. This same idea is also expressed by the fact that it is the feminine Bearer of the Grail who sends him the sword. It is a good example of how precisely those weapons which are necessary to the mastery of life and of the world are presented by the anima, out of the maternal matrix of the unconscious.

[1] Such a sword is often engraved with an inscription and has precious stones set in the hilt which impart magic strength.

The development of a conscious "ego" as the centre of consciousness is a process which begins in childhood and which initiates the process of individuation. Through the development of the ego, the original state of undifferentiation and of identity with the surroundings will progressively dissolve.[2] It is essential for the individual who has to find his way in life to possess an ego with which to comprehend and meet the world face to face. It is equally necessary for the development of the individuation process, which usually sets in in the second half of life, for if the individual lacks a definite ego capable of confronting the inner world of the unconscious, the danger of being overwhelmed by unconscious contents arises. In his writings Jung has repeatedly emphasized the importance of this.[3]

As we shall soon see, Perceval's experience of the Grail is closely bound up with the development of his consciousness. The sword which he receives indicates this progress in symbolic form. Over and above this, however, it has further meanings which point to the problems of the age. As a cutting weapon it serves to separate or, metaphorically, to "differentiate", so it can also stand for the mind, especially the intellect or understanding intelligence, of whose "incisive" quality we speak. As the sword of justice it also signifies judgment, wrath[4] and vengeance. Discrimination, which means judgment with thought, is exactly what has so far been lacking in Perceval. He has followed his mother's advice in a naïvely literal manner, without reflecting upon it or allowing any voice to his own judgment; judgment was equally lacking when he so impudently surprised the young woman in the tent and when he visited the Grail Castle. The unconscious tends to remedy this deficiency—an example of its compensatory function—by presenting him with the sword. At the same time his attention

[2] Jung, "Analytical Psychology and Education," in *The Development of Personality*, pars. 127*ff*.

[3] See *Psychological Types*, p. 594.

[4] Cf. Jung, "The Visions of Zosimos," in *Alchemical Studies*, par. 110; and "Transformation Symbolism in the Mass," in *Psychology and Religion*, pars. 359–60.

is drawn to the fact that it is an outstanding weapon but one that will none the less prove unreliable on a particular occasion. There is, therefore, a situation which the sword cannot cope with, and this is a warning against wielding it blindly, an action which would certainly have suited Perceval's natural inclinations.

In many versions, in Robert de Boron, for instance, and in Chrétien's continuators, the sword is already broken when it is laid before Perceval. The reason usually given for this is that its owner has made an unworthy or treacherous use of it. One of the requirements of the knight who wins the Grail is that he be able to join it together once more, thus proving that he is the rightful, that is, the foremost and predestined, hero. This idea also plays an important part in the *Queste*, where the knight who finds the Grail (in this instance, Galahad) must prove that he is descended from King Solomon. Only such a descendant can take possession of this precious sword, "*as estranges renges*," which is on board a mysterious or mystical ship dispatched to Britain for this very purpose.[5] So the sword appears to reach at least as far back as the rise of Christianity, if not further. It could therefore symbolize an attitude of "righteousness" and of masculine judgment and understanding, going back as far as the Old Testament. This archaic form of rational judgment, which was no longer adequate to its subject, had to be surrendered, for which reason the sword was shattered. Only after he has realized through direct contemplation those unconscious contents symbolized by the Grail can Perceval restore the sword to wholeness again. Only then can a new use, which is no longer destructive, be found for the discerning intellectual mind. In certain manuscript versions[6] it is stated that the sword is only broken later, in Perceval's hand, when, in fact, he is fighting l'Orguelleus de la Lande, the friend of the young woman in the tent.[7] He throws the pieces away and carries the struggle to a victorious conclusion with the sword he has taken from the

[5] Cf. *Huth-Merlin*.

[6] Weston, *Legend of Sir Perceval*, Vol. I, pp. 136*ff*.

[7] See below for further details.

Red Knight. L'Orguelleus as his name indicates, depicts a shadow, which is not, like the Red Knight, an embodiment of affect and brutality, but rather of the *pride* of chivalry. Looked at from the psychological point of view, it is natural that a young person who sets himself a lofty ideal such as is represented by chivalry should, without noticing it, succumb to a certain arrogance. L'Orguelleus is a knight, moreover, who imagines that he has found his (innocent) lady guilty of unfaithfulness and who has consequently cruelly and mercilessly punished her. Such a demand for ideal fidelity has something all too absolute and inhuman about it. This shadow element of arrogance is more subtle and more difficult to recognize than the affectivity and aggression of the Red Knight, since it is a question of a secret and exaggerated vanity masquerading as the idea of "knightly honour." Face to face with *this* problem, the power of judgment or of thinking, which is symbolized by the sword from the Grail Castle, will obviously break.[8] The question of what this mental attitude and judgment could mean in a historical sense will be discussed more closely below in connection with the lance.

Like the sword, the *lance* or spear is also a masculine symbol. Its essential quality, however, is not sharpness or separation, but *aim* or *direction* and *impact*. This attribute is particularly marked in the javelin, the weapon of the young Perceval, and also in the arrow. This characteristic of the weapon can be understood metaphorically as perception of the goal or awareness of one's intention, or as keeping one's eye on and reaching further possibilities. Psychologically this could be compared with the function of intuition. Even though one cannot yet properly speak of differentiated functions in the case of such an early, youthful or primitive stage as that which Perceval now represents, tendencies towards the development of such functions are none the less in evidence. Perceval can scarcely be said to think or discriminate, but from the beginning a pronounced aspiration towards the goal is perceptible, for instance in his

[8] Also cf. what is said later (pp. 356, 513*f*) about the stag as the "animal soul" of Christ, and the problem of pride.

determination to become a knight and later in his unremitting search for the Grail. In this fixing of his judgment on far distant goals it might be possible to discern something like intuition, which at this stage is otherwise scarcely to be distinguished from instinctual impulse.

There are also traces of a feeling judgment present, as in the pleasure Perceval experiences on his first encounter with the knights or in his meeting with Blancheflor, though these are still very undifferentiated. The psychic functions are more or less intermingled in an individual who is not as yet very conscious. It is only with increasing consciousness that they become separated and differentiated.

The following amplifications, which point beyond the personal to a universal and impersonal meaning, may serve to clarify further the significance of the lance.

The spear is often an attribute of a particular god. Wotan and Zeus, for instance, each had his spear, Zeus' being identified with lightning or the thunderbolt. Apollo's arrows may also be compared with Wotan's spear.[9] In Celtic mythology, which is regarded by many scholars as the source of the Grail legend,[10] the sword also plays a significant part, in addition to the spear or lance. Thus, it was said of the mythical, semi-divine inhabitants of Ireland, who came from Heaven or from four cities where they had assimilated learning and the arts, that they brought a magic treasure with them from each of those places.[11] The first treasure was the *Lia Fail*, or *Stone of Destiny*, on which the Kings of Ireland stood during their coronation and of which it was said that it confirmed the legitimacy of the king by roaring. This stone was brought to Scotland in the sixth century and

[9] In the first place the lance and Grail can naturally be looked upon as a pair of opposites, alternatively as masculine and feminine symbols. They are thus interpreted by Weston, for example, in *From Ritual to Romance*, p. 71, and by Nelli in *Lumière du Graal*, p. 26. This explanation seems somewhat too simple and in this connection not convincing, even though an important role certainly attaches to the fundamental masculine-feminine pair of opposites in our story.

[10] Cf. Nutt, *Studies on the Legend of the Holy Grail*, p. 111; and Marx, *Légende Arthurienne*, pp. 129*ff*, 195*ff* and 262*ff*.

[11] Cf. Marx, *op. cit.*, pp. 129–30.

taken from Scone to England by Edward I in 1296 where, as the Coronation Stone, it was incorporated into the Coronation Chair. To this day, the rulers of Great Britain are crowned upon it. The second treasure was the *unconquerable sword* of the god Lug,[12] the third a *magic spear*, and the fourth, known as the Cauldron of Dagda (a divine being), was a *vessel* from which an entire army could be fed. These four treasures were naturally associated with the corresponding objects in the Grail legend and looked upon as proof of the Celtic or Irish origin of the latter.

Four-foldness is one of the most universal of symbols,[13] for the quaternity often appears as the expression or representation of the growth of consciousness. The conception of the world as a quaternity, originating perhaps in the four points of the compass which possess such great significance for primitive peoples, seems to have proved particularly apt and serviceable. Growth of consciousness, culture and a conception of the world go hand in hand and can therefore all be expressed by a quaternity of symbols.

The number four also refers to the so-called individuation process. This may be understood primarily as the process, observable throughout nature, of the genesis and differentiation of the individual organism. The fact that there are no two exactly identical plants or animals, let alone human beings, speaks for the unique quality of the individual, who does indeed share the same characteristics in common with all other members of the species but is equally, thanks to their specific combination, differentiated from his fellows.[14] In the psychological sense, individuation signifies a psychic process which

[12] Lug is a Celtic god of light. As such he is also a bringer of culture. He invented handicrafts, art and science and therefore corresponds to Mercury. He also invented ball games and equine sports, the activities of early Britain. Cf. McCulloch, *The Religion of the Ancient Celts*, p. 91.

[13] A reminder of a similar quarternity of symbols still exists in our playing cards, especially in the Tarot where there are the four symbols of the sword, wand, cup and pentacles (coins).

[14] Cf. Jung, *Psychological Types*, Ch. XI on "Definitions," under *Individuation.*

strives for the differentiation of the individual from the collective psyche and his development into an individual personality.[15] Individuality is indeed an *a priori* datum,[16] but it only exists unconsciously as a specific "pattern" or "predisposition" determined by the genes. The realization of individuality does not come about *eo ipso,* since it unquestionably requires a coming to terms with the environment, with which the individual often feels unable to cope. A degree of adaptation, however, is absolutely indispensable, since man is not only a solitary and isolated creature but also a collective being who requires relationships with others. He is already by nature attuned to such relationships.[17] For this reason the true individual personality consists of a union of these two opposing tendencies. The conflict between them and their reconciliation requires the development of consciousness. The process of psychological individuation is, for that reason, also a process of becoming conscious, a process which evolves conjointly with the confrontation of the individual with the outer world on the one hand and of the individual with the objective inner world (the unconscious) on the other.

In reality, the process of individuation begins at birth with the physical separation from the mother. The development of consciousness progresses with increasing encounters with the outer world. Normally this adaptation to the surroundings is the task and content of the first half of life. In the second half, the problem is that of becoming aware of the inherent individuality and its realization, in the sense indicated above.[18] This is perhaps why Perceval does not succeed the first time in winning the "treasure hard to attain," the symbol of individuation, and

[15] *Ibid.*, p. 562.

[16] *Ibid.*, p. 563.

[17] *Ibid.*, p. 562; and *Two Essays*, pars. 266*ff.*

[18] No sharp dividing line can be drawn, however, since here, as everywhere, there are exceptions, and many people, either by reason of a pronounced ability or of particularly difficult environmental conditions, are forced far earlier than others to a confrontation with themselves and with others. It is to the experiences of modern psychology, and especially to Jung's conceptions, that we owe a clear and intelligible formulation of the problem and an indication of a way to its solution.

why he has to solve other problems first before he can return to the quaternity of objects and understand their mystery.

Let us now turn to the meaning of the specific objects.

The lance plays an important part in Celtic mythology and legend, as it does in those of other races. J. Marx, in his previously mentioned book,[19] gives a series of examples. The lance of the god Lug is compared with lightning. Lances with magical attributes are abundant. Celtchar's possesses a life of its own: its strength has to be modified by dipping it into a poisonous bloody fluid; otherwise it will injure even the bearer himself.[20] Other lances return to their owners after being thrown. Bloody or flaming lances, which recall the bleeding lance of the Grail procession, often appear. As a specifically British weapon, the lance served the Britons in exile as a symbol for the recovery of their native land. In his description of a journey through Wales, which he undertook in 1188, Giraldus Cambrensis reports that the Britons of North Wales were distinguished by particularly long lances.[21] Peredur, the Welsh Perceval, was called "Peredur of the Long Lance".

In the Grail legend, the lance appears under different aspects, Chrétien introduces it as "*la lance qui saigne*" ("the bleeding lance"), but without mentioning its origin. The wounding of the Grail King is occasioned by the lance of a heathen adversary, and it is said that the curse under which the land of Logres suffers was caused by this lance. In the continuations to Chrétien's poems, a "*coup douloureux*" ("grievous blow") plays an important part in exactly the same sense.[22] The lance, however, is not only responsible for the wounding of the Grail King but, like Arthur's sword Excalibur, also serves to heal the wound it has inflicted. When the bleeding spear in Wolfram's *Parzival* is held to the wound, it is supposed to draw out the poison and relieve Anfortas' pain. In the *Queste,* Galahad heals the King by spreading blood from the lance over the

[19] *Légende Arthurienne*, p. 257.

[20] *Ibid.*, p. 133.

[21] *Itinerarium Cambriae or Itinerary through Wales*, p. 144.

[22] The motif of the lance can only be fully explained psychologically when it is clearer *who* inflicted the wound, but this can only be discussed later.

wound. In Chrétien and Wolfram, the lance is carried by a page. In the Continuation to *Perceval*,[23] Gauvain sees the bleeding lance standing in a holder; the blood flows from the iron tip down the shaft and from there into a *silver* vessel from which a *golden* pipe carries it to a similar silver vessel once more.

It was probably inevitable that with the Christianization of the legend the lance should have been identified with the lance of Longinus.[24] At the time of the rise of the Grail legend, Longinus' lance was arousing universal interest because it was supposed to have been found by the Crusaders at the siege of Antioch in 1098. It was presumably owing to this miracle that the capture of the citadel was successful. Albert von Aachen describes this episode as follows in his *Geschichte des ersten Kreuzzuges*:

> In the midst of these sufferings, of famine and of the anxieties of the siege, and of the worries concerning the ambushes and assaults which the Turks carried out unremittingly against the humiliated and despairing people of God, a cleric from Provence asserted one day that it had been revealed to him in a vision where the lance which had once pierced Our Lord's side was lying. This cleric notified the Lord Bishop Adhemar of Puy and Count Raymond of the spot where they might find the precious treasure of the lance, to wit in the church of Saint Peter, the Prince of the Apostles.

There they dug and found the lance.

> And they showed the lance that had been found in that church to all the Christian Princes and spread abroad the tidings of this discovery and wrapped the lance in precious stuff of purple. And this revelation and showing of the lance

[23] Roach, *The Continuations*, Vol. I, p. 363; or Potvin, *Wauchier de Denain*, verse 2051; and the "*Elucidation*," verse 273.

[24] Rose Jeffries Peebles gives a detailed account of Longinus' lance in "The Legend of Longinus in Ecclesiastical Tradition and in English Literature, and Its Connection with the Grail." Cf. also Brown, "The Bleeding Lance,", pp. 1–59; and Nitze, "The Bleeding Lance and Philip of Flanders."

occasioned great hope and joy for the people of Christ everywhere, and they venerated the relic with great solemnity and with countless offerings of gold and silver.[25]

A holy lance (perhaps the same one), known as the Mauritius lance because it was for a time in the possession of the Abbot of St. Maurice in the Valais,[26] was part, or perhaps still is part, of the German Imperial Regalia and was kept in the treasury of the Hofburg in Vienna until 1937.

In the ritual of the Greek Church, a "holy lance"—actually a lance-shaped knife—is used to cut up the Host on the paten, or the bread is pierced with a lance to indicate the Slaying of the Lamb. According to the liturgy of St. Chrysostom, it was carried in procession with the chalice and the paten.[27]

L. E. Iselin[28] draws attention to an interesting comparison of the lance and sword in the Syrian *Cave of Treasures*, a collection of Christian legends and fables dating from the seventh century.[29] The passage reads: "On Friday the two-edged sword was given to the Cherub, and on Friday Christ smote with the spear, and brake the two-edged sword."[30] This is very similar to the Fisher King's remark to Gauvain that they had won everything by the lance but had lost it all by the sword,[31] except that the sequence is reversed.

This amplification throws further light on the meaning of both lance and sword. As mentioned, the latter symbolizes not only the separating and discriminating aspect of the intellect, but also the judging, wrathful intervention of God in earthly affairs. In this connection, the statements of the alchemist

[25] Vol. I, p. 214.

[26] *Die Religion in Geschichte und Gegenwart* (under "lance").

[27] Cf. K. Burdach, "Der Graal;" also Jung, *Psychology and Religion*, par. 324; Anitchkof, *Joachim de Flore*, pp. 301–2; and recently, Hubert Kolb, *Monsalvaesche: Studien zum Kyot Problem*, pp. 79*ff*. Kolb completely ignores our interpretation.

[28] *Op cit.*, p. 111.

[29] Cf. the German publication of C. Bezold; or *The Book of the Cave of Treasures*.

[30] Cf. Bezold, *op. cit.*, p. 63; and Budge, *op. cit.*, p. 223.

[31] Cf. Roach, *The Continuations*, Vol. I, pp. 366–67.

Gerhard Dorn, quoted by Jung in *Psychology and Religion*,[32] gain in significance:

> After a long interval of time the Deus Optimus Maximus immersed himself in the inmost of his secrets, and he decided, out of the compassion of his love as well as for the demands of justice, *to take the sword of wrath from the hand of the angel.* And having hung the sword on the tree, he substituted for it *a golden trident, and thus was the wrath of God changed into love.*[33] . . . When peace and justice were united, the water of Grace flowed more abundantly from above, and now it bathes the whole world.[34]

Interpretations of the sword which make of it *a symbol of the divinity concealed in man*, an inner psychic god-image which transforms itself in and through itself, are also to be found in texts of the Gnosis of the Ophites and in Simon Magus.[35] At first it appears in the guise of a nature and life spirit, concealed in man, which is gradually able to transmute itself into *a divine figure within the human being.* For this reason the sword is also thought of, in the texts of the alchemists, as similar in nature to their "divine water" and to the "stone".[36] Their Mercurius serves for instance as a permeating spirit, "*penetrabilior ancipiti gladio*" ("sharper than any two-edged sword").[37] The sword signifies that life-urge which leads to the recognition of the Self.

According to the story, however, it is now broken, through treacherous misuse, indicating a false application of the intellectual faculties which are therefore no longer capable of functioning in the interests of life. This is similar to the thinking of the Fathers of the Christian Church, who used the sword of their intellect only within the framework of that which was already accepted and who, therefore, when faced with certain

[32] Par. 357; also cf. *Alchemical Studies*, par. 446, among others.
[33] Italics added.
[34] "Speculativa philosophia," in *Theatrum chemicum*, Vol. I, pp. 254*ff*.
[35] Quoted by Jung, *Psychology and Religion*, par. 359.
[36] Jung, *Alchemical Studies*, par. 89.
[37] *Ibid.*, par. 110.

prejudices, as for instance regarding the *privatio boni*,[38] could not struggle through to a direct concept based on the contemplation of inner and outer reality. The broken sword of the Grail story could, in this sense, refer to a failure in the thinking of that age, which proved unequal to the problem of the shadow and its paradoxes—the paradox, for instance, that high virtue leads to pride and through this is perverted into something evil. *This* is the reason Perceval's sword breaks in the fight with l'Orguelleus de la Lande. In the passages quoted above, the separating sharpness of the sword is set in opposition to the healing influence of the lance.[39] In contrast to the cutting function of the former, the lance aims at one particular spot, at the essential, the centre, towards which it directs its point. It may be compared with the *telum passionis* of the alchemical Mercurius, that "missile of passion" which Mercurius sends forth.[40]

In Chrétien and in Wolfram, the Fisher King is wounded by the poisoned *lance* of a *heathen* opponent. In the *Lancelot Grail*, the son of Joseph of Arimathea is wounded in the thigh by a black angel[41] and subsequently healed by another angel with the same lance, whereupon he prophesies that the lance is a sign for the beginning of the wonderful adventure in Britain. At some future time it will start to bleed, and a later descendent of Joseph will be wounded by it through both thighs. This recalls the wound by which, according to Chrétien, Perceval's father was disabled. In many versions, the lance appears to combine destructive and positive aspects in the same weapon, while also referring to the transfer of the Grail tradition to Britain. This could point to a meaningful connection, since the Grail legend had assimilated additional features from Celtic and Germanic heathendom, which was more archaic than that of the Mediterranean cultures and in contrast to the latter was

[38] Concerning the concept of the *privatio boni*, see *Aion*, pars. 74*ff*.

[39] Sometimes the lance and sword are identical in Christian legends. Cf. Iselin, *op. cit.*, p. 116.

[40] Cf. Jung, *Alchemical Studies*, par. 278. The passage is in Ripley, *Opera omnia chemica*.

[41] At that moment when he is trying to bind a devil sitting on a corpse.

much closer to nature. Also, the lance is an older weapon than the sword and for this reason symbolizes a still more undifferentiated faculty of judgment which is closer to "hitting the target" than to discrimination.

Occasionally, the lance is also called *lance vengeresse* (lance of vengeance), as in the "Merlin," while in the Spanish *Demanda di San Graal* it is *la lanza vengadora* and is described as standing in a golden vessel or hovering in the air. It is similarly depicted in the *Lancelot Grail* and in the *Queste*. In "Merlin," too, the King is wounded by the lance, which is the cause of the abnormal conditions prevailing in his country.[42] Again, in *Peredur*, the lance refers to unavenged misdeeds. According to old popular beliefs,[43] a crime contaminates the criminal, and, should he remain undiscovered in the community, it contaminates society as well. His punishment is an extirpation of a cult impurity.

It seems then that the Grail King has been "struck" by an impulse rising unexpectedly from the unconscious with which he is unable to come to terms. This impulse emerges from the heathen layer of the soul or else from a dark opponent behind whom God Himself appears to be standing.[44] The suffering of the King will endure as long as this unconscious impulse is not realized in consciousness.

The close connection between lance and Grail vessel is rooted in a medieval Christian view which is clearly expressed in a creed dating from the eleventh century. This creed was drawn up by Maurilius, Archbishop of Rouen, on the occasion of the famous Last Supper Dispute, caused by the unorthodox views of Berengar of Tours, an opponent of the Bishop. At the synod of Rouen in 1055 the entire priesthood of Normandy was obliged to swear to the following affirmation of the Doctrine of the Eucharist, the only doctrine accepted as true by the Church:

> We believe with the heart and confess with the mouth that the bread placed on the altar is only bread before the

[42] Also cf. Potvin, *Wauchier de Danain*, IV, 5.
[43] *Handwörterbuch des deutschen Aberglaubens*, under "Punishment."
[44] In so far as the wounded one is sometimes an angel.

> consecration, but through the same consecration, through the ineffable power of the Godhead, the nature and substance of bread is converted into the nature and substance of flesh; and indeed not into the flesh of anything save that which was conceived of the Holy Ghost, born of the Virgin Mary, which for us men and for our salvation was smitten with the scourge, hung upon the cross, lay in the grave, on the third day rose from the grave, and sitteth on the right hand of the Father. Similarly the wine, which, mingled with water, is placed in the cup for consecration, is truly and essentially converted into *that blood which, through the lance of the soldier, flowed happily from the wound in the Lord's side for the redemption of the world.*[45]

According to this view, it is not so much the crucifixion of Christ which is looked upon as the redeeming factor but rather the blood flowing from his side after his death. This is a fundamentally magico-archaic conception. From time immemorial, and still today, blood was and is considered to be "a very special fluid," for which the religious usage and magical practices of all people in all ages provide countless examples. One need only draw attention to the blood sacrifices in various systems of worship and to all the love, healing and maledictory magic in which blood plays a part. Consecrations and initiations are ratified, contracts sealed and crimes expiated with blood. And it can still happen, even today, that someone will sell himself to the Devil with his blood. This idea is everywhere based on the assumption that *blood embodies the life-principle and is the seat of the soul.* This belief is expressed as far back as the *Odyssey* in which, on the occasion of Odysseus' visit to Hades, the souls of the departed regain consciousness on drinking the sacrificial blood; or back to the Old Testament where it is written: "For the life of the flesh is in the blood; and I have given it to you upon the altar" (Leviticus 17:11); and: "For it is the life of all flesh; the blood of it is for the life thereof"

[45] From A. J. Macdonald, *Berengar and the Reform of Sacramental Doctrine,* p. 119.

(17:14); and: "Only be sure that thou eat not the blood: for the blood is the life; and thou mayest not eat the life with the flesh" (Deuteronomy 12:23).

It is clear that blood is essentially a mana substance and anything which possesses great mana invariably owes its effectiveness to an underlying *archetypal* idea. In this case it is the belief in the identity of blood = life = soul. The conception of blood as soul prevailed in the Middle Ages, too, according to which the Eucharistic blood represented the soul of Christ,[46] and for the same reason the Grail vessel also contained his soul.

If such mysterious power is attributed to ordinary human or even to animal blood, how much more then to the blood of Christ! In the Christian doctrine it is precisely this blood that is the means of salvation for all humanity. It strikes one as significant that it is not only the death of Christ, the actual fact of his dying, that is stressed as the redeeming factor, but just as much, if not more so, the blood shed in the process, because it is in the blood that the essentially atoning power adheres. When, in most of the versions, the bleeding lance appears as appertaining to the Grail, this is because *it is the instrument by which the redeeming blood was brought forth into manifestation.* The drops of blood flowing from its tip, which in some versions drip into the Grail vessel, naturally also symbolize the sacrificial death of Christ, eternally taking place. By reason of these views the blood became the central sacrament and mystery of the Christian ritual. At all times, but quite particularly in the Middle Ages, this concept of the blood and the ideas connected with it stirred men's feelings to their depths. Evidence for this is to be found in abundance in the writings of the Church, for the

[46] Cf. Jung, "Transformation Symbolism in the Mass," in *Psychology and Religion*, par. 335; and S. Paschasii Radberti Abbatis Corbeiensis, *Liber de corpore et sanguine Domini*, J.-P. Migne, *Pat. Lat.*, Vol. CVI, col. 69c, according to Macdonald, *op. cit.*, pp. 36 and 230. The eucharistic body and blood were, according to Candiotus of Fulda, the body and *soul* of Christ; and Christian Drubmar says: This blood is the image of the soul of Christ. (Quod sanguisible animae Christi figuram tenet.) J.-P. Migne, *Pat. Lat.* Vol. LVI, col. 69c and see A. J. MacDonald, *Berengar and the Reform of the Sacramental Doctrine*, pp. 36 and 230.

Church took great pains to grasp the wondrous mystery intellectually, and in the accounts of pious believers who sought, through self-abnegation and participation in the mystery, to experience the meaning of Christ's suffering. Many miracles also occurred in connection with the Communion chalice or the Eucharistic bread, from which we can see how actively fantasy too was occupied with this matter. An expression of this interest in the mystery—so deeply moving to human beings—and, to a certain extent, an expression which may also be regarded as the Church's answer, was the introduction, around the end of the twelfth century, of the Elevation of the Host into the ritual, so that the Host was shown to the congregation for the first time apart from the Communion service. In his article, "*Die Verehrung der Eucharistie im Mittelalter*" P. Browe[47] writes, "As greatly as they had previously feared to see the holy mystery unveiled, the people now pressed forward to behold the uplifted Host." The same author remarks that by the middle of the thirteenth century, the Elevation was almost universally practised, although it had not been known before the end of the twelfth. Previously it had been expressly forbidden to look upon the holy object.[48] This need "to see the holy mystery unveiled" is characteristic of the great spiritual awakening of Western man which was taking place at that time and being manifested in such an impressive manner in every sphere of life. The intellectual movements of scholasticism, the works of secular literature, art and architecture, the founding of convents and monastic orders, the Crusades, chivalry and *Minnedienst* are

[47] Chapter II.

[48] "In the early days the unbaptized were excluded from the celebration of the holy mysteries. The catechumens received no instruction concerning the sacrifice and the Eucharist. These were first spoken of after baptism. Especially were they rigorously forbidden any view of the holy things, because, according to Augustine, experience teaches that what is withheld from people is the more desired by them." The rational discussion of the Eucharistic mystery was rejected as irreverent and presumptuous by the early medieval theologians. In his treatise, "De veritate corporis et sanguinis Christi," addressed to Berengar, Adelmannus (1060) says that God hates those who wish to probe too deeply into these matters ("odit enim Deus nimis scrutatores"), *ibid.*

eloquent witnesses to the astonishing awakening and revival of the spirit, the intensity and many-sidedness of which has been exceeded in no other epoch.[49]

The Grail legends also belong to this springtide of the spirit; they too are an expression of this spiritual awakening. The Perceval story likewise expresses an endeavour to gain a clearer understanding of the Christian doctrine and its ritual, observances and mysteries which were devoutly participated in and which caused the most profound impression without, however, being comprehended. It is understandable then that a reliquary which contained the blood of Christ should have possessed tremendous numinosity and that the lance by which the blood of the Redeemer was made to flow should also have attained to an almost divine significance. The same motif, wherein the blood is hidden by Nicodemus in a leaden vessel, is also found in the *Légende de l'Abbaye de Fécamp.*[50] By many roundabout ways this vessel arrived at Fécamp and there became a renowned wonder-working blood-relic.

The cloister of Fécamp was not, however, the only place to rejoice in a relic of Christ's blood.[51] Equally famous was the Saint Sang de Bruges,[52] brought from the Holy Land in 1149 by Count Dietrich of Flanders and presented by him to the city of Bruges,[53] where the Chapel of the Holy Blood is still one of

[49] An effort has even been made to explain the whole Grail procession as the triumph of the Church over the Synagogue, but this could only be a partial aspect. Cf. Holmes and Klenke, *op. cit.*, p. 73; and Mario Roques, *Le Graal de Chrétien et la Demoiselle du Graal, passim.*

[50] Cf. A. Langfors, *Historie de l'Abbaye de Fécamp.*

[51] In addition to this relic, Fécamp possessed another of a different kind. One day when the priest of a neighbouring church was celebrating Mass, the wine in the chalice was turned into blood and the bread into flesh. The startled priest brought them to the cloister of Fécamp where the chalice was sealed up with its contents and immured in the High Altar together with the knife that had been laid on the altar.

[52] Cf. J. B. Malou, *Du culte du Saint Sang de Jésus-Christ et de la rélique de ce Sang qui est conservée a Bruges.*

[53] This might possibly explain why Count Philip of Flanders entrusted Chrétien de Troyes with the "translation" of the Grail story, although it contains no mention of the Holy Blood. To which may be added that Count Dietrich of Flanders came originally from Alsace where, as mentioned, the relics of Joseph were supposed to have been preserved.

the sights of interest. Long before, a bowl containing the holy blood was said to have been taken from Palestine to Europe by Charlemagne. A fragment of this bowl came into the possession of the monastery of Reichenau, of which a book, *De translatione sanguinis*,[54] gives a detailed description. Many other monasteries and churches prided themselves on owning relics of this kind.

The veneration of relics was at its height during the Middle Ages. Such veneration corresponds to the primitive, age-old need to bring divine force into relation to a particular locale or to a visible, known, material object in order to make the locale or the object more tangible and permanent. The possession of wonder-working relics enhanced the fame of a monastery or church; but a far more compelling motive for their acquisition was the conviction that every consecrated altar *must* contain relics. That relics of blood should be considered especially holy and that quite particular power was attributed to them may easily be understood in the light of the preceding remarks.[55]

In the Middle Ages, blood played an important part not only in the life of the Church but also in the work of the alchemists. "The soul . . . dwells in the life-spirit of the pure blood," as one author puts it.[56] Gerhard Dorn, already quoted, describes the arcane substance of the alchemists as "blessed rose-coloured blood".[57] As Jung explains in *Alchemical Studies*,[58] blood points to the animation of the substance by an indwelling soul, for which reason Dorn says that the alchemists spoke of their stone as possessing a soul, "because at the final operations, by virtue of the power of this most noble fiery mystery, a dark (*obscurus*) red liquid, like blood, sweats out drop by drop from their material and their vessel. And for this reason they have proph-

[54] See K. Beyerle, "Das liturgische Leben der Reichenau," in *Die Kultur der Abtei Reichenau*, Vol. I, p. 361.

[55] In *Der Gral in Wolframs Parzival* Bodo Mergell also rightly stresses the connection of the blood symbolism in the Grail with the mystical view of Christ's blood expounded in the writings of St. Bernard of Clairvaux.

[56] See Jung, *Psychology and Alchemy*, par. 396.

[57] "Congeries Paracelsicae chemicae de transmutatione metallorum," quoted from Jung's *Alchemical Studies*, par. 380.

[58] Par. 390.

Die Gab Gottes: 249

wird/ auß dem ein Track dañ entsprin-
get/der sein eignen Schwantz verschlin
get in der newen Sternschein/ vnd mit
dem vier Reißlin / die anderen dingen
sind thorheit ; Aber diß Elixir ist ein
wahrheit.

Q v Gestalt

Melusine wounding the Heart of Christ with the Lance of Longinus; a woodcut from Reusner, *Pandora: Das ist, die edelst Gab Göttes* (Basel, 1588)

Wisdom in the Heart of Christ

esied that in the last days a most pure man,[59] through whom the world will be freed, will come to earth and will sweat bloody drops of a rosy red hue, whereby the world will be redeemed from its Fall. In like manner, too, the blood of their stone will free the leprous metals and also men from their diseases. Wherefore they have said, not without good reason, that their stone is animate [*animalem*]."[60]

Inasmuch as Longinus' lance causes the redeeming blood of the Saviour to flow, it is of the greatest importance, and for that reason it is described in the first Continuation to the *Perceval* as flowing over with blood.[61] It therefore symbolizes *the human capacity for continually being able to discern what is essential in the latent symbol of God*, and this enables the symbol increasingly to dispense its inexhaustible, life-giving, spiritual strength to humanity. In so far as Christ ascended to Heaven with his body, he left no traces of his physical life on earth apart from this very blood which remained on the lance and in the Grail vessel. It is therefore the only permanent evidence of his *earthly* life and of the "substance of his soul." Thus the lance is also man's arrow of love, aimed at the heart of Christ, and it was looked upon as such in the Middle Ages.

[59] Jung, *ibid.*, translates *putissimus* as *rein* (pure; "most pure" in the English of the Collected Works), and adds that it might also be rendered as *echt* (genuine, "most true") or *unverfälscht* (unadulterated). We are involuntarily reminded of Perceval.

[60] *Ibid.*, par. 381. Cf. also the whole section in pars. 383–91.

[61] Cf. Roach, *The Didot-Perceval*, p. 208.

CHAPTER VI

Perceval's Task

THE *Pandora*, an alchemical text of 1588, contains an illustration in which a crowned figure, whose fish-tail distinguishes her as a *Melusine* (mermaid), is piercing Christ in his side with Longinus' lance.[1] In front of her stands Eve, who is to be united with Christ as the "second Adam." The Melusine is a symbol of the *aqua permanens* of alchemy. The text states that the water or the elixir "is a truth." The Melusine of the *Pandora* picture represents a variant of the androgynous Mercurius, and her lance, like the flaming sword of the Cherubim in Gerhard Dorn, is here transformed into an instrument of love aimed at Christ's heart, or at that psychic element which symbolizes the *Self.*

Psychologically the term "Self" denotes the psychic totality of the human being which transcends consciousness and underlies the process of individuation and which gradually becomes conscious in the course of this process.[2] The psychic totality which comprises the conscious and unconscious parts of the personality is naturally present, as an entelechy of the individual, from the very beginning. In the course of the process of maturation, however, the various aspects of totality enter the field of consciousness, thus leading to a widening of the continually changing horizon of awareness. Beyond this there is often *a numinous experience of this inner psychic wholeness.* This experience is usually accompanied by a profound emotion

[1] The *Pandora*, p. 249, described in Jung, *Alchemical Studies*, pars. 179–80, and illus. B4.

[2] Cf. Jung, *Aion*, pars. 43–67.

which the ego senses as an epiphany of the divine. For this reason it is practically impossible to differentiate between an experience of God and an experience of the Self. The manifestations of the Self, arising from the unconscious, coincide with the god-image of most religions and, when not personified, are distinguished by circular and square forms and very often (statistically considered) by quaternary formations. Jung, making use of an Eastern term, has called these structures *mandalas.*[3]

Although the figure of Christ, the Son of Man, can be regarded as one such representation of the Self, it lacks certain features which form part of the empirically known symbolism of the Self.[4] The *heart of Jesus* which is depicted as the centre of the mandala is, on the other hand, a quaternary symbol of the Self and it is therefore not by chance that it has gradually become the object of a specific ritual veneration.[5] Various medieval illustrations place the heart of Jesus in the centre of such a typical mandala,[6] while in the four corners are his hands and feet pierced by nails. In the heart itself there is a small child carrying a scourge and a wand, who personifies the divine wisdom dwelling in Christ's heart. In a fifteenth-century woodcut only the upper half of Christ's body is represented as hanging on the cross, the lower half being replaced by a large heart from which blood flows *into a chalice* held by two kneeling angels. The heart is shown four more times, once in each corner: in the first it is transfixed by the arrow; in the second, encircled by a crown of thorns; in the third, pierced by Longinus' lance and three nails; and in the fourth, winged, the moon within it and the sun hovering above between the wings. The motif of the heart stresses the *essence of human*

[3] Cf. the empirical series of individual mandalas and the collectively venerated ones in Jung, "A Study in the Process of Individuation," in *The Archetypes and the Collective Unconscious*, facing pp. 292 and 356; also *Mysterium Coniunctionis*, pars. 776*ff*.

[4] Cf. *Aion*, pars. 115–16.

[5] Cf. K. Richstätter, *Die Hertz-Jesu-Verehrung des deutschen Mittelalters*, 2nd edition, and the further literature cited there.

[6] *Ibid.*, illus. p. 33 and pp. 49, 65, 145, and illus. pp. 104 and 107.

feeling in Christ,[7] which means that a feminine element, in the form of wisdom, is clearly pressing forward for recognition, as it also does in the images, among others, of the chalice, the moon dwelling in the heart, etc. The invocations addressed to the divine heart of Jesus also contain the same feminine element. It is extolled as "the temple in which dwells the life of the world," as a rose,[8] a cup,[9] a treasure,[10] a spring,[11] as the furnace of divine love "ever glowing in the fire of the Holy Ghost," as a censer and as a bridal chamber.[12] Jesus receives the souls of the dying into his heart which "burns glowingly," "as red gold burns and melts in the fire," and the soul dissolves therein, "as water mixes with wine." All of these symbols are feminine and are therefore very closely connected with the motifs of the Grail legend and of alchemical symbolism.

In that age, too, the wounding of the heart of Christ by Longinus' spear was looked upon as a wounding by an arrow of love. A High German woodcut (between 1470 and 1490), for instance, shows the Lady Charity, with averted countenance, dispatching arrow after arrow into the heart of the King of Heaven,[13] while Oratio (prayer), another female figure, collects the downpouring blood in a vessel. In a fourteenth-century hymn,[14] Jesus says to the soul: "With an arrow of love,

[7] Cf. the sermon on St. George (written between 1250 and 1280) quoted by Richstätter, p. 61: "The Lord suffered His pure heart to be opened by a a sharp spear, that heart which is full of all wisdom and all charity and all purity. . . . For which reason he poured out the stream from His heart, that we might see that His love was complete and pure, without any dissimulation. On the Cross we should contemplate His loving heart, as that from which flows devoted love."

[8] "The Song of the Heart of Jesus" ("Summi Regis cor aveto"), by Hermann Joseph, b. 1150, quoted by Richstätter, pp. 40*ff.*

[9]
"Let me in long draughts taste
Of the juice of the pomegranate,
Out of the cup of thy heart
Quaffing the noblest wine.
After the drinking, bestow the kiss."

—Also by Hermann Joseph.

[10] Richstätter, p. 122.

[11] *Ibid.*, p. 138.

[12] Mechtild von Magdebourg, quoted by Richstätter, pp. 81 and 82.

[13] Richstätter, p. 240. Cf. illus., pp. 112–13.

[14] *Ibid.*, p. 200.

oh my bride, hast thou wounded my heart.[15] Which is why, out of love for thee, I am fastened to the wood of the Cross." And in a thirteenth-century sermon[16] the Lord says to the soul: "Inasmuch as I was dead and hung upon the cross, out of love for thee I allowed my heart to be opened with a sharp lance . . . for thy sake I became a poor stranger. Give me now thy heart, which I have sought here on earth." It is as if the *human* nature of Christ could be most clearly understood by relating it to his heart.

The picture of the Melusine in the *Pandora* produces the effect of a "darker" modification of the picture of Charity. It leads us another step deeper into purely human nature where the love of God is mingled with earthly love. As the figure of Lady Charity represents the light, so the Melusine depicts the natural, ambiguous nature of the anima. But she, too, the dark unconscious human psyche with its indwelling urge towards individuation, aims at the heart of Christ. All the pictures illustrate the tendency of the unconscious to transfer the highest value away from the conventional aspects of Christ towards his essential quality of Anthropos or the second Adam[17] as being a more complete symbol of the Self. At the same time (in so far as the wounding weapon is given the new meaning of an arrow of love) the sharpness of ethical discrimination is modified into an attitude of understanding Eros.

Christ's blood, like his heart, is also a symbol of his essential quality, the *psychic* reality of his image, at which the Anthropos figure of alchemy, the Mercurius, or the Melusine "takes aim". As Jung has shown,[18] the symbolism of alchemy served on the whole as a receptacle in which contents that were in a compensatory and complementary relationship to official Christianity found expression, and *it is therefore no accident that such close connections can be traced between alchemy and the symbols of the Grail story*. The Christian era, which began at the same time as the

[15] With reference to the Song of Songs.

[16] Richstätter, p. 61.

[17] Cf. *Mysterium Coniunctionis*, pars. 544*ff*.

[18] Introduction to *Psychology and Alchemy*.

astrological age of the Fishes, is characterized by the problem of the opposites of Christ and Antichrist, light and dark, good and evil, which had never before attained such a pitch of intensity. A curious sudden change of view may be observed during the Christian aeon of the Fishes. Until the year 1000, the age of the "First Fish," there was a unilateral extension of Christianity; after A.D. 1000, the rise of the various Holy Ghost movements were in evidence, especially that of Joachim of Floris and of other sects such as the Neo-Manichaeans, the Albigenses, the Pouvres de Lyon and, last but not least, the spiritually kindred Occidental alchemy. An affinity with the Grail legend can be seen in all of these fields of religious thought. The works of O. Rahn, E. Anitchkof and J. Evola attempt to establish connections with the Catharists, with Joachim of Floris and with Hermeticism. It would seem, however, that only single points of contact existed, which cannot explain the whole of the Grail story, so that it is more probable that the relation should be sought for in those unconscious *psychological* constellations Jung has discussed in *Aion*.

In all of these movements a preoccupation with the problem of evil of nature, of the feminine and of the divine in the individual, was manifested in a form which sought to supplement those elements that until then had been lacking in Christianity.[19] The natural symbols of psychic wholeness, or the Self, do not fully coincide empirically with the traditional figure of Christ, since the shadow is missing in the latter or else appears split off into the contrasting figure of the Antichrist. In alchemy, on the other hand, the image of the Anthropos (or of the Son of Man) was continually amplified since its earliest appearance and in the image of the *lapis* and of Mercurius was expanded into a paradoxical symbol of the Self in which the opposites were reconciled.[20] Since alchemy retained certain living aspects of the symbolism of the Self which were not ad-

[19] A connection has therefore been deduced between the bleeding spear and the synagogue, where a broken lance—as opposed to the chalice of the victorious Ecclesia—is often carried. Cf. Holmes and Klenke, *op. cit.*, p. 159.

[20] Cf. *Mysterium Coniunctionis*, pars. 544*ff*.

mitted into the Christian dogma, the continued life of some pre-Christian elements, i.e. those contents of paganism which had not yet lost their psychic value,[21] was thus made possible. In a similar way the same broadening of the religious symbols, through contents from late antiquity, Gnosticism and Islam, is to be found in the Grail story. It is therefore not inappropriate that the poets drew upon Oriental legends as amplifications. Even those versions of the story that have a Christian nuance can be clearly traced back to apocryphal writings which include legendary material from antiquity and the East. In the *Lancelot Grail* especially, in the works of Robert de Boron and in the *Queste*, many motifs, such as the legend of Solomon, which stem from Oriental fables are to be found side by side with the Celtic motifs.[22]

The legend of Joseph of Arimathea, based on the work known as the Gospel of Nicodemus,[23] was generally known at that time.[24] Joseph of Arimathea enjoyed particular veneration in Lorraine, which is not far distant from Montbéliard and the nearby village of Boron, the reputed birthplace of Robert, and this may also have had an influence on the author's selection of

[21] Cf. Jung, "Answer to Job," in *Psychology and Religion*, pars. 553–758.

[22] Robert de Boron appears to have been the first to have made a connection between the legend of Joseph of Arimathea and the *Matière de Bretagne*, out of which he created an entire cycle of romances. Cf. P. Zumthor, *Merlin*, p. 115; E. Brugger, "L'Enserrement Merlin," and Weston, *Legend of Sir Perceval*, Vol. II, Ch. I.

[23] The Latin work known by this name was translated from the Greek and consists of two originally unconnected parts, both ascribed to the fourth century. The first part, also known as the "Acta" or "Gesta Pilati," contains the story of the Passion; the second is an account of Christ's descent into hell, the overcoming of Satan and the freeing of the soul. Cf. W. C. von Tischendorf, *Evangelia Apocrypha*, Ch. 2 and 12*ff*.

[24] There were various rhymed French versions of the Gospel of Nicodemus, as well as similar renderings in other languages. *Trois versions rimées de l'Evangile de Nicodème*, published by G. Paris and J. Ulrich, volume for 1885. According to de Lincy, *Essai sur l'Abbaye de Fécamp*: "The Gospel of Nicodemus has come down to us in Greek. It was probably written in vernacular Hebrew in the fifth century at the latest. Gregoire de Tours is one of the first to have made use of it. It was translated into Anglo-Saxon, French, English and German in the twelfth and thirteenth centuries.

the material.[25] *The return to Celtic and Germanic mythological material on the one hand, and to some apocryphal traditions of early Christianity on the other can all be explained psychologically by the same need: to complete the Christ-image by the addition of features which had not been taken sufficiently into account by ecclesiastical tradition.*

Further parallel motifs or traces of possible influences point even further back to the legend of Alexander in late antiquity, details of which recall the description of the Grail Castle to a really remarkable degree.[26] In this story Alexander, on his march to India, comes to a mountain with two thousand five hundred sapphire steps leading to its summit. At the top he finds the "House of the Sun," a magnificent palace with doors and windows of gold. There is also a temple of gold with a golden vine bearing grapes of precious stones before its gate. Upon a golden couch inside the temple lies a *beautiful white-haired old man, sumptuously robed and nourished solely on incense and balm.* He asks Alexander whether he wishes to see the holy trees of the sun and moon and to question them about his future. Close to these trees, which prophesy Alexander's early death, is another tree without leaves or blossom upon which sits a purple and gold phoenix bird.[27] The same story is to be found in the German song about Alexander by the parson Lamprecht,[28] but in the song the "beautiful old man" is asleep and Alexander,

[25] Relics of Joseph of Arimathea, supposed to have been taken there by Fortunat, Patriarch of Grado, were said to have been found at Moyenmoutie. Nitze, *Roman de l'Estoire dou Saint Graal*, p. vii, is of the opinion that Robert came from this region. According to Hucher, *Le Saint Graal*, Vol. I, p. 41, a village called Boron, in the neighbourhood of Fontainebleau, was Robert's place of origin, while Brugger, "L'Enserrement Merlin," p. 59, considers that he was an Anglo-Norman.

[26] These amplifications are due to the kind suggestions of Prof. Emil Abegg.

[27] This description is taken from the French prose romance of Alexander, dating from the thirteenth century. Together with its prototype, the "Historia de Préliis," which was written by a Church elder named Leo, it has been edited by Hilka, in *Der altfranzösische Alexanderroman*. According to J. Zacher, *Pseudokallisthenes*, p. 108, the Church elder was thought to have transcribed the story in Constantinople where he was travelling on behalf of the Dukes John and Marinus of Campania (941–65), and to have brought it back with him to Italy.

[28] H. Weismann, *Das Alexandergedicht des XII. Jahrhunderts vom Pfaffen Lamprecht.*

who does not venture to awaken him, retraces his steps. All of these poems about him are, in the final analysis, based on a record of the legend of Alexander known as the novel of Pseudo-Kallisthenes, written, probably in Alexandria, about A.D. 200.[29] It contains a "letter from Alexander to his mother" in which we read as follows:

> We sailed away from the river and reached a large island, a hundred and fifty stadia distant from the land, and there found a *City of the Sun*, on to which had been built twelve towers of gold and emerald. . . . In the centre of the city was an altar constructed of gold and emerald and having seven steps. On top stood a chariot to which horses were harnessed and a charioteer of gold and emerald. But on account of the fog one could not see all of this clearly. The priest of the sun, an Ethiopian . . . told us . . . that we must depart from that place. . . . We therefore turned back and came to the sea of Lysus and there found a high mountain. We climbed to the top and saw beautiful houses full of gold and silver, and also a great city wall of sapphire with a hundred steps. Inside and out were statues of demi-gods, bacchantes, satyrs and initiates, but the old Maron [a type of Silenus figure] sat on a beast of burden. *In the middle of the temple stood a bed, whereon lay a man clothed in silk. I could not actually see his face but I saw his size and his strength.* In the centre of the temple a transparent golden crown was hanging from a golden chain. *A precious stone, which lit the whole temple, took the place of a fire.* A golden cage, with a large bird inside, was also hanging from the ceiling. The bird in a human-sounding voice, called out: "Alexander, desist henceforth from setting thyself up against the gods. Turn back home and do not, through recklessness, hasten thy passage to the heavenly paths."[30]

This story contains features which recur in the Grail legend, in particular that of the beautiful, white-haired old man lying on the sumptuous bed. He recalls the Grail King who is described, in almost the same words, as white-haired, beautiful,

[29] See Zacher, *ibid.*
[30] *Ibid.*, Book III, Ch. 28.

magnificently clothed and lying on a couch. Of the old man in the story of Alexander it is said that he is nourished solely on incense and balm, like the old Grail King who is served from the Grail and who feeds only upon the Host.

Incense and balm are the fragrant foods of the gods. The palace is called the House of the Sun. There is also a temple and the holy trees of the sun and moon, from which a place of worship may be deduced, while the trees remind us of Paradise. The *Gran Saint Grail* describes how Joseph, in his wanderings with the Grail, came to the town of Sarras, the home of the Saracens, where there was a temple of the sun.[31]

In Alexander's letter the locale is quite plainly depicted as a holy place with a numinous atmosphere. The beautiful man is described as very large and strong; his face cannot be seen clearly, he seems to be a sleeping god or a statue of a god that moves. The vine points to Dionysus, as do the statues of bacchantes, satyrs and initiates, and as does the "old Maron," one of the characters in the legends of Dionysus. Under the designation of Zagreus, Dionysus was the focal point of the Orphic mysteries and brings us to Orpheus whose name Robert Eisler translates as "fisher."[32] The Grail King is called the "Rich Fisher." At a later date "Orpheus the Fisher" became, like Christ, the "Good Shepherd." In his other aspect he was also called the vine and was, in turn, closely linked with the Grail.[33] Furthermore, when the text tells us that "a precious stone, which lit the whole temple, took the place of a fire" this recalls the great hall of the Grail Castle where a fire burned continually before the couch of the Grail King and where the Grail shed such a brilliance that the light of the candles was dimmed. It also reminds us that in Wolfram the Grail itself is a stone. There are, therefore, so many parallel motifs that it seems possible that the writers who elaborated the Grail story derived these features in part from the legend of Alexander

[31] Von Schroeder's interpretation of the Grail as a "vessel of the sun," mentioned in Chapter I, might also be considered in this light, namely as an archetypal parallel.

[32] *Orpheus—The Fisher*, Ch. II, pp. 114–15.

[33] *Ibid.*, pp. 18, 22–23, 51*ff* and 280–81.

which had already been translated into Latin in the fourth century and was generally known at that time.

Another legend which was widely known and very popular in those days and which contained a similar description of a wonderful temple palace was that of Prester John[34] which bore many resemblances to the story of Alexander. In it the temple-tomb in India where Thomas the Apostle was buried is described as a magnificent palace of gold and precious stones, illuminated by two carbuncles. The Apostle himself, with red hair and beard, lay in the tomb uncorrupted and as fresh in appearance as if he were asleep, occasionally moving his hand when devout worshippers brought offerings.[35] L. J. Ringbom, in his comprehensive work *Graltempel und Paradies*,[36] has tried to take up L. E. Iselin's old hypothesis to show that the idea of the Grail Castle (especially as it is described in the *Jüngere Titurel*) came to Europe from Persia, and that this castle or temple—a mandala-shaped structure—represents Paradise, or a spiritual Beyond, whose prototype he sees in the Parsee sanctuary of the holy fire at Siz (Gazak).[37] It is the pattern of the royal tomb as well as a sanctuary at the centre of the world[38] and an image of the whole universe.[39] Ringbom also compares its structure with that of Western mandalas[40] and with the mountain sanctuary of the Moslem sect of the Assassins, a secret brotherhood under the authority of an "Old Man of the Mountain," with which the Templars cultivated particularly close relations.[41] The Iranian sanctuary at Siz was rebuilt under the Moslem rule of Genghis Khan's successors, and one of them, Abaka Khan, took the title of "Priest-King John" (Prester John). Wolfram von Eschenbach and the author of the *Jüngere Titurel* both explicitly link the legend of Prester John with the story of the Grail temple.[42]

[34] Cf. F. Zarncke, "Der Priester Johannes."

[35] *Ibid.*, pp. 846 and 917. Cf. Zarncke, "Der Graaltempel," pp. 375*ff*.

[36] Stockholm, 1951.

[37] Ringbom, *Graltempel und Paradies*, p. 216.

[38] *Ibid.*, p. 247.

[39] *Ibid.*, p. 261. Cf. illus. of same.

[40] *Ibid.*, p. 281, illus.

[41] *Ibid.*, p. 455.

[42] *Ibid.*, p. 458. In Wolfram it is Feirefiz' son who eventually acquires the title of "Prester John."

Even if the particular historical and literary connections are not always incontestable, at any rate the enormous stimulation of a *centrum mundi* fantasy which, besides the Christian elements, reaches back to widely disseminated traditions from antiquity, the East and also in part to Celtic sources,[43] is beyond dispute. It looks as if there had been *a psychic need to amplify the symbol of the Self with many natural features.* A further complex of ideas from antiquity that probably also had an effect on the development of the Grail story is the myth of Osiris, which we will consider in due course.

All of the descriptions, from the City of the Sun in the story of Alexander to Thomas the Apostle's sepulchre in the legend of Prester John, present a picture of what is without question a mandala, *a symbol of the Self.*[44] Significantly, in the legend of Alexander, the limitations of the young world conqueror are pointed out to him each time he encounters the symbol. He is sent back from the City of the Sun, and when he is close to the old man in the temple, a bird with a human voice calls out to him, "Alexander, desist henceforth from setting thyself up against the gods." In the *Historia de Prêliis* and in the French versions, his death is foretold him. It is precisely the Self, as the inner "guide," which tries to reduce the man striving for Olympus to his human proportions. Perhaps there is a corresponding significance when the turbulent young Perceval is banished from the Grail Castle and can only find it again after he has achieved the necessary maturity.

The amazing enrichment of the Grail story through Celtic and Oriental symbolism and the symbolism of antiquity is, therefore, a phenomenon of the age which found its parallel in medieval alchemy.[45] As Jung has shown,[46] the latter represented an undercurrent that compensated and supplemented the lacunae and the conflicts in the Christianity which ruled the

[43] Brown, "The Bleeding Lance," pp. 37–38, traces the Grail Castle back to the Celtic idea of a castle turning on its axis.

[44] Cf. *Psychology and Alchemy*, pars. 325 *ff.*

[45] Cf. *ibid.*, *passim* and especially par. 263; and *Mysterium Coniunctionis* throughout.

[46] *Psychology and Alchemy*, par. 26.

surface areas. For this reason many alchemists themselves compared their sought-for substance and their stone to Christ, setting them up as parallels to him,[47] and in so doing felt unconsciously that their work was a continuation of Christ's work of redemption. Had they understood this consciously, they would have had to realize, as Jung says,[48] that they had themselves stepped into the position of Christ, inasmuch as they could really only bring their work of redeeming the Spirit of God in matter to a successful conclusion under the guidance of the Self, the "inner" Christ. They did not, however, become conscious of the fact that Christ is a symbol of the Self. In our story, Perceval, like the alchemists, is also called to a specific work of redemption, for which reason he is placed in a mysterious secret historical relation to Christ. It is as if he had to carry the process of becoming conscious in the Christian aeon a stage further, in that he had to ask the question about the origin of evil (the mystery of the wounding of the Grail King by an enemy) and about the Grail. He must discover the meaning of the vessel that contains the blood of the Crucified One; he is faced with problem of discovering *the form in which the essential psychic life of the figure of Christ continues to exist and what it means.*

These connections with the historical past and with the central symbols of Christianity place the objects carried in the Grail procession in a very broad, transpersonal psychological context. Looked at from this angle the story of Perceval's development cannot be understood only as an example of the coming to consciousness of one individual but also as *a symbolic representation of a collective evolution, conditioned by the age.* Seen in this light *the figure of Perceval himself becomes a symbol and represents an archetypal content.* The fact that he is destined by a long line of ancestors to achieve the redemption of the Grail Kingdom, together with the essential genuineness of his nature and all the character traits of the fairy tale hero which he has assimilated, suggest that he himself should be interpreted as an Anthropos figure which, like the Mercurius-*lapis* of the alchemists, should compensate and amplify the Christ-image

[47] *Ibid.*, par. 451. [48] *Ibid.*, par. 452.

then dominating the collective consciousness.[49] He forms a parallel figure to the *homo altus* or *homo quadratus* of alchemy, the true and total man or the divine component in man which gradually emerges from the depths of the maternal womb of the unconscious and releases specific areas of the psyche previously cut off from life. Of interest and bearing on the relation to alchemy is the name of Perceval's ancestor, Uther Pendragon, which Vincent de Beauvais interprets as Dragon's Head (*caput draconis*).[50] In alchemy the dragon is considered to be the *prima materia* of the *lapis*.[51] In the old text *Scriptum Alberti super arborem Aristotelis*[52] there is a description of eight concentric circles which correspond to the celestial spheres. The fourth circle contains an evil dragon which came forth from the planets, and the fifth is called "the head and the death of the dragon." This head "lives in eternity" and is known as the *vita gloriosa*, and "the angels serve it." According to Jung,[53] the *caput draconis* is here clearly equated with Christ, for "*angeli serviunt ei*" unmistakably refers to Matthew 4:11, where Christ has just repudiated Satan. But if the dragon's head is identified with Christ, then the tail must be equivalent to the Antichrist or the Devil. The dragon opposed the *imago Dei*, but through the might of God this image was implanted in the dragon and constitutes its head. "The whole body obeys the head, and the head hates the body, and slays it beginning from the tail, by gnawing it with its teeth, until the whole body enters into the head and remains there for ever." The dragon's head is therefore the substance out of which the philosopher's stone originated. It is highly significant that the name of Perceval's ancestor, Uther Pendragon, is interpreted as Dragon's Head, since this establishes Perceval as a parallel to the alchemical

[49] *Ibid.*, pars. 412*f.*

[50] *Speculum historiale*, Book XX, Ch. 49.

[51] Cf. *Psychology and Alchemy*, par. 530.

[52] Albertus Magnus in *Theatrum chemicum*, Vol. II, p. 456, quoted by Jung in *Alchemical Studies*, par. 416. The Latin reads: "Totum corpus sequitur caput et ipsum caput odit corpus et interficit ipsum incipiendo a cauda cum dentibus ipsum corrodere quousque totum corpus intrat in caput et in eo permanet sempiterne."

[53] Cf. *Alchemical Studies*, par. 390.

lapis, or to the "purest" and "simplest man" whom the alchemists identified with their stone and in whom they saw a *redeemer of the macrocosm*. When Perceval has to solve the riddle of the Grail, this means that he should make his own psychic problems and his extensive inner nature conscious. The sphere which he has to redeem, the Grail Castle, brings him into contact with specific "apocryphal" contents representing the psychic background or matrix of the Christian symbols, in other words, the collective unconscious. As Jung explains in *Aion*, a group of archetypal images have crystallized themselves around the figure of the historical Jesus, which in itself is scarcely discernible. This has the effect of turning Christ into a true symbol of the Self. To this group of images belong in particular the fish, the lamb and the cross. (Unfortunately it is not possible, within the limits of this volume, to go more closely into the comprehensive examples that Jung has assembled or to study the details of his explanation. An acquaintance with the content of his work must therefore be assumed.) This process of amplifying the Christ-image proceeded with greater freedom in the near-Christian traditions of the Middle Ages than it did in the official promulgations of the dogma. In that way, fantasies, feelings and emotions rising up from the unconscious, as well as audacious new thought contents, had a better chance of finding expression in those traditions, so that it could in fact be said that the living essence of Christ, his blood, lived on especially intensively in such interpretations and that in transforming itself, it also developed further.

It is as if Perceval were in himself the embodiment of that natural man who is faced with the problem of evil and of the relation to the feminine and through these with the task of a greater development of his own consciousness, so that by many a circuitous route he accomplishes the redemption of the Grail Kingdom whose ruler he finally becomes.[54] It is very pertinent

[54] This is said in contrast to Amelia Klenke's interpretation, which only sees Perceval as a prototype of the Christian man. Cf. Klenke, "The Spiritual Ascent of Perceval." Max Wehrli, "Wolfram von Eschenbach," also sees Perceval as the spiritual Christian man *par excellence*.

in the story that the land to be redeemed is bound up with just those early days of Christianity when the Christ-imago was crystallizing out of the matrix of the collective unconscious and at the same time, by its one-sided insistence on the light side, was casting off its shadow, the image of the Antichrist.[55] It is as if a further enrichment of the symbol of the Self, from out of that same matrix, were taking place in the Grail story, by which the continued tearing asunder by the opposites might be ended and their reconciliation striven for. For this task the individual human being serves as a *vessel*, for only when the opposites are reconciled in the single individual can they be united. The individual therefore becomes a receptacle for the transformation of the problem of the opposites in the image of God. With this reflection that each human being represents a place of transformation and a "vessel" in which God may come to consciousness, we come to the discussion of the central theme of our story, the Grail.

[55] This is a literal translation of a text of Valentinus, quoted by Irenaeus, *Adversus haereses*, II, 5, i. Cf. *Aion*, footnote par. 75.

CHAPTER VII

The Central Symbol of the Legend: The Grail as Vessel

IT SEEMS ONLY natural that in the maternal domain of the unconscious—for thus we can interpret the Grail realm—Perceval should find not the personal mother but the mother *sub specie aeternitatis*, the primal image of the mother, the wondrous vessel. It is so self-evident that this is a symbol of the feminine and, as that which receives, contains and supports, of the maternal in particular that we shall not cite too many examples that bear on it but refer the reader to Jung's *Symbols of Transformation* where this aspect of the vessel is dealt with in detail.[1] Divested of the personal and viewed as an object, the vessel does not explicitly represent a human reality but rather an idea, a primal image. As such, it is of universal significance and is found in untold myths, legends and fairy-tales, of which only a few of the most appropriate will be quoted here.[2]

The symbolic meaning of the vessel goes back to the earliest of times and can therefore be termed an archetypal conception. It is one of the first manifestations of culture and as such is possessed of a magically significant, numinous character. This is apparent for example in a legend that Herodotus tells of Targilaos, the ancestor of the Scythians.[3] Four objects

[1] Particularly pars. 298, 450 and 407. Cf. also *Psychology and Alchemy*, par. 338.

[2] It has already been mentioned in Chapter I (Introduction) that in the Vedic scriptures the sun and moon appear as divine vessels, the sun as a pap bowl, the moon as a vessel for soma, and an attempt has been made to see in them the archetype behind the Grail vessel. Cf. von Schroeder, *Die Wurzeln der Sage vom heiligen Graal*, pp. 8*ff*.

[3] *Historiae*, Book IV, Ch. 5.

(ποιήματα), a plough, a yoke, an ax and a bowl (φιάλη), fall from Heaven in the presence of Targilaos' sons. Neither of the two elder brothers are able to take hold of them for when they try to the implements glow with fire. When the youngest approaches them, however, the fire is extinguished. He carries them home and is acknowledged king of the entire nation.[4] Here, four objects that distinguish the culture hero again have a numinous quality.

That the vessel is so frequently considered to be life-giving or life-maintaining is readily understandable when we realize how extremely important it must have been for earliest man to possess a receptacle in which, for instance, water, the stuff of life *par excellence*, could be transported or stored. According to Jung's definition, the archetypes represent innate predispositions to human behaviour in certain life situations and the ability to grasp their meaning. The image of the vessel could therefore correspond to such a "pattern," to a possibility inherent in the psyche of finding or producing a vessel and of discovering its uses.

Thus, in nearly all mythologies there is a miraculous vessel. Sometimes it dispenses youth and life, at other times it possesses the power of healing, and occasionally, as with the mead cauldron of the Nordic Ymir, inspiring strength and wisdom are to be found in it. Often, especially as a cooking pot, it effects transformations; by this attribute it achieved exceptional renown as the *vas Hermetis* of alchemy.

Let us begin by citing a few vessels from Celtic legends which exhibit a more or less close relation to the Grail story. Irish legend tells of Dagda's cauldron, one of the four treasures belonging to the semi-divine Tuatha De Danann; it could feed an entire army without becoming empty. In Welsh legend, too, there are many such vessels. Those who had been slain could be brought back to life in Bran's magic cauldron, merely forfeiting the power of speech in the process.[5] The cauldron of Caridwen[6]

[4] Cf. O. Glaser, *Skythenkönige als Wächter des heiligen Goldes*, p. 277.

[5] See *The Mabinogion*, the Mabinogi of "Branwen the Daughter of Llyn," p. 37.

[6] *Ibid.*, Mabinogi of "Taliesin," pp. 263*ff*.

contained a beverage of wisdom and inspiration similar to the Nordic *Sinnreger*. The cauldron at Tyrnog was also one of these receptacles; when meat for a coward was put into it, it would not cook, while meat for a brave man was cooked at once. The basket of Gwyddno Gahanhir (Welsh: Mwys)[7] was one of the Thirteen Precious Things of the Island of Britain. When food for one man was placed therein, it was found on opening to contain sustenance for a hundred. According to J. Rhys, it offers the closest parallel to the Grail.[8] From the description it can be visualized as a sort of basket or chest. The word also means a measure. In Old Cornish *muis* or *moys* means table. In Irish, the charger on which John the Baptist's head lay was called *mias*; the meaning of the word is associated with the Latin *mensa* and is in fact very closely connected with the meaning of the Grail. It was said that this basket finally disappeared with Merlin when he withdrew into his house of glass on the Isle of Bardsey. According to Loomis,[9] the original model of the Grail was an Irish horn of plenty, and the word *cor* (horn) was confused with *cors* (body).[10]

Yet another vessel must be mentioned here. A poem by the Welsh bard Taliesin describes Arthur's journey to Annwn, the underworld, and the theft from that place of a vessel in many respects suggestive of the Grail. A passage from a rather obscure text,[11] a poem known as the "Preideu Annwn",—"The Plundering (or Spoils) of the Underworld"—will indicate this similarity:

Will fame not fall to my lot, when I let my song be heard?
The first word from the cauldron, when was it spoken,
In Caer Pedryvan, which four times rotates?
By the breath of nine maidens it was tenderly heated.
Is it not the cauldron of the world below?

[7] *Ibid.*, notes, p. 328.

[8] *The Arthurian Legend*, pp. 312*ff*.

[9] *Arthurian Tradition*, p. 172.

[10] For a contrary view, see Nitze, "The Fisher King and the Grail in Retrospect;" also Holmes and Klenke, *op. cit.*, p. 177.

[11] Cf. *Le Morte d'Arthur*, Introduction by J. Rhys, p. xxxiii; and T. W. Rolleston, *Myths and Legends of the Celtic Race*, p. 410.

And what is its nature?
A round of pearls encircles its rim.
For the coward it cooks no meat, neither for the breaker of
oaths;
A shining sword will be raised against him
And in Lleminawg's hand will remain.
At the gate of the Underworld the lamp did burn,
When with Arthur we went—a splendid venture;
None but seven from Caer Vedwyd returned.

The rim set with pearls is reminiscent of the gem-studded Grail which was also tended by young women. This vessel also did not permit the unworthy to share in the distribution of its blessed effects.

It will be useful here to make a brief survey of the meanings of the word "grail," of the forms which the vessel takes and of the peculiarities attributed to it in the various stories.

As we have already noted, the chronicler Helinandus traces the word back to the Latin *gradale* or *gradalis*, meaning a rather deep plate or dish. In F. Diez's *Etymologischem Wörterbuch der romanischen Sprachen* we find under "*Graal*":[12] Old French *greal*, *grasal*, Provençal *grazal*, Old Catalonian *gresal*, a vessel, cup or bowl of wood, earthenware or metal. *Grazal*, *grazau*, *grial* are still in use today in the south of France to denote various receptacles. The French *grassale* (basin) may also be noted here. The word *grasal* (grail) is still found in certain dialects of southern and eastern France. R. Bezzola equates it with *garalis* and quotes a passage from a will of the Emperor Henry I (873), where "*garales argenteos cum binis cochleariis*" are mentioned.[13] P. Borel[14] maintains that the word must come from *grais*, "*Parce que ces vaisseaux sont faits de grais cuit*" ("Because these vessels are made of cooked earth"). *Vaisseau de grès* also means hard-fired earthenware crockery (stoneware). Diez considers this to be unlikely and is of the opinion that "a better case can be made for suggesting *crater*, for which Middle Latin

[12] "*Grada*" in original, p. 602.
[13] *Le sens de l'aventure et de l'amour*, p. 254, note 18.
[14] *Recherches*, p. 242, quoted in Diez, *op. cit.*, p. 602.

used the term *cratus*, from which the derivation *cratalis*, Provençal *grazal*, French *graal*, could easily have evolved." H. and R. Kahane[15] and C. Gossen[16] have also recently admitted to sharing this view.

Borel's questionable derivation of the word *graal* from *grès* (stone) does, however, follow an association of mythological ideas, since in Wolfram the Grail is a *stone* which was said to have come from heaven[17] and was called *lapsit exillis*, which was taken to mean *lapis elixir* by some, and *lapis exilis*, meaning a small, inferior, inconspicuous stone,[18] by others. The word *grès* is closely connected with *grêle* (hailstone) and *grésil* (hoarfrost) which, as the round white stone coming from heaven, reminds us of manna and at the same time suggests the consecrated wafer which was brought to the Grail from heaven every Good Friday in order to renew its nourishing power. Conversely, *grêle* also accords with *exilis*, since it likewise signifies *lean, thin*. Another interpretation cited by Helinandus, but more as a popular meaning, derives *graal* or *greal* from *gratus* (pleasing, acceptable) and *gratia* (pleasantness, satisfaction, goodwill, grace, reward), the French *agréable* (agreeable) from *gré* (wish). This interpretation is repeatedly vouched for in the works themselves. Robert de Boron's "Joseph of Arimathea", for instance, tells us that:

Par droit Graal l'apelera
Car nus le Graal ne verra
Ce crois je, qu'il ne li agrée.[19]

[15] "Wolframs Gral und Wolframs Kyot."

[16] "Zur etymologischen Deutung des Grals." Cf. also Herbert Kolb *Monsalvaesche*, pp. 140*ff.*

[17] According to another tradition it is considered to have been a precious stone which fell out of Lucifer's crown when he was cast out of heaven.

[18] In one passage in Arnaldus de Villanova the *lapis philosophorum* is described as *lapis exilis*. Cf. Johannes Jacobus Mangetus, *Bibliotheca Chemica Curiosa*, Vol. II, p. 88, where it says:

Hic lapis exilis
extat precio quoque vilis
spernitur a stultis
amatur plus ab edoctis.

[19] Verse 2659.

In the *Didot Perceval* we read, "*Et por ce l'appelons nos Graal, qu'il agree as prodes hommes*" ("And this why we call it Grail, because it please us as men"). Nascien, in the *Estoire du Saint Graal* of the Lancelot Grail cycle,[20] says "*Car tout mi pensez sont acomplit puis ke je voi chou que en toutes coses*" ("For all my thoughts are completed since I see things which are in all things"). Merlin, in the poem of that name,[21] says of the Grail:

Et ces gens claiment cel vaissiel,
dont ils ont celle grâsce—Graal.

All these men call this vessel
from which they have this grace—the Grail.

In spite of the somewhat derogatory evaluation of this derivation (Helinandus describes it as popular and Nutt as punning),[22] it does not fit too badly, since on the one hand the Grail is a wishing object, while on the other the effects of grace proceed from it. In Wolfram the wishing character is particularly clear. Of the Host, which on every Good Friday is placed on the stone (that is, the Grail) by a dove, it is said:

dâ von der Stein enpfaehet
swaz gouts ûf erden draehet
von trinken und von spîse
als den wunsch von paradise:
ich mein' swâz d'erde mac geberen.

From that the stone derives
whatever good fragrances
of drink and food there are on earth,
like to the perfection of Paradise.
I mean all things the earth may bear.

[20] Hucher, *Le Saint Graal,* Vol. II, p. 306.
[21] Paris and Ulrich, "*Merlin,*" *Roman en prose du XIIIe siècle.*
[22] *Studies in the Grail Legend,* p. 76.

And in Book V, verse 430*ff*:

man sagete mir, diz sage ouch ich
ûf iuwex iesliches eit,
daz vorem grâle waere bereit
spîse warm, spîse kalt,
spîse niuwe unt dar zuo alt,
daz zâm und daz wilde.

Whatsoever one reached out his hand for,
he found it ready
in front of the Grail,
food warm or food cold,
dishes new or old,
meat tame or game.

And verse 451:

môrag, wîn, sinopel rôt,
swâ nach den napf iseslîcher bôt,
swaz er trinkens kunde nennen,
daz mohte er drinne erkennen
allez von des grâles Kraft
diu werde geselleschaft
hete wirtschaft vome grâle.

Whatever drink one held out his goblet for,
whatever drink he might name,
mulberry juice, wine, or red sinopel,
he found the drink in his glass,
all by the power of the Grail,
whose guests the noble company were.[23]

The Grail is therefore a real *Tischleindeckdich*, a horn of plenty, a wishing object or vessel such as also frequently appears in fairy-tales in the form of pots, baskets, cups or cloths. The connection of *gratum*, *gratia*, *grâce* with the Christian relic is obvious and accords with the concept of the Grail as a relic of

[23] *Parzival*, Book IX.

this kind. Another attempt at a derivation, which, however, is certainly incorrect, equates *san greal*, as it is often written, with *sang real* (royal blood), meaning the blood of Christ, which was thought to be contained in the Grail.

Yet another explanation, advocated among others by P. Paris, is that the designation of Grail came about because the story was originally included in a gradual, a book used for church services, and so named because it contained the gradual, a hymn set to musical intervals. Actually, the obvious and well-attested derivation from *gradale* (dish) could suffice, except that it seems to belong to the nature of the vessel that new associations to its meaning are continually being sought for. It is remarkable how this also finds expression in speech: words present themselves as related, or as in some degree manifestly pertinent, and even if the connection cannot be proven scientifically, they do nevertheless indicate the ambiguity of the designated object in a manner which is satisfying in a feeling way and which allows its many facets to light up. All of this indicates that it is not simply a matter of a mere vessel but of a symbol.

W. Hertz's book, *Die Sage von Parzifal und dem Graal*,[24] gives us a few more examples of the changes which time has brought about in the meaning of the word. As a designation of the highest value, the word "Grail" appears in religious songs and in *Minneliedern*. Mary is compared to the Grail, even God himself is called "the Highest Grail." The beloved is described as the Grail of the heart (Reinmar von Zweter), or a pure woman is spoken of as the Grail which must be fought for.[25] With time the word took on more and more the meaning of a banquet and an entertainment. Thus, about 1280 a play about a young woman called Frau Feie (from Sophia) was presented in Magdeburg, a kind of tournament in which a camp called *der Gral* was pitched. In Brunswick in the fifteenth century, the Grail was an important popular festival, taking place every seven years and held

[24] Pp. 33*ff*.

[25] J. Fischart mentions it as being synonymous with the Venusberg in the *Gargantua*.

for the last time in 1481. The word *grâlen* was used to indicate loud sounds of noisy rejoicing, rather in the sense of *bawling*. In the sixteenth century, *gralisieren* or *kralisieren* (to make a cheerful noise) also came into use in High German with the substantive *Krales*. "To go to the *Grals* (or *Grollus*)" meant to go to a feast. In religious poetry, too, the Grail became a place of pleasure. In an old prayer from Bremen, for example, the eleven thousand virgins dance in the heavenly Grail before the Virgin Mary.

By degrees, the word took on a more questionable nuance. Thus, the Dutch chronicler Veldenaer wrote towards the end of the fifteenth century: "Some chroniclers assert that the Knight of the Swan (Lohengrin) came from the Grail, as the earthly Paradise was formerly thought to have been called; that, however, is not Paradise but a sinful place which is entered as the result of high adventure and is only departed from again by means of high adventures and good fortune." A chronicler of Halberstadt in Saxony says: "The historians are of the opinion that the Knight of the Swan came from the mountain where Venus lives in the Grail." In the round mountain of St. Barbara near Pozzuoli there lived, so runs the legend, a great company of bewitched men and women who were forced to spend their lives there in dancing and lechery until the Day of Judgment.[26] Among the Germans of the sixteenth century the legend and the word vanished from popular speech; in Frisch's German-Latin dictionary of 1741,[27] under *Graal* (grail) it simply says, "An old play which was performed with dancing and shouting."[28] Thus F. Locke asserts quite rightly that the symbol of the Grail is an archetypal image of polyvalent meaning.[29]

Just as the word is certainly ambiguous and as its meaning changes, so the Grail itself and the events associated with it are not everywhere the same. The impression is often clearly conveyed that with the emergence of the subject, a proliferation

[26] Cf. A. de la Sale, *Le Paradis de la Sibylle*, p. lxxxv.
[27] *Deutsch-lateinischem Wörterbuch*.
[28] Quoted from Hertz, *op. cit.*, p. 36.
[29] *The Quest of the Holy Grail*, pp. 3 and 7.

of fantasy set in which never tired of devising new arrangements and combinations, similar to the profusion of ornaments, flowers, animals, saints and monsters that confront us in Gothic cathedrals. The formation of such different styles and the modifications which the material underwent in the process bear witness to the fact that it possesses an inherent psychic life of its own which will not allow itself to be confined to any one specific pattern. In Chrétien it is introduced as *a* grail, not *the* Grail, for this was, as we have seen, the designation for a particular type of vessel. Further on, it is described as being of pure gold, set with precious stones and with such a brilliant light streaming from it that nearby candles lost their brightness.

It is not clearly stated here that the Grail provides food, merely that with every course the vessel is carried uncovered past those at meat. In other versions, it does provide food for those at table. In the description of Gauvain's visit to the Grail Castle, it is called *le rice Graal* and the point is made that it goes around the table serving food without being carried by anyone.

In later continuations of the romances centering around Perceval, as well as in most of the other works, the Grail is expressly referred to as the vessel used by Christ at the Last Supper which later came into the possession of Joseph of Arimathea.[30] The Grail also dispenses food in those versions which have a more religious bias. When he is in prison, Joseph of Arimathea is miraculously fed and comforted by it, as he later is during his wanderings with his family.

In the *Queste del Saint Graal,* it appears in a wondrous manner at Whitsuntide, just as King Arthur is sitting down to supper with his knights. "A clap of thunder sounded, followed by a brilliant ray of light. The Grail then entered, covered with white velvet, without being carried by anyone, and the chamber was filled with a pleasant fragrance. As it went round the table each person was served with the food he desired."

In Heinrich von dem Thuerlin's *Diû Krône,* the Grail is described as a reliquary casket containing a piece of bread, of which one third is presented to the Grail King. Besides this,

[30] According to another version, Joseph had had it made.

a *toblier* (probably a beaker, tumbler) in which there are three drops of blood is mentioned, so that here we already have an unmistakable allusion to the Eucharistic sacrament. This finds unequivocal expression in the works of an outspokenly religious nature[31] in which the Grail, called *le Saint Vaissel*, becomes the vessel of the Mass, the chalice or ciborium, and the Grail Service the Mass. In Chrétien Perceval learns from the hermit that the Grail contains the Host which serves the Old King for food. From the vessel containing the blood of Christ to the chalice of the Mass is only a short step.[32]

In the *Perlesvaus*,[33] King Arthur attends a Grail service celebrated by a number of hermits. The story recounts that "at that time there was no chalice in King Arthur's realm. In the mystery of the Mass, the Grail appeared in five forms which, however, may not be mentioned because no one may speak of the mystery of the sacrament, excepting he who by divine grace is fitted to do so. King Arthur saw all these transformations, the last of which was into a chalice, while the hermit who had sung the Mass found on the corporal-cloth a letter saying that it was the Will of God that his body should be consecrated to his memory in that cup." We have already discussed the meaning of the blood and referred to the mysterious and numinous effect the idea of a relic of the blood of Christ must have had upon the people of that age. But it is not only in the veneration and the attempt to grasp the significance of Christ's blood that deep emotional and archaic reactions are touched; the symbol of the vessel in which it is preserved naturally causes an equally profound impression. That the "soul-substance" should be preserved in a funerary vessel conforms to a particularly archetypal concept which has its roots in antiquity and the East. At the burial of certain African chieftans, for instance, the fluids secreted by the corpse are collected in a

[31] Especially in the *Lancelot Grail*, the "*Queste*" and the *Perlesvaus*.

[32] The Grail was thus actually interpreted as the Eucharistic chalice. See Holmes and Klenke, *op. cit.*, p. 172, and the literature there cited; also Mario Roques, *Studies in Philology*, XLIV, pp. 413–14. Sometimes the Grail was identified with the ciborium *or* the chalice.

[33] Verses 7220*ff.*

leather bag or receptacle and buried apart as being especially "holy". According to the natives the animal that incarnates the soul of the deceased and which represents the survival of the soul of their kings comes out of this bag.[34] Similarly, in Egyptian burial rituals all of the easily corruptible parts of the body of the dead Pharoah were separately interred in four canopic vases. These, for the most part, had lids in the form of the heads of the four sons of Horus, who brought about the resurrection and ascension of their grandfather. They were the agents for the resurrection of Osiris. In later times Osiris himself was represented as a receptacle with a human head.[35] It is as if the vessel contained the magic soul-substance of the god; it does not, therefore, seem out of order to attribute a similar meaning to the Grail.

The vessel containing Christ's blood is a symbol that emerges with absolute spontaneity. It is the main motif of the story, the Grail motif.[36] It is as though it contained the living remnant of Christ and *his soul-substance, that element out of which a mystical continuation of his being is made possible.* For this reason a connection with the myth of Osiris cannot be dismissed out of hand, for there is a tradition which points in that direction, namely the *Légende de l'Abbaye de Fécamp*,[37] already referred to. In this legend it is Nicodemus who, with a knife, scrapes the dried blood from Christ's wounds and conceals it, first in his glove, then in a lead container, a small cylinder according to the description. He hides the cylinder in the trunk of a fig tree. Because of a threatened invasion of Sidon, where he is residing,

[34] Cf. Frobenius, *Erythräa, Länder und Zeiten des heiligen Königsmordes*, pp. 128*ff.*

[35] Cf. H. Bonnet, *Reallexikon der ägyptischen Religionsgeschichte*, under "Kanopus."

[36] Certainly, in the poems of Chrétien and Wolfram, the Grail is depicted either as a precious vessel that is not described in any greater detail, or even—in Wolfram—as a stone, but in Robert de Boron it is unequivocally a vessel containing Christ's blood. In the Continuations the Grail is generally understood in this sense.

[37] Cf. Langfors, *Histoire de l'Abbaye de Fécamp*, *passim*; and Mergell, *Der Gral in Wolframs Parzival*, pp. 100*ff*, and the literature cited there, as also pp. 107–8.

and in obedience to a divine command, he entrusts the tree to the sea; it is carried to the West and washed ashore on the coast of Normandy, near Fécamp. There the trunk again takes root and puts forth leaves. Owing to the remarkable influences that emanate from the spot, a church and later a monastery are founded there, although the holy blood hidden in the trunk is not yet discovered.[38]

The similarity between this story and the Grail legend is remarkable,[39] not only in detail but also because in both the vessel containing the holy blood remains hidden for a long time and is noticed only because of the strange effects it produces. The Fécamp version clearly suggests the "myth of Osiris" reported by Plutarch,[40] in which the coffin of Osiris is washed ashore at Byblos in Phoenicia, the land of the origin of the fig tree, and is concealed in a bush of heather which grows up around it. It therefore seems probable that traces of the myth of Osiris survive in the Grail story. But even if no historical connection does exist, the same archetype appears none the less to have manifested itself once again. The aspect of the Grail as a sepulchre is very clear in Robert de Boron's version. In the

[38] According to the legend this first happened in 1171 during the rebuilding of the burned-out church. Actually a scroll was said to have been found earlier, on which it was written that "*le prix del mont*" ("the prize of the world") that had come from Jerusalem was in this church but without its being known where.

[39] The similarities of expression may also be compared. The opening of Book One of the Fécamp story reads as follows:

> Cel qui de contes s'entremeit
> Celui sa cure et s'entente meit
> *A rimer la plus heute estoire*
> *Mande salus premièrement.*
> A tout cheny qui parfaitement
> Jhesu Crist emoient et servent
> Et qui la sou amour deservent.

And the *Roman de Perceval* opens with these lines:

> Chrétien qui autant et . . .
> à rimoier le meilleur conte
> per le commendement le conte
> qui soit conté cort real.

[40] *Über Isis und Osiris.*

Latin version of the Gospel of Nicodemus,[41] Joseph of Arimathea says to Christ, who appears to him in prison, that to prove he really is the saviour he should show him, Joseph, where he laid the body. Whereupon Christ takes him by the hand and leads him to the grave. In our version Christ delivers the cup to Joseph instead, thus hinting that the Grail is synonymous with the grave. This is the point at which the Grail story diverges from the Gospel of Nicodemus and follows its own course. At the time of the formation of the Grail legend, emotions were deeply stirred by the idea of the Holy Sepulchre, and it was this idea that imparted such inflammatory motive power to the Crusades, if it did not actually cause them. The task of freeing the Holy Sepulchre from heathen powers formed the central aim of the undertaking. This aspect of the Grail motif, and the way in which the literal freeing of the Holy Sepulchre gradually became an inner goal as well, has been brilliantly elucidated by Helen Adolf. She has also pointed out the aspect of the Holy Sepulchre as that place where the mystery of resurrection came to pass, thereby giving the sepulchre an especially numinous character.[42]

In every age and every land, holy graves have enjoyed veneration on account of the blessed effects emanating from the remains of those buried within them. With Christ's sepulchre the case is different, in so far as Christ was resurrected and the grave consequently left empty. Furthermore, its authenticity is by no means certain, since it was said to have been choked up with rubble and only discovered as the result of a miracle three hundred years later when the Emperor Constantine had it dug for. In the intervening centuries heathen holy places had occupied the site.[43] If, in spite of this, the sepulchre was considered to be precisely the most important object of devotion in Christendom, this was because something of far greater moment was concealed behind and beyond the concrete actuality,

[41] W. C. von Tischendorf, *Evangelia Apocrypha*, p. 382.

[42] *Visio Pacis*, *passim.*

[43] Cf. article entitled "Heiliges Grab," in *Die Religion in Geschichte und Gegenwart*, 1910.

namely a symbol or an idea. The great riddle of death has naturally occupied the human spirit from time immemorial, as is witnessed by the ideas that have attached themselves to its visible and, so to speak, its enduring expression—the grave.

The cult of the grave is one of the very earliest manifestations of religious conviction and appears among nearly all races and in the most varied stages of culture. Great significance is attributed to the graves of saints in the non-Christian worlds of China, India and Tibet, while the most holy place in all Islam is the Grave of the Prophet. The grave plays an important part not only in religion but also in popular superstition,[44] where magical powers of the most diverse kinds are attributed to it. In fairy-tales and legends, too, wonderful things come to pass in connection with graves, as in the German version of the well-known story of Cinderella, where the mother's grave possesses the power of granting wishes, and beautiful clothes or golden apples fall from the tree growing above it. For the most part the place of burial is looked upon as the home of the dead, from which either the deceased or his spirit can still exercise his influence. It was said of the Tuatha De Danann that they withdrew into the burial mounds where they live on and occasionally appear to men. As mentioned, every consecrated altar in a Roman Catholic church must contain relics, so that it is at the same time also a grave; often it is even shaped like a sarcophagus.

Like the vessel, the grave has a maternal meaning, since the mother is not only the place of birth but also, as Mother Earth, that which receives the dead back into herself. The primal image of the mother is suited for this dual aspect of life and death.[45] Both the food- and drink-imparting, life-bestowing aspect and the aspect of death and the grave are exhibited by the Grail. The mystery of coming into being and of ceasing to

[44] *Handwörterbuch des deutschen Aberglaubens*, under "Grab."

[45] More precise information on this matter may be found in Jung's *Symbols of Transformation*, "Symbols of the Mother and of Rebirth," pars. 300–418, and also in his "Psychological Aspects of the Mother Archetype," in *The Archetypes and the Collective Unconscious*, pars. 148–98. Cf. Erich Neumann, *The Great Mother*.

be is bound up with the image of the mother; this explains why Mysteries with this process as the content of their ritual were connected with the cult of mother goddesses such as Demeter and Isis.[46]

The great and genuinely vital mystery of the death and resurrection of the god also forms the central point of the Christian religion. Through the sacrificial death of Christ the believer is not only assured of the remission of sins but also of resurrection and life everlasting. The idea that new life can be produced through sacrifice, especially bloody sacrifice, is as old as mankind itself. The life-bestowing property of the Grail is therefore conditioned in a two-fold manner, on the one hand through its maternal significance and on the other through the sacrificial blood it contains. If in our story prominence is now given to the vessel in its meaning as grave, and especially the grave of Christ, this is because it is there that the mysterious transition from death to life, the resurrection, took place. Equally, the Eucharistic chalice is where the ineffable mystery of transubstantiation is consummated. Indeed, this event is represented in the Mass as eternally taking place, just as, although in a somewhat different sense, the succession of life and death is also an unending rhythm. The idea of the Communion cup as the grave of Christ and therefore as the place of his death and resurrection seems to have been familiar to the Middle Ages, as is indicated in a passage from Honorius of Autun, which reads:[47]

> When the priest says, "*Per omnia saecula saeculorum*," the deacon comes before him and elevates the chalice. He covers a portion of it with a cloth, then returns it to the altar and covers it with the corporal, enacting the part of Joseph of

[46] Prof. Kerényi brought out this connection very skilfully in a series of lectures, "Seele und Griechentum."

[47] "*Dicente sacerdote: Per omnia saecula saeculorum, diaconus venit, calicem coram eo sustollit, cum favone partem eius cooperit, in alteri reponit et eum corporali cooperit praeferens Joseph ab Arimathia, qui corpus Christi deposuit, faciem eius sudario cooperuit, in monumento deposuit, lapide cooperuit. Hic oblate, et calix cum corporali cooperitur, quod sindonem mundam significat, in quam Joseph corpus Christi involvebat. Calix hic, sepulchrum; patena lapidem designat, qui sepulchrum clauserat.*"

Arimathea who took the body of Christ down from the cross, covered his face with a sudarium, laid the body in the grave and covered it with a stone. That which is here offered, and also the chalice, are covered with the corporal, which signifies the linen winding sheet in which Joseph wrapped the body of Christ. The chalice signifies the grave, and the paten the stone with which it was closed.[48]

In our story, the Grail vessel, as mentioned, is depicted as a prefiguration of the Communion cup and the service of the Grail as similar to the Mass. It differs from the Mass however; instead of a sacrifice another transformation takes place. The wine does not have to be transubstantiated, because the sacrificial blood is already in the vessel, nor is there anything that can be clearly recognized as a death and resurrection mystery. Perceval's assumption of responsibility for the Grail could of course denote a renewal of the Fisher King, the more so since the King dies after installing his successor in office.[49] In the version of the legend under discussion, as in most of the other versions, the sick king becomes healthy and "*toz muez de sa nature*" ("quite transformed") as soon as Perceval asks the question, only to die three days later.

This interpretation seems superficial. The type of renewal wherein the son steps into the father's shoes is far too natural and well known to be able to express the transformation that is meant by the mystery of resurrection. We must therefore try to probe the symbols more deeply and for that purpose will consider another aspect of the grave. The grave cannot be looked upon only as the place of transformation and resurrection, but

[48] *Gemma Animae*, Book I, Chap. XLVII; Migne *Pat. Lat.*, Vol. 172, quoted by Birch-Hirschfeld, *Die Sage vom Graal*, p. 221. This same point is also independently emphasized by Helen Adolf in *Visio Pacis*.

[49] J. L. Weston, *From Ritual to Romance*, supports the view that the Grail legend is a relic of pagan Oriental cults, especially that of Adonis, therefore of the dying and resurrecting god. She corroborates her theory with numerous examples from Frazer's *Golden Bough*. It is, however, more a question of an analogue. On the other hand there does appear to be a real connection with the Osiris legend via the story of the Abbaye de Fécamp.

must also be viewed as the state of being dead or buried. There seems to be a special significance attached to precisely this aspect of our story. In the grave life has vanished, it is not manifest but concealed. This brings us to another age-old conception, that of the hidden treasure and, in connection with it, to the following train of thought:

Hidden treasure is a preferred ingredient of legends and fairy-tales. According to popular belief,[50] this treasure is imagined as being within the earth, in such places for instance as where the grass grows more luxuriantly, where the snow never lies, where a meteorite has fallen or where the rainbow touches the earth. The acquisition of buried treasure is made more difficult by its power to change location. Thus it is said that treasure moves away, it grows, rises or falls. It only comes to the surface of the earth once every seven hundred years, at which time it announces its presence by little blue flames, the so-called "treasure fire." The efflorescence of the treasure generally takes place at night and only at particular times that are propitious for excavating it. Treasure is frequently not recognized since it appears in the guise of a valueless object. The riches lying under the earth are seldom unguarded. Either a good or an evil spirit watches over them, facilitating or hindering their removal, as the case may be. Most frequently it is the Devil who is encountered as guardian, although often enough it is poor souls or little grey men who have acquired gold in a questionable manner and therefore have to atone to the treasure until it is dug up. Their salvation depends on the successful removal of the hoard. This is often reserved for a particular man of a particular age and having particular attributes. The heroes who have withdrawn into the hills, like Barbarossa or King Arthur, are also inhabitants of the treasure mountains. The typical motifs of the land of the dead can also be detected in the legends of treasure mountains; they were originally the dwelling place of the dead. The belief in treasure must therefore be rooted in the custom of burial gifts, and the earliest

[50] Cf. *Handwörterbuch des deutschen Aberglaubens*, under "*Schatz*" *and* "*Schatzhüter*."

legends about treasure would have been stories of robbing graves. We have also seen the Grail as a treasure of this kind. For instance, it manifests itself only at a certain time and only *one person* is able to find it. Certain it is that this deeply-rooted concept of the hidden treasure contributed to the fact that the summons to liberate the Holy Sepulchre awakened such a resounding echo. It is not without reason that these ideas are the cherished children of the imagination. They are deeply embedded and should not be brushed aside as mere infantile wish-fulfilment fantasies. The treasure seeker's instinct is not directed solely towards concrete objects for, as is known, there are treasures of another kind, so that one can imagine the things in varied and different ways. The idea of being dead or in the grave as a psychic condition is sometimes reflected in philosophical views. In the *Gorgias* for instance, Plato has Socrates say: "Well, life as you describe it is a strange affair. I should not be surprised, you know, if Euripides was right when he said, 'Who knows, if life be death, and death be life?' And perhaps we are actually dead, for I once heard one of our wise men say that we are now dead, and that our body is a tomb."[51] The same is meant in Heraclitus' dictum, "We live the death of the Immortals, they live ours."[52] Very similar is the Christian doctrine of the body as a prison. This idea was worked out in extraordinary detail in those systems of Gnostic doctrine which spoke of the descent of the soul into the physical world and of its imprisonment there, and above all in the teachings of Mani with their Zoroastrian influence. According to Mani, who accepted the opposing realms of light and darkness as existing from eternity, the entire material world, together with everything that lives in it, is the grave of the light element which has vanished or been imprisoned within it. The work of redemption consists in releasing this light element from the darkness of matter and in its reunion with the realm of light. Attention has often been called to the fact that these Gnostic ideas may be connected to

[51] "Gorgias," in *The Collected Dialogues of Plato*, pp. 274–75.

[52] Vide H. Diels, *Fragmente der Vorsokratiker*, p. 164.

the Grail stories by way of the Catharists and Albigensians.[53]

The idea of the hidden treasure finds its most far-reaching and individual elaboration in alchemy. This elaboration proceeds from the assumption that something precious, i.e. a spirit, is concealed or bound in the substance, the *prima materia* or *vilis*, and that the work of the "royal art" consists in freeing or transforming it.[54] Consequently, according to the alchemistic view, to be dead and buried—an incomprehensible state of existence—is looked upon as the primary condition and as the starting point for the *opus*, in contrast to the general view that death and burial come at the close of life.[55] From this it may be concluded that the life worked on in the *opus*, or through the Grail, was different from visible, physical existence, as Christ's empty grave also denoted the dawning of a new and differently conditioned life. This difference did not, however, appear to refer to an existence after death, but to one which would run its course during this life, though on another level.

It is natural to suppose that things buried or hidden merely refer to something unconscious which only needs to be dug up or uncovered, like a treasure raised to the light of day. The concept of an empty grave, however, seems to point further. It could be a question here of something so concealed and invisible that it is as if it had never existed at all, something which did not merely need to be uncovered but which to some extent had to come into existence first. This then would be that other life referred to above, not the natural, bound-to-nature life of the

[53] As mentioned, specific traces of these views may be detected in the Grail legend, for which reason Rahn makes the suggestion, in *Der Kreuzzug gegen den Graal*, that the Grail should be looked upon as a Manichaean or Catharistic relic, and the Grail legend interpreted as a veiled description of the Manichaean-Catharistic mysteries. This, however, seems questionable, even though Catharistic ideas were very widely disseminated at that time, especially in the south of France (cf. Anitchkof, *Joachim de Flore*, *passim*) and, as the crusade against the Albigenses showed, were considered to be so heretical that a disguising of the same might well have been desirable.

[54] Cf. Jung, *Psychology and Alchemy*, *Psychology and Religion* and *Mysterium Coniunctionis*.

[55] Cf. Jung, "The Relations between the Ego and the Unconscious," in *Two Essays on Analytical Psychology*.

body but the life of the inner man, transcending nature, that encompassing personality which Jung has called the Self.[56] In the dreams and fantasy pictures of modern man this hidden, invisible something is occasionally depicted as a meaningful and numinous void. There is one picture in which an egg-shaped void, from which rays stream forth, forms the centre of a world or of a mandala with an empty centre.[57] The words of Meister Eckhart beautifully express what is meant by this image: "Everything must be lost, the soul must exist in unhampered nothingness," or "Whosoever would come to God must come as nothing."[58] Or, expressed in Eastern imagery: "In the purple hall of the city of jade dwells the God of Utmost Emptiness and Life."[59] The Confucians call it "the centre of the void." A nothingness, a void, is therefore the inescapable condition for the emergence of the Self.[60] The Self is not already present from the beginning in a comprehensible form, but manifests itself only through the outer and inner realizations of a life lived to its end. For this reason Jung has likened it to the crystal lattice[61] present as a potential form in a solution but which first becomes visible in the process of crystallization, although crystallization does not necessarily take place. The Self is therefore not complete, but is present in us as a potentiality which can become manifest only in the course of a specific process. Certainly, the Self is not invariably realized through the unfolding of the natural biological life processes. There appear to be many lives where this does not come to pass.

Then how and by what means can the Self become manifest? It is realized to that extent in which it is lived in the experience of daily life. It is not achieved, however, when it appears in symbolic form in dreams and inner images, nor is it when

[56] Cf. *ibid.*, par. 399.

[57] Cf., for instance, *Psychology and Religion*, par. 136.

[58] Büttner, *Meister Eckeharts Schriften und Predigten*, pp. 202*f*, 206.

[59] *The Secret of the Golden Flower*, p. 22.

[60] Indian Yoga teaching also speaks of a void (the void of consciousness) that must be established before the Self can be perceived. Cf. Heinrich Zimmer, *Der Weg zum Selbst*; and J. W. Hauer, *Der Yoga als Heilsweg*, pp. 29 and 129.

[61] *Psychology and Alchemy*, par. 325.

consciousness acquires a specific degree of clarity, nor yet when a psychological function has attained a high degree of differentiation. Important as consciousness undoubtedly is—and rightly utilized consciousness is an invaluable means of help for the realization of the Self—it is not by itself the determining factor. For it does not depend so very greatly on knowledge and ability or upon some degree of intelligence, but rather upon the use which is made of these attributes and above all, on the psychic attitude a person adopts in the face of the various circumstances of his life and fate. As the threads of fabric are woven into a pattern, so the Self as the living garment of divinity is woven out of the many decisions and crises, in themselves possibly insignificant, by which we are affected in the course of our lives. Such occasions present themselves at every level of life and intelligence and in every milieu. Whether or not they lead to a manifestation of the Self depends solely on our own response. Many of us have observed that children, even small children, when faced with some difficulty, possess an attitude which many adults could only envy. That "something," the lack of which we experience as soullessness, is a "someone" who takes a position, who is accountable and who feels committed. Where this higher, responsible ego is lacking there can be no Self. Ethos and the Self are therefore mutually interdependent. For this reason, too, an attitude of "beyond good and evil," such as has been commended in many quarters in modern times and especially since Nietzsche, is the best way to prevent the emergence of the Self.

From the foregoing we can see that a fascination can emanate from something empty. It longs for completion like an invisible form which calls out for substance; the individual is conscious of the existence of this summons and of the growth of this attraction, but without knowing what it is that calls to him. The influence emanating from the hidden Grail could be likened to such a summons.

A further characteristic of the Grail is that it distinguishes between good men and sinners, in that its beneficial effects are perceived only by the former. A vessel possessing a similar discriminating function also appears in Celtic mythology. Manawyddan, son of Lir, a divinity of the sea, owned, among other precious objects, a cup which broke whenever a lie was told. The same trait is found in an old Irish tale, "The Vessel of Badurn" (from *Irish Ordeals*):

> Badurn is the name of a king. His wife went to the fountain on one occasion, and there saw two women, carrying a bronze chain between them, come out of the fairy hills. When they saw the woman coming towards them they vanished into the fountain. She followed them in and in their home she saw a wonderful method of ordeal. This was a crystal vessel or cup that had the peculiarity that when someone spoke three lying words it divided itself into three parts in his hand, and when anyone uttered three true words the pieces united again. Badurn's wife begged for the vessel, which Badurn then kept in order to discriminate between truth and falsehood.[62]

Through *disintegration* the vessel indicated that a lie was being told, and through *unification* it bore witness to the truth, as though to illustrate the way an individual's soul is similarly affected by his words. He who lies deceives himself and disintegrates in the process, whereas he who tells the truth "heals" his soul and makes it whole. It is a temptation at this point to think of that vessel filled with *νοῦς* (understanding and consciousness) which is mentioned in the *Corpus Hermeticum* and which, as Hermes taught his pupil Thoth, was sent from heaven to earth so that men, plunging into it, might understand the purpose for which they were created.[63] A vessel of this kind also played a part in the Gnostic mystery celebrations of late antiquity. In Hans Leisegang's study, "The Mystery of the Serpent,"[64] an illustration is given of a bowl that appears to

[62] Quoted by A. W. Thompson, *The Elucidation: A Prologue to the Contes del Graal*, p. 41.

[63] W. Scott, *Hermetica*, Vol. I, p. 151. With this compare Jung, *Alchemical Studies*, par. 96.

[64] In *The Mysteries*, Vol. 2 of the Papers from the Eranos Yearbooks. See Plates I and II.

have originated in an Orphic community.[65] On it sixteen naked men and women, in reverential and worshipping attitudes, stand around a coiled and winged serpent, the symbol of the Redeemer and Son of God in the Orphic Gnosis. The serpent leads them towards the development of consciousness. A text of the Perates[66] says: "Now no one can be saved and rise up again[67] without the Son, who is the serpent. For it was he who brought the paternal models down from above, and it is he who carries back up again those who have been awakened from sleep and have reassumed the features of the Father." In this bowl the Logos-serpent is clearly being worshipped by the initiates. According to the views of the Gnostic Naassenes, another vessel, known as the cup of Anacreon, mediated a similar gnosis (knowledge) of God. This sect believed that there was an androgynous original being who had to be redeemed from matter. The Greeks called him "the heavenly horn of the moon" and in a state of ecstasy declared:

> Bring water here, boy, bring wine.
> Immerse me in stupor and frenzy.
> My tankard tells me
> Speaking in mute silence
> What I must become.[68]

Probably the Persian-Arabic legend of the cup of Jamshyd, in which all the mysteries of the world could be perceived, and the stories of Solomon's miraculous cup can be traced back to just such Gnostic sources.[69] The writer Ibn Malik recounts a vision of Mohammed's which the latter commanded Malik to des-

[65] In the possession of Jacob Hirsch, Lucerne, until 1957. In the auction catalogue it figures as "Important work of art from the estate of the late Dr. J. Hirsch, A. Hess AG, Lucerne, No. 105." I do not know who bought the bowl or where it is now.—*M.-L. von F.*

[66] Hippolytus, *Elenchos*, V, 17, 8; quoted by Leisegang, *op. cit.*, p. 230.

[67] From the abyss of the world.

[68] Cf. Leisegang, *Die Gnosis*, p. 126; and Jung, *Psychology and Alchemy*, par. 550.

[69] For the part played by a mystical cup in the legend of Solomon, in general, cf. Kampers, *op. cit.*, pp. 81*ff.*

cribe as follows: "On the night when I ascended to Heaven I glimpsed, under a canopy, a goblet of such penetrating brightness that all the seven heavens were illuminated by it. Around the goblet was a prayer written in green characters. [According to a second manuscript[70] the goblet itself was green.] . . . A voice declared, 'Oh, Mohammed, the All Highest God has created this goblet for thine englightenment.' "[71] That Gnostic traditions survived into the early Middle Ages is proved by the *coffrets gnostiques*, boxes found in Provence on which are portrayed naked initiates.[72] Gnostic cult objects, presumably through the agency of Arabic and especially Sabean culture, reached into Sicily, Spain and the south of France. It is therefore not beyond the bounds of possibility that certain influences which affected the Grail legend could have originated there. The vision of the Gnostic alchemist Zosimos of Panopolis in Egypt (third century A.D.), in which he saw a cosmic altar in the form of a bowl,[73] is related to the vessel mentioned in the *Corpus Hermeticum* in which men acquired *νοῦς* (consciousness). In a dream Zosimos saw an altar in the form of a shallow bowl in which men in torment were being cooked and thereby sublimated into a state of spirituality. In another of his works, Zosimos mentions the *krater* (mixing bowl) of Poimandres[74] in which he advises his *soror mystica* to immerse herself. "The *krater*," says Jung, "is . . . a font or piscina, in which the immersion takes place and transformation into a spiritual being is effected. It is the *vas Hermetis* of later alchemy . . . uterus of spiritual renewal or rebirth."[75] In this *krater*, which is the subject of the books of the *Corpus Hermeticum*, Henry and Renée Kahane even see the actual source of Wolfram's idea of the Grail. They assume that this book came to Spain via the

[70] The Dresden Library.

[71] Quoted from Kampers, *op. cit.*, p. 85.

[72] J. de Hammer, *Mémoire sur deux coffrets gnostiques du moyen age*, described and illustrated in *Psychology and Alchemy*, par. 184 and Fig. 70.

[73] Interpreted and commented on by Jung in *Alchemical Studies*, pars. 85*ff*.

[74] *Ibid.*, pars. 96*ff*.

[75] *Ibid.*, par. 97.

agency of the Sabeans and thus to the notice of the mysterious Kyot—Wolfram's source.[76]

In alchemy the vessel is at times identical with its contents. The *Rosarium*, a fifteenth-century text, says: "One is the stone, one the medicine, one the vessel, one the procedure, and one the disposition," [77] and the *Aurora consurgens*, another text of the same period, declares that the vessel is the *aqua permanens*, the arcane substance itself.[78] The "Liber quartorum," a Latin translation of a Sabean text, emphasizes that the vessel is "like the work of God in the vessel of the divine seed (*germinis divi*), for it has received the clay, moulded it, and mixed it with water and fire." [79] "This," says Jung, "is an allusion to the creation of man, but on the other hand it seems to refer to the creation of souls, since immediately afterwards the text speaks of the production of souls from the 'seeds of heaven.' In order to catch the soul, God created the *vas cerebi*, the cranium."[80] Thus, the symbol of the vessel is also applied to the soul. Caesarius of Heisterbach gives an excellent example of this: "The soul is a spiritual substance of spherical nature, like the globe of the moon, or like a glass vessel that is furnished before and behind with eyes and 'sees the whole universe'."[81] In this case the vessel or soul thus has a relation to the whole cosmos and its creation.

The emergence of human consciousness can be compared to the Genesis story of creation. On the first day God divided the light from the darkness and called the light day and the darkness night. Psychologically translated, this would mean that on the same day the light of consciousness emerged from the chaos of

[76] "Proto-Perceval und Proto-Parzival," and the further literature there cited.

[77] "Unus est lapis, una medicina, unum vas, unum regimen, unaque dispositio." 1550 edition, fol. AIII; quoted by Jung, *Alchemical Studies*, par. 113.

[78] (Part II) *Artis Auriferae*, I, p. 203; quoted by Jung, *ibid.* Cf. the numerous passages on the identity of the vessel and its contents from the texts there quoted.

[79] *Theatrum Chemicum*, Vol. V, p. 148; quoted *ibid.*

[80] *Ibid.*

[81] *Dialogus miraculorum*, IV:34, and I:32; quoted *ibid.*

undifferentiation, night, the unconscious, also came into being as an absolute and independent opposite to consciousness. "Unconscious" is the negative of "conscious", which is there, presupposed to exist. Small children have no individual unconscious because they have no corresponding consciousness. They have their being in a dreamlike, twilight state out of which, with increasing consciousness, they awaken into an ever higher, more consolidated consciousness, oriented towards the outer world. With consciousness, the unconscious therefore also comes into existence. If we follow the Genesis story further we read that on the fourth day, after the firmament which separates the waters above from those below has been created and when the lower waters have been collected together to form the seas so that the dry land can appear and bring forth vegetation, God speaks: "Let there be lights in the firmament of the heaven to divide the day from the night; and let them be for signs, and for season, and for days, and years: And let them be for lights in the firmament of the heaven to give light upon the earth: and it was so. And God made two great lights; the greater light to rule the day, and the lesser light to rule the night: he made the stars also."

The great light of day, the sun, may be compared to the mind, the lesser light which rules the night to the soul.[82] After the earth, as solidity and consciousness, had been separated from the sea, the surging, fluctuating unconscious, the soul came into being as if arising from the water. Is it not her whom the ancients worshipped as Aphrodite, the foam-born, and who is still called upon today as Stella Maris? Morgane, the sea-born, is the name given to the fairy, skilled in magic and healing, who holds sway in the world of the Breton stories, the same otherworldly we experience as the realm of the unconscious and of dreams. It was also she, the Lady Soul, whom those heroes of chivalry saw and sought behind the real woman. In truth, service and worship were offered her without it always being known that such was the case.

[82] Cf. *Mysterium Coniunctionis*, Ch. III, "The Personification of the Opposites", pars. 104 *ff*.

In a quite particular sense the winning of the soul was the problem of that age. If we keep to the analogy of the Genesis story, the soul, the light of night, makes its first appearance after the creation of a world which it can assimilate. Mankind, or at any rate Western man, had obviously reached this stage at the rise of Christianity. The growing consciousness of the soul coincided with this phenomenon, indeed the highest value was attributed to the soul in the Christian religion. The part played in Christianity by suffering and the Passion clearly indicates (in contrast to some other religions) that a *feminine element* is included and is of importance, and that the soul could be described as the organ of suffering. Tertullian's saying, "*Anima naturaliter christiana*" ("The soul is Christian by nature"), can also be understood in this sense. The process of realizing or becoming conscious of the soul was greatly intensified in the Middle Ages and was manifested not only in religion but also in the secular *Minnedienst*, to which, moreover, a pronouncedly religious character adhered, so that the process finally came round again full circle to its true foundation, the soul.

Adam de Saint Victor's beautiful song, written during the time the Grail stories were being produced, also harmonizes with this spirit:

Salve Mater salvatoris
Vas electum, vas honoris
Vas caelestis gratiae
Ab aeterno vas provisum
Vas insigne, vas excisum
Manu sapientiae.

Chosen vessel, vase of honour,
Vase of heaven's grace
From eternity foreseen,
Noted vessel, vessel carved
By wisdom's hand.

In a special sense, therefore, the soul is that wondrous vessel which is the goal of the quest and in which the life-giving power inheres, whose final secret can never be revealed, but must ever remain hidden because its essence is a mystery. In that age the alchemists, who sought it in the "soul in matter," were also devoting themselves to this same mystery.

CHAPTER VIII

The Grail as Stone

As JUNG HAS pointed out,[1] the vessel (*vas*) in alchemy is a true symbol, representing a mystical idea and exhibiting correspondingly extensive connections of meaning. The legendary writer of antiquity, Maria Prophetissa, says of it that "the whole secret lies in knowing about the Hermetic vessel." [2] The vessel is always One, and it must be round like the vault of heaven so that celestial influences can contribute to the work. It is also often called a matrix or uterus, in which the *filius philosophorum* (son of the philosophers) is born, and at the same time it is, in a mysterious way, identical with its contents.[3] For instance, it is simply the *aqua permanens* itself. Mercurius is "our true hidden vessel, and also the Philosophical Garden in which our sun rises and ascends." [4] It is *itself* the *lapis philosophorum.*[5] Inasmuch as it contains and gathers up dispersed matter, it can also be interpreted psychologically as a *concept*, a concept that is not, however, arbitrarily attributed to the unconscious by consciousness, but that develops from the unconscious itself, as a result of observing it with painstaking care.

In this sense it is a *theoria* in which the unconscious explains itself.[6] Modern depth psychology has rediscovered a similar way of using the manifestations of the unconscious psyche as a "vessel" in order to assimilate its contents. This is the method

[1] *Psychology and Alchemy*, par. 338.
[2] *Ibid.*
[3] *Alchemical Studies*, par. 115.
[4] *Psychology and Alchemy*, par. 338, note 19.
[5] Jung, *Alchemical Studies*, par. 115.
[6] Cf. this concept in *Aion*, par. 249.

known as "active imagination", which Jung defines as "an active evocation of the inner images *secundum naturam*." [7] This means that one does not fantasy aimlessly into the blue but, on the contrary, tries to grasp the meaning of the inner object in its quality of a faithfully reproduced mental image.[8] It is a very real achievement of thinking and imagination. The process produces symbolic stories or dialogues with an inner partner who personifies the unconscious, and these activities bring about a mutual rapprochement and synthesis of the conscious and unconscious halves of the personality. At the same time there arises in consciousness an attitude that is willing to take the contents of the unconscious into lasting consideration and, as far as possible, to understand and incorporate them into real life. In a way, the individual becomes like a vessel for the inflowing contents of the unconscious. In this sense the German mystics use the word *vaz* (vase) as a designation for man.[9] That the alchemical vessel has to do with visual understanding is also seen in a statement by Senior quoted in a treatise by Theobald de Hoghelande (sixteenth century) to the effect that "the vision" of the Hermetic vessel "is more to be sought" than the "scripture." [10] By beholding it, man attains νοῦς, the higher consciousness, which is found in the vessel.[11] So the vessel also becomes a uterus for the spiritual renewal or rebirth of the individual.

In early times, the contents of the vessel, the arcane substance, had already been compared to the waters of the Nile or to the dismembered Osiris, thus admitting to its secret, divine nature.[12] The vessel, therefore, also appears to represent an

[7] Cf. *Psychology and Alchemy*, par. 219.

[8] Cf. *ibid.*, and Jung's commentary on "The Secret of the Golden Flower," in *Alchemical Studies*, pars. 18*ff*.

[9] Examples from Grete Lüers, *Die Sprache der deutschen Mystik des Mittelalters*, pp. 285–86. Cf. for example, Mechtild von Magdeburg: "wellen wir es nit verstopfen mit eigenem willen, so vlüsset unser vesselin immer über von gotz gabe." ("If we do not try to stop it up with our own will, then our little vessel will always overflow with God's gifts.")

[10] Quoted in *Psychology and Alchemy*, par. 350.

[11] Cf. *Alchemical Studies*, par. 96.

[12] *Ibid.*, par. 97.

inner readiness for relating to the archetype of the Self.[13] In this connection it should be noted that to the nations of north-western Europe, Christianity was a product of what was to them the remote and more advanced Mediterranean culture, which had been grafted on to their own primitive and barbaric mentality. Because they possessed no intellectual instrument, no differentiated thinking with which to grasp its meaning, there was no alternative for them but to allow the new and foreign faith they adopted to sink down until, in the depths of the soul, it animated a latent archetype. In this way it was therefore more fundamentally and securely assimilated than it would have been by an understanding based merely on intellect or feeling.

Whether such a process of spiritual appropriation takes place on a large or a small scale, in the collective or in the individual, it is inevitably attended by a profusion of associations from the individual soul, for this assimilation consists precisely of such associations. These contributions are naturally not *eo ipso* orthodox. They do not fit into a conscious, universally valid and appropriate conception, but are just as they happen to be in the soul of the person or race concerned. Even should such unorthodox ideas be condemned as heretical by a church whose main concern must be to lay down a uniform creed, great importance attaches to them, none the less, just because they do serve the process of assimilation.[14]

[13] *Ibid.*, par. 115. Jung continues: "Dorn calls the vessel the *vas pellicanicum*, and says that with its help the quinta essentia can be extracted from the prima materia (*Theatrum chemicum*, I, p. 442). The anonymous author of the scholia to the "Tractatus aureus Hermetis" says: "This vessel is the true philosophical Pelican, and there is none other to be sought for in all the world" (*Theatrum chemicum*, IV, p. 698). It is the lapis itself and at the same time contains it; that is to say, the self is its own container. . . . The thought and language of alchemy lean heavily on mysticism: in the Epistle of Barnabas (Lake, *Apostolic Fathers*, I, p. 383), Christ's body is called the 'vessel of the spirit' (τὸ σκεῦος τοῦ πνεύματος). . . According to the teachings of Herakleon, the dying man should address the demiurgic powers thus: 'I am a vessel more precious than the feminine being who made you. Whereas your mother knew not her own roots, I know of myself, and I know whence I have come.'" *Ibid.*, pars. 115–16. Cf. also the further explanations of the symbolism of the vessel, *ibid.*, pars. 117*ff.*

[14] For this reason it would seem that one could unhesitatingly grant the

A new realization first becomes alive and effective when it succeeds in reaching beyond the limits of consciousness into the depths of the soul and there unites with a corresponding archetype. The feminine and maternal symbol of the vessel can also be understood in this sense as the place, similar to the mother's womb, where significant factors, previously invisible or only existing *in intellectu*, acquire life and form. There would appear to be a connection here with the idea that after its arrival in Britain, the Grail fell into "captivity" or disappeared into a "beyond" or into concealment. This situation might be looked upon as a kind of incubation.

As Jung has shown in *Psychology and Alchemy* and *Mysterium Coniunctionis*, medieval alchemy, like the Grail legend, also mirrors a similar process in the assimilation of Christianity, a process *which at the same time represents a reshaping and a further development of the Christian contents.*[15] For this reason, the vessel signifies not only the possibility of psychic assimilation, but is also *a matrix in which the archetype of the Self is transformed even further.* On account of this, its divine content, the alchemical vessel has the value of a mystery. Thus, an old text called "Practica Mariae" (Maria Prophetissa) says of the vessel that it is "the measure of your fire" and that the Stoics had hidden it because it was the *corpus toxicum* (toxic body) that transformed the Mercurius, the water of the philosophers.[16] As the arcane substance, however, it is not only the water but also the fire. So that the "Allegoriae sapientum" say: "Thus our stone, that is the flask of fire, is created from fire."[17] The poisonous and dangerous qualities and the fiery nature of the alchemical vessel are also characteristic of the Grail. The *Lancelot Grail* recounts how Mordrain, a companion of Joseph's who wanted to see the Grail unveiled and who approached closer than was allowed, was

right of existence to unorthodox conceptions, in the confidence that ideas which accord with the truth—as is the case with the Christian idea—cannot perish, even if their form perhaps undergoes a certain mutation.

15 Cf. the Introduction to *Psychology and Alchemy*.

16 Cf. *Alchemical Studies*, par. 113.

17 *Ibid.*, and further examples in *Psychology and Religion*, pars. 354*ff*.

deprived both of sight and of the use of his limbs so that thenceforth he, like the Fisher King, was quite helpless. On one occasion in the *Queste*, Lancelot comes to the Grail Castle where, attracted to a room by a bright glow, he enters and sees the holy vessel standing on a silver table. He also goes too close and a breath of hot wind blows in his face; he is convinced that his face is scorched. His hearing and sight disappear and he falls to the ground as if dead. He loses the power of speech and lies for twenty-four days and nights without speaking, unable to move.

In this motif we see that the Grail represents a genuine mystery. In most of the mystery cults of antiquity there were holy objects which were kept wrapped up in baskets (*cista*) and which might not be seen by the uninitiated.[18] Among primitive peoples, too, the fetish or the contents of the "war bundle" or "medicine bag" are similarly mysterious, and the unauthorized person who looks at them out of curiosity experiences similar consequences.[19] In this way the dangerous, overwhelming quality and the numinous essence of the archetypal content find expression.[20] This might explain to some extent why the book of the Grail, as well as its mystery, were shrouded by such an extraordinary taboo.

For instance we read in Wauchier's Continuation:

Les grans merveilles qu'il trova
Dont maintes fois s'espoënta
Ne doit nus conter et dire,
Cil qui les dist en a grant ire
Car c'est se croi du Graal.
S'en a grant anui et grant mal
Cil qui s'entremet del conter
Fors si come il doivent aler.

[18] Concerning this, cf. M. Dibelius, "Die Isisweihe des Apuleius und verwandte Initiationsriten," illus. 4, p. 16*ff.*

[19] Cf. Paul Radin, *The Trickster*, p. 117; and Hastings, *Encyclopaedia*, under "fetishism".

[20] Cf. Rudolf Otto, *The Idea of the Holy, passim.*

Of all the marvels which he found
And which so often he did fear,
May no one speak a word.
Whoever speaks of them will be in peril,
For 'tis the secret of the Grail,
And evil can befall the man
Who talks of it in any way
Except the way it should be told.[21]

And in another passage (the "Elucidation"):

C'est del Graal dont nus ne doit
Le secré dire ne conter.

About the Grail, of whose mystery
None may speak or tell.

In Robert de Boron, it is said of the book:

La sunt li grant secré escrit
Qu'en numme le Graal et dit.

There the great mystery is written
Which is called the Grail.[22]

The alchemistic equation of the vessel with its contents, the stone, also turns up, strangely enough, in the Grail story. In Wolfram von Eschenbach, the Grail is called a stone, of which it is said:

Ûf einem grüenen Achmardi
truoc sie den Wunsch von pardis,
bêde wurzeln unde rîs,
daz was ein dinc, daz heiz der Grâl,
erden wunsches überwal.[23]

[21] Roach, *The Continuations*, Vol. I, p. 355, verses 19933–40.
[22] Nitze, verse 929.
[23] Bartsch, Book V, verses 350*ff*.

Upon a deep green achmardi
she bore the perfection of Paradise,
both root and branch.
This was a thing called the Grail,
which surpasses all earthly perfection.[24]

And further on:

Sie lebent von eimen Steine
des geslähte ist vil reine.
Hât ir des niht erkennet,
der wirt iu hie genennet:
er heizet lapsit exillis.[25]

They [the Knights of the Grail] live from
a stone
of purest kind.
If you do not know it,
it shall here be named to you.
It is called *lapsit exillis.*[26]

This *lapsit exillis* (which W. Hertz renders as *lapis electrix*) has caused much speculation. Because of the reading, *lapsit ex coelis*, there was a wish to interpret the Grail as a meteorite,[27] for in antiquity, meteorites were considered to be λίθοι ἔμψυχοι—stones with a soul.[28]

[24] Hertz, p. 116. [25] Bartsch, Book IX, verses 1083 *ff.*

[26] Hertz, *op. cit.*, p. 242.

[27] P. Hagen, *Der Graal*, Ch. IV. Cf. also F. Ranke, *Zur Symbolik des Grals bei Wolfram von Eschenbach.*

[28] Owing to changes in the letters (often hard to decipher in the manuscripts) a *lapis betilis*, i.e. a "Baetylos." This, according to Roscher's *Lexikon der griechischen und römischen Mythologie*, is "a name stemming from Semitic origins, and taken over at a late date by the Greeks and Romans, for sacred stones that were assumed to possess divine life, λίθοι ἔμψυχοι stones with a soul, created by Uranos; these, set up in holy places, were venerated with anointings and garlands, or, in the hands of private persons, were used for divers superstitions, for magic, and for fortunetelling. They were meteoric stones fallen from the sky." The expression "stone with a soul" suggests the maxim quoted by Jung and attributed to Ostanes, one of the earliest of the alchemists, concerning the "stone that has a spirit," to be found on the bank of the Nile. *Psychology and Alchemy*, par. 405. The older literature is to be found in Helen Adolf, *Visio Pacis*, p. 200.

According to Wolfram–Kyot, the Grail was discovered by Flegetanis, a pagan natural scientist who read about it in the stars.[29] Many scholars believe that in Flegetanis they discern the well-known mystic Thabit ben Qorah, who lived in Bagdad from 826 to 901, who translated Greek alchemical writings and who also appears as Thebed in Latin alchemistic literature.[30] But according to P. Hagen the Arabic for Flegetanis is Felek-Thani, which is the name of the guardian of the second planetary sphere, that of Mercury.[31] According to Wolfram, Flegetanis' writing was found by the Provençal Kyot in Dolet (Toledo), and after lengthy researches, he also discovered a chronicle in Anschouwe (Anjou) which agreed with Flegetanis' story. As R. Palgen has noted, this *one* source which Wolfram mentions points unequivocally to Arabic or Sabean astrology and alchemy.[32] The alchemists' stone was also explicitly called the *lapis exilis*[33] in some verses ascribed to Arnold of Villanova and mentioned in the fifteenth-century "Rosarium philosophorum":

Hic lapis exilis extat precio quoque vilis
Spernitur a stultis, amatur plus ab edoctis.

This insignificant stone is indeed of trifling value;
It is despised by fools, the more cherished by the wise.[34]

[29] Cf. Ringbom, *Graaltempel und Paradies*, pp. 463–64, and the literature there cited.

[30] *Ibid.*, p. 469. Thabit is referred to as "Thebed" in the "Liber Platonis quartorum," in Book V of the *Theatrum chemicum*, Vol. V, p. 114. Cf. also Palgen, *Der Stein der Weisen.*

[31] Cf. Ponsoye, *L'Islam et le Graal*, p. 26, which would also point to Sabaean alchemistic conceptions. Cf. also Kolb, *Munsalvaesche*, p. 155. According to Moses Gaster, "The Legend of the Grail," p. 898, Flegetanis was a Jew.

[32] Among Lucifer's angels Wolfram reckons "Astiroth and Belcimòn, Bêlet and Radamant" (*Parzival*, 4, 63, 10/11). These, according to Iselin (*op. cit.*, pp. 40–41), are *the same divinities that were considered to be the founders of the town of Harran* (*Syrische Schatzhöle*, I, p. 37 = II, pp. 154*f*). Here again we find a connection with the world of Sabaean culture.

[33] Also in the medieval text, "Iter ad Paradisum der Alexandersage." Cf. Mergell, *Der Gral in Wolframs Parsifal*, p. 3.

[34] Cf. *Psychology and Alchemy*, par. 246, note 117.

As Arnold was probably born about 1220, Wolfram, who was writing before that date, cannot have borrowed the term from him, but astrological and alchemical ideas were certainly not unknown to him. Many scholars accordingly rectify *lapsit exillis* into *lapis elixir.*[35] Vincent of Beauvais[36] refers to the philosopher's stone of the alchemists under this appellation (about 1260) when quoting Avicenna's *De arte Alchemia.* The expression cannot actually be traced in the latter although it does contain a comparison between the *lapis* and the *elixir. Lapis elixir* is, however, a familiar alchemical term.

Extremely significant, and also pointing to the realm of alchemical ideas, is the additional belief, according to Wolfram, that the Grail stone was left behind on earth and guarded by those angels *who had remained neutral during the strife between God and Satan* and who are sometimes spoken of as *zwivelaere* (doubters)—

di newederhalp gestuonden
dô strîten beguonden
Lucifer und Trinitas
zwaz der selben engel was
die edelen und die werden
muosen ûf die erden
zuo dem selben steine.

those who took neither side
when Lucifer and the Trinity
fought—
those angels,
noble and worthy,
who were compelled to descend to earth
to this same stone.[37]

S. Singer[38] maintains that this is a widespread idea which stems from Catharistic circles. It is therefore those angels who

[35] Cf. Ringbom, *op. cit.*, and the further authorities there cited, as well as Mergel, *op cit.*, pp. 2–3 and 17.

[36] *Speculum naturale*, I, p. 476, quoted by Ringbom, *op. cit.*, p. 463.

[37] Verse 471, pp. 15*ff*.

[38] *Wolfram und der Gral*, p. 19.

were opposed to the rending apart of the divine inner opposites and who sought to maintain a state of balance and to hold fast to the original unity of the God-image who now watch over the Grail.[39] In alchemy, the *lapis* represents a similar light-dark unity of the divine opposites. The alchemical Mercurius, who is identical with the stone, is also considered to be *duplex*:[40] good with the virtuous and evil with sinners. He is a god-image in which the opposites appear to be united.[41] He is identified now with Christ, now with the Devil, he is masculine and feminine, he is a twin (*geminus*), he is at the same time both Adam and Eve, an old man and a boy.[42] He is a figure of the Anthropos and of the saviour which, engendered by the unconscious, compensates and completes the light figure of Christ, a *deus terrestris et absconditus*, and as such is an essential part of the Self (the God-image) which, as the Whole, represents a *complexio oppositorum*.[43] The figure of Baphomet, which the Templars were supposed to have worshipped, also appears to have represented such a comprehensive light and dark god-image. Baphomet was described as an androgynous being with two faces and a long silver-grey beard, or with a head of copper, that answered questions in an oracular style.[44] Some of these secret traditions lived on with the Knights Hospitalers in Rhodes, where they were rediscovered by the alchemist Bernard of Treviso and related to his own alchemical ideas. By such devious routes, the mystical concepts of certain Oriental sects influenced by Gnosticism seem to have infiltrated—partly in combination with alchemical ideas—into the European

[39] According to the Wartburgkrieg, on the other hand, the Grail was said to be a precious stone that fell out of Lucifer's crown when he was expelled from heaven. There the idea of the *lapsit ex coelis*, of its having fallen from heaven, is likewise expressed.

[40] Cf. "The Spirit Mercurius," in *Alchemical Studies*, especially pars. 267–69.

[41] *Archetypes and the Collective Unconscious*, pars. 553*ff*.

[42] *Ibid.*, also pars. 556*f*, 689.

[43] *Ibid.*, par. 555.

[44] Cf. C. A. Campbell, *Die Tempelritter*, pp. 328–29 and 347. Cf. also Evola, *Il Mistero del Graal*, pp. 136*ff*. Concerning Baphomet, see also Adolf, *Visio Pacis*, pp. 111*ff*.

world of spiritual thought.[45] Wolfram's authority, Guiot–Kyot, was supposed to have sojourned in Jerusalem and at the court of Frederick Barbarossa and to have had personal experience of the Templars,[46] who were considered to be the guardians of Solomon's Temple. Solomon had already become in those days an archetypally magnified figure of the Old Wise Man; he was united with the ghostly Queen of Sheba and he guarded vast hoards of riches.[47] His throne and ring are obvious symbols of the "treasure hard to attain," [48] meaning the Self, and he therefore naturally appears as a figure of authority in the literature of alchemy.

That Wolfram was not unacquainted with alchemical ideas may also be deduced from the description of the Grail as the stone[49] through whose power the pheonix is consumed by fire in order to arise rejuvenated from the ashes. This allegorical figure played an important role in alchemy.

The phoenix legend[50] makes no mention of a stone, but explains that the bird amassed inflammable resins in its nest. In another context, however, the *Lancelot Grail* speaks of the bird Serpilion which was burnt by Pirastite, a stone it had brought from the Vale of Hebron for the purpose of warming its young, which were then fed by it as the Grail also fed those whom it protected. This is a combining of the figures of the phoenix and the pelican. Serpilion probably means "serpent bird," [51] a notion related to the Persian *semenda* which appears to have

[45] Cf. W. F. Wilcke, *Geschichte des Tempelherrenmordens*; and Ponsoye, *L'Islam et le Graal*, Chs. V and VI.

[46] Cf. Kampers, *Das Lichtland der Seelen*, pp. 20–27 and 23–24.

[47] Cf. W. Staude, "Die äthiopische Legende von der Königin von Saba."

[48] Cf. Kampers, *op. cit.*, pp. 24*ff*.

[49] One must indeed assume that Wolfram obtained this divergent conception from his authority, whom Chrétien refers to as Kyot, unless it is regarded simply as a misunderstanding attributable to Wolfram's faulty knowledge of French. Although he admits to this himself, he has none the less inquired into the meaning of the central subject of his poem. Also, the exhaustive treatment of his conception indicates that it is not based on a mere error. It is therefore more probable that he did actually make use of another source.

[50] Herodotus, *Historiae*, Book II, Ch. 68.

[51] Cf. Iselin, *op. cit.*, p. 53, footnote 3.

been a combination of snake and bird, a symbol that well illustrates the instinctive dual nature of the unconscious.

The motif of the phoenix and the stone in Wolfram therefore links the image of the Grail with ideas of a decidedly alchemical nature.[52] The epithet *exilis* (poor, mean) hints at a well-known feature of the philosopher's stone, which is repeatedly described by the authors as worthless, as having been thrown out on to the dunghill or as trodden underfoot in the street. In antiquity the alchemist Zosimos[53] had already stated that the *lapis* was "despised and highly honoured, not given and given by God" (*ἄτιμον καὶ πολύτιμον, ἀδώρητον καὶ θεοδώρητον*).[54]

It has been further surmised that the conception of the Grail as a stone arose through some confusion over the figure of the stone table—of which we will speak later—or because the Grail had been imagined as a sort of portable altar on which the Host brought by the dove was laid.[55] This conception of the stone as an altar paten associates it once again with the stone used to close Christ's sepulchre. According to Eastern legends this was said to be the same stone struck by Moses in the desert to provide water for the Children of Israel[56] (Exodus 17:6; I Corinthians 10:4). The alchemists compared it to their *lapis*. Thus, the *Aurora consurgens* describes the *lapis* as a treasure house "founded upon a sure rock." This rock "cannot be split unless it be . . . smitten three times with the rod of Moses, that waters may flow forth in great abundance, that all the people both men and women drink thereof." [57]

Here again, Wolfram has mixed up ideas that were, in a

[52] Cf. Mergell, *Der Gral in Wolframs Parsifal*, pp. 32*ff.* Cf. also Werner Wolfs, "Der Vogel Phoenix und der Graal," pp. 73*ff*; and Kolb, *op. cit.*, pp. 126*ff.* These two authors, however, completely ignore the alchemical traditions.

[53] Marcelin Berthelot, *Collection des anciens alchimistes grecs*, III, II, I, Vol. I, p. 114, and III, VI, 6, Vol. I, p. 122.

[54] As an example cf. also the *Turba philosophorum*, pp. 122 and 142.

[55] Kampers, *op. cit.*, and T. Sterzenbach, *Ursprung und Entwicklung der Sage von Heiligen Graal.*

[56] Iselin, *Der morgenländische Ursprung der Graalslegende*, where the part played by the stone in Oriental legend is thoroughly considered (especially pp. 7*ff*, 61*ff* and 73*ff*).

[57] *Aurora Consurgens*, p. 323.

certain sense, related. The qualities mentioned, especially the bestowal of youth and longevity, are attributed to the Grail in almost all the versions. They are the same properties as those ascribed to the *lapis philosophorum*. Another line of thought leads back to the Ark of the Covenant, which Solomon had placed in his Temple at Jerusalem. It stood upon a rock (*lapis*) and contained four things: Aaron's rod, Moses' Tables of the Law, golden candelabra and the urn holding the manna from heaven. The sacred urn had disappeared from the earth (it was thought that it might have been hidden in a cave under the paving-stones) and was surrounded by much mystical speculation.[58]

Again, the four objects might be taken to refer to the four functions of consciousness. If we have related the sword and lance to the psychological functions of thinking and intuition, then the Grail, in so far as it is marked by a power of selection and in so far as its effects (a joyous heart, for instance) are bestowed only upon the worthy, can be compared with the function of feeling. This function also discriminates, for it is also concerned with consenting or refusing.[59] This, however, is only one aspect of the Grail, which has so many meanings that it cannot simply be understood as the feeling function only. It is "a stone of purest kind"[60] and requires purity from its guardians. It may only be carried by a pure virgin without guile, in whose hands it does not weigh heavily, whereas a base person would be unable to lift it.[61] Similarly, the Arabic alchemist Alphidius says of the stone that its mother was virginal, its father had not known her. The *Aurora consurgens* plainly calls it "the stone of chastity," [62] so here too there are close contacts with alchemy.

[58] Cf. *Psychological Types*, pp. 470 and 554–56.

[59] Wolfram, Book IX, verse 1162.

[60] *Ibid.*, verse 1336.

[61] Cf. "Liber *Alphidii*," in the Codex Ashmole; and *Aurora Consurgens*, pp. 332–33.

[62] Cf. Wolfram, verses 492, 25*ff*:

> eines tages der künec al eine reit
> . . . ûs durch aventiure
> durch freude an minnen stiure
> des twanc in der minnen ger.

If all its various aspects are summarized, whether as a wonderful stone, as a vessel or as a relic, the Grail is found to possess the following characteristics. It dispenses material food according to taste and imparts spiritual solace. It preserves youth and generally maintains life. In one instance it heals knights wounded in battle. It radiates light and a sweet fragrance, it rejoices the heart, and whoever sees it can commit no sin that day. It discriminates between good and evil. To the unbaptized it remains invisible. It makes known the will of God by means of writing which appears upon it. Only he who is destined by heaven and whose name is written thereon can find the Grail. Nor does it allow its defender to have any loves other than the one the Grail prescribes for him. This latter characteristic was the misfortune of Anfortas, who chose as his friend the beautiful Orgeluse.[63] In her service he went in quest of fame as a knight,[64] and in battle received from the poisoned spear of a heathen adversary the wound that refused to heal. *Through this event the Grail acquires a psychological significance which points in the direction of Eros.* It is as though the vessel were expressing an opinion on the man's choice in love; in other words, it guides his relations to the anima. In the medieval *Minnedienst* there was, as Jung has shown,[65] a tendency towards an individual realization of the anima on the one hand, and in the direction of a personal relation to the woman on the other. Because of the increase in the cult of the Virgin, however, both tendencies were cut short. As a result the anima was no longer taken into account, save as an archetypal symbol. As the fate of Anfortas shows, the moment of individual choice is fraught with great danger. The Grail nevertheless appears to have acted as a guiding symbol in the midst of the entanglements engendered by the anima, in that, as an image of the absolute totality of the individual, it established the process of the latter's development in the service of a higher goal.[66]

The Grail's many wonderful attributes, which qualify it as a

[63] Book IX, verse 1363. [64] Book IX, verse 1380.
[65] *Psychological Types*, p. 300.
[66] *Two Essays*, pars. 391*ff* and 399.

"treasure hard to attain," and its analogy to the alchemical stone, which in Wolfram actually goes as far as identification, justify its being taken *as a symbol of the Self*. Inasmuch as it is in many versions a relic of Christ's blood, it is clear that this symbol of the Self has a connection with the Christ-image. In this respect the funerary aspect and the blood indicate particularly that the Grail is concerned with that stage of psychic development which, *after his earthly death*, carries on Christ's effectiveness *in this world* and preserves his "soul substance" throughout the ages. As described in the Gospels, the figure of Jesus is indistinct and inconsistent and, as explained in detail by Jung in *Aion*, it has only acquired its significance because all the contemporary symbolic images of the Self, such as the fish, the cross, the Son of Man and others, have crystallized around it from out of the depths of the collective unconscious. For this reason the figure of Jesus has become identical with the concept of the Self and has thus acquired that substantiality and reality which constitute its central significance for our Christian culture. All the contemporary projections of the archetype of the incarnate God, the Self, which were constellated in the soul of man in those days have, as it were, attached themselves to it. This tremendous significance would later have fallen away from the figure of Jesus if individual man—beginning with the Apostle Paul—had not again and again had inner psychic experiences which they apprehended as being identical with Christ. That psychic power which continually sustains the life of the Christ-symbol can, accordingly, be understood psychologically as the innate pattern of individuation which time and again and in all ages can engender a Christ-like image of the Self in every human being and in this way assure its survival in the world of men.

From this point of view, the Grail can also be taken as an image of the *transcendent function*. By this term Jung understands the psychic synthesis of consciousness and the unconscious, through which it becomes possible for the psychic totality, the Self, to come into consciousness.[67] This function is therefore also

[67] *Psychological Types*, and "The Transcendent Function," in *The Structure and Dynamics of the Psyche*, pp. 67*ff* (including pars. 131–93).

responsible for the continual maturation and transformation of the God-image, the Self, and for this reason can very well appear symbolically as the vessel in which the "soul substance" of the god is preserved.

Although, as we have seen, the vessel and its contents are really identical, there is yet a subtle difference in the choice of images. As Jung has shown,[68] the stone in alchemy signifies the inner spiritual man. Its divine attributes distinguish it as a particle of God concealed in nature, an analogy to the God who, in Christ, came down to earth in a human body, subject to suffering. On the other hand, the "cheapness" of the stone (*lapis exilis*, *vilis*) alludes to the fact that every human being is its potential bearer, even its begetter. In this way the alchemical symbol of the *lapis* compensates for the overly exalted and remote spirituality of the ecclesiastical image of Christ, which is too far removed from the natural earthly man.

It could be objected that the wafer of the Host before its consecration also consists of lifeless matter and that consecrated it becomes the Body of Christ. The passionate interest of medieval thinkers in the problem of transubstantiation indicates how deeply significant was this question of the incorporation of the material element into the area of speculation about God. But the mystery of the Eucharist clearly did not suffice for an answer. Perhaps the amount of the material substance there involved was too small, for which reason the alchemists, going their own way, searched more deeply into this problem of the god inhering in lifeless matter. Some alchemists (such as Petrus Bonus, Melchior Cibinensis and the author of the *Aurora consurgens*) did, however, perceive the analogy of the transubstantiation in the Mass with the alchemical opus.[69] "In the image of . . . the lapis the 'flesh' glorified itself in its own way;" says Jung, "it would not transform itself into spirit but, on the contrary, 'fixed' the spirit in the stone. . . . The Lapis may therefore be understood as a symbol of the inner Christ, of God in

[68] *Alchemical Studies*, pars. 394*ff*. Cf. also *Psychology and Alchemy*, pars. 406*ff* and 480*ff*.

[69] Cf. *Psychology and Alchemy*, pars. 480*ff*.

man."[70] Looked at from this point of view, the stone represents a *further development of the Christ symbol, reaching downwards into matter*. "Without knowing it," says Jung, "the alchemist carries the idea of the *intimatio* (*Christi*) a stage further and reaches the conclusion . . . that complete assimilation to the Redeemer would enable him, the assimilated, to continue the work of redemption in the depths of his own psyche."[71] By this means he can even free the divine spirit imprisoned in matter. He achieves this, not as an ego but acting in the capacity of the Self;[72] hence the symbol of the *lapis* "came not from the conscious mind of the individual man, but *from those border regions of the psyche that open out into the mystery of cosmic matter*." [73]

The *lapis* of the alchemists represents a symbol of the Self which is certainly analogous to Christ, but its image, by returning to the depths of matter and the physical, is enriched beyond that of Christ by a darker side that complements it. Consequently, while the essential material substance of that content is emphasized in the symbol of the stone, the aspect of the vessel stresses another facet of the same symbol, i.e. the importance which attaches to the psychic *comprehension* of the Self. A vessel is also a material thing, but it serves the purpose of containing other physical substances. This specific function of the symbol therefore indicates that the image of the Self, Christ, is practically nonexistent *unless it is realized in the human soul*.

We are concerned here with part of a long continuing process of historical development in the course of which the God-image, first experienced as completely transcending consciousness, gradually leaves its place of projection on to a "metaphysical" reality and penetrates more and more into the human realm. To begin with, this approach appears mirrored in the mythologems of the god-man (Gilgamesh, Tammuz, Osiris) in the various versions of the myth under consideration; the next step consists in the doctrine of the incarnation of God in one

[70] *Alchemical Studies*, par. 127.
[71] *Psychology and Alchemy*, par. 452. [72] *Ibid.*
[73] *Alchemical Studies*, par. 127.

particular, historically real person, Jesus, whereby God descended fully into the here and now of human reality. Because of the importance of this event the person of Christ increasingly became the chief object of theological speculation in the Reformed branches of Christianity. However, this descent of God into the human realm would have remained incomplete—especially as the historical figure of Christ already belonged to a very distant past—if a further step had not been constellated: *the realization of the actual existence of the god-man in the soul of every single human being.* The medieval mystics were the first to give expression to this realization with the intensity of individual experience, and in addition the legend of the Grail appears as a parallel rich in imagery. *In this sense the vessel or the stone signifies the whole psychic man* (not his ego) *as a realization of divinity reaching right down into matter.* In so far as the person becomes increasingly conscious, qualities and knowledge which had previously been unconscious and therefore attributed solely to God come more and more within his sphere of influence. This has now gone so far that, thanks to his understanding of matter, man could at this moment release world-annihilating explosions compared with which the acts of destruction committed by the gods of mythology seem puny indeed. Where this increasing consciousness of the God-image in man may yet lead is beyond speculation. In any event it lays upon the individual a moral responsibility previously barely dreamed of, as well as a great obligation to strive for higher consciousness, which means taking his own individuation seriously.

In this sense Perceval faces us as a symbol of modern man before whom this colossal task is laid. The stone or vessel indicates the goal, that is, the need to realize the total man. That the aspect of the stone is more prominent in alchemy while the vessel appears more often in the medieval poets is perhaps due to the fact that as "natural scientists" the alchemists were seeking more the content, the divine spirit in the material, whereas the emotional grasping and shaping of the same problem lay closer to the hearts of the poets, for which the feminine symbol of the vessel appropriately stands. A further connection lies in the fact that seeing the Grail imposed a *question* on the beholder but did not impart direct knowledge. It symbolizes more an emotional readiness to receive, which is still in the realm of the anima and has not yet been more clearly formulated. The nature of the Grail question will be investigated later, but first the remaining symbols carried in the procession should be discussed.

Wounding the Heart of Jesus

The Heart of Jesus, a fifteenth-century woodcut

CHAPTER IX

The Table, the Carving Platter and the Two Knives

THE TABLE, one of the remarkable objects in the Grail Castle, is, as a symbol, related to the Grail in many respects. A feminine and maternal meaning attaches to it, especially in this context where it is used for a *meal*. The Latin *mensa* (table, and also food) comes from *metior* (to measure, to mete out, allot, apportion). *Mensis* (month—in connection with which the moon was thought to be the measure of time) comes from the same root, *me* (to measure). The moon is known as a feminine symbol, the mother (*mētēr*), as she who measures out the food. The idea of measuring brings us back to the vessel once more, in so far as this is also a measure. In the Grail stories the table is described as being of great value. In Wolfram's Grail procession, where it is carried immediately after the lance, the table is of translucent garnet hyacinth (a reddish stone)[1] with two ivory supports. In Chrétien these supports are of ebony which neither rots nor burns and is therefore imperishable, and the table top is of ivory. Thus, the table is important, not only because the meal served by the Grail is eaten at it or because, as in Wolfram, the Grail is placed upon it; a further meaning of real importance attaches to it in the Grail stories. These stories belong for good reason to the *Histoires de la Table ronde*. Arthur's Round Table denotes a circle of chosen knights, principally his court, and to some

[1] The garnet and the hyacinth (jacinth) are frequently confused or identified, and described as *rufus vel coeruleus*, red or blue. For example, cf. F. Zarncke, *Der Graaltempel*, p. 483. It is really a corundum (cf. Kampers, *op. cit.*, p. 120) that is found in three colours—red, yellow and blue.

extent represents an archaic pre-form of those archetypal images that Perceval beheld in the Grail Castle. We have seen, for instance, that, at Perceval's first meeting with Arthur, the King was "incapable of action;" like the Grail King, he too was crippled (though only temporarily). At that meeting a vessel, the golden cup that had been stolen, also played an important part.

King Arthur's Round Table had been inaugurated by his father, Uther Pendragon, at the bidding of Merlin, his counsellor skilled in magic. It was the last of three important tables mentioned in the *Queste del Saint Graal*:

> *Vos savez bien que puis l'avenement Jhesucrist a eu trois principaus tables ou monde. La premiere fu la Table Jhesucrist ou li apostre mengierent plusor foiz. Cele fu la table qui sostenait les cors et les ames de la viande dou ciel. . . . Et icele table establi li Aigniax sans tache qui fu sacrefiez por nostre redemption.*
>
> *Apres cele table fu une autre table en semblance et en remembrance de lui. Ce fu la Table dou Saint Graal, dont si grant miracle furent jadis veu en cest pays au tens Joseph d'Arimacie, au comencement que crestientez fu aportee en ceste terre.*[2]

> You know that since the advent of Jesus Christ there have been three most important tables in the world. The first was the Table of Jesus Christ, at which the Apostles ate on several occasions. This was the table that sustained bodies and souls with food from heaven. . . . And the Lamb without blemish that was sacrificed for our redemption established this table.
>
> After this table there was another *in the likeness and in remembrance of it*. This was the table of the Holy Grail, of which great miracles were once seen in that country, in the time of Joseph of Arimathea, when Christianity was first brought to this earth.

The Grail, by virtue of whose grace Joseph and his multitude of four thousand were fed, was placed upon this table; Joseph,

[2] Pauphilet, *La Queste du Saint Graal*, pp. 74–75.

in obedience to a divine command, had established it on the pattern of the table of the Last Supper.

In Robert de Boron, Joseph's brother-in-law Brons catches a fish which is put on the table beside the Grail. This is why the guardian of the Grail is known as the Fisher King. This second table, which reminds us of the first, is, in accordance with the divine command, expressly described as *square*. The third table, Arthur's, on the other hand, is *round*. Concerning it, the *Queste* says:

> *Apres cele table fu la Table Reonde par le conseil Merlin, qui ne fu pas establie sans grant senefiance. Car en ce qu'elle est apelee Table Reonde est entendu la reondece del monde et la circonstance des planetes et des elemenz el firmament; et es circonstances dou firmament voit len les estoiles et mainte autre chose; dont len peut dire que en la Table Reonde est li mondes senefiez a droit.*[3]

> After this table the Round Table was set up, on the advice of Merlin; nor was it established without great symbolic significance. For what is meant by being called the Round Table is the roundness of the world and the condition of the planets and of the elements in the firmament; and the conditions of the firmament are seen in the stars and in countless other things; so that one could say that in the Round Table the whole universe is symbolized.

This reminds us of other tables, partly historical, partly legendary. Charlemagne, who with his twelve peers recalls Christ and his Apostles, as well as being a prototype of Arthur and his Round Table, was said to possess a precious table[4] on which the universe was depicted in three circles. The first circle showed the earth and its atmosphere, the second the sun, moon and planets, and the third the fixed stars; a table therefore that depicted the cosmos.

Perhaps, as B. F. Kampers suggests in his aforementioned

[3] *Ibid.*, p. 76.

[4] Cf. Eginhard, *Vie de Charlemagne*, p. 18; and Kampers, *Das Lichtland der Seelen*, p. 29.

article, Charlemagne's table was copied from Solomon's famous table which, according to legend, was made, like the Genoese *sacro-catino*, from a gigantic emerald, was three hundred and sixty-five feet long and most richly set with pearls and precious stones, or else it was made entirely of gold. (This may be compared with Chrétien's description of the Grail: "*De fin or esmeré estoit, pierres precieuses avoit el graal de maintes menieres.*"—"The Grail was of fine gold, set with precious stones of countless variety.") It was part of the legendary treasure of Solomon which, after the fall of Jerusalem, was supposed to have been taken to Rome and later to have fallen for the most part into the hands of the Gothic kings. According to contemporary Frankish accounts this treasure included an *orbiculus* or Missorium, i.e. a portable altar of solid gold, encrusted with gems.[5] When the Saracens conquered the kingdom of the Western Goths, their commander Tarik was supposed to have asked about "Solomon's table" immediately upon his entry into Toledo and to have received the answer that it was being guarded in a stronghold belonging to the nephew of the last king of the Goths. There is a striking similarity between "Solomon's table" and the Grail guarded in the castle by the king or his nephew. The coveted table was then found in the Gibel Suleman, a mountain or hill in the town of Medinet Almaida, or Civitas Montevicina, called the "Town of the Table." Arabic fairy-tales and Spanish romances still preserve the memory of this treasure hoard of Solomon, which was subsequently kept in Spain and known there as the Gothic treasure.[6] The aforementioned letter of Prester John,[7] which was very celebrated in those days and was known to Wolfram von Eschenbach, gives an account of a similar table, perhaps the same one, made from an emerald and supported by two amethyst uprights. Here again it is an emerald. The green colour seems to be significant, since in Wolfram the Grail is also

[5] Kampers, *op. cit.*, pp. 26*ff.*

[6] It is very possible, as Kampers surmises, that this tradition contributed towards the formation of the Grail legend. It could also elucidate the otherwise unexplained localization of the Grail Castle in Spain.

[7] Zarncke, *Der Priester Johannes.*

carried in on a green achmardi. As the colour of vegetation and, in a wider sense, of life, green is obviously in harmony with the nature of the Grail. The land began to show green again when, in the Grail Castle, Gauvain asked the question about the lance. In ecclesiastical symbolism green is a colour of the Holy Ghost[8] or of the *anima mundi*,[9] and in the language of the mystics it is the universal colour of divinity.[10]

In alchemy the emerald also plays an important part, in connection with the famous *Tabula smaragdina* on which the essence of the alchemical work was inscribed in thirteen sentences from Hermes Trismegistus.[11] This text, according to the most varied stories of its discovery, was found in the tomb of an Egyptian king, or on a stele, and probably goes back further than Gābir to still older, possibly even Greek, sources.[12] The emerald was considered to be the stone of Hermes,[13] and in a text by Apollonios, *On Primal Causes*, he says of it:

> I say that the emerald is a jâqūt [that is, a corundum] because at the start of its formation it is coagulated as a jâqūt in all its parts. Its colour is red by nature. Because of the intensity of condensation in the redness, blackness arises out of it, so that it becomes sky-coloured. But on account of its hardness and coarseness the celestial hue withdraws to the interior and that part of the red which has remained pure appears outwardly on the surface area and becomes yellow. Therefore it becomes yellow on the outside and blue on the inside. Now the heat boils it violently and mixes the two colours, its outer colour with its inner colour, and green is produced by them both. Thus it acquires a green colour and is called emerald, but its origin is the jâqūt. Because the jâqūt is one of the stones related to gold and is the root of all (precious) stones, as gold is the chief (the noblest) of the smeltable

[8] Cf. *Psychology and Religion*, par. 151.
[9] Cf. Ponsoye, *L'Islam et le Graal*, p. 74.
[10] Cf. Grete Lüers, *Die Sprache der deutschen Mystik des Mittelalters*, p. 187.
[11] Cf. Ruska, *Tabula smaragdina*.
[12] *Ibid.*, p. 121.
[13] *Ibid.*, p. 116.

> bodies. The fire does not affect the jâqūt, neither does the iron file it.[14]

This description contains the colour changes of the classical alchemical works (*nigredo*, *rubedo*, *citrinitas*, *viriditas*) and closely relates the emerald to the incorruptible gold. To precious stones it is what gold is to metals, an everlasting, incorruptible substance, the goal of the *opus*. In this context the green colour actually achieves the meaning of life itself. In the alchemical texts the *benedicta viriditas* (the blessed green) also serves as a sign of the beginning of the reanimation of the material.[15]

Therefore, the table might perhaps, even if only indirectly, be related to the sensation function,[16] first, because it bears material food, and second, because as the cosmic table it represents a sensory awareness of universal reality.

In so far as the table is made of stone, it suggests the stone of the Grail, and inasmuch as it serves a meal, either an ordinary or a ritual one, it is, like the Grail, life-sustaining. It serves as a "supporting base" to the Grail itself and for that reason has a slightly different nuance of meaning. In the *Philosophia reformata*, an alchemical work by J. D. Mylius (1622), four goddesses are shown sitting at a round table.[17] As Jung explains, they represent the four seasons and the four elements, which in a literal sense appear to be "combined" around the table. The table, therefore, is more associated than is the vessel with *the human endeavour towards a synthesis of the totality*, which then expresses itself in the vessel, the Grail.

L. E. Iselin has shown that the motif of a magic stone plays an important part in Eastern tradition as the foundation stone of the world and as the cornerstone (a symbol of Christ) which was established in Zion (Isaiah 28:16) and "which the builders refused" (Psalm 118:22).[18] The holy Name of God was engraved on it and it was said to have been on view in front of the

[14] Quoted *ibid.*, pp. 154–55.
[15] Cf. *Alchemical Studies*, par. 102.
[16] Because, in general, green symbolizes the sensation function.
[17] P. 117. Cf. *Mysterium Coniunctionis*, par. 5.
[18] *Der morgenländische Ursprung der Graalslegende*, p. 63.

Ark of the Covenant in the Temple at Jerusalem.[19] It accompanied the Children of Israel through the wilderness, and Joshua the son of Nun was said to have laid that particular stone on Christ's grave.[20] It thus also became the altar stone "which gives life to all men," [21] since Christ's body as the Host lies upon it. The transition from altar stone to altar table was no great step, especially since in the East there circulated a legend dating from the eleventh century about a red stone that angels had brought from Sinai to Jerusalem, where it became the altar table of the Last Supper. Another story may be found in the fifth sura of the Koran (verses 112–15). Here the apostles ask Jesus whether God can send them a table from Heaven. Whereupon Jesus prays: "Lord, our God, send us a table from Heaven, that it may be a feast day for us, and it shall be a sign from Thee, to the first and the last of us. Feed us, for Thou art the best provider." Jesus' prayer is heard. Nevertheless, God threatens that those who thereafter remain unbelieving will be severely punished. As the main course a *fish* appears on the table. Subsequently, on account of man's sins, this table is taken from him again. This Islamic tradition obviously includes elements reminiscent both of the Grail in its aspect as stone and of the part played by the table in the story. This table is a wonder-working object that unites believers and brings divine wrath down on the heads of unbelievers—a symbol of the Self in which the synthesis of the many and the element of judgment are contained.

The "sun table" (ἡλιακὴ τράπεζα) has played an important role as far back as the Orphic mysteries of antiquity. Proclus[22] recounts that Orpheus was acquainted with Dionysus' mixing vessel (κρατήρ) and had seated many other people at the sun table. Vessel and table appear in a remarkable manner to be symbolically united and to allude to the initiation into the mysteries of Dionysus. We are reminded, furthermore, of the

[19] *Ibid.*, p. 56.

[20] *Ibid.*, p. 39, according to the *Syrische Schatzhöhle.*

[21] *Ibid.*, p. 61.

[22] *Commentaries on the Timaeus of Plato,* p. 378; cf. *Mysterium Coniunctionis,* footnote 23 to par. 5.

curious passage in which Hippolytus, one of the Church Fathers, recounts the part played among the Naassenes by the cup of Anacreon. With the help of the four elements, God created the world of forms, and this world is the cup to which the previously quoted passage concerning the cup of Anacreon refers. The cup is therefore connected with the *realization of the divine in the four elements.*[23] The table, for its part, bears the cup, and round it sit those who desire to partake of the mystery of the cup. The table's function in providing the supporting base for the essential symbol of the Self equates it with the ancient Egyptian myth in which the square floor of heaven, made of a sheet of iron, is supported at the four points of the compass by the four columns of Shu, god of the air, so that it is shaped like a table. The four supporting pillars are identical with the four sons of Horus, who assist their grandfather Osiris in ascending to heaven where he becomes the one universal god.[24] As Jung says, the opposing elements must come together in a common effort to help the *one* achieve totality. This motif resembles Ezekiel's vision of the heavens (Ezekiel 1:22): "And the likeness of the firmament upon the heads of the living creature was as the colour of the terrible crystal, stretched forth over their heads above." Also verse 26: "And above the firmament that was over their heads was the likeness of a throne, as the appearance of a sapphire stone: and upon the likeness of the throne was the likeness as the appearance of a man above upon it."[25]

Here the four-legged sheet of metal bears the figure of the "Son of Man," and we meet the same image again in the Gnostic *Codex Brucianus*, where the Monogenes, the only begotten son, is also described as standing on a table.[26] This table and the sheet of metal with four wheels of Ezekiel's vision form the vehicle for, or the basis of, *the empirical Self.*[27] Its

[23] For a close comparison see *Psychology and Alchemy*, pars. 527*ff.*

[24] For close comparison see *Aion*, par. 188; and *Alchemical Studies*, pars. 360–62.

[25] Cf. *Aion*, pars. 188–91.

[26] Cf. Charlotte Baynes, *A Coptic Gnostic Treatise*, pp. 70–73.

[27] Cf. *Mysterium*, par. 273.

quaternary structure resembles the *foundation of the god-image.* It is as if the Self required the consciousness of the individual, consisting of the four functions, as the basis for its realization, since the quaternity, in contradistinction to the circle, symbolizes *reflected wholeness.*[28] Compared with the vessel, the table is for that very reason more connected with the human effort to achieve consciousness. By its means all the dissociated aspects of the personality will be made conscious and brought into unity. A symbol of the incarnate deity, the "Son of God" or, in the Grail story, the wondrous vessel which constitutes a feminine analogy to the Son of Man, then appears on the table for the first time. The awarding of equal value to both aspects well reflects the psychological perception that "God cannot be experienced at all unless this futile and ridiculous ego offers a modest vessel in which to catch the effluence of the Most High."[29]

It only remains to mention the plate which figures in Chrétien and the two silver knives referred to by Wolfram.

Little information can be offered concerning the part played by the silver plate that was carried in the Grail procession. Advocates of the liturgical theory see it as the paten or the object known in the Greek liturgy of St. Chrysostom as the discus that is carried with the other objects.[30] In the Welsh *Peredur* the Grail is replaced by a dish (*discyl*—clearly related to "discus") on which is carried the severed head of the Lord of the Castle's kinsman, who has to be avenged. It has also been suggested that the word *tailleor* should be understood as "knife," from *tailler* (to cut). In Wolfram, there are two silver knives which serve to scrape the poison from the wound, while in the legend of the cloister of Fécamp, famous on account of its *Saint Sang*, knives with which Nicodemus was supposed to have scraped the blood from Christ's wounds are also mentioned. The more general opinion, however, is that *tailleor* seems more likely

[28] *Ibid.*, par. 261.

[29] *Ibid.*, par. 284.

[30] Cf. Hilka, *Der Percevalroman*, p. 683. According to Lot-Borodine, "Le conte . . .," the *gracl* is the ciborium, and *tailleor* is a vessel to catch the blood. Cf. also Holmes and Klenke, *op. cit.*, p. 189.

to mean "plate." Moreover, in Chrétien another, secular *tailleor d'argent* (silver plate), on which the hind is carved, appears immediately after the first.

It might also be supposed that the plate was used to serve the Host to the King. The fact that the plate is of silver permits association with the alchemical *lapis* when in the state of the *albedo*, because the stone is then white or silver like the moon. The plate, moreover, is a "round" object—a symbol of the Self, like the *lapis*. However, while the table represents a more collective aspect of the process of bringing the Self into consciousness—it brings many persons *together* for a communal meal—the plate is an illustration of *a more individual application* of that same transcendent function, since it is from a plate that the single person eats his share of wholeness.

Wolfram himself gives the following explanation of the knives. The sick king suffered severely at the changes of the moon, when he was seized by a chill and his flesh became colder than ice. The spear was then laid on the wound so that the hot poison ran down into it and the cold was drawn out of the body. It then stuck to the spear like ice, and it was impossible to remove it until Trebuchet, the wise smith, forged two silver knives with which it could be scraped away. Apart from this reference, the knives appear nowhere else in *Parzival*. An effort has been made to explain them as a misunderstanding on Wolfram's part, in that he took the word *tailleor* (plate) as *tailler* (to carve) and therefore wrote of silver knives instead of the plate.

The knives, however, are to be found in another work that may have played a specific, even if unrecognized, role in the development of the Grail legend. This was the legend of the Holy Blood of Fécamp[31] which, like the story of Joseph of Arimathea, is based on the Gospel of Nicodemus. This tradition relates that at the consecration of the first monastery church at Fécamp a beautiful white-haired man entered and placed upon the altar a knife, on which it was written that the church should be consecrated to the Holy Trinity. This knife is probably

[31] Cf. Langfors, *Histoire de l'Abbaye de Fécamp.*

meant to be the same that Nicodemus used to scrape away the blood. When the blood was discovered, a small cylinder containing a piece of iron "like a part of a lance" was also found. This throws light on the peculiar circumstance that in *Parzival* the two silver knives which serve to scrape the poison from the sick Anfortas' wound when his condition is especially severe are carried in the Grail procession.

Finally, the knives are also connected with the small lance or lance-like knife used in the above-mentioned Liturgy of St. Chrysostom. In the preparation for Communion, which is meant to symbolize the slaying of the Lamb, a square piece of bread is cut out of the consecrated loaf and marked with the form of a cross. The four loosely connected pieces produced in this way symbolize the Lamb of God that is to be slain.[32]

In the various versions, these knives appear to have the unchanging function of carrying on or completing the work of the lance. Either they clean the lance or they clean Christ's body of the blood that flowed from the wound inflicted by Longinus' lance. In the Fécamp version the knife even seems to have been made from the iron of the lance. In itself, the knife, like the sword, represents a psychic function, i.e. discriminating thought and judgment. The doubling of the knife in Wolfram indicates, however, that this function—thinking—is as yet only nascent[33] and even partly identical with the enlightening impulse (the lance) on its way up from the unconscious, or else that it is only now separating out from it. The knives, in so far as they take the place of the "broken sword" of conscious traditional thinking, certainly represent a new type of thinking which, taken from the unconscious itself, is for that reason more adequate to deal with its contents than merely conscious reflection would be. This new mental attitude would seem to be the precursor of the alchemistic turn of mind and of the psychological way of thinking which stemmed from it. It was destined

[32] Iselin, *Der morgenländische Ursprung*, p. 111. Cf. *Psychology and Religion*, pars. 331*f*.

[33] Concerning the doubling of a motif with reference to the *status nascendi*, cf. Jung, *Kindertraumseminar*, p. 72; and S. Hurwitz, *Die Gestalt des sterbenden Messias*, p. 211.

to eliminate the Grail King's poisonous blood substance and, in the most literal sense, the "dried-on" blood, i.e. the no longer effective psychic essence of the Christ symbol. But because the Grail stories were written by poets, this new form of understanding was considered from the purely symbolic angle and was apprehended visually as it emerged from the unconscious. The alchemists, on the other hand did exert themselves to extract from matter, i.e. from the unconscious itself, a *sensus naturae,* or "light of nature," and a way of thinking, the symbolic or essentially psychological thinking that is contained within it. For this reason, many of their texts recommend working on the head or skull or brain of a human being so as to extract the "thinking" from it.[34] The thinking thus taken from the unconscious is clearly symbolized here by the two knives and is intended to protect the lance or *imago Christi* from the desiccated residue—that is, behind the *Imago Christi* stands the Self, and what the Self attains is cultivated by a thinking achieved through self-knowledge and is thereby protected from the sterilizing effect of the intellect.

We have now enumerated the most important objects observed by Perceval in the Grail Castle. Their psychological meaning seems, on the whole, to point to the individuation process as being the aim and object of the way of development decreed for him. The experience in the Grail Castle, which can be taken as a dream or vision through which the hero is given the direction of his life's task, forms the first stage in his achievement of consciousness. This stage consists in a union of this world with that world beyond consciousness, i.e. a contact between consciousness and the unconscious, and in the integration of the totality symbolized by the quaternity of objects. On the other hand, in a more extended sense Perceval himself represents a type of analogue to Christ, which may be compared to the *homo altus* or *homo quadratus* of the alchemists, as someone in whom the progressive workings of the Holy Ghost seek to become manifest.

[34] Cf. *Liber Platonis quartorum,* in the *Theatrum chemicum,* Vol. V, p. 186; and *Mysterium,* par. 730.

CHAPTER X

The Continuation of Perceval's Quest

LET US RETURN once more to our story. Perceval, departing from the Grail Castle without having learned anything concerning what he saw there, continues on his way. He notices fresh hoofprints on a path leading into the forest. Following them he arrives at an oak tree beneath which a weeping maiden sits lamenting over a warrior whose head has been cut off and whose body she is holding in her lap. When Perceval greets the girl, she tells him that her friend was killed that very morning by a knight. She asks Perceval where he spent the previous night, since there is no house for miles around; when he tells her, she exclaims, "So you were with the Fisher King?" Perceval replies that he has no idea whether his host is a *King* or not, although he had indeed seen him fishing. He then learns from her that the Lord of the Castle is a King who has been wounded in battle by a javelin through both hips so that he can neither walk nor stand. As he is in no condition to ride or hunt, he sometimes has himself taken out in a boat for a short time in order to fish, for which reason he is known as the *roi pêcheur*. He has had a house worthy of a rich King built for him in the forest where his men and falcons hunt; and there he likes to live.

When Perceval tells her of his reception at the Castle, the damsel asks, "Did you see the Grail? Who carried it? From whence did it come? Where did it go?" When she hears that he did not ask any of these questions she exclaims: "God help me, this is serious! What is your name, friend?" Although he has not until then known his own name, it suddenly occurs to him that he is called *Perceval li Galois* (Perceval the Welshman). She comments: "Not Perceval li Galois but Perceval the Unfortunate, because you neglected to ask about the Grail. So much would have been restored if you had only asked. The sick King would have been healed and his limbs made strong again. He would have governed in his own country once more and all would have been well. But now worse troubles will result, both for you and for others. You have behaved so incompetently on account of your mother, whose death you were responsible for. Because she died of the pain caused by your departure."

The girl reveals herself as Perceval's cousin. She had previously lived in his mother's house and this is the reason she is so well informed about him. She is no less distressed by Perceval's failure to ask about the Grail than she is over the death of her friend. Perceval is deeply shocked to hear of his mother's death. Where should he go now? He had meant to search for her.

Idle lamentation is not his way, however. He is stimulated to further action; he invites the girl to go with him, instead of tarrying with the dead man whom he promises to avenge. She indicates the direction taken by the murderer but refuses to follow Perceval until she has buried her friend. Suddenly she notices Perceval's sword and asks him where he acquired it. She knows that it has not yet come in contact with human blood or been drawn in danger. She also knows who made it and warns Perceval not to rely on it, for it is treacherous, it will break when used in battle and can only be repaired by Trebuchet, the smith who forged it. Whereupon they part.

Perceval later encounters another girl coming towards him on a wretched nag and in equally sorry plight herself, quite ravaged and ill-treated. It is the same young woman from whom he had stolen a ring and a kiss in the tent and who is now being rigorously punished by her jealous knight, l'Orguelleus de la Lande (the Pride of the Land). Perceval promises to make amends for the injustice done her. An opportunity soon presents itself, for the proud knight arrives in person and is challenged by Perceval. L'Orguelleus is overthrown and, together with the young woman, dispatched to Arthur as prisoner. When the King hears that the two have been sent by the "Red Knight," as Perceval is now called on account of the colour of his armour, he resolves to seek out the man who has been missing for so long and sets out with his court to find him.

That evening their tents are pitched for the night in a forest clearing. By chance, Perceval also spends the night quite close to the same spot; when he awakens in the morning fresh snow has fallen. Even before catching sight of the camp, he spies a flock of wild fowl which, chased by a falcon, is fleeing before it with a great clamour. One bird is wounded and falls to earth, but when Perceval runs to fetch it it has already flown away, leaving three drops of blood on the snow. Perceval stands like one spellbound, for the red blood on the snow reminds him of Blancheflor's countenance and transports him into a state of profound meditation.[1] Servants from Arthur's camp catch sight of him and report to the King that a knight, to all appearances asleep on his horse, is outside the camp. The King sends one of his companions to fetch him. Perceval, however, sees and hears nothing and wins the fight which ensues without awakening from his dream state. The same thing happens with a second knight. Finally Gauvain arrives, to find Perceval still in the same mesmerized condition. However, the sun has partially dried two of the drops of blood, with the result that his reverie has diminished. He accepts Gauvain's message and explains why he was so spellbound. He is brought to Arthur who greets him most joyfully. The company then turns back to Caerleon, where that night and the following day are given over to feasting. On the third day the rejoicing comes to a sudden end with the arrival, on a dun-coloured mule, of a loathsome damsel, hideous to behold, as if she had been spawned in hell. She wears her hair plaited into two short black braids, her neck and hands are black as iron and her eyes small as a rat's. She

[1] The motif of the drops of blood on the snow also appears in the Irish legend of Deirdre, cited in T. W. Rolleston, *Myths and Legends of the Celtic Race*, p. 197, as well as in "The Singing, Soaring Lark" and "Snow White" in Grimm's *Fairy Tales*. Cf. Erich Köhler, *Die drei Blutstropfen im Schnee*, p. 421. Köhler says the three drops represent *le caractère sans issue de l'amour courtois* (the issue-less nature of courtly love).

has a nose like an ape's, lips like a donkey's, teeth like the yoke of an egg and a beard like an ox, to which are added a hump in front and behind and bandy legs. In her hand she carries a scourge. She rides up to the King and greets all the company—except Perceval, whom she reviles for not having asked about the Grail and the lance when he was with the Fisher King.

You were with the Fisher King
And saw the bleeding lance.
Was it so irksome then
To open your mouth and ask
The reason why those drops of blood
Spilled from the white iron?
And of the Grail you saw
You equally did not inquire
And did not ask
What rich man was served therewith.
Had you but asked the wealthy king,
Who is in such great distress,
Then his wounds would have been healed
And he would possess his land again
Which he will never more regain.
Do you know what will happen
If the King should forfeit his land
And he should not be healed?
Women will lose their men,
Countries be laid waste,
Maidens will be helpless and abandoned
And many knights on that account will perish—
All this through you.[2]

Turning back to the King, she asks if he has heard of the Chastel Orguelleux (Castle of Pride). In that castle, where she will spend the night, there are five hundred and sixty-six knights, each with his lady. Whoever desires to accomplish knightly deeds need only repair thither, where he will find opportunities in abundance. But the greatest prize is to be won

[2] Verses 4652 and 4675.

at Montesclaire where a maiden is besieged. Whoever shall raise the siege and free the damsel will win the highest fame and, in addition, will acquire *l'espée as estranges renges*—the sword with the strange baldric. With this, she leaves the Round Table.

Some of the knights, Gauvain among them, decide to go to Chastel Orguelleux, while Perceval asserts that he will spend no two nights in the same place until he has learned who is served by the Grail and the meaning of the bleeding lance.

The next section of Chrétien's text is concerned with Gauvain's adventures, so we will pause here and consider what has happened to Perceval, on the psychological level, in this part of the story.

First he meets a weeping girl who is holding a dead man in her lap. It turns out that she is a near relation, a cousin brought up in his mother's house, and is therefore very closely related to him. It does not seem to be by chance that she should be a cousin, for the Grail Bearer, who is the King's niece, is also Perceval's cousin or aunt. In her, as already suggested, we can see a manifestation of the anima. Indeed she, like everything in the Grail Castle, appears *sub specie aeternitatis*; she does not appear in direct relation to him but only indirectly (in that she sends him the cloak or sword). She is the anima, for she lives as a divine archetype in the unconscious, too exalted and distant to be addressed.

When Perceval meets the anima again, in front of the castle gate, it is as a girl related to him who is lamenting over a dead man. With her he can talk. She is therefore a more human form of the anima, with whom he can enter into a personal relation. The dead man over whom she weeps actually represents an aspect of Perceval himself; he heedlessly observed a wonder without using his head or asking about it and therefore, from the point of view of the Grail world, he is like one dead.

That this girl and the Grail Bearer are both Perceval's matrilineal kin is highly significant; it illustrates an aspect of the anima that touches on the problem of incest. As Jung has explained in "Psychology of the Transference," [3] incest is

[3] In *Practice of Psychotherapy*, particularly par. 431.

probably based on a genuine fundamental instinct which could be described as kinship or endogamous libido; i.e. it arises out of an authentic urge in the individual which aims at holding the family together and protecting it from the disruptive influences of the outer world. Opposing this instinct there is, however, a contrary gradient of exogamous psychic energy which actually causes strange and distant things to appear alluring, thus counteracting inbreeding and the psychic stagnation connected with it.

An attempt to reconcile these two basic psychic tendencies in the sphere of erotic relationship is to be found in the custom of the cross-cousin marriage which exists among many primitive peoples and can also be traced in the past of many more civilized nations. According to this practice, a man must marry a cousin on the mother's side, almost the nearest female relation except the actual mother or sister. In the course of time the exogamous tendency became fully established everywhere, on the sociological level. But since the opposing endogamous tendency is based on a real instinctual foundation, it did not disappear, but persisted, principally as the idea of incest among the gods and representatives of divinity, as for example the ancient Egyptian god-kings. In the same way, in the world of alchemical symbolism, the King and Queen celebrated an incestuous *hieros gamos* (divine marriage). At the same time, the alchemical symbolism reveals the goal in whose service the endogamous gradient of energy is now placed. It is no longer the family but the inner psychic components of the individual that it holds together; i.e. it has been internalized into the urge towards individuation.[4] Over against the disintegrating manifestation of psychic collectivity, the endogamous urge works in the direction of a psychic consolidation of the individual which is symbolized by the alchemical *lapis*. Therefore, when the niece or daughter of the Grail King, who is himself a brother of Perceval's mother, carries the Grail in the castle, or in other versions presents Perceval with a sword or cloak, she is, as it were, personifying the *endogamous aspect of the anima* and thus

[4] Concerning the whole development, cf. *ibid.*, pars. 420*ff.*

that anima function which furthers the process of individuation. For this reason Blancheflor, whom he abandoned out of longing for the mother, may be understood as a representative of the opposite, i.e. exogamous, aspect of the anima. It is chiefly through her that Perceval is freed from the mother and initiated into the world of experience and finds his own inherent being. Through her, he discovers his masculinity and at the same time acquires experience of a real woman. But had he remained with her, he would not have been able to meet the other, inner aspect of the anima, namely the Grail Bearer. In so far as the image of the anima would not have been experienced independently of the outer woman, the previously mentioned danger of *accidie* turns out, in a deeper sense, to be the peril of remaining stuck in the projection and of failing to carry out the process of individuation. To be sure, Perceval did not understand this consciously when he left Blancheflor but was simply following the urge to action which summoned him to further adventures. For this reason the three drops of blood on the snow recall Blancheflor, and he is compelled to meditate about her.

Just as he left Blancheflor without understanding the deeper meaning of his conduct, so he omits once again to ask about the meaning of the Grail carried by the figure of the endogamous anima and as a consequence is expelled from the Grail realm.

The girl with the dead man in her lap also conveys the idea of a *pietà*. She suggests the suffering mother bewailing her divine son-lover, i.e. that aspect of Perceval which qualifies him as the "divine son of the mother," as a type of Christ or redeemer figure. Through his death in the Grail realm—that world of the future-prefiguring archetypal images—Perceval, as a human being conscious for the first time, is now actually born into this world, the world of the circle of Arthur's knights from which he had set out. And even though he was expelled from the Grail world as a sinner, he nevertheless obtained something from that world, an intimation of the anima as an inner figure guiding him towards the process of individuation. Certainly he is not bound to her permanently, and she only appears to him in transient meetings, as, in changing form, now helpful and attractive, now antagonistic and often even dangerous, she entices and guides him towards his goal.

This uncommitted, still distant and not really personal relation to the anima corresponds to an earlier stage than the one in which there exists a strong and lasting tie to the Lady Anima, such as that between Dante and Beatrice and other well-known couples.[5] In the Breton stories there are also similar pairs of lovers, such as Tristan and Isolde and Lancelot and Guinevere. But these figures represent less of a relationship than of an unqualified *participation mystique*, expressed, to take one example, by a knight immediately losing his reason when his lady is angry with him and rushing off into the forest, where he falls into an animal-like condition until, by chance, he is reunited with his love. Such catastrophic happenings are the result of a total projection of the anima. In so far as the anima is equivalent to the soul, which as is well known represents the life principle, the separation from the object of projection naturally results in a loss of soul and life. As long as the anima is so completely projected, the soul is also still externalized and for that reason, the individual is endangered. The cultivation of an individual relationship, as was practised in the *Minnedienst*, was concerned with overcoming this state of *participation* and with substituting a more conscious and personal relation. But together with this more conscious relation, as we know from our understanding of modern psychology, a discrimination between the real woman and the anima as the archetypal soul-image must also be made; at the same time, insight into the function of the anima as a guide to higher inner wholeness forces its way into consciousness.

This girl with the dead man in her lap reproaches Perceval because he omitted to ask where the Grail was being carried and who was served from it. In like manner she informs him that his mother has died from the suffering caused by his

[5] In this connection it is interesting to compare Linda Fierz-David's masterly interpretation, *The Dream of Poliphilo*. There, a higher stage of this development has already been reached and is expressed in the striving towards and jealous fostering of an individual relation to the anima.

leaving her, and that because of this sin of which he was not conscious, he was unable to ask the questions concerning the Grail. He is therefore made conscious of his offence. His name, of which he had been ignorant, suddenly occurs to him. He becomes conscious of himself as an individual.

Herein lies a very old and profound realization: that the growth of consciousness concerning oneself proceeds simultaneously with an awareness of guilt. This realization is already expressed in the biblical story of Paradise, providing the occasion for the concept of original sin, as well as in the Eastern belief in *karma*, equivalent to a debt that has to be paid, which the individual brings with him into his present life.

Perceval is now no longer the *cher fils, beau fils*[6] but Perceval the luckless, conscious of his guilt. Certainly he has not, like Adam and Eve, partaken of the Tree of Knowledge. On the contrary he has failed by *not* eating of it, by *not* asking, *not* becoming conscious of the mysterious thing that he has seen. Thus he becomes a sort of compensatory figure to Adam, and we shall see that this role is one for which he is further destined.

Perceval has therefore incurred a twofold guilt: he did not attend to his mother and he did not ask about the Grail—and the latter offence is actually described as a consequence of the former. It can thus be said that because or for so long as he did not ask about his mother, he also did not ask about the Grail. This is enlightening when it is considered that, as its primal image, the Grail takes the place of the mother, so that in a more profound sense it is the same sin. A similar offence against the feminine principle is mentioned at a much later stage of the story. The evil Espinogre, whose ghostly hand is connected with the mystery of the Grail, is said to have murdered his mother in the Chapel of the Black Hand. On Perceval's first appearance at Arthur's court, the Queen has suffered the outrage of having the wine from the stolen cup spilled over her.

In Wolfram, too, there is a passage that has relevance here, where something similar is expressed in more biblical language.

[6] Cf. Wolfram, *Parzival*, ed. W. Stapel, p. 67.

Trevrizent is there telling Parzival about Adam and Eve and how one of their sons, out of rapaciousness, robbed his grandmother of her virginity.[7] To Parzival's objection that "that could not very well have happened", Trevrizent proceeds:

> The Earth was Adam's mother,
> He was nourished by her fruit;
> Yet she is fittingly called virgin.[8]
> When Adam's son his brother slew,
> Merciless and scornful of good,
> And stained the pure Earth's lap
> With blood from Abel's head,
> There was she robbed of her virginity.
> Then strife sprang up among men,
> And so it has been ever since.[9]

This offence of Perceval's against the feminine principle appears to have had four unfortunate results. First of all there was the woman he robbed of a ring and kissed by force, thereby plunging her into misfortune. Next there was the death of his mother, then his failure to ask about the Grail and finally his recollection of the forsaken Blancheflor. In a certain sense it was always the same offence he committed: that of acting too unconsciously. It was not so much that what he did was so wrong as that he was not conscious of the other person involved

[7] Book IX, verse 922.

[8] Here we also have a correspondence between the earth, which was Adam's mother, and Mary, the Virgin Mother of God.

[9] Book IX, verse 941.

> Diu erde Adâmes muoter was,
> Von Erden frucht Adâm genas,
> Dannoch was diu Erde ein maget.
> Noch han ich in niht besaget
> Wer ir den magetum beham.
> Kains vater was Adâm:
> Versluoc Abeln um krankez guot
> Dô ûf die reinen erden'z bluot
> Viel, ir megetuom was vervarn:
> Do huop sich erst der Menschen nît:
> Also wer er iemer sît.

in his actions. To conclude, it is certainly *no* sin that he should leave his mother, since, as we saw earlier, he had to leave her to go forth into life; but he no longer concerned himself about her after the separation took place. Because he did not know what he was doing, he did not allow himself to be enriched by the suffering that the conflict between having to remain with his mother *and* having to leave her might have awakened in him. Kissing the girl in the tent was guileless naïveté, and he never suspected that her friend, one of his own shadow figures, would misconstrue it so severely. Leaving Blancheflor so as not to be guilty of *accidie* was proper, but he did not realize the emotional suffering he was thereby imposing both on her and on himself. His real offence actually lay in the primitive unambiguousness of his behaviour, which arose from an unawareness of the inner problem of the opposites. *It was not what he did but that he was not capable of assessing what he did.* His one-sided attitude accords with an identification with the masculine logos principle, whereby the emotional and feeling side of the anima the conflict and suffering which result from such an attitude are not given sufficient consideration.[10] This is why he now comes upon the image of the suffering anima and is reminded of Blancheflor by the blood of a wounded bird. In this connection the image of wild game birds pursued by a falcon has a deeper significance. In the poetry of the Minnesingers, the falcon is a symbol of the man in love, acting like a bird of prey hunting its game.[11] In Wolfram, for instance, when Gahmuret catches sight of the Queen of Wales, it is said that "the noble hero raised himself up like a falcon that eyes its prey."[12]

The duck, on the other hand, quite often appears in fairy-tales as a counterpart of the bride.[13] Thus in a Russian tale a father says to his son: "Go to Moscow. There is a pond there. In the pond is a net. If the duck goes into the net, take it; if

[10] Cf. *Alchemical Studies*, pars. 463*ff*.

[11] In medieval mysticism the words "to hunt" generally stood for the desire of love. For examples, see Lüers, *op. cit.*, pp. 204–5.

[12] Wolfram, *Parzival*, Book I, p. 41.

[13] Cf. A. de Gubernatis, *Die Thiere in der indogermanischen Mythologie*, p. 575.

not, then pull the net out." The son returns home with his predestined bride. In many other fairy-tales the duck is an emblem of the bride or wife put under a spell by a witch.[14] This describes the anima as still being under the influence of the mother image, as not yet having taken on human form but appearing only fleetingly in the shape of an animal which then suddenly disappears.

It is as though Perceval receives from the unconscious a sign, in the image of the falcon that injures the game, which impels him to contemplation; for in the language of the auguria (bird auspices) he is told what has really happened to him; his masculine *Logos* has violated his soul, which lives by the feeling relationship. His attitude to Blancheflor was like that of a bird of prey. He saw her as a prize and took possession of her. Feeling was damaged, however, because his appropriation of Blancheflor still did not exemplify a human relation, and the spilt blood seems to accuse him of an unconsciously committed injury. As mentioned, blood symbolizes the soul, but also in this case its suffering, to which Perceval has not given sufficient consideration. The drops of blood in the snow display the colours red and white, the classical colours of alchemy where they indicate the masculine and feminine principles that have to be united. The classical pair in alchemy are the "red man or slave" (*servus rubeus*) and the "white woman" (*mulier candida*). It is therefore not by chance that since his first battle Perceval has himself been called the Red Knight and has united himself with Blancheflor, the "white flower." [15] This singular nuance in the two names supports the interpretation that Perceval represents a correspondence to the *homo altus* and the *lapis* of the alchemists. Furthermore, drops of blood on snow are a widely disseminated motif in fairy stories and in that context sometimes have the function of establishing a guiding clue by which the goal is attained. Therefore, to follow traces of blood means, in the psychological sense, to follow the gradient of

[14] Examples in Gubernatis, *op. cit.*, pp. 575*ff*.

[15] Red and white are also favourite colours in the language of the medieval mystics.

psychic energy, i.e. to follow the secret impulsion of the soul.

Perceval realizes all this through the encounter with the anima. We therefore see what an important part she plays in the achievement of consciousness. In the course of making her acquaintance, that quite particular form of consciousness known as *conscience* is awakened in him.

An interesting connection between "name" and "anima," which is found in J. Rhys' *Celtic Folklore*,[16] remains to be considered. The author poses the question: With which part of the person is his name associated? Rhys sees an answer in the fact that the Old Aryan words for "name," such as the Irish *ainm*, Old Welsh *anu*, Old Bulgarian *imen*, Sanscrit *nâman*, Latin *nomen* and Greek *onoma*, are remarkably like the Irish and Welsh words for "soul." For instance, in Irish *ainm* is "name" and *anim* is "soul, anima." In certain cases they are declined alike and therefore often confused by students. Rhys traces both back to the very oldest Aryan word for "breath," because the soul was looked upon as the breath of life, which is certainly expressed in the words *Atem*, *atmen* ("to breathe," in German), *anima*, *animus* and *breath*. A similar connection is hinted at when Perceval learns his own name at the same time that he becomes acquainted with the anima. Attention must be drawn to the fact that the name "Perceval" could not until now be satisfactorily explained. The literal translation, "pierces (or penetrates) the valley," seems the likeliest and would imply that the hero was destined to penetrate the dark valley of the unconscious. In the *Perlesvaus* it is emphasized that the name means *per-les-vaux*, i.e. "for the valleys." The boy was thus christened in remembrance of the fact that his father had lost some valleys belonging to him or because he penetrates the mystery of the valley that leads to the Grail.[17] Wolfram himself explains the

[16] Vol. II, p. 625.

[17] Cf. Nitze, *Perlesvaus*, p. 218; Loomis, *Arthurian Tradition and Chrétien de Troyes*, p. 489; and Marx, *La Légende Arthurienne et le Graal*, p. 68. Another interpretation is "par lui fait" or "par lui vaut," "made by him" or "valued by him." This explanation is too vague, however, for it to be possible to draw psychological conclusions from it. According to Hilka and some others the name is not French at all.

name as meaning "right through the centre," for "with the plough of faithfulness great love ploughed a deep furrow through the centre of his mother's heart." [18] The name would thus be connected with the idea of the centre and the heart, a meaning really invented by Wolfram, which nevertheless expresses Perceval's symbolic nature extremely well.

Apart from the anima, Perceval is also made aware of his task, which he has now clearly recognized, and his goal, of which, in spite of future wrong turnings and detours, he will never again lose sight. The ability to set a goal and to follow it consistently is an important achievement in the course of human development. Children and primitives are not yet really capable of it. They act from instinct and allow themselves to be determined by any momentarily arising impulse. They still lack the will necessary for any action conscious of its aim and for which ego consciousness is a prerequisite. Perceval has now obviously achieved this consciousness. It could be considered as an essential result of his initiation, his first visit to the Grail Castle.

[18] *Parzival,* p. 83.

CHAPTER XI

The Suffering Grail King

It can now be seen that the encounter with the anima actually corresponds to a further increase of consciousness in our hero. From her he learns, among other things, that the Lord of the Castle has been so badly wounded in battle by a javelin that he can neither walk nor ride, so that fishing is his only pastime. Hence his name.

This name has caused much speculation and has yet to be clearly or satisfactorily explained. A. Hilka, the editor of the *Perceval*, believes that the name continued to be used because Perceval met the King by chance when he was fishing. This seems unlikely, since he is regularly called "the Fisher King" even when he is not in the least concerned with angling. In the "Joseph of Arimathea," Joseph bids his brother-in-law Brons go fishing, and the latter brings back to the Grail Table a fish that satisfies the hunger of everyone present. For this reason it is thought that the guardian of the Grail is known as the Fisher King. It does not ring true, however, that a much later Grail King, in addition to all of the earlier ones, should have been called after this one event, the less so as the Grail itself provided nourishment, without the presence even of a fish. Certainly, in the manuscript illuminations fish is usually seen on the table, along with other foods like bread, although there is no special mention anywhere of fish being eaten. On the contrary, the hermit informs Perceval that the Grail does not contain fish, but rather the Host.

A meal of fish undoubtedly played a part among the early Christians, as can be seen in the catacomb frescoes.[1] The fish,

[1] Cf. Eisler, *Orpheus—the Fisher*, p. 209 and Fig. LV; and F. J. Dölger, *Ichthys, passim.*

as the symbol of Christ, seems to have been a part of the sacramental meal in those days. We also find the meal of fish in the Gospels: the feeding of the five thousand on five loaves and two fishes, and particularly the meal by the Sea of Tiberias, where the risen Christ appears to the disciples as they are fishing and partakes of a meal of fish with them.[2]

St. Augustine writes: "At this meal, which the Lord gave to his seven disciples and at which he served them the fish they had seen on the fire of coals, together with the loaves of bread and the fishes they had caught, it was Christ who had suffered, who was in reality the fish that was broiled."[3] Prosper of Aquitaine speaks of the "great fish which itself satisfied the disciples, and at that time gave itself to the whole world as a fish." [4] In the Talmud it is said that: "Only the son of a man with the name of a fish could lead the Children of Israel into the Promised Land, namely Joshua, the son of the fish (Joshua the son of Nun)."

In other religions, too, the fish is often the saviour. In this guise he appears as the redeemer of mankind in the Brahmanic legend of Manu: "For the salvation of nature Vishnu took on the form of a fish."[5] The Assyrian fish man Oannes brought written characters to men and taught them wisdom, science and the arts. Celtic legend also has a "salmon of wisdom" that lived in a spring surrounded by hazel bushes and got its wisdom from eating the nuts that fell from the trees. A merging of this idea with the Christian one is to be found in a Breton legend in which Saint Corentin fed a King who had got lost

[2] "As soon then as they were come to land, they saw a fire of coals there, and fish laid thereon, and bread.

"Jesus saith unto them, Bring of the fish which ye have now caught.

"Simon Peter went up, and drew the net to land full of great fishes, a hundred and fifty and three: and for all there were so many, yet was not the net broken.

"Jesus saith unto them, Come and dine. And none of the disciples durst ask him, Who art thou? knowing that it was the Lord."—John 21:9–12.

[3] *In Evangelium Johannis Tractatus*, CXXIII, Sec. 2.

[4] *De Promiss. et praedic. Dei*, II, 39. Cf. J. Scheftelowitz, "Das Fischsymbol in Judentum und Christentum," pp. 1*ff* and 321*ff*, especially p. 14.

[5] King Bhartari of Benares had a fish that kept him informed of all that took place in the "Three Worlds," *ibid.*, p. 327.

while hunting, together with his retinue, on the flesh of a wondrous trout he kept in a well.[6]

The fish, living in the darkness of deep water, is often illustrative of a content of the unconscious that lingers below the threshold of consciousness and in which instinctual and spiritual aspects are still merged in an undifferentiated state. Therefore, the fish is an inspirer, a bringer of wisdom and, at the same time, a helpful animal—at once insight and redemptive, instinctive impulse.

In *Aion*, Jung deals extensively with the symbolism of Christ as the fish; reference can therefore be made to that work.[7] In many religions the fish, as already mentioned, is chiefly a symbol of the redeemer,[8] and has therefore also been equated with Christ. At the same time the extraordinary revival of fish symbolism in early Christianity is certainly not without a synchronistic connection with the beginning of the astrological Age of the Fishes.[9] The fish emerged at that time as an image out of the depths of the unconscious and became associated with the figure of Christ.[10] In a special sense, therefore, the fish represents that aspect of Christ which marks him as a content of the unconscious, a manifestation, as it were, of the unconscious Self. In this connection, its animal nature refers to the instinctual impulses, consisting either of biological urges or of convictions and emotions. When these emerge from the unconscious, they can either oppress or else "nourish" and enrich consciousness. In so far as the fish symbol became linked with the figure of Christ, it formed a bridge to the psychic nature of man and enabled him to receive the figure of Jesus into his psychic matrix. In a Coptic magic papyrus, Christ is depicted as a fisherman angling for himself in the form of a fish.[11] He is the one who makes his own nature

[6] This is taken from the works mentioned above. The dolphin, sacred to Apollo, and actually incarnating him, is also described as the saviour of those in danger.

[7] *Aion*, Ch. VI–IX, especially pars. 127*ff*.

[8] Cf. *ibid.*, Manu, Oannes, Ea, etc.

[9] Cf. *ibid.*, pars. 128*ff*.

[10] *Ibid.*, pars. 285–86.

[11] Cf. A. Kropp, *Ausgewählte koptische Zaubertexte*, Vol. III, Diagram II, Cf. illus., pp. 196–97.

conscious and in this respect points the way to a higher consciousness for others. At the same time he is also an image of that unconscious process by which Christ became the archetype of the Self and thus a content which can be subjectively experienced by human beings, and which emerges from the background of the psyche, surprising, terrifying, bringing insight or redemption.

However, our story speaks not of a fish but of a fisherman. The fisherman, likewise, is a very well-known figure in myths and legends. In his book *Orpheus the Fisher*, R. Eisler provides abundant information about a great or "divine" fisherman.[12] According to him, the name Orpheus could mean "fisher." The fisherman is naturally someone who draws something up from the depths of the waters. As a fisher Orpheus, too, would have drawn up the fish with his magic music. He also suggests our Fisher King, in so far as magical powers were also attributed to the latter. Among other matters, Eisler cites a Greek story of a rich fisherman which he connects with the Fisher King of the Grail story. In this tale the angler finds a golden cup in the belly of a fish he has caught. Each time he pours wine into the cup it is filled with gold coins. "When the fisherman has become a rich man through the power of this cup, he devotes himself to music and learns to play the lyre so wonderfully that no heart is able to withstand the enchantment of his melodies."[13]

In point of fact this fisherman with the wondrous wine goblet and the magic lyre suggests the Fisher King, to whom, however, no pronounced musical ability is attributed. At most, it could be pointed out that in general, the Celtic fairy folk were considered to be very fond of music and that in many respects the Grail King seems to have been a fairy King.[14]

Having taken the Grail Castle to be an otherworldly realm and since, according to the Celtic conception, that world was

[12] *Passim.*

[13] Eisler, *Orpheus—the Fisher*, pp. 103–4.

[14] Concerning the Celtic background see Helaine Newstead, *Bran the Blessed in Arthurian Romance*; and Eithne O'Sharkey, "The Maimed King in Arthurian Romance."

thought to be either in the water, as an island, or else to lie beneath it, it follows that the ruler of the Grail Kingdom must in any case have had a close relation to this element. Connections between the Fisher King and the widely venerated Celtic sea god Manannan (Welsh Manawydan), son of Llyr, may thus be assumed.[15] The Tuatha De Danann elected him as their chief; he conferred invisibility and immortality on the gods and gave them magic food. Furthermore, he was supposed to have possessed various magical objects, among them a sword, the Answerer, that cast dread over all who beheld it, a tablecloth that produced food when whirled around and a cup or bowl that broke when a lie was told.[16] Both of these latter treasures forcibly suggest the Grail legend.

Christ, however, is not only the fish but also the fisher who appointed his disciples, and especially Peter, to be fishers of men. Since the Grail King is nourished exclusively on the Host, he can hardly, for that reason, be dissociated from these Christian motifs;[17] instead, we should address our attention to the meaning of this symbol within that context.

Among primitives, the King, especially in his original role as chief of the tribe, represents in his own person the centre of the life of the people.[18] In him the divine "spirit" of the tribe is incarnated, on him depend the psychic and physical welfare of the people, even to the rain and the fruitfulness of fields and livestock. Psychologically he represents a symbol of the Self become visible in a human being, to which the entire social and psychic organization of his people is adjusted.[19] That the king is an incarnated symbol of the Self, visible in the life of the society, is, however, also connected with the fact that on the more primitive cultural levels he is always ritually killed if he

[15] Cf. Marx, *Légende Arthurienne*, p. 195; cf. also, E. Brugger, "Die Nodons-Nuadu Hypothese als Erklärung des Namens des Fischerkönigs and Holmes and Klenke, *op. cit.*, p. 201.

[16] D'Arbois de Joubainville, *Celtic Mythological Circle*, p. 188. Cf. also Dorothy Kempe, *op. cit.*, p. xxii.

[17] Regarding this description of the Grail King as the *Roi Pêcheur*, cf. Mergell, *Der Gral in Wolframs Parsifal*, p. 115.

[18] Cf. Frazer, *The Golden Bough*, Vol. II, "Adonis, Attis, Osiris," p. 161.

[19] Cf. *Mysterium Coniunctionis*, par. 498.

shows signs of illness or old age, so that the "spirit" of the tribe may function better in the body of his successor. Frazer has collected numerous examples of the ritual killing of the king. He has also shown that traces of this ritual murder survive in many of the customs of more civilized races, such as the Sed festival of the Egyptians and even in the present-day King Carnival.[20] So that the same archetypal motif seems to be involved when the Grail King is old and unable to die. Helen Adolf thinks that the Grail King is a symbol of a "stricken society," [21] and H. B. Wilson considers him to be "mankind in a fallen state." [22] In the chapter in *Mysterium Coniunctionis* entitled "Rex and Regina," [23] Jung has shown that this mystery of the killing and renewal of the King also persisted as a symbolic conception in alchemy, which indicates the great and universal significance of this idea. In the same work he has also explained that the image of God prevailing in collective consciousness requires renewal from time to time, because the dominant attitude of consciousness is only "right" when it accords with the claims of both consciousness *and* the unconscious. Only then can it combine their opposing tendencies into unity. If, on the other hand, the ruling attitude is either too weak or incomplete, then "life is consumed in unfruitful conflict." [24] But if the old attitude of consciousness is renewed through its descent into the unconscious, then from the latter there emerges a new symbol of wholeness which is as son to the old king. As we know, Perceval is elected to be the "son" in the Grail legend, but in the beginning this process of transformation is somehow arrested so that the old king cannot die nor can Perceval relieve his suffering.

A similar condition is described in the *Historia regum Britanniae*[25] which relates of King Cadwallader (d. 689, according to

[20] Cf. Frazer, *op. cit.*, Vol. I, p. 231. These connections were known to both Weston and Nitze.

[21] Adolf, *Visio Pacis*, Ch. 5.

[22] "The Grail King in Wolfram's *Parzival*." M.L.R., *LV*, 4, 1960.

[23] Pars. 349–543, and especially pars. 541*ff*.

[24] *Ibid.*, par.

[25] Ed. Faral, Vol. III, pp. 299 and 302.

Cult bowl from the community of the Gnostic Ophites

Alchemistic oven

Geoffrey of Monmouth) that he ruled peaceably to begin with, but that after twelve years he became ill, whereupon dissension broke out among the Britons. As a result of this reprehensible civil strife, the rich land was devastated. It then suffered from further calamity in the shape of famine. Everywhere the necessities of life were lacking, "*excepto venatoriae artis solatio*," for the only solace or recourse left them was hunting, just as angling was the Fisher King's only remaining consolation. The famine was followed by a frightful pestilence that depopulated the country. The survivors banded together and migrated to Armorica, singing with great lamentation, as their sails spread above them: "Woe unto us sinners on account of our frightful misdoings." Might the lamentations that broke out at sight of the lance or the King's litter in the Grail Hall be a memory of this? In Armorica the emigrants were received by Alanus, the king of the land. (In various versions of the Grail story, Perceval's father, or even the Grail King himself, is called Alain li Gros.) In consequence, Britain was laid waste and deserted for eleven years. After some time, Cadwallader begged Alanus for help in winning back his former dominion, where the Angles had firmly established themselves during his absence. But when he planned to fit out a fleet, he heard an angel's voice telling him that he should refrain from this undertaking, for the time was not yet ripe. The voice further bid him make a pilgrimage to Pope Sergius in Rome, where, after making atonement, he would be received among the saints. Because of his faith, the Britons would regain their island when the proper time arrived. *This would not come about, however, until they had brought his relics from Rome to England.* In addition, the relics of other saints, hidden on account of the heathen invasion, should also be found, and then at last the lost kingdom would be regained. As mentioned, the lance served as a symbol of the kingdom that was to be recovered.[26] The relic, according to a

[26] This passage is highly reminiscent of the story of the sick King and the "détruisement du pays de Logres," the devastation of England, the original cause of which is repeatedly assumed to have been fraternal strife of some kind.

manuscript entitled *Romans des la Table ronde* (in the Bibliothèque de l'Arsenal in Paris), refers to a rumour spread abroad in Britain[27] that the Most Holy Grail, in which Joseph of Arimathea had taken up Christ's blood, and the vessel in which, with his own hand, Christ had consecrated his body and blood for the first time, as well as the lance that was thrust into his side, were in Britain. They had been brought there by Joseph, *but no one knew to which place*. According to this manuscript, the search for the Grail owed its existence to this rumour, which in its turn could have arisen out of the allusion to hidden relics in the *Historia regum Britanniae*, the discovery of which would have coincided with the restoration of the kingdom of the Britons.

In this version it is the King's sickness that causes the conflict to break out; the ruler is no longer able to hold the opposites together. From this originates the complete devastation of the land, the stagnation of psychic life. Restoration is delayed, i.e. the process of renewal is suspended for a long time. Psychologically the relics represent the possibility of a further development of the Christian symbol, which, however, was long postponed on account of the predominance of regressive pagan tendencies.

The consequences of the relic's or (in Robert de Boron) the Grail's concealment is a condition of dearth and sickness,[28] therefore a situation in need of redemption. This calls to mind the archetypal concept of a lost Paradise. It has already been pointed out that this is the situation in the Grail realm.[29] It is, however, remarkable that this unfortunate result does not appear to have been in operation from the beginning but seems to have become evident only at a certain moment, a moment,

[27] Cf. P. Paris, *Romans de la Table ronde*, Vol. II, p. 267.

[28] Chrétien de Troyes, *Li conte del Graal*, verses 4670*ff*:

Dames en perdront lor mariz,
terres en sont essilliees
et pucelles desconseilliees,
qui orfelines remandront,
et maintes chevalier en mourront.

[29] The "Elucidation" expresses this most clearly of all.

clearly, when the possibility of discovering the hidden thing had developed. In many versions it is especially emphasized that the wonders would begin at a particular moment in time.

> Then, in all those lands where the lance is to be found, wonders will begin, and they so great and terrible that all peoples will be amazed, and all these marvels will occur solely on account of the knowledge of the Grail and the lance. For the desire for it will be so great among the virtuous then on earth, that they will be determined to undergo the terrifying adventures of worldly chivalry, simply that they may come to know the miracle of the Grail and the lance.[30]

The Grail, therefore has the characteristics of those hidden treasures of which it is said that from time to time they "blossom," and that when they do the moment has then arrived when they can be brought to the surface. Should this fail to occur they will disappear again. The *merveilles de Bretagne* were one such sign of the "flowering of the treasure"—a call from the hidden value that someone should come and find it. At the same time this summons also indicates that the psychic values in the depths of the unconscious are constellated whenever the dominant ideal in consciousness, the King, no longer possesses enough life to ensure the union of the opposites.

As we have seen, the figure of the old Grail King, who is nourished solely on the Host, cannot be dissociated from the context of these Christian ideas. He obviously represents a Christian dominant in the collective consciousness, or alternatively the prototype of the Christian man. He is not really Christ himself, but it is as if he personifies that element in the figure of Christ that has been admitted into tradition and consciousness and which has thereby become the ruling ideal that influences and impresses itself on society. He therefore also represents the collective man who has been formed by the traditional Christian image. But like all Kings, this ruler too has

[30] Hucher, *Le Grand Saint Graal*, Vol. II, p. 311.

become old and in need of renewal or of redemption by a successor.

Although the Grail King appears to represent the prototype of Christian man, it must not be overlooked that he also possesses some of the features of the sea kings and rich fishers of the pre-Christian Celts and of antiquity, and these figures seem to provide him with a pagan shadow. It is as if what had already happened to the historical figure of Jesus was now being repeated in the Grail King. As the archetypal image of the fish crystallized around the historical figure of Jesus,[31] so the fairy king who rules in the water is an archetypal image that attaches itself to the image of the Christian king and enriches him with characteristics arising from the depths of the unconscious. Thus, the Grail King is, as it were, the archetypal image of Christian man, but Christian man as he is viewed from the perspective of the unconscious.[32] Seen in this way he throws a remarkable "shadow."

Together with that of the king of fairies and of fairy-tales, another complex of ideas has attached itself to the figure of the Grail King: the motif of the sleeping old man who will awaken one day and bring back a new and happy age, a paradisal kingdom. This complex of ideas is imbued with the old conceptions of the sleeping Kronos-Saturn, the motif, already quoted, of the sleeping old man in the legend of Alexander and its variants, and the theme of the Apostle Thomas resting uncorrupted in his place of burial in India, as well as other parallels. These ideas are connected, moreover, with that of an anticipated earthly golden age or kingdom.[33] In the German variants especially, this Eastern, and particularly Persian, motif is developed anew,[34] obviously because it was suggestive of a content being constellated in the unconscious. This content is expressed by the Germans in the motif of the "old man

[31] Concerning the motif of the renewal of the king, in general, see *Mysterium Coniunctionis*, Ch. IV, "Rex and Regina," *passim*.

[32] Cf. *ibid.*, par. 129, footnote 67.

[33] Cf. Evola, *Il mistero del Graal*, p. 126; and Ringbom, *Graltempel und Paradies*, pp. 133*ff*.

[34] By Wolfram von Eschenbach, and in the *Jüngere Titurel*.

asleep in the mountain," which has been applied to Barbarossa (in Switzerland to William Tell) and to many other heroes. As Martin Ninck has shown, this is really nothing less than the *figure of Wotan*, which survives in these legends of emperors and empires.[35] It is Wotan who is waiting to reappear in this world meaning that the shadow aspect of the suffering Grail King is connected with a dark heathen god-image that has not been taken into account by the prevailing attitude of consciousness.

The Fisher King of the Grail legend is therefore not only remarkably iridescent in outward appearance but is also suffering, being either lame or ill. We could find no suitable parallels in Celtic legend to add to this theme. On the other hand, the motif of the ailing King in need of healing and redemption is widely distributed in fairy-tales. Psychologically this exactly reflects the fact that again and again *the outwardly crystallized conception of the Self, after becoming a content of collective consciousness, grows old* and must therefore be transformed, rejuvenated or replaced by another form. This has to happen in order for the eternally self-renewing psychic life to flow up from the depths and for its ungraspable, eternally fresh and unexpected aspects to be retained.

A connection between the motifs of suffering and fishing is to be found in a Jewish tradition, quoted by J. Scheftelowitz in his article, "Das Fischsymbol in Judentum und Christentum."[36] It is strange how Eastern and Western themes are interwoven in these Grail stories, not only in those versions which deal with the obviously Oriental legend of Joseph of Arimathea, or in Wolfram where the prototype of the Grail story appears to have originated in the pagan-Jewish Orient, but also in Chrétien, whose story in other respects exhibits the characteristics of a Breton fairy-tale. Scheftelowitz refers to the popular Jewish belief that at the end of the Age of Leviathan a "pure fish" will be caught by the Angel Gabriel, so that it may be divided up and served as food to the pious. Inasmuch as they eat of its flesh, the eschatological fish—the Leviathan—acts as a

[35] *Wodan und germanischer Schiksalsglaube*, pp. 133*ff*.

[36] Pp. 9–10.

remedy for the righteous.[37] At the very time the Messiah comes, this messianic fish will be partaken of. "The Messiah will first appear when the sick one yearningly craves for the fish that he can find nowhere."[38]

When Perceval makes his appearance, the Grail King is in precisely the condition of the "sick one who yearningly craves the fish." In reality, the King is *fishing for the redeemer*, who then actually appears in the form of Perceval. This is enlightening, since the condition of the Grail realm and its King, sickly and in need of redemption, is the essential point of the quest. The crucial matter here is less the winning of the Grail than the redemption that accompanies it.[39] But how is it that the Christian Grail King longs so for the fish, the redeemer, when the latter has already appeared in the person of Christ? Something of the curiously revived eschatological expectations that gripped Christian humanity around the year 1000 and later, and which have already been briefly discussed, appears to be reflected here. In this connection it would seem particularly significant that the sect of the Cathari professed to believe in a "Revelation of John," in which the following is recounted:

Before his fall, Satan one day visited the earth, which was still covered by the primal waters, and on descending into them, found "two fishes lying upon the waters, and they were like oxen yoked for ploughing, holding the whole earth by command of the invisible Father from sunset to sunrise."[40] Here

[37] This messianic fish of Judaism is closely connected with the Messiah. Humanity, with its burden of guilt, is thought of as being diseased, so to speak, for which reason it is in need of healing, i.e. of the forgiveness of sins. This healing occurs in the messianic age: "And then God will heal his servant" (Book of Jubilees 23:10—a little known apocryphon, not in the collections). Cf. Scheftelowitz, *op. cit.*, pp. 61*f.*

[38] *Talmud Sanhedrin*, 98a, quoted *ibid.*, p. 9. For further examples of the motif of the fish, cf. Kampers, *op. cit.*, pp. 74*ff.*

[39] In the more religio-mystical forms of the story—the *Queste du Saint Graal* for instance—Galahad, the hero, is clearly conceived of as an analogue to Christ. Something may here be perceived of the eschatological state of mind which was prevalent about the year 1000 when the end of the world was expected, and it is equally possible that parts of the Grail legend actually stem from that time.

[40] Quoted from *Aion*, par. 225.

it is an account of *two* fishes that must certainly, as Jung points out, be interpreted as "ruling powers," [41] as if they were divine primeval figures still existing in the unconscious. Both together can hardly refer to Christ, for which reason Jung surmises that, in view of the heretical beliefs of the Ebionites and later of the Bogomils, the *two* fishes could allude to their idea of the two sons of God. These sects taught that God had two sons, Satanaël the elder and Christ the younger. The two fishes would seem to refer to these two sons of God, as well as to the zodiacal sign of the Age of the Fishes. The doubling of the fishes asserts symbolically that this world-month is ruled by two principles, Christ-Antichrist or Christ-Satanaël, which must, however, finally work together side by side (like oxen yoked to the plough) in order to take possession of and cultivate the earth. The change over from the first to the second fish took place around the year 1000.[42] With this year, says Jung,[43] it was as if a new world began, a world that manifested itself in religious movements such as those of the Bogomils, Cathari, Albigenses, Poor Men of Lyons and the Holy Ghost Movement of Joachim of Floris. Here, too, belonged alchemy and its development into modern natural science, which finally merged into anti-Christian rationalism and materialism. In fact, the Age of the Second Fish has something inimical to Christianity within it which, nevertheless, also works along similar lines, i.e. in the direction of achieving greater human consciousness. Might it not be this second fish for which the Grail King looks so longingly?

Before we pursue this problem further, however, we must ask ourselves still more precisely *why the Grail King and kingdom are in such great need of redemption*. It is only in Robert de Boron that the King is infirm simply from old age; in most versions he has been wounded as well. In Chrétien, the lamenting damsel, Perceval's cousin, tells him only that in battle the Fisher King had been hit in both hips by a javelin. In Wolfram, Anfortas was wounded by the poisoned spear of a heathen, who was likewise striving

[41] *Ibid.*, par. 229.
[42] Cf. *ibid.*, par. 231
[43] *Ibid.*, par. 235.

for the Grail. The King, however, was not at the time fighting in the service of the Grail but for love of the beautiful Orgeluse. The arrogance[44] and sinful worldliness of his opponent are there given as the true cause. The hermit who speaks to Parzival about this also admonishes him not to adopt a haughty deportment, recommending humility and modesty. The iron from the spear, that had been embedded in the wound, must undoubtedly have been removed by a doctor, but the poison remained in the body and prevented its healing in spite of the application of every imaginable cure.

Wolfram's allusion to the King's suffering as being more particularly acute at the time of the new moon and as connected with the ascension of Saturn is highly significant. To anyone of that period it would immediately convey important astrological associations. The moon's dangerous and uncanny side is particularly in evidence when she is new.[45] Writing of the Church as Luna, Augustine says, "Whence it is said: They have made ready their arrows in the quiver, to shoot in the *darkness of the moon* at the upright of heart."[46] At this moment, the sun enters into conjunction with the moon and, infected with her instability and perishable nature, is darkened into the *sol niger*, for the moon has a strikingly nether-world quality. To her belong the snake, the tiger, the Manes, the Lemurs and the *dii infernales.*[47] In connection with our theme, this dark aspect of the moon requires very particular attention. Paracelsus says of moonlight that it is a "*humidum ignis* [moisture of fire], of a cold nature"[48] (the Grail King is chilled and the poison in his wound is like ice), for which reason it is very receptive to poison. If a menstruating woman looks at the moon, it will be poisoned, and "when (the moon) grows new and young, [it] is of a poisonous kind." Feminine consciousness and the feminine in general, as well as man's anima, are personified by the moon; Jung has equated these qualities with the con-

[44] Expressed in the name "Orgeluse."

[45] Cf. *Mysterium Coniunctionis*, pars. 154*ff*, on "Luna," and pars. 375.

[46] *Ibid.*, par. 20.

[47] *Ibid.*, par. 216.

[48] *Ibid.*, par. 215.

ception of Eros.[49] Consequently, there is somehow a dark feminine element at the back of the Grail King's wound. Two versions of the Grail legend, in which this dark feminine element is expressly mentioned, accord with this argument. In the Welsh *Peredur*, which contains very archaic elements on the whole, the laming of the king is brought about by *the witches of Gloucester*, wild amazonian females who obviously intend to harm the Fisher King. Peredur succeeds in getting one of them into his power. She tells him that she knows she is fated to suffer humiliation at his hands, but that he is destined to learn the knightly arts and the handling of arms from the witches. He then follows her into the witches' palace where he remains for three weeks. At the end of this time he is allowed to choose a horse and weapons for himself and to proceed once more upon his way. (The Irish hero Cuchulainn had the benefit of being educated by Scatach, the goddess of war.)[50] These wild, warlike creatures are the descendents of destructive and terrifying feminine deities, such as Kali in India or Cybele of Asia Minor. The witches also killed a cousin (an unknown one, to be sure) of Peredur and it is the cousin's head that is brought in on the charger in place of the Grail. This dead man, whom Peredur must avenge, has appeared to him in the form of various maidens. He allows Arthur and his followers to be called to battle against the witches, who are annihilated. Their misdeeds are thereby expiated and the dead man avenged, although no mention is made of whether or not the lame king regains his health.

In any event, a destructive feminine element, resembling the above-mentioned dark side of the moon, emerges from behind the Grail King's illness. This relation of the witch to the moon (Hecate) is well known. That the witch-madness should have begun precisely at the height of the Christian Middle Ages is certainly not without significance in connection with this complex of symbols. A too intense and one-sided spiritualization and the fact that only the collective and light aspects of the feminine found expression in the Cult of the Virgin

[49] *Ibid.*, par. 224.

[50] Cf. C. G. Gollum, "Die schöpferische Muttergöttin," p. 250.

animated a dark feminine side and endowed it with a dangerously demonic quality[51] which, in these versions, presses threateningly upon the King, the prototype of the Christian man.

A further story, known as the *Elucidation*, which, as its name implies, sought to clarify the connections that were at that time already quite obscure, illuminates a somewhat different aspect of the same problem.[52] The story recounts how the "*détruisement du pays de Logres*" ("destruction of the land of Logres"), about which so much had been foretold, had come to pass. At one time there were living in that land, in certain *puis*, i.e. burial mounds or grottoes of springs,[53] maidens who used to refresh tired hunters or wanderers who came that way with food and drink. It was only necessary to go to one of the *puis* and state one's wishes and immediately a beautiful damsel would appear, carrying a golden bowl containing all kinds of food (also a kind of grail). A second maiden would follow, with a white hand towel and a second dish containing whatever the newcomer had wished for. The maidens served all wayfarers thus, until one day a king named Amangons ravished one of them and stole her golden bowl. His people followed this bad example and the maidens never again came out of the grottoes to revive wanderers. From that time on the land went to waste. The trees lost their leaves, grass and flowers withered, and the water receded more and more. "And since then the court of the Rich Fisher which made the land to shine with gold and silver, with furs and precious stuffs, with foods of all kinds, with falcons, hawks and sparrow-hawks, could no longer be found. In those days when the court could still be found, there were riches and abundance everywhere. But now all these were lost to the Land of Logres."[54]

[51] Cf. *Psychological Types*, pp. 292–93.

[52] The author is not known. It is quite certainly not Chrétien, for he must, in any case, have been acquainted with Wauchier's Continuation, if he was not Wauchier himself.

[53] *Puis* can mean either.

[54] The devastation of the Land of Logres also had a historical basis in the above-mentioned story of King Cadwallader, related in the *Historia regum Britanniae.*

In King Arthur's time, when his knights heard these stories they took upon themselves the duty of finding those *puis* again and of protecting the maidens who dwelt within them. They also swore vengeance on the descendants of the villain who had insulted them. They gave alms and prayed that God might re-establish the *puis*, but however much they searched, they heard no voices and saw no maidens coming forth. But they did find something strange instead. In the forest they often met beautiful damsels under the escort of well-armed knights, with whom they fought for possession of the maidens. In this way King Arthur lost many brave knights, but he also won many. The first of the captured knights was called Bliho Bliheris, who knew so well how to tell a tale.[55] When questioned about the Fisher King's court and about the maidens riding through the forest, he said that they, as well as their escorting knights, were descended from the *demoiselles des puis* who had been wronged by King Amangons and his people. Amends could never be made for the resultant injury. Like Arthur's knights, who desired above all things to find those *puis* again, these knights too rode through forest and plain with their ladies, seeking the court of the Rich Fisher from which had emanated joy and lustre. Unheard of adventures befell those who sought the vanished court (these were the "*enchantements du pays de Logres*"). In King Arthur's time Sir Gauvain found the court of the Fisher King, who was learned in magic and could take on a hundred different forms. It was recounted how the land began to grow green again when Gauvain asked the question about the lance. But even before that it had been found by a young boy, who had not his equal in the whole world. This youth had then come to the Round Table. At first he was considered foolish and uncouth, but later he won great esteem and searched long in the whole land until he finally found the court. This was the Welsh Perceval. Any number of such and similar stories, in which fairies or elves give hospitality to men or else marry them,

[55] The hypothetical original form of the story is attributed to this singer and poet, Bliho Bliheris or Bleho Bléheris. Cf. Marx, *Légende Arthurienne*, p. 56.

still live on to this day in Irish and Welsh tradition. J. Rhys[56] informs us that the descendants of such unions are called *Pellinge* (ostensibly because one such fairy was called Pell or Penelope) and that in Wales, as late as the nineteenth century, people maintained that they had known such families. Of interest is the similarity between the designation "Pellinge" and the name Pelles or Pellam, borne by the Fisher King in a few versions, which in its turn, suggests the name of the Welsh god of the underworld, Pwyll.

According to these stories, the destruction of the Land of Logres was caused by the violation of these fairy maidens and the theft of the bowl. Thus, a wrong against a feminine being and a plundering of nature were perpetrated. It is interesting and remarkable that the origin of the trouble was looked upon as an offence committed against the fairy world, i.e. actually against nature. The motif of the plundering of the fairy world appears in numerous legends and fairy-tales, such as the legends of the Swan Maidens and the Rheingold. It is always a question of something either unlawfully won from, or done to, nature which results in a curse. Although he stole from the upper and not the nether gods, Prometheus' theft of fire certainly belongs here, as does the eating of the forbidden fruit in Paradise.

The fairies and maidens in the hills do not so much personify evil in feminine form as they do a purely natural aspect of the anima. They are, as it were, the soul of the spring or tree or place and, equally, what man feels psychically in such places. In the passage under consideration, this aspect of the anima is known to have been injured in the past, and because of this misfortune has befallen the land. The growth of masculine consciousness and of the patriarchal logos principle of the Christian outlook are concerned in no small measure with this development. They have certainly made possible that emancipation of the human mind which has given man mastery over nature. That which has been stolen from nature must, at the

[56] *The Arthurian Legend* and *Celtic Folklore, passim.* Cf. also Eithne O'Sharkey, *op. cit.*, p. 420, who sees the Grail King as the ruler of an earthly paradise, like Enoch or Elizeus.

same time, however, be understood as something "torn from the unconscious." Looked at from the point of view of the unconscious, becoming conscious clearly appears as guilt, a genuinely tragic offence, since it is only in this way that man can become what he has to be. But a deadening and violation of nature, which imply a tremendous loss of soul, have gradually resulted from the achievement of consciousness effected by Christianity.[57] The feminine symbol of the Grail, and its meaning, point to a compensation originating in the unconscious, by means of which the feminine and the soul of nature may once again achieve recognition.

In view of all this, it is not surprising that the moon, as a symbol of feminine consciousness and of the anima, should be connected with the suffering of the Grail King. In Wolfram, along with the moon's cycle, Saturn also plays a part in his suffering, especially

dô der Sterne Saturnus
wider an sin zil gestuont

—when the planet has completed its revolution—which is noticeable in the wound and is marked by snow in summer. Then the King's agony becomes intolerable and, in order to alleviate it, the spear is held in the wound from time to time:

da half ein nôt für andern nôt
Dez wart daz sper bluotec rôt.

The one trouble was helpful for the other,
therefore the spear was red with blood.[58]

The connection with Saturn is highly significant, since in the astrology of antiquity, Saturn was considered to be the star of Israel and of the Old Testament Yahweh.[59] In the medieval view, however, Saturn was thought to be the domicile of the

[57] Cf. Emma Jung, "The Anima as an Elemental Being," in *Animus and Anima*, pp. 62*ff*.

[58] Book IX, verse 9, 711.

[59] *Aion*, par. 128.

Devil.[60] He was depicted as lion-headed, like the demiurge Ialdabaoth of certain Gnostic systems, and was considered to be a "black star" and an evildoer, to whom belonged donkeys, dragons, scorpions, vipers, foxes, cats, mice, night birds and other devilish creatures.[61] While Christianity, according to medieval tradition, originated in a conjunction of Jupiter, the kingly planet, and Mercury, the Judaic religion was under the domination of Jupiter and Saturn, and the Antichrist under that of Jupiter and the moon.

In antiquity, the ass, which was considered to be particularly lustful, was sacred to Saturn, who for that reason was also venerated as the god of fertility. Psychologically he is connected with the demon of sexuality in which the shadow and the dark and animal side of the divine are especially conspicuous. This dark background to Eros was, however, very largely repressed by Christian man[62] and for that reason, has turned into a dangerous opponent. This also explains the relation of Saturn, inimical to the King, to the destructive or impaired feminine principle of nature, as shown in the above-mentioned versions. It is the same world of chthonic instinctuality, of ecstasy and its wisdom, which is embodied in these various figures and which bears the blame for the suffering of the Grail King.

The conjunction of moon and Saturn (both planets have a share in the King's suffering) signifies, according to Albumasar, "doubt and revolution and change." [63] Here Saturn is clearly related to the dark aspect of divinity. Indeed, according to certain views, Christianity is also ruled by Jupiter and Saturn,

[60] Richard Reitzenstein, *Poimandres*, p. 76; and Jung, *ibid.*

[61] Cf. A. Bouché-Leclerq, *L'Astrologie Grecque*, p. 93. In antiquity Saturn was called "the old man." Also cf. *Aion*, par. 129. Cf. also the Spanish sources which Herbert Kolb, *op. cit.*, pp. 154*f*, mentions which show that such ideas were known in Spain, especially in Toledo, from where Wolfram's Kyot might have picked them up. For Wolfram's astrological knowledge, see Deinert, *Ritter und Kosmos im Parzival.*

[62] Concerning the sexual nature of the injury, cf. Weston and also Marx, *Légende Arthurienne*, pp. 181 and 191–93. In Wolfram it is the king's absent-mindedness, caused by sexual desire, that administers the *coup douloureux.* Cf. Clovis Brunel, "Les 'hanches' du Rois Pêcheur," p. 37.

[63] See *Aion*, par. 130, note 35.

for which reason the Christian aeon has been characterized from the very beginning by a combination of the most extreme opposites.[64] These antitheses are personified in the figures of Christ and Antichrist. It is therefore significant and obvious that in so far as the Grail King represents Christian man, he should have been injured precisely by Saturn, the malefic spirit opposed to Christianity.

In a remarkable way, the Grail King himself seems at times to change places with Saturn. In the adventures of Gauvain, which in many respects follow the same course as the Perceval story, Gauvain comes to a castle that in many ways matches the Grail Castle, even to the extent of appearing to be identified with it in many versions. Beside the steps leading up to this magic stronghold a man is sitting on a bundle of gladioli. He has a wooden leg, inlaid with gold and silver and set with precious stones, and is whittling an ash staff with a small knife.[65] He takes no notice of the entering hero and his guide, nor do they address him. "That man with the wooden leg is very rich," whispers the guide to Gauvain, "and you would certainly have to hear some unpleasant things were I not escorting you." The owner of the wooden leg is apparently the builder of the miraculous castle, an astrologer. He corresponds to Clinschor in Wolfram's *Parzival* and to Gansguoter[66] in Heinrich von dem Thuerlin's *Diû Krône*. He appears as an ill-omened parallel to the Fisher King, who is also occasionally called *le riche roi méhaigné* (the rich maimed king).

His wooden leg marks this uncanny figure as a personification of Saturn who, in medieval illustrations, is often depicted as having a wooden leg.[67] Everything that has so far been said to

[64] *Ibid.*, par. 130.

[65] It is possible that this figure was created owing to a confusion on Chrétien's part between the words *eschaquier* or *eschac* (chessboard) and *eschacier* (man with a crutch); see Loomis, *Arthurian Tradition*, pp. 445*ff*. This shows how an unconscious conflict can be projected into any possible motif.

[66] Cf. Hilka, p. 757. According to other romances this classic doorkeeper carries a gilded lump of silver. He is therefore most certainly an alchemist.

[67] Cf. *Psychology and Alchemy*, Fig. 223.

characterize Saturn, the perpetrator of the King's injury, must now also be applied to the King. He is here portrayed as being himself the *sol niger* of the alchemists, as the dark shadow of the principle of consciousness[68] or as that obscurely and imperceptibly negative element which participates in the apparently clear and light nature of consciousness. However, in so far as the sun is traditionally a god-image,[69] Saturn also represents an aspect, present although unrecognized, of the god-image dominant in man's consciousness. From this aspect emanate dangerous influences.[70]

The gladioli, on which the man with the wooden leg sits, point, however, in a different direction from that of Saturn, since the iris, as explained by M. Ninck,[71] is one of Wotan's symbols—of the love engendered by him and of German kingship. It could accordingly be suggested that this paradoxically dark aspect of the highest Germanic god is also involved in the action. It is at the same time both mysterious and meaningful that the magician should have been cutting precisely an ash stick when Gauvain meets him, for ash is *the* wood above all for Germanic spears, and the Grail King was struck by the spear of a treacherous opponent, sometimes described as invisible. In a mysterious sense the wounded and the wounder are one, and because medieval man did not understand the unconscious impulse implied by the spear-thrust, the dark daimon now cuts away at another spear. This produces the effect of an uncanny premonition of that devastating spear-thrust that Wotan has inflicted on the Christian humanity of today.

Since we shall return later to this aspect of the dark, Clinschor type of magician, when discussing the figure of Merlin, we will not go further into the matter now except in its relation to the wounded Grail King.

It is not always either the feminine principle or Saturn that

[68] Cf. *Mysterium Coniunctionis*, par. 113.

[69] *Ibid.*, par. 130.

[70] According to Mergell, p. 115, St. Bernard of Clairvaux calls God himself a fisherman (*piscator*).

[71] *Wodan und germanischer Schiksalsglaube*, p. 222–23.

hovers behind the King's injury. On the contrary, many other causes are given in the versions that remain to be mentioned. In the Continuation to the *Perceval*, for instance, the King was wounded by a fragment of the ill-omened sword with which his brother was treacherously murdered. A similar story, which certainly contains points worth noting, is told in the "Merlin." There (as in Wauchier) a knight, in the company of another knight named Balain, is mysteriously murdered. The murderer is Garlan, a brother of the Grail King, who rides around in a state of invisibility and kills his victims with an invisible lance. In order to have his revenge, Balain seeks out the court of King Pellehan, as he is here called, where Garlan, who is only invisible on horseback, is serving at table. Balain reproaches him with his treachery and kills him, whereupon great tumult breaks out. The King desires to avenge his brother, and at the same time Balain's sword breaks. Balain hurries from room to room, pursued by King Pellehan.

> Finally he came to a sumptuously furnished apartment, where stood a bed covered in cloth of gold, in which someone lay. By the bed stood a table of pure gold, supported on four silver feet, on which there was a wondrous lance of extraordinary workmanship. The weaponless Balain quickly seized this lance and with it wounded the pursuing Pellehan, who sank unconscious to the floor. At the same moment the castle collapsed with a deafening crash and Balain lost consciousness.[72]

Merlin had prophesied to Balain that he would inflict the *coup douloureux* as a result of which three kingdoms would be laid waste for a period of twelve years and their populations deported.[73] Malory then adds:

> The lance with which Sir Balain struck King Pellehan was the lance which had pierced the body of Jesus as He hung

[72] Paris and Ulrich, *Merlin*, Vol. II, pp. 27–28. Cf. also Malory, *Le Morte d'Arthur*, II, Ch. XV–XVI.

[73] Cf. *Merlin*, Vol. I, p. 321.

> from the Cross: it had been brought to Britain by Joseph of Arimathea, whose corpse it had been that lay on the bed, and from whose kin King Pellehan was descended. . . . King Pellehan's wound remained open until Sir Galahad, many years later, cured him.

This tale throws a strange light on the otherwise obscure sequence of events. In the *Livre du Saint Graal*,[74] two kingdoms, known as *tière gaste* (wasteland), were plunged into misery and laid waste as a result of the murder of Lambor, the Grail King, by Varlan. This had been prophesied by Joseph of Arimathea:[75] "An outstanding King, by the name of Arthur, will one day reign in a country called Britain. At that time, as the result of the blow of a single sword, such great and wonderful adventures will take place in that land, that the whole world will be amazed by them. These will endure for four and twenty years."[76]

In the "Merlin," the King wishes to avenge his invisible and sinister brother. He therefore tries to stand up for his shadow and is wounded in the process. In some mysterious way, he has thus become identical with the demonic powers. The conclusion is reached that on the one hand, the Grail King is a Christian man who has been wounded by a dark adversary, while on the other, he has become this dark opponent and now appears demonic himself. When consciousness is incapable either of grasping or knowingly integrating a spontaneously emerging impulse (the lance) or content (the enemy who throws it), the individual will instead be unconsciously possessed by it. This explains the demonic nature of the wounded King, hinted at in many versions, which is also expressed in his role of "Lord of the Fairies and Magicians." At the same time it should not be overlooked that in Germanic mythology, Wotan is the Lord of

[74] Hucher, III, p. 294.

[75] *Ibid.*, p. 160.

[76] In the *Queste du Saint Graal* the wounding of King Pelles, as he is there called, is the result of his boarding "Solomon's ship," which has drawn in to the coast across from Ireland, and drawing the sword of David, which is kept on the ship. As a consequence he is wounded in both hips by a lance, and cannot be healed until the coming of Galahad.

Love and of all swan maidens and water nixies.[77] He is a dark "father of the anima," i.e. a spirit that rules over the world of Eros and seeks his positive and negative expression in ecstasy, demonism and the dark compulsiveness of the instincts. This dark spirit of nature, standing in opposition to the one-sidedness of Christianity, has assailed and crippled the Grail King.

The nature of the injury is also revealing; it is a wound in the region of the hips, which is taken by many to indicate an injury to the King's sexuality. This suggests the motif of Jacob's struggle with the dark angel at the ford, during which his thigh is thrown out of joint.[78] At this place of crucial passage, Jacob is attacked by a dark figure, who seems at first to be his shadow brother Esau but is subsequently revealed as a dark aspect of Yahweh himself. Jacob defends himself hand to hand, whereas his later spiritual brother, Job, vindicates himself more through his straightforward loyalty and consciousness.[79] In a later continuation of the same motif it is Joseph of Arimathea who is wounded by a *black angel*. This assault by the dark aspect of God against a chosen human being who is called upon to grapple with the dark divinity and at the same time to serve as a vessel for the realization of the totality of God[80] is therefore an ever-recurring motif in the history of Judeo-Christian religious consciousness.[81] Perceval's father and the Grail King are both overtaken by this fate without being able, however, to master the problem. For this reason the question is posed anew to Perceval.

The motif of the one-legged king is also found in alchemy. Albertus Magnus once described the stone as *monocolus* (uniped—having one foot).[82] The same motif appears in an alchemical codex of Abraham the Jew, in which the figures of *two* one-footed kings are depicted bound together like Siamese twins.[83]

[77] Cf. Ninck, *op. cit.*, pp. 140 and 221*ff.*

[78] Concerning the parallel themes in the stories of the Fisher King and of Jacob, see Holmes and Klenke, *op. cit.*, pp. 103 and 201. Also cf. *Symbols of Transformation*, par. 524.

[79] Cf. "Answer to Job," in *Psychology and Religion*, pars. 638–42.

[80] Reference must be made to "Answer to Job" here.

[81] The Germanic parallel to this archetype is the fate of Baldur.

[82] Cf. *Mysterium Coniunctionis*, pars. 720*ff.*

[83] *Ibid.*

From the inscription it is clear that the reference is to the duality in unity of Mercurius and to the coming into consciousness of the opposites. As Jung says, the one figure "is the mirror-image of the other. This indicates a relationship of complementarity between *physis* and spirit, so that the one reflects the other."[84] Following the discrimination of the opposites, which results from the "dark night of the soul", a reunification of the opposing elements takes place in alchemy, in the image of the *coniunctio* of King and Queen.[85] This one-footed man of the Grail story, on the other hand, represents the King's shadow which is still cut off (being likewise wounded in the leg), that other half whose place in alchemy is taken by the Queen.

To sum up, it can be said that the Grail King accordingly personifies the principle of Christian consciousness confronted with the problem of *physis* and of evil. It is as if the dark aspect of divinity had attacked him in order to awaken him to a more conscious religious attitude. But he cannot himself solve the problem within the structure of the outlook he personifies. He therefore has to await a successor who shall free him. His condition is analogous to that of the alchemical Rex as he is described in the "Aurelia occulta", for instance. There he says:

> I am an infirm and weak old man, surnamed the dragon; therefore am I shut up in a cave, that I may be ransomed by the kingly crown. . . . A fiery sword inflicts great torments upon me; death makes weak my flesh and bones. . . . My soul and my spirit depart; a terrible poison, I am likened to the black raven, for that is the wages of sin; in dust and earth I lie, that out of Three may come One. O soul and spirit, leave me not, that I may see again the light of day, and the hero of peace whom the whole world shall behold may arise from me.[86]

This champion of peace is the alchemical stone with which, in the Grail legend, Perceval is equated.

[84] Cf. *Mysterium Coniunctionis*, par. 722. [85] *Ibid.*, par. 724.

[86] *Theatrum chemicum*, IV, pp. 569*f*, quoted by Jung, *ibid.*, par. 733. Cf. also Jung's elucidation of the motif of the ailing Grail King, *ibid.*, par. 375.

CHAPTER XII

The Figure of Gauvain; Perceval's Return to Christianity

WHILE PERCEVAL IS lost in reflection about the Grail King and his suffering, the story turns to Gauvain, who represents a sort of double to Perceval. In many versions, *Diû Krône* for instance, Gauvain is the real Grail hero, while in the Continuation he is in the forefront to such an extent that many competent judges[1] advocate the view that he was really the original hero and that only later, owing to the Christianization of the story, was he supplanted by Perceval, as the latter, in his turn, was subsequently replaced by Galahad. This, however, does not seem likely. On the other hand, one is struck by the way the two heroes in our poem proceed along parallel paths, in the course of which Gauvain exhibits certain more archaic features, for instance the peculiarity that, according to some versions, his strength waxes from midnight to midday and thereafter wanes, a motif that marks him as a sun hero.[2]

The two protagonists represent a classical pair of heroes, who may be compared with Gilgamesh and his dark brother, Enkidu, or with Castor and Pollux, Odysseus and Ajax, Mithras and Sol, or with those heroes who were always accompanied by a servant, such as Moses and Joshua ben Nun, Elijah

[1] Weston, *The Legend of Sir Perceval*, Vol. I, p. 249. According to the view advanced in Vol. II, p. 201, the probable author of the original version was a certain Bleheris from Wales.

[2] Cf. Kampers, *op. cit.*, p. 40; E. Wechssler, *op. cit.*, p. 137; and Marx, *La Légende Arthurienne et le Graal*, pp. 66–67. Also cf. Loomis, *Celtic Mythology*, pp. 39–40. The name derives either from *Gwalchmei* (falcon) or possibly from *Gwallt A(d)vwyn* ("he with the beautiful hair"), Marx, p. 67, footnote 2.

and Elisha, and many others. In his work, *Die Gestalt des sterbenden Messias*,[3] S. Hurwitz has explained this motif of the dual hero or redeemer in greater detail[4] and has quoted many more examples. According to Jung the doubling of a motif usually indicates that a content is just stirring on the threshold of consciousness.[5] The doubling of the heroes in the Grail legend might therefore be an assertion that a new image of the redeemer and hero is being constellated. His state of being one thing rather than another has not yet, however, been fully determined. Compared with the above-mentioned pairs, Gauvain would represent Perceval's shadow brother, since he is not so successful as the latter in the solution of the task. In Wolfram, Gawan (Gauvain) actually depicts a kind of preliminary stage of Parzival himself. He is "only" the perfect Christian knight, whereas Parzival acts in a far more human manner. He also wrestles individually with the religious problem. Thus, he is characterized as a hero who strives spiritually in order to achieve a wider development of consciousness, whereas Gawan proceeds along paths already firmly established. In Chrétien there is no evaluation of the two figures, who instead complete each other, as is also indicated in Wolfram.

In contrast to Gauvain's role of the shadow brother, it now seems that it is precisely *he* who is the sun hero and who should therefore be equated with Gilgamesh—if we compare the Grail legend with the Babylonian epic—rather than with his shadow brother Enkidu. But when we consider the curious enantiodromia that, from the year 1000 on, tended to reassess all Christian contents, it appears to be quite meaningful that it should be the sun hero (embodying the principle of collective consciousness still dominant in the first half of the fish aeon, as it had been in the pagan world) who should have been repressed into the shadow, while the earthy, natural, mortal Anthropos, of the Enkidu or Pollux type, should, conversely, be raised up to the place of the highest guiding principle. In Wolfram's version,

[3] *Studien aus dem C. G. Jung Institut*, Vol. VIII.

[4] Especially pp. 208*ff*.

[5] Jung, *Kindertraumseminar*, p. 72.

the two fight together,[6] without recognizing each other, and after the encounter Parzival calls out:

"*Ich hân mich selber überstritten.*"

"I have been fighting against myself."

And Gawan replies:

"*Du hast dir selber an gesiget.*"

"Thou hast conquered thyself."[7]

Accordingly, Gauvain probably represents an outgrown aspect of Perceval himself, very likely the one-sidedness of consciousness so clearly shown in his early history, his naïve ideal of chivalry that caused him to offend against the feminine principle, an offence of which he is now gradually becoming aware. It is a very remarkable fact that just at the time of the high flowering of chivalry, a hero (Perceval), whose most essential characteristics were a spiritual search and an undoubted lack of certainty, amounting even to a burden of guilt, should take the stage alongside the perfect Christian knights (Gauvain, Galahad) as the most important figure in the Grail legend. A higher value is placed on the more human hero than on the conventional noble knight, for to be able to doubt oneself, to grope one's lonely way, step by uncertain step, appears to represent a higher achievement of consciousness than naïvely to follow collective ideals. The Christian attitude of mind, with its one-sided emphasis on the struggle for good, exposes a person to the risk of a certain aggressive pride that comes clearly to the fore in Gauvain, in contrast to which Perceval's uncertainty strikes modern man as being far more sympathetic and understandable.

Gauvain belongs to King Arthur's circle of knights, to which Perceval is admitted before his experience in the Grail Castle and to which he returns after his banishment from the Grail

[6] This is comparable to the struggle between Gilgamesh and Enkidu in the Gilgamesh epic, before the two were reconciled and set out on their adventures together.

[7] Book 14, verse 305.

realm. The part played by Arthur's Round Table in comparison with the Grail Kingdom thus gradually becomes clearer. The circle of knights around Arthur mirrors the symbol of the Self as it was manifested in the first half of the Christian age, an image in which the light, spiritual, masculine aspect of Logos predominated one-sidedly and whose vital expansion served the civilizing purpose of overcoming pagan and animal primitivity. Arthur's knights, in particular, devoted themselves to this task. At this stage, the problem of the shadow, of the individual inner opposite, is not yet constellated but is still projected outwardly on to the barbarian opponents who must be overcome. Only when "the time was fulfilled" and the second half of the fish aeon had begun was the problem of the darkness in the inner life of the individual constellated. This is the reason for the Grail King being wounded by an *invisible enemy*, as it is also the reason that it is no longer Gauvain, the Christian knight, in the sense of the Arthurian circle, who is the greatest hero, but Perceval, the guilty one who, however, in contradistinction to the others, reflects upon the problem of the Grail.

In any event, Perceval returns to Arthur's circle which, psychologically speaking, corresponds to a regression. It is as if he had encountered the Grail problem too soon; furthermore, the cultural task of the Christian ideal had not yet been completed, and it was necessary that it first be fulfilled. For this reason, it is precisely Gauvain, the exclusively Christian knight, fighting unreflectingly for what is recognized to be right, who appears just at this moment, while Perceval is seeking the "lost God" and his own soul. The contrast between Perceval and Gauvain may also be considered as the contrast between introversion and extraversion. The stories centring round Gauvain are concerned only with an uninterrupted chain of outer actions. However, as soon as the hero is obliged to experience something concerning the fate of the Grail Kingdom, he quite characteristically falls asleep. Perceval, on the other hand, reflects on his experience again and again. *His* way is one of inner realization, even if he does temporarily regress to the outer life in the adventures of Arthur's circle.

Since Gauvain personifies a shadow aspect of Perceval, it is necessary to go briefly into his adventures, at least in so far as they are connected with the Grail, even though this complicates the presentation and draws it out somewhat.

When they receive the Loathly Damsel's challenge, Gauvain and fifty knights are arming themselves for the march. Suddenly, a strange knight enters at the door. He turns to Gauvain, reproaching him with having attacked and wounded his lord without previous provocation, for which reason he accuses him of treachery. Gauvain naturally disputes this, but wishes none the less to follow his accuser, who is called Guingambresil, and to justify himself by fighting him in single combat in the presence of the King of Escavalon. When he wishes to present himself for the fight, he arrives, without knowing it, at Guingambresil's stronghold. The male inhabitants are out hunting and his opponent's unsuspecting sister receives him in the friendliest manner. The two find much favour in each other's eyes. However, a suspicious serving man surprises them at their *tête-à-tête* and accuses Gauvain, whom he recognizes, of having killed the girl's father. The local inhabitants storm the castle. Gauvain and the damsel have only a chessboard and chessmen at hand with which to hold off the attackers. At this moment, fortunately, Guingambresil returns from the chase, with the King of Escavalon. They deplore the violation of the laws of hospitality by the burghers. Accordingly, they decide to postpone the contest for a year, during which time Gauvain is to go in search of the bleeding lance, "the lance by which it is said that one day the Kingdom of Logres will be destroyed," and deliver it to the King. In the event that he does return with it, the dispute will be settled then and there. In this way Gauvain sets out on a quest that tallies exactly with Perceval's, since the lance and the Grail are kept in the same place. These two objects of their respective searches would appear to confirm the above interpretation of the two heroes. Gauvain, the Christian knight, must seek the masculine symbol, the lance, that will destroy the kingdom; he therefore has to track down the enemy's dark hiding place. Perceval, on the other hand, is searching for the feminine, containing vessel or stone, i.e. a symbol of totality which transcends the problem of the opposites and thus succeeds in uniting them. Gauvain's adventures in Guingambresil's castle are only the first of a long succession of adventures with women. In this matter, too, he is set in opposition to Perceval, since the latter, as the son of the widow, is by nature closer to the feminine and less in need of a personal confrontation with it than is Gauvain, who will have to serve the "mother" and women for a long time to come. His act of freeing the women in the Castle of Marvels, where they are held prisoner by a magician, clearly forms a parallel to the deliverance of the Grail realm and in this light, becomes understandable.

A man naturally has the tendency to identify with his masculinity, and, as is well known, the acceptance of his feminine side is a severe problem for him. He is therefore inclined to act unjustly towards the feminine. It may indeed seem strange that special emphasis should be laid on wronging the feminine element just at that time when such a high value was being attributed to woman in the *Minnedienst*. It must not be overlooked, however, that woman was only loved externally; the manly ideal was always that of a one-sided and absolute masculinity. We can also see, in the further course of historical development, how fitting was such an admonition to redeem the feminine, for the age of the honouring of women, which did not last very long, was followed by the persecution of witches. The *Minne* was therefore turned into its opposite, and woman was stigmatized as the Devil. During the Reformation, her image was even expelled from the Church,[8] with the result, ever more clearly shown, that life has increasingly vanished from Protestantism. Another phenomenon that set in approximately with the Reformation, and which could not easily be reconciled with a cult of woman or of nature, was the scientific attitude, which undoubtedly gave its stamp to the whole modern age. If it is desired to unveil nature, then reverence must step aside, because it produces emotional restraints that are not very

[8] Owing to the repudiation of the cult of the Virgin. Cf. *Psychological Types*, p. 310.

serviceable to this purpose.[9] Our age is not one of respect for nature but rather one of nature's domination or even spoliation. But there, too, in the increasing use of technique and mechanization, something similar to Protestantism is becoming evident, that is, the loss of soul by which mechanization is accomplished. It is therefore high time that a little attention should again be accorded the psyche.

The chessboard with which Gauvain and his beloved defend themselves is an ingenious motif, for in chess, a game that requires the most concentrated attention, two sides, black and white, confront each other, and a well-nigh all powerful queen stands beside a somewhat helpless yet nonetheless vitally important king. All of these symbols, objects and psychic functions are elements to which Gauvain, the knight, must still submit himself for the sake of his further development, while Perceval, his shadow figure, is trying to investigate more profound problems, though it is true he is scarcely at home with them yet.

The story now returns to Perceval, who has been wandering about for five long years. *During this time he has completely lost all remembrance of God* and has never once entered a church. He only looks for knightly deeds and curious adventures, of which he finds so many that he is able to send Arthur sixty conquered knights as prisoners.

One day on his wanderings, he meets three knights with their ladies, all on foot and wearing penitential, garments. The company is amazed that Perceval should be strolling around armed on the holy day of Good Friday. Does he not know that on this day one should carry no arms? The knights and ladies have just come from a hermit, to whom they made their confessions and from whom they received absolution. On hearing this, Perceval weeps and desires to go to the holy man too. They

[9] It is interesting, all the same, as Linda Fierz-David points out in *The Dream of Poliphilo*, that there it is the anima who, by becoming objective and to the point, proclaims or prepares the way, so to speak, for the scientific attitude.

show him the way, which he takes, shedding tears of repentance. He finds the hermit in his chapel ready to celebrate Mass and is summoned by him to confession. For five years, he admits, he has quite forgotten God and done nothing but evil. When the hermit asks why, Perceval tells him that he once visited the Fisher King and there saw the bleeding lance and the Grail but did not ask about them. That omission has weighed so heavily on him that he has abandoned his faith in God, has thrust Him out of his mind. Altogether, he would have preferred to die. The hermit then asks to know his name and on hearing it says with a sigh:

> "Brother, a sin of which you are unconscious has done you this injury. Your mother died of grief when you left her. You are to blame for her death, and that is the reason you were unable to ask about the Grail and the lance. You would have met with many more troubles had not the departed offered up intercession for you. You were ill advised not to inquire where the Grail was being taken. He who is served from it is my brother; the Rich Fisher is his son, and your mother was our sister. (Perceval is therefore a cousin of the Grail King.) Do not imagine that perchance the Grail contains pike, lamprey or salmon, i.e. a fish. No, it is only by the Host that is brought to him in this Grail that the holy man maintains life!"

> "*Tante sainte chose est li graaus*
> *Et il est si esperitaus,*
> *Qu'a sa vie plus ne covient*
> *Que l'oiste qui el graal vient.*"

> "Such a thing is the Grail
> And so spiritual is the King
> That for his life nothing is fitting
> Save the Host that comes in the Grail."

For fifteen years the Fisher King has not left the room to which the Grail is brought.

After greeting Perceval as his nephew, the hermit grants him absolution and, as penance, advises him to go to a church and hear Mass every day. Thus can he once more attain to honour and finally be admitted to Paradise. He gives him further admonitions which Perceval promises to observe and before his departure teaches him a prayer as well, whispering it in his ear but forbidding him to say it except in moments of the greatest danger.

Et li hermites lo consoille
Une oreison dedanz l'oroille
Si li ferma tant qu'il la sot;
Et an cele oreison si ot
Assez des nons nostre Seignor,
Car il i furent li greignor
Que nomer ne doit boche d'ome,
Se por peor de mort des nome.
Quant l'oreison li ot aprise,
Desfendi li qu'an nule guise
Ne la deïst sanz grant peril
"*Non ferai je, Sire, fet-il.*"

And the hermit confided to him
A prayer within his ear
That he closed as soon as he heard it;
And in that lofty orison
Were so many names of Our Lord
That may not pass the lips of man
For fear of death from that name.
When he had taught him that prayer
He forbade him on any occasion
To say it except in great peril.
"I will not do so, Sir," said he.

After receiving Communion on Easter Day, Perceval sets out on his way once more.

In this section we learn that Perceval has lost his belief in God, which his mother had taught him, and once again he is reminded of her death. The death of the mother could therefore be interpreted symbolically as the "death of the soul,"[10] i.e. as *a total loss of contact with the unconscious.* But when the soul is dead, then "God is dead" too, since it is only in the vessel of the soul that God's activity becomes perceptible to man. Because he did not ask about the Grail, Perceval no longer understands himself and is cut off from the source of his own inner being. The hermit who helps him on his way therefore personifies a tendency towards introversion and towards a renunciation of the world as a first exercise preparatory to solving the Grail problem. In his religio-sociological study, "La Chrétienté et l'idée de la Croisade," A. Dupront explains how, at the time of the Crusades, the ideal of the forest hermit was revived once more.[11] In contrast to the clerics who had become worldly-minded, the hermit personified pure spirituality and all the popular eschatological and spiritual trends of the age, in which the coming of the Antichrist and the end of the world were awaited.

The hermit informs Perceval that the Grail does not contain fish[12] but the Host on which the King is fed. Thus, the Grail is presented as a purely symbolic vessel, providing spiritual, not physical, sustenance. It could be said that it plainly signifies a stage in the development of the human spirit, when man is no longer satisfied with the materialistic view or with the effectiveness of working things, but goes beyond this and endows the concrete with a symbolic meaning. Undoubtedly, natural man also recognizes the non-material properties of things. But to him they are not symbolic, they are magical, which means that they are practical and just as concrete as a real object. The ability to form symbolic concepts is something different and presupposes a somewhat higher degree of consciousness. By this achievement, an extremely important step on the path towards spiritual development is accomplished: the transition from the

[10] Regarding the image of the mother as a personification of the unconscious in a man, cf. *Aion*, pars. 20–42.

[11] Especially Vol. I, pp. 129 and 133.

[12] Cf. H. and R. Kahane, *op. cit.*, p. 341; and M. Plessner, "Hermes Trismegistus and Arabic Science," p. 45.

natural-magical to a spiritual or mystical *Weltanschauung*. Perceval now experiences this transition through the teaching of the hermit.

The difference between the magical and the mystical mentality may perhaps be characterized by the fact that in the magical attitude of mind the ego is very much to the fore, in the sense that either it is affected by unknown powers or else tries itself to work upon those powers. In any event, the aim of magic is for the ego to obtain mastery over these unknown forces and, through them, over men and things. The mystical attitude, on the other hand, sets no store by the ego but strives to reach above and beyond it and even reaches its own culmination in the ego's dissolution. It might possibly be said, therefore, that the magical attitude of mind corresponds to a level of development or of consciousness in which the ego is not yet sufficiently conscious or consolidated, for which reason it has to be forcefully emphasized.

It often happens that people who behave in a markedly egocentric way are basically in constant danger of being absorbed by other people or situations, so that in such cases the egocentricity may be looked upon as a kind of bulwark against this tendency. It is of course essential that an ego should be present, otherwise there could be neither growth of consciousness nor any other spiritual development, and even a self is not thinkable without the preliminary stage of the ego. The mystical attitude, on the other hand, accords with a stage or phase in which the ego is already sufficiently consolidated and in which the task of reaching out beyond the ego to an "other self" or to something lying beyond. It is not a question, then, of a stage of development reached by mankind or a nation for all time; in single instances this gradual transition can also still take place in the life of the individual today. Moreover, the two phases often subsist side by side in a complementary relationship. By and large, it can well be said that the nature religions, or even pagan antiquity, exhibit more of a magico-egotistical character, while Christianity, with its otherworldly orientation, corresponds to the mystical outlook. A union of these two attitudes is to be found in alchemy where, on a higher level, the two aspects of archaic magic and purely spiritual mysticism are reunited. Among Western peoples, the change-over from the more concretistic to the more spiritual type of thinking became clearly noticeable from about the time of Charlemagne and led, from the twelfth to the fourteenth centuries, to a golden age of mysticism.

An early representative of the spiritual symbolic attitude of mind was John Scotus Erigena (about 877), who wrote about the Eucharist at the behest of King Charles the Bald (823–877), Roman emperor and King of the West Franks, and who advocated the view that it was not a concrete but a symbolic body that inhered in the Sacrament and that influenced the feelings of the spirit in a mystical way.[13] This view was, however, condemned as heretical. Ratramus, a monk of Corbie, wrote his famous work, *De corpore et sanguine Domini*, at the request of the same monarch. "Your Highness desires to know," he thus addresses the King, "whether that which the mouth of the believer receives in church becomes the flesh and blood of Christ in reality, or *in mysterio*, that is, in a mystical manner."[14]

In his exposition Ratramus says: "It is Christ's body, but not corporeal, but spiritual, and it is Christ's blood, but not corporeal, but spiritual. For which reason nothing here is to be understood in a corporeal sense, but in a spiritual one."[15]

Another passage reads: "That which is seen is not the same as

[13] MacDonald, *Berengar and the Reform of Sacramental Doctrine*, Ch. III.

[14] Migne, *Pat. Lat.*, Vol. CXXI, Ch. LVI: "Quod in ecclesia ore fidelium sumitur, corpus et sanguis Christi quaerit vestrae magnitudinis excellentia, in mysterio fiat aut in veritate."

[15] "Est quidem corpus Christi sed non corporale, sed spirituale, et sanguis Christi, sed non corporalis, sed spiritualis. Nihil igitur hic corporaliter sentiendum: sed spirituale."

"Non idem sunt quod cernuntur et quod creduntur. Secundum enim quod cernuntur, corpus pascunt corruptibile, ipsa corruptibilia, secundum verum quod creduntur animas pascunt in aeternum victura ipsa immortalia."

"Ex his omnibus quae sunt hactenus dicta monstratum est, quod corpus et sanguis Christi quae fidelium ore in ecclesia percipiuntur, figurae sunt secundum speciem visibilem; at vero secundum invisibilem substantiam, id est divini potentiam Verbi, vere Corpus et Sanguis Christi existunt."

what it is thought to be. What is seen feeds the perishable body and is itself perishable; but what is believed feeds the immortal soul and is itself immortal." And further: "From what has been said it follows that the body and blood of Christ, which the mouth of the believer receives in church, are images in a visible form: in their invisible substance, i.e. in the power of the divine word, they are, however, in very truth, the body and blood of Christ."[16]

A particularly famous supporter of this doctrine was Berengar of Tours (first half of the eleventh century), whose views occasioned the dispute known as the Second Eucharistic Controversy. Berengar taught that the body and blood of the Lord were not "real" in the Eucharist but a specific image or likeness ("*figuram quandam similitudinem*"). He was thus a forerunner of the Reformers, especially of Zwingli. His views were most strongly opposed and anathematized by the Church. The controversy was protracted over many years and raised a great storm, especially in France. In connection with this dispute, the problem of the conception of the Eucharist was again brought into the light of day (books were written about it), and miracles that had occurred in relation to the Eucharist were reported, such as the one at Fécamp, already mentioned, where bread and wine were said to have been transformed into real flesh and blood under the hand of the priest.

It is perfectly possible that the Grail stories also contain echoes of this long-drawn-out dispute. The transition mentioned above points clearly in this direction, in that at one moment the Grail is a wonderful, magically operating object (stone vessel), supplying real food as desired, while in other versions it is a symbolic object from which emanates not material food but spiritual-psychic effects.

Perceval's turning to the Christian hermit may accordingly be understood as a step away from egoistic chivalry, in the direction of a greater spirituality, and thus as a first step towards a fresh approach to that which was seen in the Grail Castle. It so happened historically, too, that the mysticism of the high

[16] Cf. *The Archetypes and the Collective Unconscious*, par. 28.

Middle Ages, with its intensification and animation of the Christian symbol, was chiefly developed out of the spiritual movements that emerged in the second half of the fish aeon, around the year 1000. This mysticism survived in various forms of Protestantism averse to the secular representation of religious contents. One result of consistently living this trend to the utmost has been, as Jung explains, a complete "spiritual poverty," a renunciation of all visible symbols and an unconditioned turning inward of the individual to the depths of his own soul, to the unconscious. Contemporary man has reached this point, always supposing that he has not taken the demonic path of materialistic, totalitarian "isms" instead, thus choosing to stagnate in that condition of Perceval's in which he has lost God and is senselessly striking at a shadow outwardly projected on to an "opponent". It also turns out that the hermit is a brother of Perceval's mother and of the rich Fisher's father. In a matriarchal order of society, the mother's brother is granted the standing of a godfather. Psychologically he is a representative of the mother's animus and thus portrays that spiritual destiny which Perceval received from his mother and which predestines him to become the Guardian of the Grail.

Thus, after Perceval, owing mainly to the failure of this task, has returned to the naïve knightly ideal of Arthur's Round Table, a return which, as already indicated, must be interpreted as a regression, he once again finds the connection to the intensified spiritual tradition in Christianity, to that spirit which animated a Joachim of Floris or, in the mendicant orders, a Francis of Assisi. In this spirit it is possible to discern a certain relationship to the modern psychology of the unconscious, in so far as in the one case the highest value is attributed to the spontaneous life of the soul, with its dreams and visions, and in the other to the meaning of the experiencing individual (in contrast to the collectivism of the religious orders). The question of the origin and reality of evil and of the dark side of God, a problem with which our age is ever more inexorably faced, is not yet solved by this means. Thus, when the hermit stresses that the Grail does not contain fish but only the Host, it is meaningful for Perceval, but we know today that it was precisely a fish for which the King was longing and that his spiritualized nourishment from the Grail was *not* healing his wound. Perceval, who symbolically anticipates modern man's way of individuation, is not, at this stage of his journey, however, in a position to ask the decisive question. But he has at least acquired hope once more.

CHAPTER XIII

Gauvain's Adventures

THE STORY NOW returns to Gauvain who, in the course of his adventures, comes to a castle in front of which a girl is sitting under a tree, admiring herself in a mirror. She begs him to bring her her palfrey from a nearby garden, although a knight, she tells him, will try to hinder his doing so. This does not bother Gauvain. He brings the horse whose head is white on one side and black on the other. The beautiful maiden behaves in a haughty, amazonian manner; nevertheless she consents to ride off with Gauvain. After a few unpleasant and dangerous adventures and fights, in which the young woman has a hand, they come to a river on the far bank of which can be seen a magnificent castle with five hundred windows. In every window is a woman or maiden in beautiful, bright coloured clothes.

While Gauvain is fighting with a knight who has pursued him, the young woman, who now appears in a malicious light, suddenly disappears. A skiff crosses the moat from the castle, with a ferryman who tells Gauvain that the young woman is more evil than Satan and already has the deaths of many knights to her account. The air is somewhat uncanny on the river bank, for this is "*une terre sauvage*" ("a savage land") "*tote plainne de granz mervoilles*" ("full of great marvels"). Therefore, Gauvain ought not to tarry there but should take shelter with the ferryman. They set off across the river, and Gauvain finds a hospitable welcome in the man's house.

The next morning Gauvain learns from his host that the latter, although he performs the duty of ferryman, does not know for certain to whom the castle belongs. It is well guarded by five hundred self-drawing bows, always kept at the ready, which come into action as soon as anyone approaches the castle with hostile intent. He relates further that the castle was built by a rich and wise queen, of exalted birth, who brought great possessions of gold and silver with her when she came to live there. Her daughter, likewise a queen, who also has a daughter herself, accompanied her. The palace is guarded by sorcery; a learned astronomer, brought by the queen, has devised an amazing phenomenon by which no knight who exhibits cowardice, envy, avarice or any other weakness will be able to abide there. There are, in addition, approximately five hundred squires from different countries who are of all ages and who are all anxious to earn their spurs. Old widowed ladies who have been robbed of their possessions also live in the castle, as well as orphaned maidens who have taken refuge with the queen. All of them live in the foolish belief that one day a knight will come who will fight for their cause, who will restore the old ladies' properties, help the maidens find husbands and make knights of the squires. It looks as if this is a situation for which Perceval is responsible, one of the results of not having asked about the Grail. As his cousin, the Loathly Maiden, says to him:

Dames en perdront leurs maris,
Terres en sont essilliées
et pucelles desconseilliées
qui orfelines remandront
Et maint chevalier en morront.

Ladies will lose their husbands,
lands will be ravaged,
disconsolate maidens
will remain orphans,
and many knights will die.

But it will be easier to find a sea of ice than a hero who will be able to remain in this Castle of Damsels. If a sagacious and high-minded knight, handsome, candid, brave, loyal and without falsehood or envy should arrive, he would be able to become master of the castle and to lift the magic spell. Gauvain resolves to hazard a visit, in spite of the warnings of his host, who takes him to the steps leading to the castle. At the bottom of the steps is the man with the wooden leg, sitting on a bundle of gladioli, whom we have already discussed.

Gauvain and the ferryman enter the palace, the gate of which is fitted with hinges and bolts of gold. One of the doors is of carved ivory, the other of ebony, and both are richly ornamented with gold and stones of magic power. The floor of the apartment they enter is paved with many-coloured stones, artistically worked and brilliantly polished. In the middle of the room stands a bed; its posts are of gold, the curtain braidings of silver, and wherever the curtains are crossed are hung little bells. A costly coverlet is spread over the bed, and at each of the four posts is a carbuncle that sheds as much light as candles. Carved dwarfs with grotesque faces form the feet of the bed, and the feet stand on rollers so that the bed moves at the slightest vibration. The walls of the apartment are of marble, hung with precious materials and set with countless windows, through which all who arrive and leave the castle can be observed.

Gauvain examines everything minutely, then tells the ferryman that he sees nothing that could justify the latter's warning about the castle. In spite of his guide's assurance that it is certain death to lie down on the bed, Gauvain is resolved to try it. He also refuses to leave the castle without having seen its inhabitants. Since his entreaties are of no avail, the ferryman leaves the apartment. Gauvain, in full armour, sits down on the magic bed, whereupon a shriek resounds from its curtains, the bells hanging from them begin to ring, the windows spring open and magic breaks loose. Crossbow bolts and arrows fly in through the windows at Gauvain, who is unable to see whence they come or who is shooting them. Then the windows close of their own accord. While Gauvain is occupied in removing missiles from his shield, a few of which have hit him so that he is bleeding, a door opens and a gigantic lion hurls itself upon him, driving its claws into his shield and dragging him to his knees. He succeeds in getting to his feet, however. Drawing his sword, he cuts off the lion's head and both paws, which remain firmly embedded in his shield. Exhausted, he sits down again on the magic bed. Then his host, the ferryman, with joyful countenance, enters and informs him that he has freed the castle from magic forever and that its inhabitants, old and young, are ready to serve him.

The meaning of this excerpt from Gauvain's adventures has in part been anticipated in the description of the wooden-legged man and of the astronomer who was also the builder of the miraculous castle. If we take the latter as the Saturnian demon of sexuality and as Wotan, the lord of instinctual ecstatic *Minne* (love), this will explain the devilish bed that he has built and on which the hero is struck by invisible arrows (the *tela passionis* of the alchemical Mercurius) and also the lion as an outbreak of animal greediness and overwhelming passion.

As long, however, as the unconscious still assails the individual in such an untamed, animal fashion, the one-sided Christian attitude of the "knight" is still indicated. For this reason the alchemists advised cutting off the lion's paws;[1] in one version it is the mother whose hands must be amputated.[2] In alchemy, therefore, the lion that has to be overcome is associated with the mother imago. A Queen grandmother and a superfluity of women and untried men (squires who have not yet become knights) all live in this magic castle, thus indicating a purely matriarchally structured region of the soul, which is compensated by Gauvain's one-sided solar masculinity. Inwardly, the civilizing task of overcoming the more elementary forms of instinctuality has to be carried further. And even if, in the story of Perceval, the unconscious outlines new tasks for the development of the unconscious, tasks which reach still further into the future, these adventures of Gauvain show that the Christian task of overcoming chthonic pagan nature continues and must continue. Like alchemy, and for the same reason, the Grail legend is not an antichristian symbolic tale but depicts further development and completion of the Christian task in which the value of the first half of the fish aeon is united with that of the second, "like oxen side by side at the plough."

[1] Cf. *Psychology and Religion*, pars. 351*ff*. [2] *Ibid.*, par. 361.

The process in which the Christian symbol sinks down into the maternal depths is exemplified in the figure of Perceval, to whom falls the task of asking the question about the Grail. Simultaneously, a civilizing achievement, which consists of suppressing brutal instinctuality and emotionality, continues on the level of outer accomplishment, so to speak. This is the level of Gauvain's achievement. Historically, this accords with an external missionary activity, as realized in the Crusades, or especially in the struggle with Islam. Gauvain's enchanted castle could actually be associated in quite a few ways with the Moorish world. It has a curiously ambivalent character. One of its doors is of ivory, the other of ebony—white and black—which is reminiscent of Homer's description of the land of dreams, where there are also two gates, one of horn, the other of ivory, from which true and false dreams proceed. The young woman who leads him to the castle indicates this same ambivalence. Her horse is black and white, half dark and half light, and heretofore she has lured all the knights to destruction. Yet in the long run,she is not evil, only unfortunate, and wishes to be redeemed herself. The motif of the opposites of black and white recurs once again in the symbol of the chessboard. Since the castle was built by an astronomer (which in those days also meant an astrologer) this realm is influenced by ideas that point to the Islamic world. Wolfram, indeed, claimed to have obtained his material from a pagan astronomer. At the time of the Crusades, the Christian Crusader knights came into close contact with the mysterious traditions of the East, and the solution of the problem of *Minne* as presented in the primitive institution of the harem must have made a deep impression on them, since in the *Minnedienst* they too were seeking a solution of the anima problem that should transcend Christian conventions. The harem, however convenient in many respects, is none the less far too primitive a solution. Certainly, sexuality is not repressed, but beyond that there is no individual psychic relationship between man and woman, therefore its adoption by the knights subject to the *Minnedienst* would have meant a regression.

The lion that attacks Gauvain, as well as the magic arrows of passion that wound him, can therefore be understood as a temptation to fall back into a primitive situation, in which the erotic problem appears to be solved on the sexual level, through polygamy, but at the price of sacrificing the possibility of psychic relationship.

After he has overcome this image of instinctuality and thus exorcised the bed—the place of union in love—from such influences, there immediately appears a troop of squires who throw themselves down before Gauvain and offer him their services. Whereupon a beautiful maiden with a gold fillet in her hair and escorted by many other maidens enters and, in the name of the Queen, greets him as their lord and the foremost knight. The Lady of the castle would have him know that he is at liberty to climb the tower to see the view in all directions. Gauvain does so but learns from his guide, the ferryman, that he will not be able to hunt in the surrounding countryside and that he may never again leave the castle. Far from pleased by this intelligence, he makes his way back to the chamber and, thoroughly out of sorts, sits down on the magic bed. This is reported to the Queen who, with her daughter and a large retinue, comes to him in an effort to restore his good humour. When greetings have been exchanged, she asks whether he belongs to Arthur's Round Table. When he replies in the affirmative, the Queen inquires whether he knew King Lot (Gauvain's father), how many sons Lot had, and what they were called. Finally, she asks him about King Arthur. The King is healthier, more nimble and stronger than ever, Gauvain replies. She ponders whether this is possible. It has been a hundred years since Arthur was a child! She then asks about Queen Guinevere, whom Gauvain, who is one of the Queen's knights, extols in the highest terms. (The passage is quoted here because it is significant concerning the role and influence of women in those days.)

Tot ausi con li sages mestre
Les petiz anfanz andoctrine

Ausi ma dame la reine
Tot le monde ansaigne et aprant.
Que de li toz li biens desçant
Et de li vient et de li muet.
De ma dame partir ne puet
Nus qui desconseilliez s'an aut;
Qu'ele set bien que chascuns vaut'
Et que an doit a chascun feire
Por ce qu'ele li doie pleire.
Nus hon bein ne enor ne fet
A cui ma dame apris ne l'et,
Ne ja nus n'iert si desheitiez
Qui de ma dame parte iriez.

As a wise master
teaches small children,
so My Lady the Queen
teaches and instructs everyone.
All good comes from and moves through her.
No one goes uncomforted
from My Lady's presence.
She well knows the worth of each
and what to do for each
in order that she may please him.
No man does good or honour
to whom My Lady has not taught it,
and none is so discontented
that he may part from My Lady in anger.

It should be the same for him, too, the Queen tells Gauvain, and he straightway perceives that his joyous mood is returning. At this point a meal is brought in and Gauvain and his companion are magnificently served by the damsels and squires. The meal lasts as long as a day at Christmas time, as it is said. Afterwards there is dancing and other entertainment, then everyone retires for the night. Gauvain sleeps in the magic bed which is now quite harmless.

The next morning he again climbs the tower, from which he catches sight of the malicious young woman and her knight. The two queens come to bid him good morning:

> *Cist jors de vos soit liez et joieus*
> *Ce doint icil glorieus pere*
> *Qui de sa fille fit sa mère!*
>
> May the day be full of joy for you
> that the glorious Father gives,
> who, of his daughter, his mother made!

He asks whether they know the lady and the knight. "May the fires of hell burn her!" exclaims the Queen. "She brought you here yesterday evening, but do not concern yourself over her. She is too evil and malicious." He should also not bother himself about her escorting knight, the Queen advises, for fighting with him is no light matter. He has already killed many other knights, here at the ford, before their eyes. Gauvain begs for leave of absence, since he wishes to talk to the malicious damsel. The Queen tries to restrain him. He really should not leave her castle, she says, on account of such a worthless person; altogether, he ought never to go out at all, for by so doing he might cause them some harm. Provoked, Gauvain replies that in that case he is poorly rewarded if he is not to be permitted to leave the castle that he has liberated. He does not wish to be a prisoner there. The ferryman comes between them and persuades the Queen to let Gauvain go, "since he might otherwise die of anger." He must promise, however, to return in the evening if he is still alive. Gauvain further requests that he not be asked his name for eight days, to which the Queen agrees.

Being captive of the Queen, from which captivity Gauvain only escapes with effort, is reminiscent of Odysseus' adventures with Calypso and Circe, each of whom wanted to keep him with her forever. The image of the mother wants to confine the one-sided manly hero, and our surmise that the vanquished lion has a considerable connection with the matriarchal world and the problem of the instincts is therefore not beside the point.

Had the ferryman not interceded for him, Gauvain would hardly have freed himself. This ferryman plays such a vital role in Gauvain's adventures that it is worth while to consider him more closely. A ferryman is a well-known figure in myths and fairy-tales. Usually, he takes people to the other shore, whether it be to the land of the dead (Charon), or to hell (in the fairy-tale of the Devil with the Three Golden Hairs, for instance). As one who "leads across" he is connected with Mercurius, who also plays the part of psychopomp between one world and another. "*In habentibus symbolum facilis est transitus*" ("For those that have the symbol, the passage is easy"),[3] as an alchemical text says. The ferryman therefore appears to personify the transcendent function which aspires towards a synthesis of the psychic opposites.

The ferryman's presence protects Gauvain from the malice of the man with the wooden leg at the castle entrance, for he is the positive aspect of that same wooden-legged man, that part of the dark spirit of nature which is not one-sidedly opposed to consciousness but which is capable of mediating the opposites and of assisting in the further development of consciousness. It is also owing to him that the Queen allows Gauvain to go free. This emphasizes still more clearly his prospective function of pointing into the future.

Gauvain thereupon goes to the river, where he fights with the knight guarding the ford, a friend of the malicious young woman. He vanquishes the knight and hands him over to the ferryman. He then invites the evil maiden (who is, to all appearances, a parallel to the hideous messenger of the Grail) to come with him. She refuses and requests instead that he fetch her some flowers from the far side of the river, as her knight was wont to do. The women of the castle watch with horror as he rides away with her. With a daring leap, Gauvain springs across the river and in the meadow on the opposite side meets a knight with falcons and hunting dogs. It is the handsome Guiromelanz, one-time friend of the malicious damsel, from whom Gauvain

[3] Johann Daniel Mylius, *Philosophia reformata*, p. 182, quoted in Jung, *Practice of Psychotherapy*, note to par. 460.

learns that no one has yet dared to cross the dangerous ford and that the evil damsel has sent him across it in hopes that he will perish in the attempt. Her name is l'Orguelleuse de Logres, the Proud One of England, from whence she comes. Guiromelanz, who has introduced himself, cannot believe that Gauvain has been in the Castle of Marvels and slept in the magic bed, and therefore takes him for a mountebank. But when he hears of the fight with the lion and observes its paws still hanging from Gauvain's shield, he falls on his knees to beg forgiveness for his doubts. He asks Gauvain whether he has seen the old queen and whether or not he asked her who she was and from whence she came. Gauvain had not asked the questions and is informed that the Queen is King Arthur's mother, Ygerne. He does not believe this, for Queen Ygerne has been dead and Arthur motherless for sixty years. Guiromelanz maintains his assertion, however, and tells Gauvain that after Uther Pendragon's death Queen Ygerne moved here with all her goods and chattels and had the castle built for her. The other queen is her daughter, the wife of King Lot and Gauvain's mother. Gauvain, who has not mentioned his name, says that Gauvain is well known to him but that he has had no mother for something like twenty years. Guiromelanz insists that he is better informed: Gauvain's mother came to this place years ago and bore a child who is now the tall and beautiful young woman in the Queen's castle. She is Guiromelanz's friend and the sister of a brother, "may God confound him." If he were standing here before him, the knight declares, he would cut off his head or tear his heart from his body. His own father was brought to his death by Gauvain's father, and Gauvain himself has killed one of his cousins, which is the reason Guiromelanz hates him so intensely and must have his revenge. He gives Gauvain a ring to take to his sister, the beautiful Clarissant, and tells him the name of the Castle of Marvels: La Roche de Champguin (or Sanguin in many manuscripts; in Wolfram it is Rosche Sabbins). Green, red and scarlet cloth is dyed there and used for trade.

Finally, Guiromelanz desires to know the name of his *vis-à-vis* and learns with amazement that he is none other than the bitterly hated Gauvain himself. He regrets not having his weapon to hand, but they arrange for a combat to take place in a week. Gauvain must invite King Arthur and the whole court, and Guiromelanz will send for his people, since a contest between two outstanding knights would be such a spectacle that it would be a pity if as many knights and ladies as possible were not present. The fame of the victor will then be a thousand times greater than if no one had witnessed the combat.

Gauvain agrees to this and returns across the dangerous ford. The malicious damsel, at sight of him, sinks to her knees in repentance and implores his forgiveness. She explains that it is owing to grief over the death of her beloved, at the hands of Guiromelanz, that she has become so wicked and treacherous, and that she has lived in the hope that one day she will succeed in so enraging a knight that he will kill her. He, Gauvain, should now execute her. This he does not do; he invites her instead to go with him to the castle. They are transported by the ferryman and are welcomed at the castle with much joy. Gauvain presents his sister with Guiromelanz' ring and declaration of love, which she reciprocates although they have never seen each other save in the distance across the river. Gauvain, however, does not yet reveal his identity and so remains unrecognized by his mother. He sends a squire to Arthur, who is staying in the neighbourhood, with the message that he should appear before Roche Champguin in five days' time so as to be present at the contest between him and Guiromelanz. In addition he commands that Queen Guinevere be especially invited to come too. The squire is taken across the river and rides directly to Arthur in Orcanie. Great joy reigns in the exorcized Castle of Damsels. The Queen orders the bathhouse to be heated and five hundred tubs prepared, in which the squires must all bathe prior to donning fresh, gold-woven, ermine trimmed clothes. They spend the night standing vigil in the church, and the following morning Gauvain, single-handed, buckles spurs on to the right foot of each one of them, girds on their swords and dubs them knights.

During this time, Arthur is holding court in Orcanie, where

anxiety is occasioned by the long absence of Gauvain. When the King sees all his knights assembled and Gauvain not among them, he falls into a swoon. The company hastens to his assistance, and a commotion breaks out in the hall. A lady, Lore, notices this from a bower and, dismayed, hurries to the Queen, who inquires what has happened. . . .

At this point Chrétien's poem breaks off abruptly. The first continuator, previously identified as Pseudo-Wauchier (Gautier), takes up the story again at the same place, probably fairly soon after Chrétien's death (between 1190 and 1212),[4] and continues:

. . . While the knights are concerned about the unconscious Arthur, Gauvain's messenger arrives and everything is resolved into gladness and rejoicing. Preparations are made for immediate departure in response to Gauvain's invitation to his fight with Guiromelanz. In the Castle of Damsels, meanwhile, Queen Ygerne has made herself known to Gauvain as Arthur's mother. With the arrival of Arthur and his following, the encounter between the two contestants of equal rank is organized with great pomp. The combat proceeds undecided, until Arthur, allowing himself to be moved by the despairing Clarissant, brings about the reconciliation of the opponents. Guiromelanz wins Clarissant as wife and is invested with lands by Arthur.[5] In Wolfram's version, Orgeluse, who pledges herself to Gawan, renounces her hatred of Guiromelanz, and he desists from his quarrel with Gawan.

It is not possible to go into all the details of Gauvain's adventures since this would lead us too far afield, but two motifs should be stressed, for they also reappear in Perceval's adventures and are closely connected with the problem of the Grail. One is the unavenged, or to be avenged, murder of a cousin or

[4] Loomis, *Arthurian Literature*, pp. 212*ff*.

[5] The various texts differ considerably here. C. Potvin's edition of the text, the only one hitherto available, is based on the Mons MS. This version is used here, since other texts are not accessible.

brother; the other is Arthur's falling unconscious before the tournament of the hostile knights.

This is not the first appearance of the motif of the unavenged murder of a relative. It is repeated in some form or other in connection with nearly all of the principal figures in the Grail legend. As we have already mentioned, in many versions the Grail King himself is implicated in some such murder. On one occasion, he is wounded by the spear of a pagan adversary while fighting in the services of an anima figure whom the Grail has forbidden him to follow. Here, the heathen opponent is clearly recognizable as a shadow figure of the King. Psychologically this would mean that, together with the emancipation of consciousness made possible by the Christian religion,[6] an *Orgueil* (pride) has also been secretly generated, which for its part has then constellated a negative pagan demonism, leading to a destructive estrangement from instinct and nature. The other versions all illustrate with different nuances something of the same problem, while, as we shall see later, Perceval also is subsequently checkmated, during a visit to a water nixie's castle, by an invisible opponent who has obviously been constellated against him by the anima. This adversary also corresponds to the invisible being who kills the knight accompanying Gauvain, or who maliciously slays the Grail King's brother who has brought about the Grail King's illness and the calamity that has overwhelmed the land. The King has clearly not succeeded in his confrontation with the shadow. As has been pointed out, he has a one-sided nature and the invisible, i.e. unrealized, "other" who has caused his wound is in part responsible for its not being able to heal until Perceval fulfils the task. Here, as with Gauvain, it is a case of making reparation for the wrong committed.

The idea that a crime must be avenged is part of the primal attitude of mankind, so to speak. It accords with one of primitive man's most intimate feelings, which could be described as an *archetypal "judgement."* From it originates the obligation for revenge or reparation, to which great importance is attached on

[6] Jung, *Psychology and Religion*, pars. 444f.

certain levels of culture. (Celtic legend is full of it.) It would be incorrect to explain this as nothing but the instinct for revenge. Rather, concealed behind it is the idea that because of crime committed or suffered, the world falls into disorder and that to some extent *Tao*, the cosmic order, is disrupted. On account of the incalculable consequences that can result, it is absolutely essential to make amends for the offence committed. Nowadays, of course, we question that this should be permitted to happen in the form of bloody vengeance, and label such revenge as "primitive." Our so-called progress consists in the fact that we do indeed prohibit revenge. At the same time, however, we no longer acknowledge the fundamental fairness and purport of this basic feeling, by which means we exempt ourselves from responsibility. Nevertheless, something very significant lies hidden behind it, that is, the profoundly religious sense of common responsibility for world events and the attempt to align the individual in the cosmos as a necessary and meaningfully functioning member of the great work of creation. Thus, vengeance also achieves its significance as the releasing impulse of restitution.

In the Continuation to the *Perceval,* the problem of injustice is somewhat more complicated, for there the Grail King has wounded himself *on a piece of sword on which his brother was treacherously slain.* This brother again represents that same aspect of the king, the Christian man, that has remained unconscious. He is a part of the King's shadow, and it is he, not the King, who wields a traitor's sword. He symbolizes the possibility of dangerous unconscious behaviour. In general, as a cutting weapon, the sword refers to the discerning, discriminating function of consciousness, and a function of this kind has, according to the mythological testimony of the unconscious, robbed Christian man of his shadow. This must certainly allude to the cutting off of the natural, primitive man which has been brought about by Christian thinkers with their doctrine of the *privatio boni.* The amputation of the natural man, the inner brother, has a direct repercussion on the Grail King himself. He is injured as if by recoil, since the misuse of thinking, which in the Middle Ages was forced into service against the problem of evil, has finally impaired the integrity of the dominant Christian consciousness itself.

The form given to the wounding of the Grail King, as recounted in the "Merlin" and summarized above, also points in the same direction. It is not the murdered man but the murderer Garlan who is *an invisible errant brother of the King.* Balain kills this murderer at King Pellehan's court, but the King pursues Balain into a room where the wounded Joseph of Arimathea lies in bed. (We recall that the latter was wounded by a black angel.) There Balain wounds King Pellehan who was considered to be the most virtuous man of his age. This development will be gone into at a later stage of our inquiry. For the moment it is already clear that again and again we come upon the motif of a brother or relative of the Grail King who is sometimes killed, sometimes himself a murderer whose fate, either directly or indirectly, entangles the King in his troubles. And now the same motif is found in connection with Gauvain, who meets a knight who wishes to avenge himself on Gauvain for the murder of his father by a cousin. Perceval will find himself in a similar situation when he later discovers that the Red Knight, whom he killed at the beginning of his adventures and whose armour he appropriated, is related to him.

Whenever a motif appears in such numerous repetitions or modifications, it indicates, psychologically, that it is not understood in consciousness, and that it will therefore emerge in ever new forms in an effort to gain attention. This motif of the shadow brother is undoubtedly connected with the contradictory nature of the Christian aeon and with the rending apart of the opposites in this age. Jung has shown in *Aion* that this problem is reflected in the figures of Christ and Antichrist or in the two Sons of God, Satanaël and Christ, or in the original Gnostic speculations about the twin or double nature of Christ, which points to a sundering of the opposites in the symbol of the Self.[7] This religious problem, and with it the personal problem

[7] Cf. *Aion*, pars. 77, 131*ff*, 134. Also cf. Hurwitz, *Die Gestalt des sterbenden Messias, passim.*

of the indwelling shadow, obtrudes itself upon the Christian man, the Grail King, and upon Perceval, his appointed successor, and here Gauvain too is finally obliged to confront it.

While the opponents are preparing themselves for combat, i.e. for a conscious confrontation of the Christian knight (which Gauvain represents) with his shadow opponent, King Arthur faints from anxiety, because Gauvain has not yet arrived. The latter, as we have already remarked, mirrors that still naïve world of Christian consciousness that, without any concept of the inner opposites, has set itself a civilizing task and projects the adversary on to the pagan who still has to be overcome. Arthur, therefore, *cannot* watch a confrontation of ego and shadow or be aware of their mysterious relationship as yet. This realization would be too unbearable. His fainting is thus very significant.

That Chrétien de Troyes should die at precisely this point in his writing is likewise very remarkable. It rather looks as if he too had been unable to understand the problem and had therefore been slain by the invisible arrows of the dark god. His continuator does well at first. He reconciles the opponents through the meditation of an anima figure and Arthur regains consciousness. But the problem is not solved in this way and therefore reappears in another form in the Continuation. There now follow various adventures for Arthur and Gauvain that need not be more closely pursued, as they do not really belong to the Grail legend. We find a connection with the Grail story again when Arthur and his followers march up to Chastel Orguelleus in order to rescue the imprisoned Giflet Fis Do, who has wanted to reap for himself some of the knightly fame promised by the Loathly Maiden.

After the capture of Chastel Orguelleus, their return journey leads the knights to the stronghold of Brandalis de Lis, whose sister has had a son by Gauvain. The child has just unaccountably disappeared and the knights, together with the King, resolve to go in search of him. On the other hand, its father, Gauvain, prefers to go to court with his lady friend in order to present her to the Queen. "I would indeed be foolish," he says, "if I wished to look for the child; I leave that to his two uncles" (Arthur is Gauvain's uncle, as Brandalis is the young woman's brother)—an attitude that clearly suggests matriarchal or otherwise archaic conditions in which the uncle is more important than the father. Arthur charges Gauvain to tell the Queen that in a month's time she will come to a certain crossroads where he will meet her. On the appointed day, she goes there with her knights and ladies to await the King. Tents are pitched and the time beguiled with all manner of pastimes. Towards evening an unknown knight approaches along the road but hurries by without any form of greeting. The Queen, annoyed by this lack of civility, sends Keu after him to bring him back, for she wishes to know his name. The knight, however, refuses to turn back, unseats Keu who threatens him, and rides on. Displeased, Guinevere then sends Gauvain after the stranger. Gauvain begs him most forcefully to return to the Queen. The knight assures Gauvain that he would willingly return to oblige him, but that he has an important and most urgent affair from which he cannot withdraw. Gauvain, however, finally succeeds in persuading him to ride back to the Queen's camp. As they reach the camp the stranger suddenly falls from his horse, mortally wounded. He is able, however, to entreat Gauvain, in keeping with his promise, to take over his task.[8] For the purpose, Gauvain should put on the stranger's armour and mount his horse, which will carry him to the appointed place. Now for the first time, Gauvain notices that the stranger has been pierced by a javelin, and he weeps for grief and shame that this should have happened to a knight whom he is accompanying. Of the perpetrator of the crime there is not a trace.

The dead man is brought before the Queen, is undressed and shown to be very handsome and is lamented by the entire company. Unmindful of the rapid fall of night, Gauvain arms himself at once. It is his intention to fulfil his promise to carry

[8] The slain knight also appears in Malory's *Le Morte d'Arthur*, Book I, pp. 60–61. There the unknown, lamenting knight rides past Arthur without stopping and at the latter's bidding is brought back by Balain and killed by the invisible Garlon while in his company. Also cf. the draft of the *Merlin* mentioned above.

out the unknown man's business, of whose nature, however, he is totally ignorant. But he trusts himself to the stranger's horse and does not intend to return until he has avenged the dead man.

Thus, Gauvain sets out and rides wheresoever the horse carries him. The night is very dark. In a chapel at a crossroads a light is burning. Gauvain enters, for it is stormy and raining, with flashes of lightning from time to time. Suddenly he sees a black hand claw its way in through a hole under the altar and extinguish the altar light. He hears a wailing voice, and his horse is terrified.

Mais la mervelle qu'il trova
Dont maintes fois s'espoventa
Ne doit nul conter ne dire
Cil ki le dist en a grant ire,
Car c'est le singnes del Graal
S'en puet avoir et paine et mal
Cil ki s'entremet del conter
Fors ensi com il doit aler.

But of the marvel that he found,
Of which he was terrified time and again,
No man may speak or tell.
Whoever speaks of it has trouble,
For it is the Grail's sign.
Pain and trouble could come to him
Who undertakes to tell it
Differently from the way it should be told.

Troubled and full of fear, Gauvain rides on till morning, when to his amazement he perceives that he has crossed the whole of Brittany and Normandy. Without halting, he rides on through a great forest and when, towards evening, he comes to the sea, he is so tired and hungry that he can scarcely hold himself up in the saddle. But the horse jogs along, allowing him no rest. He comes to a road over which trees are arched like a roof, so that it is dark and uncanny beneath them. At the end of the road, in the far distance, Gauvain sees a bright glow as if from a fire. When he tries to turn his horse aside from the road, it rears up like a mad thing, and finally he has to acknowledge defeat. By midnight he still has not reached the glow. His steed carries him further and further until in the end he arrives at a great hall where a vast multitude of people are assembled. They welcome him joyfully, as one whose arrival has been longingly awaited. He is led to a huge fire, relieved of his armour, and a *green* cloak is laid over his shoulders. After sitting by the fire a while, he notices that the assembled company is looking at him with dismay and saying to each other, "My God, who is that? It is not he!" Whereupon, one after another, they leave the hall. The vast apartment, recently so full of people, is now empty. Gauvain, alone, sees that a coffin is standing in the middle of the room. A pall with a cross worked in gold is spread over it, and on the cross lies a sword broken in two. Four candles are burning at the head and feet of the dead person, and from four gold and silver pillars hang four censers that fill the room with thick smoke. Anxiously, Sir Gauvain crosses himself. Everything strikes him as very uncanny. Then he sees a valuable silver cross, adorned with precious stones, carried towards him by a priest followed by a procession of holy men, all in magnificent robes. They begin to celebrate the Mass for the Dead. The censers are swung over the bier, and the hall again fills with people who surround the coffin lamenting loudly. When the service is ended and the censers are hung up again, "the god disappeared, the corpse remained," as the text puts it ("*Li dious s'en vait, li cors remaint*"). Bemused with amazement at the incredible scene he has just witnessed, Gauvain crosses himself repeatedly and offers up a fervent prayer. He then sits down—he has been standing a long time—and covers his face with his hands.

Here we again encounter the motif of a knight struck by an invisible enemy. This dead man, named Goon du Desert, was a brother of the Fisher King. He had been assassinated by the nephew of an opponent he had slain; the sword of the murdered man broke under the treacherous blow and the Grail King himself was injured by a fragment of the weapon as he tried to remove it from the wound. From the way the people receive

Gauvain,it is clear that they have mistaken him for the awaited redeemer of the Grail. They discover, to their disappointment, that he is not, and that he is therefore in no position to avenge the crime against the dead knight.

Psychologically, the dead man can be looked upon as the part of psychic life which is not taken into consideration in the Christian collective attitude of consciousness and which has therefore been weakened and is attacked by a "traitor." The manner in which the knight is laid out, between four gold and silver pillars, with four censers, marks the dead man as an aspect of the Self. And when the text strangely relates that after the Mass for the Dead or the bearing away of Christ's Body, "the god disappeared, the corpse remained," it must surely be understood to mean that the presence of Christ in the transubstantiated Host is not capable of including *this* aspect of the Self, i.e. this aspect is not activated by the Incarnation of Christ and its perpetuation in the Mass. The dead knight is the object on which the sword of traditional thinking is shattered. He is therefore the paradoxical Anthropos which one-sided Christian thinking, by granting reality only to the light aspect of the Self in Christ, cannot understand. The traitor, however, is the person who, for the sake of this incomplete aspect of the Christian symbol of totality, is willing to murder the essentially paradoxical personification of wholeness, the chthonic brother of the Christian attitude—just as today materialists and apostles of enlightenment jettison the whole soul of man and its living possibility of development along with the symbol of Christ. On the other hand it would have been in the interest of the Grail King, who represents Christian consciousness, to make himself responsible for this complementing aspect of the Christ symbol, for it does not run counter to the Christ image but completes it as a brother.

The ghostly black hand which extinguishes the altar candles is considered to be the "sign of the Grail." Here the reference is to the previously mentioned dangerous aspect of the Grail which, however, only manifests itself against unauthorized persons who lack understanding.

While Gauvain, "bemused with amazement," is thinking over his experience, without, naturally, being able to understand it, a noisy bustle causes him to look up. The people who were in the hall on his arrival are back again. Servants are bringing in linen and cutlery and laying a table. While this is happening, a handsome knight wearing a golden crown comes out of an adjoining chamber, takes Gauvain by the hand and leads him to the table with a great show of honour.

Lors vit parmi la sale aler
Le rice Gréail ki servoit.

Then he saw passing through the room
The rich Grail serving.

First, it lays bread before the knights and pours wine into golden goblets. Then food is served in great silver dishes, up to ten courses, all with the utmost hospitality. Gauvain is much amazed that no servants are to be seen but that the Grail serves the diners by its own power, in which it is remarkably swift, now here, now there.[9] After the various courses have been brought in and removed, always by the Grail, everything disappears the moment the King orders the table to be cleared. Gauvain is alone once more in the hall with the coffin. He then perceives a lance-holder and in it a lance that is bleeding profusely. From the iron tip, the blood flows down on all sides into the holder and from the holder into a silver vessel from which it is carried through a golden pipe into another similar vessel. While Gauvain gazes in astonishment at this marvel, the King enters carrying the sword which belonged to the knight who was killed in front of the Queen's tent. He bids Gauvain stand up, and walking over to the bier with him says, weeping:

"What a misfortune that he lies here,
For whom the whole world longs.
God grant he may be avenged
And the land thereby redeemed."

[9] According to the Montpellier MS.

This remark confirms the supposition that the slain man represents the complete Anthropos, the Saviour, whose coming at the end of time is also prophesied in the Apocalypse of John. In other words, he is a complete symbol of the Self, as is the philosopher's stone in alchemy.[10]

This "brother of Christ" has been murdered by the destructive shadow of Christian consciousness, that is, by the materialistic rationalism engendered by this consciousness and its wrongly directed thinking. The bewitched land is the realm of the soul, which suffers under this event and impatiently looks for redemption.

The duality of the vessels united by a golden pipe is a curious motif. In itself, the doubling of a symbol, as mentioned before, generally indicates that it is constellated on the threshold of consciousness, but it is not yet realized in its essential nature. Perceval perceived one vessel. Gauvain, on the other hand, saw two. It is as if the attitude of consciousness of the Christian knight, as personified by Gauvain, would split the essence of the psychic being or else maintain it in a state of lasting cleavage. The golden pipe connecting the two vessels points to the fact that the split is not total but is bridged again and again by Christ's blood, as is actually the case in the Christian doctrine of redemption. The inner unity of the soul, however, is endangered.

We recall that Gauvain had to seek the bleeding lance, while Perceval's task was to find the Grail. Here in the hall Gauvain now sees both. The dwellers in the Grail Kingdom think at first that he is the awaited Grail hero and therefore put on him the green cloak, which, accordingly, appears to be the hero's attire. This corresponds to the same trend in Wolfram, where the Grail is a stone that is carried in on a green silk cloth. The colour green, the *benedicta viriditas* of alchemy, is considered to be the colour of the Holy Ghost[11] and implies growth and the life of vegetation, the spirit of nature itself. In contradistinction to the scarlet of worldly Kings, this green cloak can therefore be taken

[10] Cf. *Psychology and Religion*, par. 738.
[11] Cf. *ibid.*, par. 151.

as a sign that the Guardian of the Grail is a King in nature, or a ruler of the realm of the natural soul.

Gauvain, the type of the Christian knight, is not called to this kingship. The King draws the sword and Gauvain sees that it is broken in two. The missing part is lying at the dead man's feet. The King hands both pieces to Gauvain, with the words: "If God so wills, this sword shall be joined together by you. Let us see what He has decreed." Gauvain attempts it but does not succeed in joining the parts.

The King then takes him by the hand and leads him into an apartment where many people, knights and others, are present. They sit together on a couch, and the King tells Gauvain that he should not fret because he cannot accomplish the task for which he came. His fame as a warrior is not yet sufficient. Perhaps, should he come back again one day, he may then succeed. No one can carry out the enterprise without having first joined the sword together, and only the world's foremost knight is capable of achieving that.

"He who should have undertaken it has remained in your country," the King continues, "I do not know what is holding him there. We have awaited him so ardently. Your coming here shows great daring; should you desire anything here, it will be bestowed on you with pleasure, and should you wish to ask anything about the marvels that you have seen here, we will also willingly tell you what we know."

Sir Gauvain, who has ridden for two nights, longs to sleep, but he suppresses his fatigue in order to hear about the wondrous things he has witnessed. He asks about the bleeding lance, about the sword and about the bier. "No one has yet dared to inquire about them," replied the King, "but no secret will be kept from you. I will tell you the whole truth. First, the lance. It is the one with which God's Son was pierced in His side. Since that time it has always bled thus and will go on bleeding until the Day of Judgment. Many, both Jews and sinners, who saw the Lord bleed in those days will then be in great dread. But for us it is a gain, since we have been ransomed by the blood. By the piercing of that lance we have won so much—it is impossible to say how much—and by that other blow, dealt by this unlucky sword, we have lost everything. Never did a sword deliver such an evil blow as this, which has brought misfortune to Kings, princes, barons, noblewomen and maidens. You will of course have heard of the destruction of the land of Logres, on account of which we came here? That sword stroke was the cause of it. I will tell you who met his end thereby and at whose hand." The King begins to weep, but when, still in tears, he starts to continue his story, he notices that Gauvain has fallen asleep. Not wishing to awaken him he breaks off his tale. Gauvain sleeps till morning and on waking finds himself under a bush on the seashore, weapons and horse at his side. There is no sign of any castle. He is ashamed that he fell asleep and so missed the further explanation of the wonders he had seen and that he neglected to ask by what means the land might have been repopulated, for the King had been eager to give an answer.

Gauvain eventually consoles himself with the reflection that when he has achieved still greater fame as a warrior, he will seek out the castle again and learn everything. In the meantime, he resolves not to return to Britain until that future day. As he pursues his way, he notices that the land which had been desolate the day before is now green, the streams running with water. This is the erstwhile devastated kingdom. At midnight, the very moment he asked about the lance, God permitted the waters to take their courses again, so that everything has become green once more. The land should also have become populated, but this has not happened because Gauvain asked no further questions. The people he meets bless him and praise him as their deliverer. They must thank him for what he has done, they tell him, but at the same time they hate him because he did not want to hear what purpose was served by the Grail. Gauvain, having no inclination to tarry any longer, prefers to seek out new adventures in order to achieve still greater renown, so he wanders for a long while without returning to his native land.

Gauvain's story seems to have come to an end. His one-sided attitude as a Christian knight permitted him to sleep through the tidings concerning the mystery of the Grail, i.e. he remained unconscious of it. He only asked about the lance, which did indeed revive nature in the land of the Grail but did not redeem its people, as was to be expected from the duality of the Grail vessel which he beheld. Gauvain's subsequent wanderings indicate an aimless psychic restlessness, for he is not "contained" in anything, because he did not apprehend the mystery of the vessel. His roamings reflect the meaningless unease which, at the end of this aeon, is taking an ever stronger hold on Christian man and turning him into a restless, adventure-seeking wanderer.

CHAPTER XIV

Perceval's Further Adventures

THE STORY IN the Gautier Continuation now returns to Perceval, whom we find sunk in thought, always in search of the Grail. It is not necessary to interpret each single incident and adventure; we will limit ourselves rather to singling out those episodes that are most suited to our purpose—to expound the meaning of the quest, the search for the Grail.

When Perceval hears from a knight whom he has defeated that at Mount Doulourous (the Grievous Mountain) there is a miraculous pillar to which only the noblest knight will be able to tie his horse, he longs to make the attempt. On his way to the mountain he comes to a swiftly flowing river, the same river at which he had formerly met the Fisher King. He would not be far, therefore, from the latter's castle, if he could only manage to get across the river to the beautiful, inhabited country he sees on the other side. He rides the whole day without finding a crossing. Finally, on the slope of the river bank, he reaches a castle that he has a mind to visit. He finds the gate locked, however, and has to gain entrance through a hole in the wall. Inside, a maiden is sitting under an almond tree, combing her hair; she is already apprised of the fact that he wishes to cross the river and is willing to conduct him across on her mule. "*Estrangement fut viste et bele*"—she is remarkably "nimble and fair."

At the river bank she unties a skiff, jumps in with her mule and invites Perceval to do likewise. Things would have gone badly for him had not some workers in a nearby quarry shouted to him not to step into the boat because the maiden is planning his death. It is her *metier* to perform such misdeeds. He accordingly does not get in, despite her attempts to persuade him, but is ferried across by the quarrymen. They also point out to him the way to the Fisher King.

Instead of going directly to the Fisher King's castle, Perceval first visits another castle which he has seen not far from the river. He rides into the courtyard through the open gate. Two tall fir trees grow there, but no inhabitants are to be seen. He dismounts, ties up his horse, leans his shield against the wall and goes into the great hall. There he sees lance holders, a pack of hounds and, in the centre of the hall, a magnificent ivory couch. In front of it stands a chessboard, fashioned of gold and azure, the pieces, encrusted with precious stones, set out as if inviting a game. Perceval seats himself and makes a move, whereupon the figures on the opposing side begin to move of themselves and soon checkmate him. The chessmen then set themselves out again and the game starts once more, with the same result. Perceval is mated three times running. Furious, he sweeps up the pieces into a corner of his cloak and is about to throw them out of the window, into the water below, when suddenly a young woman rises from the depths and restrains him. She is wearing a red dress strewn with shining, twinkling stars, and is of an enchanting beauty. Emerging as far as the waist, she upbraids him for wanting to throw her chessmen into the water. He promises not to if she, in return, will grant him her company. She agrees and allows him to lift her in through the window. When she presses against him his heart behaves so strangely that he begins to sigh. When she asks what is troubling him, he kisses her and would have desired still more had she not told him that if he would win her love he must first hunt the white stag in the nearby park and bring her its head. Then she will give herself to him. He should take her small white hound, which the stag would certainly not be able to escape, but he must not lose it or forget his weapons.

The dog, white as snow and with a gold-worked leash (cf. Titurel), is brought in and Perceval sets out. He finds the stag, which the dog brings to bay beside a high cliff, and cuts off its head. While he is thus occupied *une pucelle de malaire* (an ill-omened maiden) rides up, lifts the hound on to her horse and gallops swiftly away. Perceval calls to her that she must return the dog, but she refuses, for she is highly incensed that he has killed her stag without her permission. She adds that the woman who instigated him to this action certainly did not love him or she would not have required such a deed of him. He tries to overpower her but is repulsed with the remark, "*Force à faire n'est mie drois*"—if he uses force he will regret it.

She sends him, however, to a nearby tomb on which there is the figure of a knight to which he must say: "Vasall, what doest thou here?" She will then return the hound. Perceval does as he is directed, and in response to his summons a knight in black armour rides out of the tomb on horseback to attack him. Perceval puts the stag's head and the hound in a meadow. While the fight is on, a passing knight steals both the head and the dog. Perceval, in consequence, falls the more furiously upon his adversary, wounding him so seriously that he hastily withdraws to his tomb. Disappointed, Perceval sets off after the thief. In the course of his search, he again meets the *pucelle de malaire*, who once more mocks him that his friend, the Star Woman, will be extremely obliged to him for losing the stag's head.

This part of the narrative repeats Gauvain's experiences in many respects, but with significant modifications due to Perceval's more complete humanity. Here too, the hero comes to a ford, the place of an arduous psychic transition, where he likewise meets a dangerous and beautiful anima figure, similar to Orguelleuse de Logres with her black and white horse. This anima, however, is riding a mule, and since this motif will turn up frequently it must be briefly interpreted. In that it combines the characteristics of the noble steed of the knight with those of that contemptibly lustful beast of burden, the donkey, the mule represents a *coniunctio oppositorum* on the animal level. It is sterile and cannot itself beget or give birth. As with the black and white horse belonging to Orguelleuse de Logres, it refers to an ambivalence or else to a union of the opposites in the realm of instinct. Certainly, this union has taken place in a living creature, but, even, so it is too unconscious (an animal), as well as being subject to an ambiguous anima figure, for it to be assessed positively. It could indeed mean a regressive reconciliation of the opposites, perhaps to the level of Eros in Islam as previously described. The mule's rider is "nimble and fair," which could also hint at an enticing short-term solution, through backsliding to an already overcome instinctual pagan attitude, but this would imply a renunciation of the Christian ethical feeling value. Perceval escapes this danger but does not go on to the Fisher King, although he could now do so. Instead he calls on the lovely chatelaine of a nearby castle, who is a water nixie.

Her castle suggests the *château des pucelles* (Castle of Damsels) in Gauvain's story, although it is inhabited by only *one* anima figure, thus pointing to a higher, more individual stage of relationship to the anima. Contact with her begins with the game of chess, which represents a spiritual confrontation and discussion. In the course of the game, Perceval is each time checkmated by his invisible partner. His masculinity, still naïve and unswerving, is confronted with something totally irrational and incomprehensible, and he is forced to admit that there are powers that cannot be overcome by daring and courage alone. The unseen opponent mates him each time, i.e. he proves to be *unquestionably superior*, and it may therefore be surmised that the invisible partner is a correspondingly superior figure of the Self or, more precisely, of the aspect of the Anthropos that Perceval does not yet embody. Through the game of chess it is made clear to Perceval that he is confronted by a superior psychic factor that had already been at work in all of the foregoing unhappy experiences and had always checkmated him. But because he cannot see this figure and is therefore unable to apprehend his own greater task, he reacts with a characteristic outbreak of affect and starts to fling the chessmen into the water; again a short-term reaction. A red-robed female figure then arises out of the water, clearly one of the *demoiselles des puis*, a mysterious nature being. That the figure of the opponent, previously often distinguished by the colour red, should have become invisible appears to bear some meaningful connection

'La Vision du St-Graal'. The gathering around the table in the Grail Service

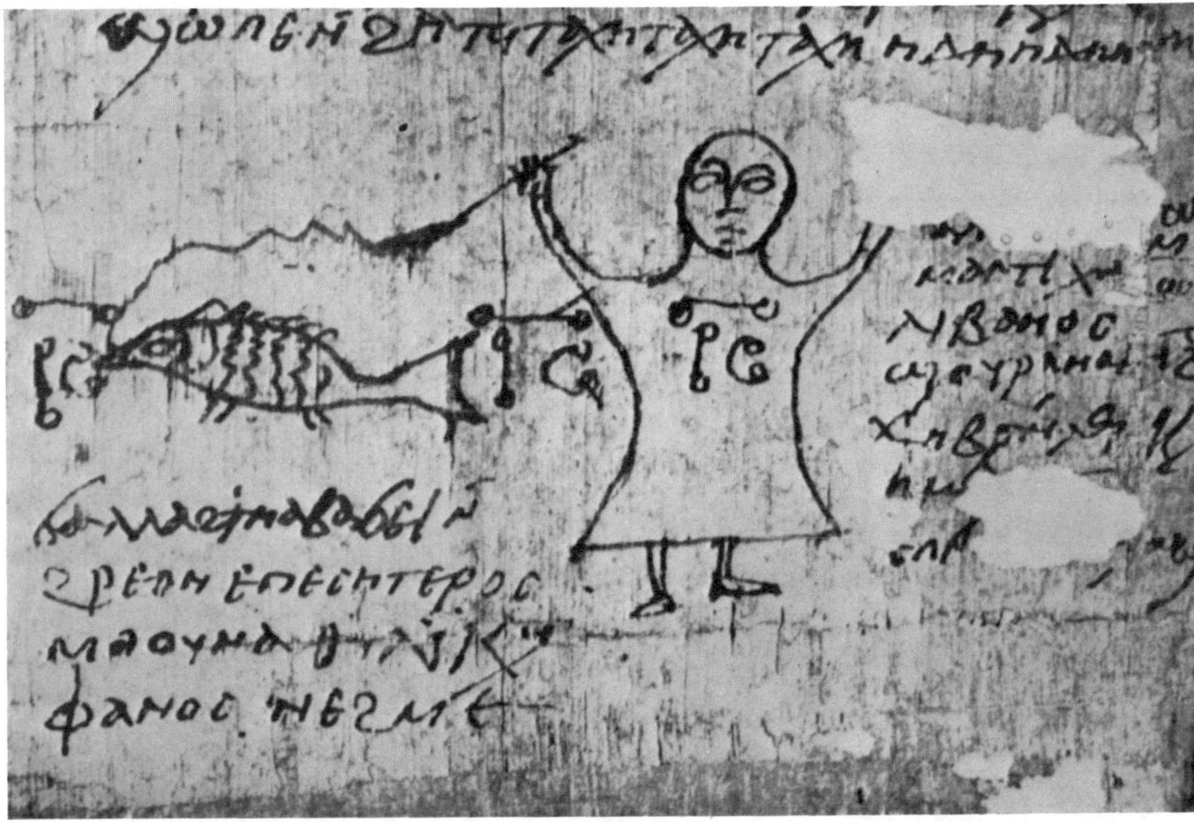

Jesus as Fisherman

to the fact that the anima is now wearing a red dress. As already indicated, this colour refers to blood, emotion and feeling, and this element has now flowed over from the shadow on to the anima, endowing her with a tremendous ascendancy in psychological affairs. In all his previous actions, Perceval has never permitted himself to be influenced by feeling and has therefore been unaware of the paradoxical ambiguity of his well-intentioned deeds. For this reason the anima imperiously sets him a task which forces him, for the time being, to relegate the quest of the Grail to the background. The anima's red robe is strewn with stars,[1] thus identifying her as a cosmic being. This figure is usually the Virgin, who wears the *blue* cloak of the firmament which is also frequently covered with stars. The star motif further distinguishes the woman of the Apocalypse, who is clothed with the sun and crowned with twelve stars. As Jung has shown in *Answer to Job*, this woman appears to be a personification of the divine Sophia (Wisdom). She represents the figure of the anima which gives birth to the *new redeemer.*[2] This saviour embodies the form of the Anthropos, which signifies a more complete personification of the Self. It is precisely this redeemer figure which, just because he should become conscious of it, weighs upon Perceval like a challenge. If the relation to this content were legitimate, the red anima figure would be an analogy to the Sophia of the Apocalypse. The cloak of heaven that she wears is, however, not blue but red, suggesting rather the purple and scarlet raiment of the Apocalyptic harlot. Furthermore, red refers to the unsolved feeling problem. The red star dress is like the morning or evening sky[3] in whose twilight the new self-manifestation of the Anthropos is announced. Since the nixie is the mother-mistress of this figure, she forbids

[1] Concerning the stars as "luminosities" of the unconscious and the motif of the *oculi piscium*, cf. Jung, "On the Nature of the Psyche," in *The Structure and Dynamics of the Psyche*, par. 394.

[2] She also appears in this guise in the alchemical text *Aurora consurgens*, where she is the mother/lover of the *lapis*. Cf. M.-L. von Franz, *Aurora Consurgens, passim.*

[3] Cf. von Franz, *Aurora Consurgens*, for a description of the figure of Sophia, pp. 191*f.*

Perceval to throw the chessmen into the water and sets him a new task, the search for the *head* of a white stag that has been laying waste to the forests. For this task she sends with him her own hunting dog, with its leash of white and gold.

The stag is a well-known medieval allegory of Christ, and in the *Saint Graal*[4] it is related that Christ occasionally appeared to his disciples in the form of a white stag accompanied by four lions (the four Evangelists). The stag knows the secret of self-renewal, for according to Honorius of Autun[5] when, from time to time, it is feeling old, it swallows a snake and from the venom of the bite loses its antlers and grows itself a new pair. Thus, says the author, we also should put off the "horns of pride" and renew ourselves. In the legend of St. Hubert, the stag represents the *bush soul* or *animal soul of Christ*[6] and in his antlers bears the Crucifix as his own spiritual aspect.[7] Jean Marx mentions that the stag is of special importance in the Celtic religion.[8] On the bowl known as the vessel of Gundestrup there is a representation of the god Kerunnus, a god with stag's horns, whose animal attribute is the stag. He is a god of vegetation and of death, of the communal meal and the intoxicating drink through which communication with the other world is established. In one of the representations on the vessel the god is shown dying as he is immersed in the inebriating beverage, while in a further portrayal he is depicted as the resurrected one, in a rejuvenated form. As the dying and resurrected god, this figure typifies, though on a more archaic level, the same archetype that Christ also personified. He is the more primitive, original image, so to speak, which was almost overlaid by the more spiritual image of Christ and which appears to have been absorbed into the

[4] Ed. Hucher, III, pp. 219 and 224. Cf. also Jung, *Structure and Dynamics*, par. 559 and note 9 to the same par.

[5] Migne, *Pat. Lat.*, CLXII, col. 847.

[6] By "bush soul" is understood a spiritual being or a "doctor" animal which is looked upon by the primitive as his life principle or double. His life is bound up with this creature in the closest *participation mystique*.

[7] For examples cf. F. Losch, *Balder und der weisse Hirsch*, pp. 152*ff*.

[8] *La Légende Arthurienne et le Graal*, p. 184.

tradition by the later images, as were the fish and lamb symbols of the Mediterranean world. According to many local Germanic legends, the stag was supposed to have caused springs to flow, or to have pointed out healing springs to men.[9] More often it shows the hunter the way to his beloved,[10] with whom it is secretly identical.[11] It also appears in legends as the summoner of the dead and entices those who hunt it to the land of the dead, forever.[12] In the sixth and seventh centuries, the custom of the *cervulum seu vitulam facere*—of acting the part of a stag or calf—still persisted in many places. This was a New Year's play in which people clothed as stags and hinds acted obscenely.[13] On Stag Monday (usually the first Monday in Lent) a jousting match took place in which the chief personage was the *Hirsnarr*, the stag jester. Geiler von Kaysersberg in his Strasburg Chronicle describes it as follows: "*Habent larvae procul dubio originem a gentilitate, sicut et der hyrtz et das wild wyb von Geispiken* (*Geisboltheim*) *Bacchus hirsutus depingebatur: his omnibus consonat hyrtz*" ("Without doubt, masks have their origin in gentility, as have the stag and the wild woman from Geispiken. Dionysos was represented covered with fur, the stag has to do with all this").[14] Here too the stag is connected with the ghosts of the dead (for the latter hover behind the masks of that season, between March and April) and with an orgiastic rite of renewal, as Marx conjectures to be the case in the cult of Kerunnus.

Kerunnus and the stag also have more than a little in common with the figure of Merlin, so that subsequently we shall have to speak in more detail about the latter. In alchemical symbolism too, the "fugitive stag" (*cervus fugitivus*) appears as a symbol of Mercurius and of the soul in matter.[15] Since in the foregoing context the stag is described as destructive, its inter-

[9] Cf. Losch, *op. cit.*, pp. 58–63.
[10] *Ibid.*, pp. 67*ff* and 72*ff*.
[11] For example, the goddess Lora in Weselburg; Losch, *op. cit.*, pp. 74*ff*.
[12] *Ibid.*, pp. 169*ff*.
[13] *Ibid.*, pp. 185–86.
[14] *Ibid.*, p. 187.
[15] Jung, *Structure and Dynamics*, par. 559; and *Psychology and Alchemy*, par. 84.

pretation brings more of its negative features into consideration, for instance, the *superbia* and the death aspect. It is almost Christ's shadow soul, i.e. a psychic component of the Christ symbol, that is unfavourably manifested in the realm of instinct. Consequently, this stag also has a certain connection with the Grail King's enemy who rides around cloaked in invisibility; it embodies an unconscious counterposition that has come into being as a result of Christianity and which works destructively when it remains unnoticed.

As a theriomorphic symbol of Mercurius, the stag carries the archetype of the Self and the principle of individuation. There are numerous representations in which the stag literally bears the quaternity symbol of the cross in its antlers[16] and points the way as a guide. In the monastery of Fischingen,[17] it appears beside St. Idda, who is hovering in ecstasy, presumably as a companion who shows the way. It represents the urge towards individuation and contains everything of which consciousness is deficient. In it lies the mystery of a constant self-renewal on the part of the Self. Because Perceval too much ignored feeling and feeling relationships, he had to become conscious of the shadow, of the nature-destroying *superbia* of Christian humanity which identifies itself one-sidedly with the Logos principle.[18] If a man becomes identified in an unbalanced way with his intellect and the fictions of his ego, he loses his relation to the anima, for which reason the unconscious torments him with emotions, irritations, lack of self-control, moods and depressions. This one-sided masculinity threatens to sever the connection with reality and to become ruthless, arrogant and tyrannical. These displeasing shadow qualities are expressed in the theriomorphic symbol, and the red-robed (therefore emotional) anima figure demands that the hero should become conscious of this shadow. She gives him her white dog as a guide. Like the stag it is also an animal, but, in contrast to the stag, it attaches itself to man

[16] Cf. Losch, *op. cit.*, pp. 152*ff.*

[17] In Canton Thurgau, Switzerland. Cf. Losch, *op. cit.*, p. 71.

[18] Concerning this typical condition cf. *Alchemical Studies*, par. 435, and also K. Schmid, *Hochmut und Angst*.

and renders him good service with its sensitive nose. It could very well represent intuition. The gold leash clearly indicates its "allegiance" to man. To begin with, however, Perceval loses this helper, then he encounters several sinister figures on his hunt for the stag. First, a *pucelle de malaire* steals the dog and tries to infect him with a mistrust of the woman who set him his task. She passes herself off as the owner of the stag, which makes her psychological meaning plain. Accordingly we have a *quaternio*: the Red Star Woman with the white dog, and the *pucelle de malaire* with the stag.

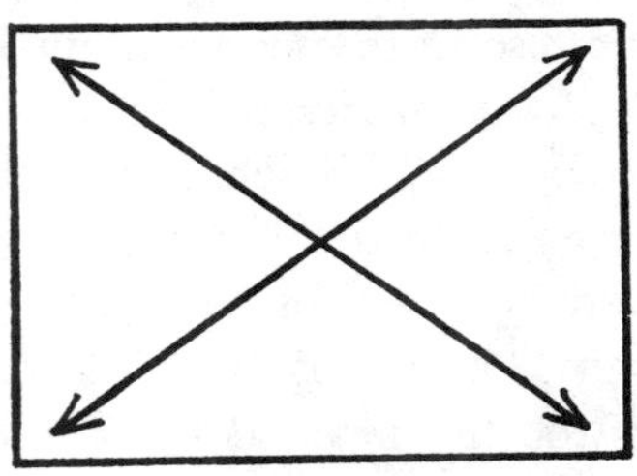

The Red Star Woman orders Perceval to hunt the *pucelle de malaire*'s stag, but instead the *pucelle* steals the Star Woman's dog. Here stag and dog are both undoubtedly the masculine partners, in animal form, of the feminine figures, and the Star Woman's task brings about a rough plan for setting up a marriage *quaternio*, an image of the Self which will later be discussed at greater length. But a quaternity does not materialize at this juncture, and this failure is certainly connected, among other things, with the animal form of the two male partners, i.e. their far too profound unconsciousness. The *pucelle* and the Red Star Woman are mutually antagonistically disposed; they fight, as do the dog and stag. The violently separative tendencies prevail, so that a stable *quaternio* cannot come into being. As the owner of the white stag, the *pucelle de malaire* probably personifies that part of the anima which, concealing itself behind the arrogance of masculine consciousness, breeds demoniacal possession and quite definitely prevents feeling from coming to consciousness. The one-sided exaggeration of the logos principle gives rise to a state of moody anima possession, and it is this that makes the welling up of genuine feeling impossible. For this reason, the *pucelle* has a secret understanding with the destructive stag. For all that—and she is therefore not only evil—she confronts Perceval with the Black Knight reposing in the tomb, i.e. the "dead" aspect of the higher Anthropos in himself, which we have already met. It turns out later that the Black Knight lives with his beloved in a state of complete enchantment and seeks a fight from time to time so as to escape the monotony of his life. His fate recalls that of the magician Merlin who, caught in the bondage of love for the fairy Vivien, vanishes from the world. The aspect of Merlin as an Anthropos figure and the meaning of a state of enchantment such as this will be considered later. For the moment, however, a compensatory motif can be discerned. Just as Perceval has too firmly evaded the problem of Eros, of the feeling relationship, so, conversely, the Black Knight has fallen too deeply into a love experience with the anima. While Perceval is fighting the knight, instead of making his peace with him, and driving him back wounded to his tomb, another knight steals the dog and the stag's head, not, as it turns out, without the assistance of the Grail King's niece, who wishes thereby to punish Perceval for his one failure to ask the question. In point of fact, the anima behaves very paradoxically, or else she splits into two opposing figures, between which consciousness is torn this way and that, until the ego begins to concern itself with the task of individuation. It is only when a man begins to have an apprehension of the Self behind the anima that he finds the foundation on which he can escape her pulling and tugging in contrary directions. On the other hand, as long as she is entangled with the image of the Self,[19] he cannot escape from her trickery, for she wishes to enmesh him in life and at the same

[19] Cf. *Psychology and Alchemy*, par. 112.

time to pull him out of it, to enlighten and to deceive him, until he has found both himself and an inner basis beyond the play of the paradoxes.

In the first place, dog and *cervus fugitivus* are lost once more. Angry, Perceval rides on and meets a hunter whom he questions about the Fisher King's palace. The man maintains that he has never heard of it, neither has he seen the knight with the stag's head. There is no shelter within a radius of thirty miles, the only person living in the forest is a hermit to whom Perceval could go. Or he could spend the night with the hunter, which he does. Next morning, the hunter tells Perceval that he should take the path to the right and it will lead him out of the wood. Perceval takes the road to the left, however, for he hears cries coming from that direction. He runs into a squire with a scratched face and tattered clothes and carrying a javelin (as Perceval once had done), who is pursued by a dog. A knight with a bloody sword in hand overtakes the fugitive and kills him. The knight refuses to answer to Perceval for his action, so there is a fight and the knight is killed. Afterwards, Perceval seeks out the hermit and tells him what has happened. The latter fetches the corpses and buries them in his chapel.

Perceval rides on and meets an aged knight on a white mule. The knight asks him whence he has come and whether he knows that he has offended against his, the speaker's, family. He is the brother of the Red Knight whom Perceval killed with his javelin in the days of his boyhood and whose death has never been avenged. Truly, he killed him at Arthur's behest, replies Perceval, whereupon the old man declares him to be exonerated, because he has not denied the act, and promises never to refer to the matter again. The knight says, furthermore, that he knows that Perceval is seeking the Fisher King and the bleeding lance, but that there are many difficulties in store for him before he reaches his goal. But, for all that, he might have seen the King's niece the previous evening. She was in a castle in the neighbourhood and told him, the old man, about a stag's head and a dog she had had carried off by one knight in order to cause vexation to another, very outstanding knight as punishment for his not having asked about the Grail when he was at her court.

In a certain sense,Perceval cannot meet with the Star Woman until he has become to the fullest extent conscious of the problem of Christianity. Otherwise, swinging from one opposite to the other, he could easily fall into the power of the nature goddess and lose touch with reality, as happened to his polar opposite, the Black Knight. For this reason, according to the curious logic of psychic events, the next episode is the horrible sacrifice of the squire carrying the javelin, the weapon once carried by the youthful fool. Perceval encounters himself in the figure of the squire, whose naïve attitude has until then prevented his becoming conscious of the paradoxical problems of the anima and of the Christian god-image, an attitude that now finally has to be sacrificed. Most regrettably, however, the sacrifice is not Perceval himself but the figure of an unknown knight, probably a new personification of the "opponent" whose outlook Perceval cannot understand and whom he therefore drives off to the land of the dead, as he previously did the Black Knight. The hermit's Christian point of view helps him quite literally to bury the problem once again. But even so, a piece of youthful folly is thereby eliminated. In lieu of the squire, the "Wise Old Man" now appears, in the guise of a knight full of years. He turns out to be the brother of the Red Knight, killed long ago. He forgives Perceval most generously for his brother's death and enlightens him concerning the disappearance of the stag's head and about his own future. He represents a helpful father figure, similar to the hermit, but unlike the latter he is not a counsellor withdrawn from the world and only sympathetic to the spirit, but a man who, in the knightly calling itself, has matured to a certain superiority and detachment from affect. He points out the way to Perceval who soon loses it again, which is not surprising, since the old man, like the evil anima figure, was riding a mule. He has that particular theriomorphic attribute in common with her, which proves the unconsciousness and sterility of any premature union of the opposites. The reconciling symbol is still on the animal level, i.e. in the condition of the animal instincts. This would mean that Perceval has indeed attained to a certain insight and maturity which do not, however, suffice for the achievement of the task set him, for which reason fate puts further hardships in his path.

It is curious that it is precisely the Grail King's niece who makes it impossible for Perceval to carry out the Star Woman's task of hunting the stag, apparently in revenge for his not having asked about the Grail. Strangely enough, the Grail Bearer acts in a similar manner towards the *pucelle de malaire*. The latter steals the dog entrusted to Perceval by the Star Woman and the former causes Garsales, the knight in white armour, to carry off the stag's head which Perceval had already won, as well as the dog, so that he has to go out of his way to gain possession of them again. Perceval finds the head, nailed to a tree and guarded by Riseult, a red-and-white-robed damsel, the beloved of Garsales. It is as if the Red Star Woman were contending, not only with the *pucelle de malaire* but also with the Grail Bearer, for possession of the stag's head. On her side the Grail Bearer is assisted by a knight in white armour and a red and white fairy, while the *pucelle* appears to be in league with the buried knight in black armour who lives enthralled in the bonds of love for a woman. The stag now suddenly appears in duplicated form, so that the structure overleaf is produced.

The head of the stag that was killed first hangs on the tree; a second stag, hunted by Garsales, suddenly appears and is killed. Thus the designs of the White Knight and his lady become evident. They kill one stag and nail the head of the other to the tree. It may be recalled that the stag signifies a theriomorphic attribute of Christ, so it is as if they wished to kill Christ's animal soul and crucify its essence (head) anew (nailing it to the tree) and, consequently, to sacrifice the theriomorphic component once again and to force on the unconscious the Christian solution, that is, the repression of the instincts.[20]

[20] This corresponds to the hanging of the sword on the tree of Paradise in Gerhard Dorn's interpretation, quoted above.

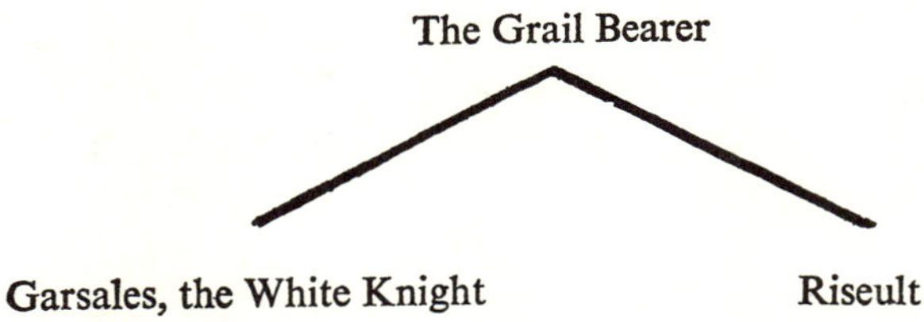

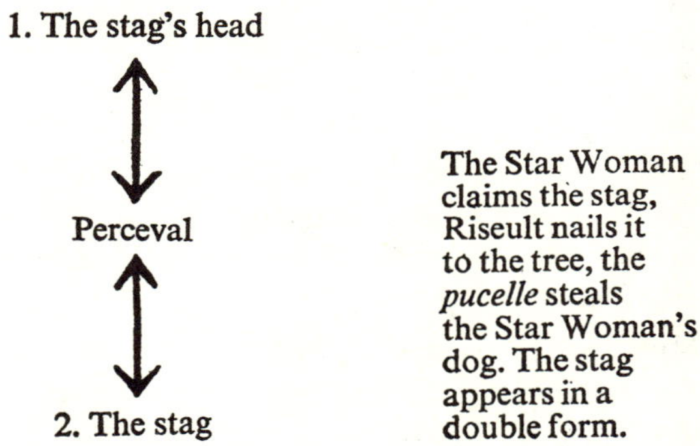

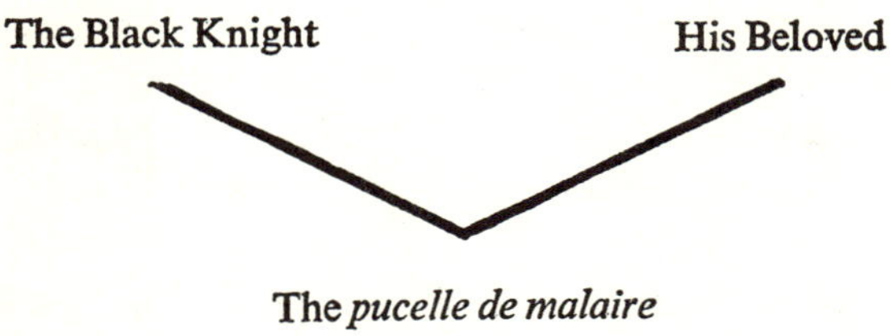

The *pucelle de malaire*, on the other hand, wants Vasall, the Black Knight who is enthralled in the bonds of love, to hunt Perceval to death and to steal the Star Woman's white dog. She represents surrender to instinct and unconsciousness. In a certain sense the Grail Bearer corresponds to the light aspect of the anima, as it is personified in the Virgin, and the *pucelle* to the dark witch-Eve aspect. The red-robed Star Woman, the

Sophia figure, intends to lead Perceval into a place beyond the opposites.[21]

After the meeting with the old knight, Perceval, full of hope, sets out on his journey again but does not notice—or notices only too late—that he has missed the way. After fighting a lion and a knight, he arrives at a giant's castle, where he does himself well at a lavishly spread table and subsequently kills the homecoming giant. The road then leads over a mountain to a river, on the far bank of which is a tent standing under a tree and beside it a white horse, a white shield and a lance of the same colour. On a stone he sees an inscription in gold letters. While he is seeking a crossing, a knight emerges from the tent and challenges him to combat because he has allowed his horse to drink at this ford. Perceval defeats the knight and learns that the ford is *le gué amourous*, the most wonderful ford in the whole world, which the knight has been guarding for five years, keeping watch that no horse shall drink there. At one time, ten damsels had dwelt under the tree, and knights had repaired thither from all parts to win their love and to distinguish themselves in feats of arms. The victors had always killed their opponents without quarter. When the damsels left the place, after a sojourn of six years, they had this information inscribed on the stone, as well as the additional intelligence that if any knight could defend the ford for seven years he would be entitled to a prize beyond all others. This is the reason the knight has remained there so long. But now that he has been defeated, Perceval should take his place. Perceval, however, does not covet this honour, and they go into the knight's tent together where they are sumptuously served and where they spend the night.

In the prose "Perceval",[22] one of Robert de Boron's trilogy, this adventure is described in somewhat different terms. There the ford is called *le gué perilleus*, its guardian knight is Urbain, the son of the Queen "*de la noire Espine*" (Queen of the Black

[21] Cf. Francis Thompson's (1859–1907) description of Christ as the "Hound of Heaven".

[22] Weston, *Legend of Sir Perceval*, Vol. II, Ch. 7.

Thorn) who lives with his beloved in an invisible castle in the vicinity of the ford. While he is talking to Perceval, a great noise is heard and the air becomes black with smoke. As they fight, a flock of black birds assails Perceval by flying around his head and trying to peck out his eyes. Defending himself, he catches one with his sword, and as it falls to earth it turns into a beautiful woman. The other birds surround the body and fly away with it. Urbain tells Perceval that the noise and smoke were caused by the destruction of the invisible castle, the voice they had heard was that of his fairy love who, with her companions, had wanted to hasten to his assistance in the form of birds.

In a different sphere, the ford, as the place of the dangerous transition, appropriately symbolizes the psychic region in which a change of attitude is necessary and where complexes that are as yet unassimilated can still be dangerous.[23] Here, as indicated by the very name of the place, it is the problem of Eros which Perceval must face. (The overcoming of the lion and the giant, a victory over concupiscence and overwhelming emotion, has already occurred and has the same meaning as that discussed in connection with Gauvain's parallel experiences.) The knight on the white horse who guards the ford of the ten maidens would portray a human equivalent of the white stag,[24] the Christian attitude that will not allow itself to be more profoundly moved by the problem of love. He is encircled by ten maidens[25] who have withdrawn, for in the face of such a conscious attitude of rejection, the anima remains undifferentiated or even disappears altogether. Perceval is reconciled to this white adversary and achieves nothing more thereby. In the second version the same problem is presented in a more interesting form, in that we again encounter the motif of the knight ensnared in the bonds of love for his mistress. Urbain, son of the Queen of the Black Thorn, is a son of the dark mother, who has therefore fallen too

[23] Cf. Jung, *Symbols of Transformation*, par. 503.

[24] Cf. the subsequent remarks about Garsales, the knight in white armour who did not wish to hand over the stag's head.

[25] The plurality of the anima figure indicates a lack of differentiation in her nature. Cf. *Psychology and Alchemy*, pars. 116–18.

deeply into the power of nature, just as Perceval will not sufficiently submit himself to her.[26]

The idea of beautiful women or fairies appearing in the form of birds accords with the universally distributed motif of the swan maiden in fairy-tales. The birds are generally white, however, and by stealing her bird skin or husk the hero wins one of the fairies as his bride. Here it is a more negative variation of the motif. The birds symbolize dark, destructive fancies and ideas.[27] Perceval, who defends himself with the sword of understanding, kills the fairy at the same time and it seems that the castle in which she lived with Urbain is also destroyed. The motif, thus altered, could be connected with the pronouncedly Christian outlook of the author, Robert de Boron, who very significantly rechristens the ford *le gué périlleus*. He rejects the problems of Eros, and the anima assumes correspondingly negative traits in his work. There is, therefore, no solution of the problem of the anima or of the psychic opposites.

After the adventure of the *gué amourous* or *gué perilleus,* Perceval comes, after several relatively unimportant adventures, to a beautiful, flourishing new town that he does not recognize at first. It is Belrepeire, the city of his most dearly beloved Blancheflor, and a joyous reunion takes place between the lovers. Blancheflor tells him that she was quite desperate when, instead of marrying her, he departed, leaving her alone in the town that had been so terribly laid waste during the siege. But when the prisoners and refugees returned she had the castle and town rebuilt. Now that he has come to fulfil his promise, the wedding can be celebrated immediately, on the following day. There can be no talk of that, says Perceval, for he has promised to undertake a task he would not relinquish for all the treasure in Friesland. As soon as this task has been accomplished he will, without fail, return to her. Blancheflor replies that of course a knight such as he must not break his given word under any cir-

[26] This question will be discussed more thoroughly in the final chapter.

[27] Concerning the significance of birds as thought beings, cf. *Alchemical Studies*, par. 338, and G. Weicker, *Der Seelenvogel in der alten Literatur und Kunst, passim,* which gives many examples of the bird as a daemon of death and as an image of death and as an image of the soul.

cumstances. She has already waited so long for him, she will go on doing so, whether it is agreeable to her or not; she would rather suffer this than not to have regard for his wishes.

> *Car damoiselle ne doit faire*
> *nule rien ki doive desplaire*
> *A son ami ne anoier.*[28]
>
> For a maiden must do
> nothing that might displease
> or annoy her friend.

Perceval spends two days with her, then leaves his distressed friend, swearing to return as soon as he can.

He once more searches for the hound and resolves to take no rest until he has found the dog and the stag's head and learned about the Grail and the bleeding lance from the Fisher King. He meets a knight and an outwardly hideous girl, fights the knight, learns from the defeated man that he is called *le Biau Mauvais* (the Evil Biau) and that his companion is the most beautiful of all women, a truth which becomes apparent after the knight arrives at Arthur's court with her.

The disappointment Perceval once more involuntarily causes Blancheflor reveals that his refusal to probe deeply into the problem of the anima is preventing him from becoming attached to the woman who belongs to him, and is forcing him instead, through the torment of an unfulfilled inner duty, to appear unrelated. The beauty of nature is thereby cast aside, together with the evil, for which reason he meets the distorted anima once more, without the problem coming to any sort of

[28]
> Puisqu'il convient qu'ele l'ait cier
> De fine amor vraie et certaine,
> Ne li doit pas grever la paine
> Qui son cœr a mis en detroit.
>
> For it is seemly that she hold him dear
> With tender love, certain and true,
> And must not cause pain to him
> Who has caused her heart to ache.

solution. Since Perceval also sends all defeated knights to Arthur's court, it is clear that he has not yet reached beyond the chivalric way of life described by these victories, and that in spite of all these noble deeds he has not developed any further. He himself, therefore, also returns time and again to the same place, namely the hermit's cell.

Resting under a tree, he recognizes the spot where he met the knights when he was a boy. His mother's house must therefore be close at hand. He finds it and is welcomed by his sister who greets him most warmly, when he reveals his name. She tells him that their mother died ten years and four months ago, after he rode away from her. They go to the hermit uncle, who lodges nearby and in whose hermitage the mother is buried. On the way, Perceval survives yet another combat in which he kills a knight who is trying to violate a girl.

Perceval attends Mass. He makes himself known to the hermit and is informed that the hermit is his father's brother. In most accounts it is the mother's brother. He is then shown his mother's grave in front of the chapel altar. Perceval laments her death and tells his uncle the story of his life and how he was with the Fisher King without asking the question about the Grail. He also gives an account of the damsel with the game of chess, of the stag's head and the hound, and of the knight in the tomb.

His uncle rebukes him for having killed a knight on his way to Mass, for whoever desires to find the Grail may shed no blood. Perceval replies that if he can first learn about the lance and the Grail and about the broken sword that can only be joined together again by one peerless knight, he will then perform everything his uncle may impose on him as a penance for this sin. The hermit invites them to a simple meal of white bread and grapes, brought to him by angels who do this every morning.

They then take leave of the hermit, who imparts more good moral precepts. Sadly, Perceval leaves his sister behind and proceeds upon his quest.[29] Once again this leads to a strange castle

[29] In other versions he brings her to the Castle of Damsels.

where he is so cordially entertained by beautiful maidens and their mistress that he thinks he must be in Paradise. It is the *château aux pucelles*, built by four lovely damsels with no man having worked on it.[30]

The next morning he awakens under an oak tree in the forest. Later in the day, he comes to a gigantic tree in whose shade a thousand knights could rest. A sumptuous tent is erected there. Under the tree, he sees a maiden in a red and white dress (the colours of the fairy world), while from the tree hangs the sought-for stag's head. He greets the girl, but she is extremely uncivil, for she maintains that he has taken her dog from her. Here is the stag's head, she informs him, but the woman in the red, star-covered dress can wait for her hound indefinitely, since she considers herself to be its rightful owner. Perceval is delighted, thinking that the dog cannot be far away. He takes the stag's head down from the tree and lays it on the grass. The damsel becomes irate and wishes for an avenger. The barking of a dog is heard, and soon a white stag appears, on its back the missing hound and behind it a knight in snow-white armour. They halt at the tree, the knight kills the stag, and a fight ensues over the stag's head. Perceval gains the victory, acquires the head and the dog, and the knight (Garsales) is sent to Arthur with the maiden (Riseult). From him, Perceval also learns the circumstances of the Black Knight from the tomb. Inadvertently, this knight had come to the land of Avalon and had there fallen so deeply in love with a beautiful maiden that he was unable ever to be parted from her again. He, now, lives with her, in an invisible castle she has built. At the entrance to the castle, she has erected a mausoleum with the effigy of a knight inside it, visible to everyone, so that her enraptured lover, who might otherwise find the time in the company of his beautiful lady hanging heavily on his hands, shall have the opportunity of fighting there with passing knights.

Although Perceval had word of his mother's death immediately after leaving the Grail Castle, it is as if he were only now fully grasping the painful occurrence to its full extent. It is a

[30] A different castle from the one known as the *Chastel merveilleux*.

well-known fact that psychically affecting events are realized step by step, so to speak. In this instance, it has taken more than ten years for Perceval to experience the full extent of his loss. Earlier, we took the death of the mother as symbolizing a state of being cut off from the unconscious, and it seems, accordingly, that throughout his unhappy experiences, Perceval has gradually become painfully conscious of this state of psychic withering and is beginning to realize that he is literally going round in circles. The knight who is trying to do violence to the girl is indeed himself in his first adventure, when he kissed the young woman asleep in the tent and stole her ring. This time, at any rate, he kills the violent man in himself and commits himself more and more to the hermit, a purely spiritual guide and father figure, who evidently helps him to become conscious of himself.

He again abandons his sister (an aspect of the endogamous anima),[31] while the "other-worldly" castle of maidens, with its symbol of wholeness, indicated by the four, remains in the background like a dream vision, without establishing any lasting connection with his masculine consciousness. All of these events anticipate the end of the narrative, pointing more and more to the withdrawal of the Grail into the Beyond. In those days, the difficulty of the inner problem was also conducive to the virtual elimination of the figure of woman from Robert de Boron's contemporary version.[32] This tendency is already apparent, in this rendering, when Perceval's father, Alain li Gros, the son of Brons, refuses to marry and only does so after his emigration to Britain, where he begets Perceval and sends him off to King Arthur's court.

Apart from his mother and sister, who are fairly shadowy and who die early, women play hardly any part in the life of de Boron's Perceval. Like his father Alain before him, he says that he will not and is not meant to have anything to do with them.

[31] Concerning this cf. above.

[32] According to the Didot MS. the dying Alain hears a voice that tells him his father is in the same country and is unable to die until his—Alain's—son shall have found him, taken over the guardianship of the Grail and learned the secret words. Nothing is said there about the mother's death.

This accords with the Christian and religious nature of de Boron's work but at the same time deprives it of important psychological components. Woman is only briefly suggested, namely as the sister who tells him of his mother's death and conducts him to the hermit uncle so that he may be absolved of his offence. The meeting is an isolated occurrence, and after some time Perceval hears that she has died. The fairy woman with the chessmen also appears, she for whose dog Perceval must search and who promises to reward him for the task with her love. In the course of many adventures he finds the dog but waives his claim to the reward, for he has no time to waste; he must press on in his search for the Grail.

In place of the anima, it is the archetype of the Wise Old Man which appears time and again to the seeker, admonishing, criticizing and showing the way. Once it is the hermit—the Grail King's brother, therefore Perceval's uncle—or again it is Merlin who, in the form of an old man with a sickle hung round his neck, meets Perceval shortly before he finds the Grail Castle for the second time and reproaches him for spending more than one night in the same place, in spite of his vow not to do so.

Compared to this version of de Boron's, which almost completely evades the subject of the anima, Chrétien's continuators at any rate have tried to give at least an anticipatory form to the problem of the feminine. Thus, in the *Queste*, Perceval succeeds in winning the stag's head and the hound for the water-woman in the red, star-covered dress. He finds the object of his search in the domain of an enraged fairy, where the stag's head is fastened to a gigantic oak tree. The oak refers to Wotan and the pre-Christian tree worship in the groves of the sacred oaks; the red and white of the fairy's dress also alludes to the same region. The angry remark she makes about the red-robed Star Woman aligns this fairy woman with the *pucelle de malaire*, whom we have already interpreted as the aspect of the anima that desires to maintain Perceval's unfortunate state of being possessed or else refuses to free him, i.e. *she is the deluding aspect of the anima*. This fairy, who strives for a "suspension" of the problem symbolized by the stag's head and therefore desires to arrest Perceval's progress, can equally be interpreted as such a figure. As has already been anticipated, the command of the Grail Bearer will continue to enforce a status quo, an unending restitution of the Christian attitude, until such time as Perceval shall have asked the question about the Grail. A mere regression into paganism would be equally meaningless, so that this state of suspension, this crucifixion of the animal soul and the agonizing conflict bound up with it, must be maintained until the growth of consciousness striven for by the unconscious, namely the question concerning the Grail, has been achieved. The White Knight remains fixed in the role of a noble, adapted, Christian knight of the old school, a regressive tendency (like Gauvain) that wishes to hinder Perceval in the performance of his higher duty. In this he does not succeed, for Perceval takes the stag's head, which means that he comes to a point where he can very nearly recognize the shadow of the Christian principle. Here once more is that curious reversal of values which we observe throughout the story. The Black Knight is really the sought-for Anthropos aspect which Perceval should integrate, while the White Knight, the bright hero, turns into the enemy who tries to impede the task set by the Star Woman. Perceval defeats him in the end, which no doubt means that he succeeds in overcoming the shadow of Christianity, namely its *superbia*, which is so estranged from nature.

From this moment on the hero's destiny finally takes a turn for the better, so we must attribute a particular importance to this event, even though it is recorded unobtrusively enough in the long succession of adventures. To be sure, Perceval has not yet discovered his Anthropos role; nevertheless he has overcome a main obstacle on the path—that is, his arrogant identification with the principle of light and logos—wherefore he immediately receives tidings of the repressed Anthropos who, so he hears, has been wafted out of this world by the bonds of his lady's love.

For this reason, the way to a new phase of life now opens up for him. As he is searching for the castle that housed the chessmen, he sees a white mule with a golden bridle standing in the middle of the path. It is already evening. Perceval, much astonished, catches sight of the owner of the mule, a beautiful damsel in a cloak, coming towards him. He offers to help her mount, but she declines and also refuses his offer of an escort. He would do better to go his own way, she tells him; he will be risking his life if he goes with her; she does not desire his company. Nevertheless he rides along at her side. In the thick forest it gets darker all the time; neither the moon nor the stars are visible and no breeze stirs. Suddenly, he sees something bright, like a burning candle, in the distance; then there appear to be five of them, and soon it looks as if the whole forest is on fire. It seems like a miracle to Perceval. He asks the girl where the light is coming from but gets no reply and then notices that she has disappeared. A sudden heavy downpour forces him to take shelter under a tree, and when the storm is over the light has vanished. He then lies down to sleep and continues his journey the following day.

Soon he meets the beautiful girl on the mule again. This time she is extremely affable and tells him that she had not wanted to ride with him because she had promised her friend not to share any other man's company until he should return. She did not notice the storm, it had been a most beautiful night, but she is able to explain the bright glow. Has he heard of the rich Fisher King who lives here in the neighbourhood, on the far side of the river? He travelled through the forest the night before and the brightness, which looked like a high-burning fire, came from the precious Grail, in which the blood of the King of Kings was received when he hung on the Cross. The Fisher King has this Grail with him in the forest. Those who see it cannot be claimed by the Devil that day; therefore the King, who is a holy man, has it carried around with him. Perceval naturally wants to hear more about the Grail, but the damsel can enlighten him no further.

Car ce est chose trop sacrée
Si ne doist estre recontée
Par dame ne par demoisele.

For it is a thing too holy
And may not be recounted
By matron or maid.

It is such a holy thing that it may be spoken of by no one except an ordained priest or a man who lives a holy life (who desires nothing that belongs to another and will not do evil unto others what evil is done unto him). Only such a one may speak of the Grail and recount the miracle, and no one may hear of it without blanching and trembling with fear.

The damsel thereupon leads Perceval to a tent where he is regaled with delicious food. She then gives him the mule, which will speedily carry him to the *pont de voirre*, a "bridge of crystal" that spans a wide river. When he has crossed over the bridge he must send the mule back. She also gives him a ring set with a stone of magic power. Provided he wears the ring he need fear nothing, but he must not lose it, for as soon as they meet again she will require both ring and mule of him. They take leave of each other and Perceval finds the glass bridge. It is only two and a half feet wide and is transparent, so that the water flowing beneath it is visible. Without hesitation the mule steps on to the bridge, but Perceval's horse, which he is leading, evidences great fear. The bridge collapses behind him with a crash. Although he imagines he is plunging down with the bridge, Perceval nevertheless trusts the mule to bring him safely across. When he looks round after gaining the far bank,he is amazed to see the whole structure in position again. Nearby he meets a knight who tells him of another extraordinary bridge, a *pont où nul ne passe* (bridge over which no one crosses), and of a tournament that is taking place at Chastel Orguelleus where it is possible to win the highest prize.

Perceval decides to go to the castle, leaving the stag's head and the dog with his new friend, *Brios de la Forêt arsée* (Brios of the Burning Forest), who gives him lodging. The following day, his host accompanies him to the *pont où nul ne passe*, so-called because it only reaches as far as the middle of the river. Perceval, as the foremost knight, succeeds in getting across in the following manner: When he reaches the middle of the bridge there is a deafening crash; the head of the bridge has been torn from the earth and swings around so that it now lies on the opposite bank, and the crossing is thus made possible. Whereupon, Brios realizes that Perceval is the best, bravest and most gallant of knights. Perceval proceeds to Chastel Orguelleus, where he defeats all comers without making himself known and in the evening returns to the bridge, where Brios awaits him. The same events are repeated the following day, and the day after that,Perceval collects the stag's head and the dog and proceeds on his way.

He comes to a grave, from which a voice is calling loudly. Dismounting, Perceval releases the knight imprisoned there. By way of thanks, the knight pushes Perceval into the grave, slams down the stone lid of the coffin and hurriedly tries to ride off on the mule. The animal, however, is not to be budged, any more than the horse, and finally the knight has to let Perceval out of the grave, for he recognizes that the latter is the best of all knights. He shows Perceval the way to Mount Doulourous, in case he wishes to perform further deeds of chivalry, and then jumps back into his grave once more.

Soon thereafter, Perceval comes upon a veiled damsel seated beneath an oak tree. She gets up on his arrival and demands that he give her the ring and the mule. She then takes off her veil; Perceval recognizes and embraces her joyfully. When she asks whether he has been to the Fisher King and asked about the Grail, the lance and the sword, and about the mysterious adventures, Perceval, somewhat embarrassed, replies that he has not been there yet,but tells her everything that has happened to him in the meantime. He returns the mule and the ring, whereupon the woman quickly rides away without saying goodbye. Alone, Perceval once more spends the night in the forest.

In this part of the story, a woman riding a mule appears once again. Although in her earlier manifestation she without doubt personified a dangerous and destructive anima figure, in this instance she proves to be helpful. Later, she again appears in a benevolent guise and reveals herself as Merlin's daughter. Although the story does not say as much, it is obvious that both riders refer to the same figure. Her more negative aspect in the early stages and the regressive significance of the mule would have been occasioned by Perceval's deluded attitude, especially by the *superbia* of the stag before it was killed.

This second mule rider gives Perceval a ring with a magic stone in it, sends him over the curious bridge of glass and then across the dangerous second bridge that turns round on its own axis. The ring with the magic stone is a symbol of the bond, in and through the Self, of the commitment to wholeness. That the daughter of Merlin should give a ring and take it back again probably indicates that this anima establishes, in a special degree, the connection with the figure of Merlin who himself represents the personification of wholeness, unattained as yet but continually influencing the story from a distance. In what follows, Merlin turns out to be extremely important; for the moment it need only be mentioned that he is probably in some mysterious way associated with the wounding and healing of the Grail King and that, like an invisible guardian spirit, he stands behind Perceval on his way to the Grail Castle. With his daughter's magic ring, Perceval can ride over the extraordinary bridge. We have already interpreted the ford or river-crossing as the "dangerous transition" that causes a significant alteration in the psychic attitude. In the same way, the ferryman who helps Gauvain also appears to illustrate the transcendent function. The bridge could therefore be conceived of as a human construction that causes the transcendent function to become a consciously realized and continually helpful attitude which takes that function into lasting consideration and makes a practical use of it. This is also indicated in the priesthood of the *pontifex*.

The first bridge is of glass, a material still very costly in the Middle Ages, to which, on account of its transparency (*diaphanitas*), spiritual qualities were attributed.[33] It almost unites the material and the spiritual. A similar glass bridge also appears in

[33] Cf. Jung, *Alchemical Studies*, par. 245.

the following form in a Finnish fairy-tale.[34] A youth is stolen by the Devil and abducted into hell, where the Devil promises him freedom if he can perform three tasks. Two of the Devil's daughters are his own but one is a human girl; the boy's first task is to choose the human daughter to be his bride. He fulfils the task, for he selects the girl on whom a fly alights, thus revealing her human nature. She then helps him solve the two remaining problems: building a glass bridge over the sea, and brewing a vast quantity of beer. The pair escape across the sea from the pursuing Devil and after many more trials and adventures are married. The glass bridge across the sea, which can only be built with the help of the anima, clearly depicts a form of spiritual understanding which makes it possible for the hero and his bride not to remain caught in the depths of the collective unconscious. The correct interpretation of a dream, for instance, can be a "bridge" of this kind, as can a religious attitude of genuine surrender to the soul, making the effectiveness of the transcendent function possible. For this reason glass is an admirable image of psychic reality in its central position between spirit and matter. In Perceval's story, the glass bridge is followed by *le pont où nul ne passe*, a still more arduous form of the *transitus*. This is only half a bridge, but it turns round on its centre when the right hero steps on to it. Being only half a bridge alludes, no doubt, to the fact that Christianity permits only the one, light half of the transcendent function to become conscious but does not allow for the psychic law of the reversal of all opposites (*enantiodromia*), which is surprisingly and frighteningly manifested in the turning round of the bridge on its own axis. It is precisely because of this, however, that Perceval is enabled to reach his goal. In doing so he walks back over the same half of the bridge, but goes forward towards the opposite bank.

This incident seemingly represents a regression which nevertheless leads forward, an impressive indication for modern man

[34] *Die Märchen in der Weltliteratur*, ed. F. van der Leyen and P. Zaunert, in a volume of Finnish and Esthonian fairy-tales, pp. 29–30, No. 29, "Der dem Teufel versprochene Königssohn."

with his apparent turning back to a quasi "pagan" attitude which nevertheless does not lose the religious and ethical values of Christianity but broadens them through further progress. The name of the bridge, *le pont où nul ne passe*, indicates the difficulty of the crossing.[35] It leads to the hero's triumph at Chastel Orguelleus. His friend, Brios of the Burning Forest, who in the meantime guards the stag's head for Perceval, probably represents the passionate man who adheres to the most essential things, while Perceval still applies himself to the outdated duties of Christian chivalry. Because to some extent he still pursues such obligations, instead of devoting himself to his main task, he is again attacked by the "knight in the grave" whom we interpreted as the Anthropos-task which Perceval has repressed. This buried knight even tries to push Perceval into the tomb in place of himself, that is, he threatens Perceval with the same remedy—total elimination from life—that the latter had inflicted on him. Perceval defends himself against the danger but without any progress being made.

The next morning, Perceval prays God to lead him to the Fisher King and then to the beautiful maiden with the wonderful chessmen. A voice calls from a bush and tells him that he need only let the hound run loose, it will show him the way. And so it comes to pass; with head down, as if following the scent, the dog runs to a castle by the river and goes straight in through the gateway. Perceval follows but sees no one. He ties up his horse and enters a beautiful hall where gorgeous tapestries hang on the walls and the floor is strewn with flowers. In the centre is an equally magnificent couch on which the hound is already lying, and beside it is the chessboard. Perceval sits in front of the board and takes a pawn. A door opens, a maiden enters, so beautiful that Perceval very nearly loses consciousness. His whole body trembles; this, he thinks, must be an angel come from Heaven to show herself to mortal men,

[35] Cf. the Shinvat Bridge of the Iranians and the Bridge al-Sirat in Islam, across which sinners plunge in their journey to the beyond. Hastings, *Encyclopaedia*, under "bridge."

Cou sambloit cose spiritable
Tant estoit bele et délitable.

Who seemed a thing of spirit,
Being so beautiful and so delightful.

When he has somewhat collected himself he hands over the stag's head and the hound, which breaks into joyous barking. The Star Woman accepts both with thanks. A meal is then served, after which she sits with Perceval at a window overlooking the river and asks him his name and everything that befell him on the search for the stag's head. In return she tells him how she came into possession of the chessboard, which had belonged to the fairy Morgana and had been made in London on the Thames. He reminds her of her promise and she grants him her love. He is not able to tarry, however, for he now wishes to get to the Fisher King as quickly as possible. He can be there the next day, she tells him, if he will keep to the right road, which she will show him. After he has armed himself for the journey, she leads him to a river where a boat tied to an oak tree awaits its passenger. He must use it to cross to the other bank, and there he will find the road that leads to the Fisher King.

Here the Star Woman reveals that it is she who has inherited the fairy Morgana's chessboard, a fact which points to a certain correspondence between the two figures. As mentioned earlier, the symbol of the chessboard undoubtedly embraces the idea of the confrontation of the opposites in the square field action, and is thus an image of the realization of wholeness. Morgana is the fairy by whom knights were sometimes entranced, and it would not have been surprising if even Perceval had suffered this fate at the hands of the Star Woman. Only the unanswered Grail question keeps him from this doom. Thus, a mysterious opposition is once more revealed between the Star Woman, who desires to take the stag's head for herself, and the Grail Bearer, who presides over Perceval's solution of the Grail riddle. The Star Woman is obviously a pagan nature goddess capable of blotting out the Christian achievement of consciousness. The

Grail Bearer, on the other hand, personifies the aspect of the anima that progressively encourages a further achievement of consciousness. For all that, the Star Woman no longer holds Perceval in her thrall, but actually sets him on the way to the Grail Castle; nature herself acknowledges the spiritual task.

In the meantime, while riding through the wood, Perceval sees a child in the branches of a tree. The child cannot give him any information about the Grail Castle but tells him instead that he will reach Mount Doulourous the following day. This proves correct. Perceval finds the famous post and ties his horse securely to it. A maiden on a white mule appears and tells him that her father Merlin built the castle, including the pillar which will reveal the foremost knight, namely he who can tie his horse to it.

Perceval rides on and towards evening sees in the distance a tree on which many lights are burning. On approaching it, he finds only a chapel with a dead knight lying on the altar. It is the same chapel in which Gauvain saw a black hand appear and extinguish the altar candles. Next morning, Perceval meets first a hunter, from whom he learns that he is near the Grail Castle, and later a young woman who explains to him that the child in the tree and the chapel with the black hand are connected with the "holy mystery" of the Grail and the lance.

A profusion of important new motifs is here introduced in compact form. It is worth while to examine these more closely. Later on, at the Grail Castle, Perceval learns that the child in the tree did not want to tell him the way to the Grail on account of his many sins, and that it had climbed higher and higher up the tree in order to indicate that man should raise his thoughts up to God or to show how large the world was.

The same motif is also to be found in an English legend printed in 1575, which describes what Seth saw in Paradise: "In the midst of paradise there rose a shining fountain, from which four streams flowed, watering the whole world. Over the fountain stood a great tree with many branches and twigs, but it looked like an old tree, for it had no bark and no leaves. Seth knew that this was the tree of whose fruit his parents had eaten, for which reason it now stood bare. Looking more closely, Seth saw that a naked snake without a skin had coiled itself round the tree. It was the serpent by whom Eve had been persuaded to eat of the forbidden fruit. When Seth took a second look at paradise he saw that the tree had undergone a great change. It was now covered with bark and leaves, and in its crown lay a little new-born babe wrapped in swaddling clothes, that wailed because of Adam's sin."[36] Jung interprets the child as Christ, i.e. Adam Secundus who, in some well-known representations of the genealogy, is depicted at the top of a tree growing out of Adam's body.

According to many Gnostic and alchemical texts, the tree means both *gnosis* (knowledge) and *sapientia* (wisdom),[37] and in a certain sense it is also man in his comprehensive form as the Anthropos. In the English legend it is clear that the babe in the tree represents an intimation of the birth of Christ who, in the days to come, will grow out of the Tree of Knowledge which has withered because of the sin of the first parents. What, though, does the child in the Grail legend mean? It is obviously not a prefiguration of Christ, whose birth and death already lay in the distant past. It is really not possible to avoid the conclusion that *it must refer to an intimation of the birth of a new redeemer*, similar to the son of the woman crowned with stars in the Apocalypse. Jung interprets that figure as a symbol of the process of individuation,[38] depicting a continuation of Christ's work of redemption in the single individual, and it is natural to interpret the child here in the same sense. So it is understandable that it shuns Perceval and only shows him the way to Mount Doulourous, for we know from the context that Perceval has not yet understood the nature of his task. The withdrawal of the child is in accordance with the later withdrawal of the Grail into Heaven, which indicates that a realization of the Self was not yet possible at the level of development in those days, and that therefore it had to remain latent in the unconscious. Even so the child sends Perceval to the pillar at Mount Doulourous, to

[36] Quoted from *Alchemical Studies*, par. 400. [37] *Ibid.*, par. 419.
[38] *Psychology and Religion*, pars. 713–17.

which only the "foremost knight" is able to fasten his horse. The column on the hill is similar to the tree in meaning; it embodies a maternal principle,[39] *the axis of the world*, the framework of the process of individuation.[40] The tree, as Jung says, "symbolizes a living process as well as a process of enlightenment, which, though it may be grasped by the intellect, should not be confused with it".[41] In many of the rites of primitive peoples a post is set up to mark the centre of the world, and around it revolves the ritual event.[42] In this sense the post is a centre, like the point of all psychic happenings. The mountain also has a similar meaning.[43] The name of the "grievous" mountain has a special significance, as if in this phase of development the Self were first experienced as that which stimulated suffering, in an analogy to the Christian Passion. The mountain is almost a parallel to the Hill of Calvary and symbolizes the anguish of becoming conscious. Tying the horse to the pillar accords with a painful binding and restriction of the animal soul, which is subjugated and bound to the centre, the Self.[44] In so far as the horse represents the instinct that carries consciousness,[45] it means that instinct, by being bound to the pillar, is concentrated on the individuation process and robbed of its free roaming motion. The pillar was set up by Merlin; therefore his figure and that of his daughter acquire an ever more profound significance; they seem to personify the *principium individuationis* par excellence.

Next, Perceval comes upon a tree on which many lights are burning; it is later explained that it is "fey," a magic tree, and that its lights are deceptive. Perceval cannot be lead astray by it because he is determined to accomplish the miracle of this world and make an end of such illusions.

[39] Cf. J. Przyluski, "Ursprünge und Entwicklung des Kultes der Muttergöttin," pp. 17*ff.*

[40] The stele erected by Solomon and the "Mountain of Purification" in Dante's *Paradiso* may be taken as analogues of a miraculous past of this kind. Cf. Kampers, *op. cit.*, pp. 60*ff.*

[41] *Alchemical Studies*, par. 413.

[42] Cf. Mircea Eliade, "La vertu créatrice du mythe," pp. 67*ff.*

[43] Cf. *Alchemical Studies*, par. 407.

[44] *Ibid.*, the chapter, "The Motif of Torture," pars. 439*ff.*

[45] Cf. *Symbols of Transformation*, par. 421.

The effect of the magic tree is as a negative aspect of the tree with the babe in it. In fact, the symbol of the tree can, in certain circumstances, have a negative meaning of this kind. Thus the Gnostic, Simon Magus, compares the universe to a tree of fire. At some future time the tree will have to be burnt, and only the fruit, after it is fully developed and has acquired its form, will not be thrown into the fire but gathered into a barn.[46] This fruit is the image of the Anthropos, the Self. The alchemists also explained their Mercurius as a sap that grows in the tree but that also burns it up;[47] he is "the *spiritus vegetativus* that pervades the whole of nature, both animating and destructive." [48] Blaise de Vigenère (1523–1569?), an alchemist who was influenced by cabalism, speaks of a "trunk of the tree of death that sent out a red death-ray." [49] There the tree becomes the coffin and death mother. This symbol of the tree and even the *lumen naturae* that streams from it are here shown to be purely negative will-o'-the-wisp which Perceval must shun. For in those days, unlike the present, the recognition of nature could have implied a dangerous loss of direction, because it would have seduced naïve medieval man into the abyss in which he would no longer have been able to find his way. The primitive in him was still too close to the surface. The sinister tree of lights grows beside a chapel on whose altar lies a dead knight, and a ghostly black hand extinguishes the altar candles at Perceval's approach. We learn later that the evil Pinogre (Epinogre) killed his mother in this chapel because she wanted to become a nun, and that because of this more than four thousand knights have lost their lives. At a later date, Perceval has to fight the Devil in this same chapel and also to fetch a veil out of a chest, lay it in a golden vessel and look after it. He must, however, bury the dead knight.

The motif of the dead knight was interpreted when Gauvain's adventures were described. It appears to refer to an aspect of the Anthropos, the Self, that is not sufficiently expressed in the Christ image, to a shadow of Christ which reposes in that spot

[46] Cf. *Alchemical Studies*, par. 459, note 8.
[47] *Ibid.*, par. 459. [48] *Ibid.*, par. 408. [49] *Ibid.*, par. 401.

where Christ's body, in the form of the Host, is preserved. Furthermore, a crime was committed in the place, a matricide that was followed by still further misfortune. It was in fact unconscious nature herself that compelled Perceval to commit matricide, but at the same time she also attacked his one-sided masculine development as an unbalanced deviation, so that Perceval should now become conscious of this paradox. This is the reason the ghostly evidence of the murder of a mother is brought to his notice. It is obvious that Christ's adversary, the Devil himself, would also be roving around in a place of this kind. The motif of matricide produces an uncanny effect when it is borne in mind that Perceval is not guiltless in his mother's death either and has, as already mentioned, offended against the feminine principle in diverse ways. It is therefore as if Pinogre were an image of a destructive side of which he had remained unconscious—an unrealized aspect of his own shadow. He is one in the long series of figures of the invisible enemy that threatens Gauvain and all the other Christian knights, as well as the Grail King, in their capacity of typifying the Christian man in general, and that, in the form of the Antichrist, finally menaces Christ himself. Significantly, Pinogre is enraged because his mother wishes to take the veil, that is, because of her unconditional submission to the Christian principle and especially to the vow of chastity. (The restitution of the veil possibly refers to this.) It is the proscription of sexuality in particular that provokes the reaction of the dark, antichristian world. When Perceval has to lay the veil in a golden vessel, this not only offers an analogy to the Grail, but the vessel could in this context refer specifically to the fact that the nun's veil must be understood psychically, so to speak, and assimilated as a psychic content. It is expressly stated that these things in the chapel were connected with the mystery of the Grail and this lends them a particular importance. Considering their inner significance it seems likely that the problem of the opposites in the Christian aeon is portrayed here, irrespective of the fact that in this instance it is not the principle represented by the King, but the feminine essence, that is damaged. Afterwards Perceval departs from this chapel. He cannot solve the problem of the shadow, so he rides on without having understood the meaning of what he has seen.

Finally he arrives at the long-sought-for goal, the Grail Castle. Servants approach him and lead him into the hall where, as in the past, the Grail King is seated on a purple couch. He asks Perceval where he has spent the previous night. Perceval gives an account of his adventures and desires to know the meaning of the child in the tree, of the tree with the lights and also of the chapel with the dead knight. The King is fully prepared to give him the information, but first they must eat. As they are sitting at the table the young woman with the Grail enters, followed by another with the bleeding lance, and a page brings a sword broken in two in the middle. Now Perceval delays no longer with his questions; he refuses to eat until he has heard the answers.

The King first explains about the child in the tree. Before he can learn any more, however, Perceval must try to join the broken sword together. He succeeds in doing this, although a tiny crack remains visible. The King says that he can see that Perceval is indeed the most excellent knight of all so far, but that even so he has not yet achieved enough. Disheartened, Perceval sighs so that all can hear it. Whereupon the King leaps up and, embracing him with much joy, greets him as the present master of his house.

Sire soies de ma maison
ie vos mes tot en abandon
Quanque ie ai, sans nul dangier
et des or vos aurai plus chier
que nul autre qui jamais soit.

Sir, be lord of my house.
Soon I will leave you
whatever I have, without any danger,
and from now on will hold you more dear
than anyone else who ever lived.

The King of the Sea calling for help, from Trismosin,
'Splendor Solis' (1582)

Stag and Unicorn, symbolizing soul and spirit, from Lambspringk, 'Figurae et emblemata' (1677)

The page who brought in the sword now wraps it in a cloth and takes it away again.

Et Perceval se réconforte.[50]

And Perceval was comforted.

With this scene, Gautier's Continuation comes to an end. Perceval has still not received the answer to the question about the Grail, nor has the Grail King been healed. The first accounts of this event are given by the subsequent continuators, especially by Manessier who takes up the thread of the narrative at this point. Obviously the continuators were not really clear about the proper ending, for the various versions differ from each other, and here once again is exhibited that remarkable shimmering uncertainty that we have already noticed in connection with the word *Grail*.

[50] Quoted from A. Rochat, *Über einen bisher unbekannten Percheval li Galois.* The volume in question, Potvin's edition of the MS., was not available.

CHAPTER XV

The Redemption of the Grail Kingdom; Perceval's End

A FRAGMENT OF the "Perceval" preserved in Bern, which accords to a great extent with Gautier's Continuation, has an ending that conforms closely to de Boron's prose "Perceval." Perceval inquires about the lance and learns that it is the one that pierced the side of the crucified Christ. He asks what the Grail is and who is served from it. At these words the King springs up—he is healed. After explaining that the Grail was the vessel in which Joseph of Arimathea received Christ's blood at the descent from the Cross, the King asks Perceval his name. He then reveals that Alain li Gros, Perceval's father, was his son (in this passage the Grail King is, therefore, Perceval's grandfather) and that Alain's mother, Enygeus, who was therefore Perceval's grandmother, was Joseph of Arimathea's sister. In conclusion he announces that Perceval will now wear the crown and reign as King and that he himself will remain alive for only three more days. The story ends with his death and burial.

In Manessier the conclusion takes a somewhat different form. There too the King tells the same story of the Grail and the lance as in de Boron and in the *Grand Saint Graal.* But in addition, Perceval learns that the Grail bearer is the King's daughter, and that the girl who carried the silver platter is the daughter of King Goon du Desert.

The Grail King decides that it is time to retire, but Perceval still wishes to know the meaning of the broken sword. Here at last we receive an explanation of the mysterious events which occurred during Gauvain's visit to the Grail Castle. Goon du

Desert is a brother of the Fisher King. On one occasion he was besieged in his fortress, Quiquagrant, by an enemy called Espinogre, whom he mortally wounded in a sortie. A nephew of Espinogre, whose name was Partiniaus, "the Lord of the Red Tower," swore to avenge him. He attired himself as one of Goon's knights, in order to approach him unobtrusively, and struck him with the sword. It broke in two at this treacherous blow. Goon's body was carried to his brother's stronghold, the Grail Castle. His daughter brought the pieces of the broken sword to the Castle and prophesied that one day a knight would come who would join the two halves together and avenge the dead man. Picking the pieces up carelessly, the Fisher King was wounded in the hip by them, and the wound will not heal until his brother's death has been avenged.

The following day, Perceval sets out in search of Partiniaus. Once again he has to undergo a number of adventures, among them a few encounters with the Devil, whom he has already fought in the Chapel of the Black Hand. He is accompanied by *le Chevalier Couart* (the Cowardly Knight) who is so greatly transformed in the process that he is henceforth known as *le Chevalier Hardi* (the Courageous Knight). In combat with a knight of the Round Table, each is so badly wounded he remains lying on the battlefield—whereupon the Grail appears and heals them both. After many other less important adventures, Perceval finally arrives at Partiniaus' castle. In front of it grows a pine tree from which hangs a shield. He throws this shield to the ground, whereupon Partiniaus comes out of the castle and a violent struggle ensues. Perceval is the victor. Partiniaus, who will accept no conditions, is killed. Perceval decapitates him and with the head sets out once more in search of the Grail Castle. He finds it, as if by chance, only after he has ridden around for the entire summer. A watchman who sees him nearing the Castle informs the King that a knight with a head hanging from his saddle-bow is approaching. The King straightway springs to his feet, healed. Partiniaus' head is impaled on a staff and set on top of the highest tower.

Then, once more, there follows the meal with the Grail

procession. When Perceval tells the company his name, it turns out that he is the son of the King's sister (not the grandson, as in the other version). He refuses, however, to accept the crown as long as his uncle is alive. He returns to Arthur's court where he recounts his adventures to the best chronicler, who is commanded by Arthur to write them down and preserve them in a casket in Salisbury.

After some time the Grail messenger arrives with news of the King's death. Perceval marches to the Grail Castle, accompanied by the entire court, who assist at his coronation and remain with him for a whole month. During this interval, the Grail serves the assembled company with the most delicious foods. Perceval gives his cousin—the Grail Bearer—and the maiden with the platter, in marriage to two valiant knights. He reigns in peace for seven years. Then he follows a hermit into the desert, where he is accompanied by the Grail, the lance and the sacred platter. He serves the Lord for ten more years. At his death Grail, lance and platter are probably carried off to heaven, for they are never seen again.

Thus our story is finally brought to a conclusion. There is a further continuation or interpolation, attributed to one Gerbert, which again retails a number of adventures but which resembles the basic story in all of the important points and, for that reason, will not be given further consideration here.

According to the Gautier version the Grail King and his kingdom are healed because Perceval asks the proper question, thereby concerning himself with the problems of the realm. In so far as the Grail region represents the unconscious, one must then assume that even at that time, it was manifesting an intensive readiness to communicate its contents to consciousness. It is therefore possible *to see this failure to become conscious on the part of contents that were ripe for consciousness as being responsible for the King's sickness*. These contents were the opposites which were not sufficiently recognized in the lack of ambiguity of the medieval Christian orientation of consciousness. Through this question Perceval becomes, so to speak, a counterpart to Adam, who was forbidden to eat of the Tree of Knowledge. He becomes the saviour who expiates the old offence through a new achievement. This role of the messiah is very clearly exhibited by the Grail hero, Galahad, in the *Queste del Saint Graal.*

In de Boron's version the moment of *kairos,* the propitious instant of time, is particularly emphasized; Perceval appears when the time is fulfilled and the Grail can be found. This is the result of the remarkable circumstance that there was a gap of four hundred years between Brons, the second guardian of the Grail, and Perceval, the third, during which time the Grail was concealed—i.e. it vanished into the unconscious—and also of the fact that the Rich Fisher was suffering, not from a wound but chiefly from the weakness of old age.

In other versions, the wounding and sickness of the Fisher King play the chief part and, like the devastation of the land and the general need of redemption, are connected with an offence that must be expiated or compensated for.

This leads back once again to Adam, the original man or Anthropos, whose redemption, from the beginning of time until today, forms the great task of mankind. We thus have a twofold tracing of the motif: on the one hand, something that has to be redeemed from a condition of unconsciousness or that is old and needs to be rejuvenated or replaced; on the other, something ailing that, as the result of a lapse, has fallen into a condition requiring redemption. This is further seen in the many versions, such as Wolfram's for instance, where there is, in addition to the Grail King who is healed, yet another old man who dies when the Grail is found. The Grail hero thus has two acts of redemption to accomplish.

In so far as it is a question of the coming to consciousness of something that was unconscious, learning and knowledge have a redeeming effect. In the story this is expressed when, again and again, Perceval is induced to give an account of his adventures, either by the Wise Old Man or by an anima figure. But how does the other salvation, that of the guilty invalid, come about?

In spite of the Christian religious character of most of the stories, redemption is not effected in a strictly Christian manner, i.e. not through faith in the Son of God, sacrificed for mankind. It does not happen in a pagan or primitive—one might also say Oriental—way, i.e. as the result of an *enantiodromia*, where development and regression unfailingly flow into each other in an eternal rhythm and cycle, the one situation being thus almost transformed and redeemed by the other, its opposite. Nor does redemption occur after the manner of the Indian doctrine of salvation, according to which everything has to be recognized as nothing but illusion. Here it happens in a different way, not through the action of a god (though naturally it is *Deo concendente*, since whosoever accomplishes it has to be destined thereto by God) and also not through nature, but solely by the unflinching exertions of a human being, Perceval; just as neither more nor less than this can be brought to the *opus* of alchemy or to the realization of the Self. It must, however, be remarked that Perceval's way to the Grail, the *opus* of alchemy and the realization of the Self all have this in common with the Christian way of salvation: they all signify an *opus contra naturam*, i.e. a way, not of the least but of the greatest resistance. This is also the reason why the archetypal images that refer to the process of individuation or that accompany it are so often Christian symbols as well, for instance the cross.

One wonders whether the emphasis on human achievement, which does not, however, consist in so-called good works or in virtue according to the law, is perhaps, in contradistinction to mere faith, a concept or contribution that Western man has added to the Christian doctrine. This would accord with his gift for action and the high value he places on individuality and personality.

In itself, deliverance as the result of the right kind of question is a universal, i.e. an archetypal, motif. Indeed,in fairy-tales it is usual for the hero who wishes to acquire the treasure to have to fulfil one or more special conditions, on the correct execution of which the result depends. One such condition is the question. There is often a prohibition on asking, as for instance in the legend of Lohengrin where it is a matter of guarding a mystery.

The mystery is generally that of the hero's descent which, most frequently, is miraculous. With Perceval the matter stands differently. Excepting in Wolfram, and in Wagner where "a pure fool, through pity wise" becomes the quintessence of Parsifal's character, the question is not based on compassion. On the contrary, in Chrétien and the others it runs: "Who is served from the Grail?" or "To whom is the Grail brought?" *This* is the question through which redemption comes about.

This seems very peculiar. He who is served from the Grail is the *old*, not the *ailing*, king and is Perceval's grandfather or uncle. By means of the question, Perceval reveals himself to be a descendant and establishes the connection with his ancestors. This again is an important feature in the initiation dreams and ceremonies of primitive peoples.

A certain Judaic custom forms a very interesting parallel to this motif. At the Passover, after the first cup has been drunk, the youngest son must ask the father about the meaning of the observance, whereupon the latter recounts the story of the Exodus from Egypt. The biblical passage (Exodus 12:25–27) reads: "And it shall come to pass, when ye be come to the land which the Lord will give you, according as he hath promised, that ye shall keep this service. And it shall come to pass, when your children shall say unto you, What mean ye by this service? That ye shall say, It is the sacrifice of the Lord's passover, who passed over the houses of the children of Israel in Egypt, when he smote the Egyptians, and delivered our houses. And the people bowed the head and worshipped."

The Grail question is: "Who is served from it?", and the expression *le service del Graal* (the service of the Grail) is used again and again. The Israelites' memorial of their exile in Egypt calls to mind the exile of the Britons. This is the closest parallel to the Grail question we have been able to find.

In our story, the old King can die only when he is able to recognize his descendant as such and can hand his property—in this case the Grail—over to him. In a few versions, for instance in de Boron's work known as the *Prose Perceval*, Perceval's father, the long dead Alain li Gros, has a dream in which the Holy

Ghost informs him that his father, Brons, is somewhere in Ireland and that the Grail is there with him. He will be unable to die until Alain's son, Perceval, shall find him and he is able to transmit the vessel and impart the secret words to his grandson. (It is possible that memories of the Briton's time of exile were still preserved in this passage.)

This taking over of the treasure, together with the mystery of the ancestors is actually, therefore, the redeeming factor. Indeed, it is not so much that the old Grail King is delivered from his sufferings as from *life* itself. In those versions, also, in which there are two kings, one sick and the other old, the king who is healed remains alive for only a few days. In this respect, *Diû Krône* has a very interesting ending. The Grail King says to Gauvain, who has asked the question, that by doing so he has redeemed many souls, both of the living and of the dead. He, the King, together with the court, are among the latter; they only *appear* to be living, whereas the Grail Bearer and her companions are *really alive*. This is especially noteworthy. It means, apparently, that in the world of collective consciousness an old king (the king corresponds to a dominant attitude), who has already lived too long, must continue to lead a semblance of life until the new life is so far advanced that it can take the place of the old.

This concept of handing over and taking over has something very archaic about it. It suggests a time before there was any writing by which knowledge could be preserved; knowledge had to be transmitted orally from father to son, carefully guarded by the father and received by the son only when he reached maturity. The almost ritual significance with which this event is invested expresses the enormous importance for man at a primitive level of culture of the fact that he can remember and transmit *knowledge*. The continuity of consciousness is, in point of fact, the *conditio sine qua non* of human mental and cultural development. The reason the redemption depends on the "question" concerning a knowledge of the ancestors is thus easily explained. It must be remembered that at that time consciousness was very much less developed than it is today. The motif of the old king is duplicated; psychologically speaking, this indicates uncertainty in most cases, as if it could signify both this *and* that. This dual motif must be examined more closely. Certain scholars have compared the old king who cannot die with the Greek Kronos who, after his overthrow by Zeus, was confined, asleep, on an island in England.[1] As Marx explains,[2] a whole group of such old-king figures are to be found in the various versions.

In de Boron's version especially, the redemptive death of the old king is expressly described. Perceval's visit to the Grail Castle follows exactly the same course as in Chrétien,except that in the former three drops of blood flow from the lance, an allusion no doubt to the Trinity. The Grail again appears during the meal at the Fisher King's castle, "and worthy relics with it" ("*et des dignes reliques avec*"). Perceval asks the familiar question, whereupon the King immediately becomes healthy and is quite transformed ("*tot muez de sa nature*"). Perceval reveals himself as Alain's son, is joyfully greeted by his grandfather, who leads him to the Grail and says, "This is the lance with which Christ was wounded on the Cross, and this is the vessel in which Joseph of Arimathea collected the blood and which is called the Grail." He then tells Perceval about Christ, about Joseph and about the Grail, and imparts secret words to him, of which the author emphasizes once again that he cannot and dare not speak.

The vessel, which radiates a wonderful melody and a heavenly perfume, is then handed over to Perceval. "On the third day," the text continues, "Brons approached his vessel, lay down before it in the form of the cross and gave up the ghost. Perceval saw David with his harp and many angels with censers waiting to carry Brons' soul to the Majesty of the Father he had served for so long. Perceval remained there, and the spell that lay over Britain and the world was broken."

In many versions,the old Grail King is of an earlier generation than the sick king and this may gives us some indication of his

[1] Cf. Nitze, *Perceval and the Legend of the Holy Grail*, pp. 318–19; and Marx, *La Légende Arthurienne et le Graal*, pp. 184 and 187.

[2] *Op. cit.*, pp. 184*ff*.

significance. As previously explained, the King in himself represents a dominant of collective consciousness and thus, at the same time, a god-image prevalent in human consciousness. The ailing Grail King corresponds to an *imago Dei* that is suspended, suffering, on the problem of the opposites; he is thus essentially the image of the Christian age and more especially of its second half. Over against him, the apparently living Grail King must have personified a still older god-image; actually, the pre-Christian, Old Testament or pagan *imago Dei*, a father figure, that is, in which the opposites were *not consciously united* but were, rather, still *unconsciously combined.* This more unconscious, archaic father-imago possesses some advantages over the god-image of the Christian age, namely its unity, but at the same time it reflects an obsolete, more unconscious condition of human consciousness.[3] For this reason, his survival is not represented in the Grail legend as a fortunate circumstance and his being enabled to die signifies a redemption. *This* king is served from the Grail because, as already explained, the Grail, as the *principium individuationis*, is the instrument for becoming whole and for the unification of God. That the old King is nourished by the Grail and for this reason does *not* die is not described as a fortunate occurence but as a cause of suffering, the unity of the god-image thus being maintained in a regressive state and not incarnated anew, on a higher and conscious level, in Perceval, the *tierz hom* (third man). *The unity of the god-image is retrospectively sought for in still surviving paganism, not in the further differentiation of the problem of Christianity.* For this reason the death of the old Grail King and his redemption at Perceval's hands signify the goal of the latter's quest. This solution cannot really be understood without going more deeply into the psychological significance of the trinitarian god-image. This will be undertaken subsequently, when we return once more to the problem of the two Grail kings.

While in the more important versions the salvation of the Grail Kingdom is brought about by Perceval asking the right question, in Manessier this is achieved by his act of vengeance

[3] For details see Jung, *Psychology and Religion*, pars. 201*ff.*

against Partiniaus. This accords with a still more radical suppression of the inner opposite and a corresponding spiritualization and denial of the primitive emotional shadow. When, therefore, after becoming King, Perceval ends his life as a hermit and the Grail is carried up to heaven with him, this does not imply a modern psychological solution but, rather, a religious, Christian one, conventional for that day. It is otherwise in Wolfram, where the story has a pronounced psychological ending. There, before taking up his office, Parzival has to fight with his black and white half-brother, Feirefiz, who is, however, not evil but merely an unbaptized heathen. Parzival does not vanquish Feirefiz but, on the contrary, recognizes him as his brother and establishes a relationship with him. It is only then that he can become the Grail King. The story thus ends with the apotheosis of two couples: Parzival is once more united with Condwiramurs, and Feirefiz, the dark brother, allows himself to be baptized and marries Repanse de Schoye, the Grail Bearer.

The formation of this quaternity is therefore the conclusion of Parzival's evolution. He has won his kingship, has reached the Castle, and he has found that centre where the Grail is and where the fire burns.

This quaternity is an illustration of the well-known motif of the "marriage quaternio," one of the most important symbols of individuation. In Wolfram's version, Parzival is a part of this quaternio. In Manessier, on the other hand, Perceval merely brings about such a quaternity inasmuch as he gives the Grail Bearer and the maiden with the platter in marriage to two knights; he himself remains outside as a hermit, and Blancheflor, for the sake of this ascetic ideal, is relegated more and more to the background of subsequent events. The Grail, moreover, is carried off to heaven, i.e. it disappears into the unconscious.

Thus a problem is touched upon in which Christian and alchemical symbolism are not in agreement. In Christianity, the teleological expectation of the "Marriage of the Lamb"[4] persists as a conception of the goal, and Christ as the spiritual king is

[4] Rev. 19:7*ff*.

the sacrifice for the well-being of his flock. As the sacrificial animal (the lamb), he is united with his bride, the Church. On the other hand, the *lapis* of the alchemists is, as Jung explains, a pronouncedly eremitical ideal, a goal for the individual. "Though likened to King Sol and even named such, it was not a sponsus, not a victim, and belonged to no community; it was like the 'treasure hid in a field, the which when a man hath found, he hideth' (Matthew 13:44), or like 'one pearl of great price,' for which a man 'went and sold all that he had, and bought it' (Matthew 13:46). It was the well-guarded, precious secret of the individual."[5] The withdrawal of the Grail probably signifies something similar, namely a symbol that confers the highest value on the individual; as such, it has no place in the community of the Church but lives on in concealment, i.e. in the unconscious, where the individual can find it. It was no mere chance that the way of life of the forest hermits, in which a search for the individual religious experience was expressed, was revived at the time of the Crusades. What this meant was a realization of monasticism on the subjective level, or an integration of the same, which would have signified an individual inner resolution of a collective tendency and aloneness with one's own inner life and the experiences resulting therefrom. But the withdrawal of the Grail symbol into heaven (which recalls the catching up into heaven of the saviour born to the woman crowned with the twelve stars, in Revelation)[6] indicates that the integration of this symbol and all that it signifies could not be achieved in the consciousness of medieval man. This is related no doubt to the fact that Chrétien's story was unable to reach an unequivocal ending, and the various continuators propounded different possibilities because there was uncertainty as to which conclusion was actually the correct one. The story of Perceval anticipates psychic problems reaching so far into the future that it could not be wholly comprehended by the medieval attitude. First of all the psychic assimilation of the Christian symbol had to proceed further. For this reason Robert de Boron, a contem-

[5] Jung, *Mysterium Coniunctionis*, par. 525.
[6] Cf. *Psychology and Religion*, pars. 711*ff.*

porary of Chrétien, did indeed undertake to shape the material along those lines. He attempted, namely, to connect the Grail legend more closely with Christian tradition, for which reason his version will be discussed in more detail in the following chapter.

CHAPTER XVI

Robert de Boron's *Roman de l'Estoire dou Graal*

UNLIKE THE POEMS about Perceval by Chrétien de Troyes, Wolfram von Eschenbach and others, which are set in a land of marvels and fairy-tales, Robert de Boron's story of the Grail exhibits a markedly Christian and religious trend. Furthermore, the hero and his adventures are far less in the foreground than are the Grail and its story. The "romance" is extant in a metrical version entitled "Josef d'Arimathie"[1] and in an exactly corresponding prose version.[2] An appended continuation deals with "Merlin," [3] and in two manuscripts of the prose version there follows yet a third part, the "Perceval."

[1] Edited by Francisque Michel, under the title *Le roman du Saint Graal*, according to the only extant MS., from the end of the thirteenth century, no. 20047 fr. in the Bibliothèque Nationale in Paris. Reprinted by F. Furnival in the appendix to Vol. I of *Seynt Graal, or the Sank Ryal*, 1861. Re-edited by Nitze, under the title, *Le Roman de l'Estoire dou Saint Graal*, in *Les Classiques français du moyen-âge*, 1927. Cf. also Nitze, "Messire Robert de Boron, Enquiry and Summary."

[2] Hucher's edition of 1875, entitled *Le Saint Graal, ou Joseph d'Arimathie: Première Branche de la Table Ronde*, contains the first part, according to a MS. of the second half of the thirteenth century known as the Cangé MS., and the same work according to the Didot MS. (named after its owner), dated 1301, as well as *Perceval, ou la Quête du Saint Graal*, likewise after the Didot MS. We are indebted to J. L. Weston for "The Prose Perceval, According to the Modena MS," Vol. II of *The Legend of Sir Perceval*, a newer edition of the "Perceval," from a MS. extant in Modena.

[3] The Merlin section may be found incorporated in a more comprehensive story entitled, *Merlin, Roman en Prose du XIIIe siècle*, edited by Paris and Ulrich according to the Huth MS., the 1886 volume of the Société des anciens Textes français. Only a fragment of the "Merlin" is preserved in the metrical version which Nitze has appended as a supplement to the above-mentioned *Roman de l'Estoire dou Saint Graal*.

In the text itself, the author of the "Josef d'Arimathie" and the "Merlin" calls himself Robert de Boron and maintains that he was the first to raise the story of the Grail from obscurity into the light of day and to translate it into French from a large Latin book. The translation was done for his patron, Gautier de Montbéliard.[4]

While there is no doubt at all as to de Boron's authorship of "Josef d'Arimathie" and "Merlin," there is no such certainty concerning the "Perceval," which is joined to the prose version. Specialist opinion on the subject is divided. On the other hand the reading public must, early on, have taken the three stories as a whole, since not only do they follow each other in the various manuscripts but also form a sequence in respect to content.

On the authority of the above mentioned publications by Hucher, J. L. Weston, and Paris and Ulrich, the three stories of "Joseph of Arimathea," "Merlin" and "Perceval" will be considered here as an integrated whole, thus also bringing the metrical version under consideration.[5] In order to give the reader an impression of the style of the story and of its prevailing atmosphere, passages will be quoted verbatim from time to time. The text begins as follows:

> It should be known by all sinners that before he came to earth Our Lord commanded the prophets to speak in his name and to announce his coming. At the time of which I speak, all men, including the prophets, went to Hell. When

[4] The fact that the Comte de Montbéliard in question went on a crusade in 1199 and died as Constable of Jerusalem in 1212, and the assumption that the work had been written before his departure, led to the conclusion that it must have originated around the year 1190, therefore roughly contemporaneous with Chrétien. According to Bodo Mergell, on the other hand, it was written ten years before Chrétien's work. According to other views the work first originated in the beginning of the thirteenth century. Cf. P. Zumthor, *Merlin*, p. 115. Whether the manner in which the one work appears to be based on the other constitutes a connection between them or whether both are based on some source unknown to us cannot as yet be stated with any certainty.

[5] In Nitze's edition.

> he had lured them all there the Devil thought he had achieved his purpose, but he was disappointed, for they comforted themselves with the thought that Jesus Christ would free them. It pleased Our Lord to come into the world, and he took up his abode in the Virgin Mary. Thus it had to be, that the race of Adam and Eve might be ransomed. He ransomed them through the Father, the Son and the Holy Ghost. These three are one and the same thing, one God. . . . How full of humility was this Lord, whom it pleased to come to earth in order to die, that his Father's work might be saved; for the Father created Adam, and Adam and Eve sinned, owing to the trick of the Enemy.

The text then describes Jesus' baptism, the meal in the house of Simon the leper, Mary Magdalene's box of precious ointment, the trial before Pilate and the betrayal by Judas. The crucifixion is only briefly alluded to. Then Joseph of Arimathea appears as a knight in Pilate's service. He "had grown fond of Christ" but for fear of the Jews has kept it hidden. After Christ is crucified, he asks Pilate for the body as repayment for services given. The request is granted, and at the same time Pilate gives him the vessel he received from the Jews in which Jesus offered up his blood the previous evening. Thereupon, Joseph, together with Nicodemus, takes Jesus' body down from the cross in order to give it burial.

> While they were washing it the wounds began to bleed, at which they were much affrighted, for they remembered the stone at the foot of the Cross that was split open by the downflowing blood. Then Joseph bethought him of his vessel and decided that the drops would be better preserved there than in any other place. So he took it and collected the blood from the wounds. He wrapped the body in a fine cloth and laid it in a sarcophagus ["*en une pierre*"] he had long possessed, meaning to be buried in it himself one day. He concealed the sarcophagus with a large flat stone so that Christ's disciples might not be able to steal the body. But he took the vessel with the blood home with him. Meanwhile Our Lord

went down to Hell, broke open its gates and released Adam and Eve and many others, according to his pleasure.

Chagrined at the disappearance of the body, the Jews throw Joseph into a concealed dungeon. No one knows what has become of him. "But he for whom he had suffered and was still suffering did not forget him; he came to him in prison, lifted the dungeon tower up from the earth and brought him his vessel."[6] At first Joseph sees nothing but a great light, and his heart rejoices and is filled with the grace of the Holy Spirit. Then he hears a voice telling him how Christ came into the world in order to save the Father's creation. The speaker reveals himself as Christ and says:

> "The Enemy, who does nothing to save lie in wait for people to incite them to evil, first seduced Eve because he saw that woman was weaker in spirit than man; and because all mankind was reduced to captivity by a woman, God desired that all should be freed once more by a woman (namely the Virgin Mary).
>
> "As the trunk bore the apple that grew from the tree by the miracle of God, so too had the Son of God to die upon the wood, in order to accomplish this salvation."

Joseph then asserts that he has long loved Christ but never dared speak to him for fear of not being believed, since he was often in the company of those who wished to bring about his death. But Christ reassures him with the words: "I left thee by thyself, because I knew what a great service thou wouldst render me, when my disciples would not dare to do so. And this thou didst out of compassion." Christ adds that he has brought none of his disciples with him because none of them know of the love between him and Joseph, and no one but himself knows of Joseph's good heart. "Thou has loved me in secret, as I too have loved thee. Our love will be revealed to all, to the great shame of unbelievers. For thou wilt have the sign of my death in thy keeping. It is here." Thereupon, the Lord produces the treasured

[6] In the Gospel of Nicodemus Christ frees Joseph from prison.

vessel which contains all of the most holy blood that Joseph collected from his precious body when he was washing it. "Thou shalt have it and preserve it, and all they into whose charge thou shalt commit it. But its guardians may only be three in number, and these three shall hold it in the name of the Father, the Son and the Holy Spirit. These three powers [*vertus*] are one and the same thing, in one God.[7] In this must thou believe." Christ then hands the vessel to the kneeling Joseph and says:

> "Thou holdest the blood of the Three Persons of the one Godhead, that flowed out from the wounds of the Son made flesh, who suffered death to save the souls of sinners. Knowest thou what thou hast gained thereby? This: that no victim [*sacramenz*] will ever be offered up. Whosoever knows about it will be the better loved in the world, and the company of those who have tidings of it and write books about it will be more sought after than that of other people."[8]

When Joseph asks how he has earned this gift, Christ answers:

> "Thou didst take me down from the Cross and lay me in thy sepulchre, after I had sat by Simon Peter at the meal and said that I would be betrayed. Because this happened at table, tables will be set up in future, that I may be sacrificed. The table signifies the Cross; the vessels in which the sacrifice and consecration will be made signify the grave wherein thou didst lay me. This is the cup in which my body will be consecrated in the form of the Host. The paten that will be laid upon it signifies the stone with which thou didst close the mouth of the tomb, the cloth that will be spread over it

[7] In the metrical version, edited by Nitze, we read:

> Et se doient croire trestuit
> Que ces trois persones sunt une
> Et persone entière est chacune.
>
> And this must be entirely believed,
> That these three persons are one
> And each is a complete person.

[8] Something similar is recounted in the legend of Fécamp. Cf. A. Langfors, *Histoire de l'Abbaye de Fécamp*, pp. 115–16.

signifies the linen that thou woundest round my body. Thus the meaning of thine action will be known to Christendom for all time, until the end of the world. It will be openly seen by sinners, and all those among them who belong to the fellowship of the believers will thereby gain eternal joy and fulfilment in their hearts, when they confess and repent of their sins. All they that are acquainted with these words will for that reason be acceptable in the world, and whosoever has absolute faith in me cannot be wrongfully condemned before the judges, nor yet fall in battle." . . . And Christ taught him words[9] that I cannot repeat, even if I wished to, without

[9] While in the prose version it is expressly stated that Christ imparted secret words to Joseph, the corresponding passage in the metrical version runs as follows:

Tout cil qui ten veissel verrunt,
En ma compeignie serunt;
De cuer arunt emplissement
Et joje pardurablement.
Cil qui ces paroles pourrunt
Apenre et qui les retenrunt
As genz serunt plus vertueus,
A Dieu assez plus gratieus;
Ne pourrunt estre forjugié
En court, ne de leur droit trichié
N'en court de bataille venchu
Se bien on leur droit retenu.

Ge n'ose conter ne retraire,
Ne je ne le pourroie feire,
Neis se je feire le voloie,
Se je le grant livre n'avoie
Ou les estoires sunt escrites,
Par les granz clers feites et dites.
Las sunt li grant secré escrit
Qu'en numme le Graal et dit.

(Verses 917*ff*, ed. Nitze)

All those who see this vessel
Shall be in my company;
They shall have fulfilment
And enduring joy.
Those who are able
To learn these words and retain them

[*Footnote continued overleaf*

having the large book in which they are inscribed. This is the mystery of the great ceremony of the Grail.[10]

Christ says, furthermore, that as often as Joseph has the need to he should turn towards the Three Powers that are *One* and to the blessed Woman who bore the Son; good counsel would then be his. *His own heart would give it to him, for he would become aware of the voice of the Holy Spirit within it.*

In contrast to other traditions Joseph is not yet freed from captivity; Christ informs him that he must endure it even longer. His subsequent release will be looked upon as a miracle in days to come. "Joseph therefore remained in captivity; the apostles did not speak of it, they knew nothing except that the Lord's body had been given to Joseph; of his love they knew nothing." Joseph's release from his incarceration in the dungeon only takes place forty-two years later. During the intervening years he is kept alive and comforted by the Grail.

The legend of St. Veronica's veil, by which the Emperor

Will be more virtuous to others,
To God more than acceptable,
Will not be able to be misjudged in court
Nor tricked out of their rights
Nor on battlefield vanquished,
So well are their rights upheld.

I dare not tell or recite
Even were I able to,
Nor have I the ability
Without the noble book
Wherein the stories are inscribed
By noble clerics made and said.
There is written the great secret
That is called the Grail.

[10] Literally the text (Cangé MS., ed. Hucher, Vol. I, p. 227) reads: "Lors il aprant Jhésu-Crist les paroles que j'à nus conter ne retraire ne porroit, se il bien feire lo voloit, se il n'avoit lou grant livre où eles sont escriptes et ce est li secrez qu l'en tient au grant sacrement qu l'an feit sor lou Graal c'est-à-dire sor lou caalice." And (Didot MS., ed. Hucher, Vol. I, p. 293): "Lors aprant Jhésu-Crist à Joseph ces paroles que je ne vos conterai ne retreirai, ne ne porrai si je le voloie faire, si je n'avoie le haut livre ou eles sont escrites, ce est li créanz que l'en tient au grant sacre del Graal."

Vespasian was healed of leprosy, is inserted here. Out of gratitude Vespasian goes to Jerusalem in order, as the text says, to avenge the death of the prophet who had healed him. Pilate is called to account—he thinks that Joseph is no longer alive—and many Jews are killed, but finally one is found who reveals the spot where Joseph is incarcerated. Vespasian has himself lowered by a rope into the dungeon, where he finds Joseph. After greeting each other Joseph asks the Emperor whether he wishes to believe in Christ who has healed him. On receiving an affirmative reply, Joseph instructs the Emperor as follows:

> "Believe that the Holy Spirit created all things, that he made the heavens, the earth, day and night, the four elements, the angels, and all things.
>
> "When he had created the angels, a number of them were evil, full of pride, envy and covetousness; as soon as the Lord saw this he had them cast out of Heaven. For three days and nights it rained angels—since then it has never rained like that again. Three groups or tribes of these angels fell into Hell, three upon earth and three remained in the air.[11] There are therefore three times three clans that fell from Heaven and brought evil and deception to earth. The others that remained in Heaven strengthen men in goodness and keep them from transgressions."[12]

After further instruction about the Fall, about Christ's conception, birth and death, Vespasian and Joseph are baptized together.[13] Then, with his family and a few dependents, Joseph

[11] Those in hell torment the poor suffering souls; those on earth deceive and mislead men and draw them into sin. Those that remain in the air use another method; they try to make people into slaves of the Evil One by appearing to them in all sorts of different forms and causing them to have foolish dreams and thoughts.

[12] "They do this to vexation and shame of those of them who hate God, who, as his purpose is, had made them out of such spiritual substance. To their vexation, God created men out of the most ordinary stuff there is, imparted life, memory and lucidity to them, and set them in the place of the recently fallen ones."

[13] By St. Clement or, according to another tradition, St. Philip, who was considered to be the evangelist to the Western races.

sets out to preach Christianity. At first all goes well with him, but after some time his circumstances gradually begin to deteriorate, for the land he cultivates yields no produce. In order to find out the cause of this, he presents himself to his vessel and prays for guidance. The voice of the Holy Spirit tells him that he is guiltless but that the guilty must be discovered and excluded from the community in the following manner: Joseph must set up a table, a square one, as is expressly stated, in memory of Christ's Last Supper. Then his brother-in-law Brons must go to the river and bring to the table the first fish he catches. Joseph must spread a cloth over the table, place the cup in the centre, before his place, and beside it the fish. "After which," continued the voice, "put thyself in my place, as I sat at the meal. Brons must sit on thy right. Then wilt thou see that he will be moved away from thee, so that there is an empty place between you. This place signifies the space Judas left when he knew that he had betrayed me. No one will fill this gap until the son of the son of Brons and Enygeus [Joseph's sister] shall occupy it." This is the seat known as the *siège périlleux* (dangerous seat) which plays an important part in this story of the Grail.

Everything is done accordingly. When the people are summoned to the table a number of them sit down, but many find there is no room, for all the places are taken except the one between Joseph and Brons. Those sitting at the table are aware of an indescribable sweetness of grace, and their hearts are filled with it. One among them, called Petrus, turning to those standing around him asks whether they do not perceive anything of this grace. They answer, "No, we notice nothing, and it is not possible for us to approach the table." To which Petrus replies, "This shows that by a sin you have brought about the famine from which we suffer." Hearing these words they are ashamed and depart from the table.

In this way, Joseph recognizes the sinners and thus, for the first time, the power of the vessel is proven. "By this vessel we are sifted one from another," explains Petrus to those rejected, "for it suffers no sinners in its vicinity, as you yourselves have experienced. If you wish to give it a name, then call it the Grail, '*parce que il agrée tant*,' which means that it is agreeable and helpful to those that can remain in its presence and fills them with such joy that they are as happy as a fish that slips back to the water out of the hand of its captor." The company is thereupon divided; the sinners remove themselves, the virtuous remain and from then on come daily, at the same time, to this service which they call the "Grail Service." This is the reason this story is called, "The Story of the Grail."

One of those who are sent away, named Moys, is not willing to acquiesce in this arrangement and begs Joseph to allow him also to have access to the table. But when he attempts to sit in the only remaining free place, between Joseph and Brons, the earth opens and engulfs him. Terrified, those at the table ask Joseph what has become of him. Joseph kneels before his vessel and addresses the question to Christ. The voice answers: "Joseph, Joseph, now is the sign of which I told thee become true; for I told thee that the place must remain empty in memory of the one that Judas vacated when he betrayed me. And I declare unto thee that it will remain empty until the third of thy family, the son of the son of Brons and Enygeus, shall occupy it. Moys was false and evil and unworthy of the grace, for which reason the ground swallowed him up, and nothing more shall be spoken of him until the one comes who is worthy to occupy the seat."

So they live long and rejoice in the grace of the vessel.

Brons and Enygeus have twelve sons. When they are grown and their parents do not know what to do with them, they turn to Joseph. Joseph is instructed by an angel to tell the brothers that whichever of them wishes to take a wife should do so; the others are destined for the service of the Lord. They all decide to marry except the youngest, Alain li Gros, who declares that he would sooner be flayed alive than take a wife. It is thus made clear that he is destined for higher things, and his father puts him in Joseph's charge so that he may receive instruction. Joseph shows him the Grail and, at the command of a divine voice, informs him that one day an heir will be born to him, to whom he must hand over the vessel. The voice also reveals to Joseph that on the following day a brilliant light will descend from heaven, bringing a letter with it. The letter is to be given to Petrus who will take it to the furthest west, to the Vale of Avalon, there to await the eventual arrival of Alain's son. The following day, when they are gathered together for the Grail service, everything happens as the voice has foretold.

Thereupon, they prepare for their departure and take their leave. Alain, as their leader, guides them to strange lands, where they proclaim the death of Jesus Christ and his Name. Petrus remains behind, so that he may receive instruction about the Grail and be a witness of its transfer to Brons. In obedience to a divine command, Brons must be the guardian of the Grail from now on. Joseph therefore is obliged to tell him all the circumstances relating to it and to impart to him the secret words that Christ taught him in captivity. "It is these holy words that are called the Mystery of the Grail."[14] There follows a very obscure sentence: "From then on scorn or imprisonment were allotted to him."[15]

[14] "Ce sont iceles saintimes paroles que l'en tient os secrez del Graal" (Cangé MS., ed. Hucher, *Le Saint Graal,* Vol. I, pp. 272–73). The Didot MS. (*ibid.*, p. 330) runs "Ce sunt iceles saintes paroles que l'en tient os secrez du Graal." The metrical version (ed. Nitze), verse 3332, runs as follows:

> Les seintes paroles dist t'a
> Ki sunt douces et precieuses
> Et gracieuses et piteuses
> Ki sunt proprement apelees
> Secrez dou Graal et nummees.
>
> He spoke the sacred words,
> Tender and precious,
> Gracious and compassionate,
> That are correctly called and named
> The secret of the Grail.

[15] The passage (Cangé MS., ed. Hucher, p. 273) runs: "Si li conmende lou vaissel et le garde de lui et dès lors en avant sera la mesprisons sor lui." Or according to the Didot MS. (*ibid.*, p. 330): "Quant tu auras ce apris et mostré à Bron, si comande le vessel et le guarde et illeuc en avant sera la prison sor lui." Whereas the metrical version, verses 3337*ff*, runs:

[*Footnote continued overleaf*

"All who hear him spoken of will call him the Rich Fisher because of the fish that he caught. Thus it must be, and just as the world moves towards destruction,[16] so too must these people go to the West. When the Rich Fisher has taken over the Grail, then must he await the son of his son, that he may hand over and commend the vessel to his keeping. And when the time is come, that he should take it over, then the meaning of the Trinity will be fulfilled between you. But thou, Joseph, when thou hast done this, wilt take thy departure from the world and enter into everlasting joy."

Joseph, as he is bid, tells Petrus and Brons all that he has been charged by the Holy Spirit, but the words Christ spoke to him in captivity he imparts only to the Rich Fisher, doing so by writing them down and showing them to him in secret. When the others hear that Joseph will have to be parted from them, they are very much afraid. After Joseph has handed his vessel over to Brons and instructed him concerning the grace and commandments, Petrus also sets out upon his way. Amid many sighs and tears, prayers and entreaties, they take leave of each other. Brons remains behind a while with Joseph, who after three days dismisses him with the words, "Thou knowest full well what thou takest with thee and in whose company thou

Quant ce averas feit bien et bel,
Commanderas li le veissel,
Qu'il le gart des or en avant:
N'i mespreigne ne tant ne quant,
Toute le mesproison seroit
Seur lui, et chier le comparroit.

(Robert de Boron, *Le Roman de l'Estoire dou Graal*, ed. Nitze)

16 "ansinc com toz li mondes va et ira en avalant, covient que trestote ceste jant se traient vers occidant" (Cangé MS., ed. Hucher, Vol. I, p. 273) or "einsi le covient estre, que ansint comme li monde vait et va en avalant covient-il que toute ceste gent se retraie en occident" (Didot MS., *ibid.*, p. 330). The metrical version (Nitze), verses 3351*ff*, runs:

Ainsi cum li monz va en avant
Et touz jours amenuisant
Convient que toute ceste gent
Se treie devers Occident.

goest; none know it so well as thou and I. Go therefore and I shall remain, according to the commandment of my Redeemer." Thus they part. The Rich Fisher, of whom so much is subsequently to be told, goes to Britain; but Joseph, in obedience to the will of the Lord, returns to the land where he was born and there ends his life.

The writer adds further:

> Robert de Boron, who has written this book with the permission of the Holy Church and at the behest of the Comte de Montbéliard, in whose service he is, says: "To know this story fully one would also have to tell what became of Alain li Gros, where he went, how he lived, who were his heirs. One would have to know what became of Petrus and of Moys, whither the Rich Fisher went and how he was traced. These four parts ought so be combined; but no one can do this unless he has seen this story of the Grail or heard it told. At the time when Robert de Boron recounted it to Gautier de Montbéliard, it had not yet been written down by anyone except in the great book. If it pleases God I will combine these parts into a whole, as I have also taken them from a whole. But first I must tell of a *Lignée de Bretagne* [noble family of Britain], because if I left out this fifth part no one would know how matters had developed, nor why I had separated them, the one from the other."

With this the story of Joseph of Arimathea comes to an end and the narrative passes on to the "Merlin."

If we have dealt at such length with de Boron's text it has been in order to convey, as far as possible, not merely the content of the story but also the distinctive character of the work and style of the author. Whether this has to some extent been successful remains in question, since it was necessary to make extensive curtailments, and especially because the individual charm of the Old French does not find adequate expression in translation.

The simplicity, indeed the artlessness and naïveté, of the story reveals that it was written not by a scholarly cleric nor by a poet such as Chrétien or Wolfram but by a layman who applied himself with touching devotion to material that possibly struck him as strange and difficult. It is just this, however, which gives the work its particular charm. The striking and significant thing about the tale is that although in part it conforms closely to the Gospel of Nicodemus it then suddenly diverges from it and, in spite of its kinship with other, similar legends, differs from it in a specific way.

Up to that point where Christ appears to the imprisoned Joseph, the beginning of "Joseph of Arimathea" accords completely with the description of the Gospel of Nicodemus. Whereas in the prototype the dungeon walls are raised and Joseph is freed in this way, in de Boron's version Christ brings Joseph the vessel that maintains him in life during the forty-two years he still has to remain in captivity. That the miraculous Grail, vessel contains a relic of Christ's blood is the *new* Grail motif, which becomes famous and which appears here for the first time.

Two further questions appear to lie especially close to our author's heart, the meaning of the Trinity and of the Mass, for these two subjects form the core of the whole story. Enlightenment on the dogma had long since been provided in ecclesiastical literature but, for the most part, was not available to the laity. It is precisely its popular character which gives its special value to our work. It bears direct witness to the exertions of a naïve, as yet rather untrained, mind concerning the most exalted things and provides important insight into the outlook of Christian people at that time.

This is the more interesting in that with all his piety and respect for the Church, which he emphasizes repeatedly, de Boron is sufficiently unprejudiced to produce quite unorthodox thoughts as well. For it is indeed thoroughly unorthodox when one who was not a disciple is expressly chosen to guard Christ's blood and to establish an institution such as the Holy Mass, or when Christ describes Joseph's act of burial as something that none of the disciples would have dared to do. These unorthodox features appear, however, to be based less on heretical views than on the naïveté of the author, who did not hesitate to endow the traditional doctrine and the ideas in the air at that time with contributions from his own thoughts and fantasies. It is an expression of his efforts to understand, and because it strikes one as being among the most interesting things about the story, we have directed our main attention to it rather than to the course of the outer events of the narrative.

Let us turn once more to our text. Christ brings Joseph the vessel containing his blood, with the specific declaration: "Knowest thou what thou hast gained by this? Thou wilt have the sign of my death in thy keeping, the blood of the Three Persons of the One Godhead." As well as the death of Christ, the vessel therefore also signifies the Trinity.

Christ says further that sacrificial tables are to be set up in future; that such tables will signify the Cross; that the vessels in which the sacrifices will be made will signify the grave; the paten will signify the stone which closed the grave, and the cloth spread over the table the winding sheet. In this way the future institution of the Mass and its symbolism are brought into relation with Joseph's action,[17] and the subject of Christ's death and resurrection is given the central place.

[17] The meanings given here are not, to all appearances, exactly identical with present-day ecclesiastical views. According to J. Braun's *Liturgischen Handlexikon*, the Church differentiates between dogmatic and moralistic symbolism. "According to the former, the altar is a symbol of Christ's body, at first only the actual body, but according to later views it is also the mystical body, i.e. the Church. According to the latter it is a symbol of the heart, the site of spiritual sacrifice. The symbolism of the accessories, such as the cup, the corporal, the paten, the altar cloths and so forth, is closely connected with, and continues, the interpretation of the altar as Christ's body."

CHAPTER XVII

The Problem of the Trinity

THE SYMBOLIC MEANING of the Grail as a container for some of Christ's blood has already been discussed, but we have to consider still more closely the trinitarian god-image which emerges with such emphasis in the de Boron version. Not only does Christ entrust Joseph with the Grail in the name of the Trinity, but it is also expressly stated that the vessel contains the blood of the Three Persons of the *one* Godhead. For that reason there will also be three successive Guardians of the Grail, and each will correspond to one of the Three Persons of the Trinity. Origen had already had some misgivings about the inner workings (οἰκονομία) of the Trinity and had allotted different realms to its Three Persons. As the greatest, God the Father comprises the existence of all being, for in himself he contains all things. The effects of the Son, on the other hand, extend only as far as the spiritual man (rational man), and the Holy Spirit affects only the saints.[1] The power of the Father is thus the greatest, but on the other hand the *value* of the Holy Spirit is the highest. While in this exposition the realms of effectiveness of the Trinity are differentiated, in the Grail story the effectiveness in time is differentiated or unfolded, since the historical time the three Grail guardians are said to correspond to the Three Persons of the Trinity, so that the Trinity, described as *individua*, i.e. indivisible, is divided into representatives that follow each other in temporal sequence. This leads directly to the previously mentioned ideas of Joachim of Floris, already widely disseminated at that time, according to which there would be three

[1] *De principiis*, Book I, Ch. III, 5. Cf. Jung, "A Psychological Approach to the Dogma of the Trinity," in *Psychology and Religion*, par. 214.

kingdoms: the Old Testament age corresponding to the Father, the Christian era corresponding to the Son, and thereafter would follow the Kingdom of the Holy Spirit. That Joachim was no stranger to the spiritually interested circles of his day appears to be an established fact; just as those circles were conversant with Catharistic ideas.[2] Joachim's idea springs from a conception—already extant in Judaism, perhaps even attributable to Parseeism—of a kingdom to be established on earth by the Messiah at the end of time. According to the Johannine conception this age, during which Satan was to be bound, would last a thousand years. After its expiration would follow the unchaining of Satan, the last great battle of the nations, the decisive victory and the Last Judgment (Revelation 20). Relying on Matthew 16:28—"Verily I say unto you, There be some standing here, which shall not taste of death, till they see the Son of man coming in his kingdom"—the first Christians were already expecting the second coming of the Messiah. When it did not come to pass it was believed that this event, or else the end of the world, would take place in the year 1000. It is not exactly clear whether it was the coming of Christ or of the Antichrist that was the more explicitly awaited. At all events, that age was exceedingly preoccupied with the latter, as is shown by various literary testimonies. Thus, already in the middle of the tenth century, Abbot Adson of Moutier-en-Der had written an *Epistola ad Gerbergam reginam, de ortu et tempore Antichristi* (Letter to Queen Gerberga concerning the origin and the era of the Antichrist).[3] At the beginning of the eleventh century Honorius of Autun wrote on the same subject,[4] and in Robert de Boron's time there were various French poems dealing with the same material.[5]

In our story, the expectation of the Antichrist is bound up

[2] With this cf. *Aion*, pars. 138*ff*; and Anitchkof, *Joachim da Fiore et les milieux courtois*, especially p. 149.

[3] Ed. E. Sackur, in *Sibyllinische Texte und Forschungen*, pp. 104–13.

[4] *Elucidarium*, Migne, *Pat. Lat.*, Vol. 172, cols. 1109–76.

[5] Cf. *Deux Versions inédites de la Légende de l'Antéchrist en Vers Français du XIIIe Sicèle*, published by E. Walberg. Cf. further, W. Bousset, *Der Antichrist*.

with Christ's second coming[6] by the manner in which the Grail hero as the *tierz hom* is the representative of the Holy Spirit, and thus of the returning Christ, while, as we shall see, Merlin, at least to some extent, represents the Antichrist.

It appears as if de Boron has indeed caught all sorts of ideas then in the air, without quite having the depth of thought to unify them. How hard this seems to have been at that time is also evident in the introductory story to the *Lancelot Grail* which runs as follows:[7]

> On the eve of Good Friday of the year 717 after the Passion of Jesus Christ, the writer lay in his hut in one of the wildest regions of Britain (White Britain), plagued by doubts about the Trinity. Then Christ appeared to him and gave him a small book, no bigger than the palm of his hand, which would resolve all his doubts. He, Christ, had written it himself, and only he who was purified by confession and fasting might read it. On the following morning the writer opened the book, the sections of which were superscribed as follows:
>
> 1. This is the book of thy descent.
> 2. Here begins the book of the Holy Grail.
> 3. Here begins the terrors.
> 4. Here begin the miracles.
>
> While he was reading, there was thunder and lightning. While he was celebrating Mass on Good Friday, an angel caught him up in the spirit, into the third heaven, and his doubts about the Trinity were laid to rest. But when on Easter Day he wanted to read more from the little book, it had disappeared. A voice said that he must suffer, and in

[6] In Bodo Mergell's work he quotes, p. 111: *Bernhard of Clairvaux*, Sermo V, Sp 12. "In priori (adventu) quidem in terris visus et cum hominibus conversatus est. . . . In posteriore vero videbit omnis caro salutare Dei nostri. Et videbunt in quem transfixerunt. Medius occultus est et in quo soli eum in seipsis vident electi, et salvae fiunt animae eorum. In primo ergo venit in carne et infirmitate, in hoc medio in spiritu et virtute, in ultimo in gloria et maiestate."

[7] According to A. Nutt, *Studies on the Legend of the Holy Grail*, the passage in Helinandus (see pp. 15–16) could be based on this story, but this is disputed. In Appendix B, Nutt presents a parallel to this story, from the legend of Brandan.

order to get the book back he should go to the plain of Walescog, then follow a fabulous animal to Norway and there he would find that which he sought. He obeyed. The beast led him to a hermit and thence past the pine tree of adventure to a knight's castle and thereafter, on the third day, to the Lake of the Queen and to a nunnery. After he had exorcized an anchorite possessed of the Devil he found the book, and after his return Christ commanded him to make a transcript of it, which he did.

Thereafter follows the Legend of the Holy Grail.

This story illustrates very well the great psychological difficulties encountered by people in those days when they wished to understand the doctrine of the Trinity. It was mostly transmitted to them only theoretically, i.e. in book form, and for that reason was lost to them again. It then had to be found once more, in relation to the animal, i.e. to the world of the unconscious or of instinct, and beside the Lake of the Queen and the nunnery, i.e. in the realm of the anima, of personal feelings and of the unconscious. Intellect alone can certainly not suffice for the assimilation of a religious content of such central significance. Only when it appears subjectively out of the unconscious can it become an experiencable reality for people and thus be understood in a more profound sense. Moreover, the exorcism of the hermit touches on the unsolved problem of evil, to which we shall return later. The anchorite clearly became "possessed" for the same reason, namely because of the problem of the assimilation of the idea of the Trinity. Because the latter content sank back into the unconscious, there was generated a sinister animation of it which overwhelmed the hermit and from which he had, first of all, to be freed.

Although at that time—and still today—the doctrine of the Trinity is primarily comprehended in a purely theological way, it also possesses, inasmuch as it corresponds to an archetype, a psychological aspect which Jung has shown in "A Psychological Approach to the Dogma of the Trinity," [8] an aspect about which

[8] In *Psychology and Religion*, pars. 169–295.

Glorification of the Body portrayed as Coronation of the Virgin Mary, *Speculum Trinitatis*, from Reusner, *Pandora*

The two hanged men, Christ and Judas. Tablet from an ivory chest, South Gaul, *c.* 425

the people of those days were already concerning themselves, albeit unconsciously. The figure of the Father, which is manifested in the Old Testament, is that of a creator and originator of all things, who turns a benevolent as well as a destructive aspect towards men. Men stand to him in a childlike relation that does not ponder the nature of this undivided, dark and light father God and is unable to exercise any criticism concerning him. "Here man, world, and God form a whole, a unity unclouded by criticism. It is the world of the Father, and of man in his childhood state." "A feeling of oneness, far removed from critical judgment and moral conflict, leaves the Father's authority unimpaired."[9] It is a condition of complete oneness with all of nature as well. In an age, however, in which the figure of a Son of God appears, the condition of human consciousness is also different; from the original unity of the *one* a part is split off which becomes its opposite or *other*, which is why, in most religions, the archetypal form of the Son of God is a figure of suffering. For instance, it falls victim to the powers of darkness and must be freed again for the salvation of the world.[10] The Son figure is usually embedded in a redemption drama told and performed as part of a cult. "The life of the God-man revealed things that could not possibly have been known at the time when the Father ruled as the One. For the Father, as the original unity, was not a defined or definable object; nor could He, strictly speaking, either be called the 'Father' or be one. He only became a 'Father' by incarnating in the Son, and by so doing became defined and definable. By becoming a father and a man he revealed to man the secret of his divinity."[11] While on the human side the image of the Father corresponds to a childlike state of consciousness, where a ready-made way of life that has the characteristics of law is uncritically accepted,[12] in the next stage, the Age of the Son, a conscious consideration of previously accepted things begins and

[9] *Ibid.*, pars. 201 and 199.

[10] *Ibid.*, par. 202. Cf. also Hurwitz, *Die Gestalt des sterbenden Messias*, *passim*.

[11] Jung, *ibid.*, par. 203. [12] *Ibid.*, par. 270.

with it criticism, judgment and moral differentiation.[13] The condition of the Son is, accordingly, one of conflict.[14] "The choice of possible ways is menaced by just as many possibilities of error. 'Freedom from the law' brings a sharpening of opposites, in particular of the moral opposites. Christ crucified between two thieves is an eloquent symbol of this fact. The exemplary life of Christ is in itself a 'transitus' and therefore amounts to a bridge leading over to the third stage, where the initial stage of the Father is, as it were, recovered."[15] This third phase, the Age of the Holy Spirit, corresponds on the human level to an attitude that, through recognition of the guiding and enlightening function of the unconscious, strives to move beyond the state of being suspended in conflict.[16] This does not mean a step back into the first phase, although a wrong turning of this kind naturally always threatens, but the submission of individual independence to the spirit, i.e. "articulating one's ego consciousness with a supraordinate totality."[17] Together with this goes the release from a faith resting merely on authority, whether such authority is psychological or that of a collective organization.[18]

The emergence in the twelfth and thirteenth centuries of so many different movements, among which the frequently mentioned teachings of Joachim of Floris are particularly significant, indicates that this problem obviously began to become acute at that time. It could not, however, be coped with without taking the nature of the Trinity more seriously into account. This is why the texts of the Grail stories, and Robert de Boron's in particular, are continually concerned with this problem. Perceval is indeed the *tierz hom*, clearly destined to play the part of the man who, growing beyond the state of conflict characterized by the condition of the Son, should become conscious of the guiding, inspiring principle in the unconscious and thus realize and recognize the inner wholeness. But, like the Grail King who suffers continual conflict, he is forced again and again to undergo battles with shadow

[13] *Ibid.*, par. 271. [14] *Ibid.*, par. 272. [15] *Ibid.*
[16] Cf. *ibid.* [17] *Ibid.*, par. 276. [18] *Ibid.*, pars. 274*ff.*

figures, indicating what a tremendous effort it costs him to accomplish the transition to this third stage. In the light of the above explanations it becomes clear what is represented by the two Grail kings. The too-old, seemingly alive king stands for the unconsciousness of the world of the Father, the wounded King for the state of conflict of the Son condition. But Perceval is the man who serves wholeness and, as the *tierz hom*, is therefore destined to redeem them both.

With the exception of the work known as the *Comma Joanneum*, which probably represents a later interpolation, the Doctrine of the Trinity is not expressly set forth in Holy scripture.[19] The First Epistle of John 5:8 says: "And there are three that bear witness in earth, the Spirit, and the water, and the blood: and these three agree in one." In the Vulgate, this threefoldness is supplemented by the late interpolation: "For three things bear witness in heaven, the Father, the Word, and the Holy Ghost, and these three are one." Inasmuch as the Grail contains precisely the *blood* of Christ, the substance that can manifest both as spirit and as water, it actually contains the substance of the Trinity, so to speak, as de Boron's version declares. In contradistinction to the Trinity in heaven, it bears witness to the Trinity *on earth* and is therefore the humanly understandable *earthly* analogy to the metaphysical Trinity, which permits the latter to become experienceable. Although for this reason the vessel containing Christ's blood calls to mind the enactment of the Eucharist,[20] unlike the Eucharistic offering of wine no Communion takes place during the Grail ceremony; mention is made only of the effect of the grace of the Grail, which radiated on to those in its presence. On the other hand, the idea of a life-giving and grace-radiating blood substance is found, once again, in alchemy. For instance, the text of the *Aurora consurgens*,[21] which probably dates from the thirteenth century, says that the Holy Spirit effects a threefold baptism—

[19] *Ibid.*, par. 207, note 1.

[20] In the legend, Christ refers to this when he explains the meaning of the table, the cup and the paten to Joseph.

[21] See von Franz, *Aurora Consurgens*, which contains the original text, an English translation and commentary by M.-L. von Franz.

"in water, in blood and in fire"[22]—and concerning the baptism in blood it says further: "When he [the Holy Spirit] baptizeth with blood, then he nourisheth, as it is said: He gave me to drink of the saving water of wisdom [Jesus Sirach XV, 3], and again: His blood is drink indeed [John 6:56], for the seat of the soul is in the blood, as Senior[23] saith: But the soul itself remained in the water (which is like to it in warmth and humidity), and therein consisteth all life."[24] This example from an alchemical text, which may be amplified by many others, shows how the blood was looked upon as the mystical carrier of the soul and even of the Holy Spirit and at the same time, how the Holy Spirit was understood on the one hand as a divine person and on the other as an alchemical substance.[25] Similarly, the Grail has, at the same time, something of both the personal and the material about it. As each represents the Person of the Holy Spirit so, equally, the Grail stands for an aspect of the Trinity that penetrates into earthly matter and thus forms a bridge to the as yet unsolved problem of the material world and of evil.

However, as the Holy Spirit, after Christ's death and ascension, can fulfil and inspire the individual human being, so is the Grail a power which counsels the individual in specific circumstances for which the orientation of collective Christian morality is inadequate or insufficient. It acts as mediator whenever the individual hears the voice of God directly and personally, whereby a connection more suitable to the new age between man and the divine is made possible, as well as a continuing realization of God's challenge to man.

There is a further problem with the doctrine of the Trinity that indicates certain connections with alchemical tradition. At the close of de Boron's account of Christ's appearance to Joseph in prison, the secret words Christ imparts to Joseph follow as something quite particularly important. Of these words it is said that they are "*the mystery of the great ceremony of the Grail*."

[22] Von Franz, *ibid.*, p. 80. Quoted in *Mysterium Coniunctionis*, par. 316.

[23] An Arab alchemist, Mohammed ibn Umail at-Tamîmî (tenth century).

[24] Von Franz, *ibid.*, pp. 85–87. Cf. Senior, *De Alchemia*, p. 58. The soul has become warm and damp in the manner of the blood.

[25] With this cf. *Psychology and Religion*, pars. 277*f*.

It might at first be thought that this concerns the words of the Consecration which the priest, acting as a surrogate for Christ, pronounces, affecting thereby the transubstantiation. This would explain the holy awe they inspire in the author, so that he implores his readers to ask no further about it. A few things, however, gainsay this supposition: for instance the aforementioned circumstance that the Grail Service is not a real Mass, and above all the fact that during it no transformation takes place. Secret words of some kind play a part in all the versions of the Grail legend. The essentially important question that the finder of the Grail has to ask the ailing king, the omission of which causes the Grail to disappear, is a somewhat different form of the same thing. In our text,these words are known to the Grail King alone and are communicated to his successor at the same time that he hands over the Grail into his care. We are therefore concerned with the tradition of a mystery. A parallel to this, which strikes one as important in this context, may be found in one of those early Christian works of Oriental origin which have already been mentioned as possible sources for the formation of this particular aspect of the Grail legend. It would be profitable to consider it more closely. This is the work known as *The Book of Adam and Eve*,[26] attributed to the third-to-fifth centuries. Primarily the book purports to establish the connection between Adam and Christ. It describes the life of the first men after the Fall in a popular, childlike, naïve way that has a certain similarity to Robert de Boron's style.[27]

A place on the Western edge of Paradise is allotted by God to Adam and Eve as their abode. They find shelter in a cave, which they call the "Cave of Treasures," and Adam says to Eve, "Be

[26] Also called *The Conflict of Adam and Eve with Satan*. Translated from the Ethiopic by the Rev. S. C. Malan. The book was originally Arabic, probably written in Egypt and later translated into Ethiopic. It was edited in Ethiopic by E. Trumpp and translated into German by A. Dillmann. According to Wallis Budge, material from this work was supposed to have been incorporated into the collection of Syrian stories known as the *Syrian Cave of Treasures*.

[27] As it has, too, with a modern American work, *The Green Pastures*, Marc Connelly's dramatization of Roark Bradford's *Ol' Man Adam and His Chillun*.

this cave our prison in this world and a place of punishment." There they experience the sufferings of existence and the continual temptations of Satan who, in order to ingratiate himself, appeals to his relationship to them, inasmuch as God has taken Adam out of his, Satan's, side, just as he took Eve from Adam's (an idea that to date we have met with nowhere else). With every possible kind of persecution and trick he seeks to bring about their downfall, but again and again they are granted strength and faith through the Word of God, which comes to them from time to time and according to which everything that happens to them is understood as pointing to Christ.

In the darkness of the cave Adam cries, "Oh, Eve, think of the Garden and its brilliance! Think of the Garden in which there was no darkness when we lived there." In the cave it is so dark they cannot see each other, but the Word comforts them: "All the suffering that has been inflicted upon you because of your transgression cannot free you from Satan's hand, nor save you. But I will do so, when I come down from Heaven and become flesh of your seed and take upon myself the sickness from which you suffer. Then will the darkness that came over you in this cave come over me in my tomb." Another time when, in desperation, they have thrown themselves over a cliff and have made a sacrifice to God of the blood that flowed in consequence, the Word of God comes to Adam: "As thou didst sacrifice thy blood, so will I sacrifice my blood upon an altar on earth." When Adam asks God for a memento from the Garden, he sends him, by an angel, golden staffs or rods with which to light the cave, as well as incense and myrrh: gold as a sign of the kingdom from which he has come, incense as a sign of the bright light that has been taken from him and myrrh as a sign of his grief. Adam keeps these things by him in the Cave of Treasures which, for that reason, is also known as the House of Concealment. The name, Cave of Treasures, is certainly connected with the treasures concealed within it. Once, when they have sacrificed a corn offering, the Word says, "Because ye have brought and sacrificed this to me, I will make my flesh thereof when I come upon earth and it shall be perpetually offered upon an altar, for the attainment of forgiveness and grace for those who take part therein in the right spirit." God therewith sends a bright fire down upon the offerings and the Holy Spirit descends upon it. God then commands an angel to take something from the offering with a tongue of fire, shaped like a spoon, and give it to Adam and Eve. Their souls will be enlightened thereby and their hearts filled with joy ("*accomplissement du cœur*" by the power of the Grail). God speaks to Adam: "Thou shalt practise this custom when temptation and travail come upon thee." (Joseph of Arimathea is given much the same advice in reference to the Grail.)

A series of similar events takes place. Each event is explained as a prefiguration of the life and Passion of Christ. We will consider but one of them. Adam, before his death, calls his sons together to bless them. He charges Seth to embalm him after his death and lay him in the Cave of Treasures until the Flood. Then his body is to be laid in a ship, and when the Flood has passed, it is to be buried in the centre of the earth, together with the gold, the incense and the myrrh. "For the spot where my body shall be laid is the centre of the earth; from there God will come and save our entire race." It comes to pass as Adam has commanded. Noah charges his son Shem to bring Adam's casket to its destination in secret.[28] No one is to accompany him except his son-in-law Melchizedek, "whom God chose out of all generations, to stand before him and adore him and to serve him beside the body of our father Adam." (As is already clear, the Grail service is also a service close to a grave.)

Noah concludes his exhortation to Shem with the words: "Know, my son, that from the time of Adam up to the present day all the Elders of Israel handed the commandments on, one to another, and studied them among themselves." Adam gave the commandment to his son Seth, Seth handed it on to Enoch, and so on until it came to Noah. "But my grandfather Methuselah also gave me an important commandment which I have observed and which I pass on to thee. Observe my words and conceal the mystery in thy heart, reveal it to no one of thy entire

[28] In many manuscripts the Grail is represented as a similar casket.

tribe, but go and lay the body of our father Adam in the earth; there shall it rest till the Day of Judgment."

Shem and Melchizedek set out on their journey. On the way the voice of Adam speaks from the casket: "The Word of God will come down unto the land which is our destination and will suffer and be crucified in the place where my body will be buried. The crown of my head will be baptized with his blood and salvation will then be accomplished. My priesthood, my gift of prophecy and my kingship will he restore unto me." When they arrive at the place, the rock splits asunder, so that there is room for the casket; they know then that this is the intended spot.

The Syrian collection of legends known as *The Cave of Treasures*[29] relates the same story even more interestingly. Noah says to his son Shem, "Take Adam's body and lay it in the centre of the earth, and Melchizedek shall establish himself there. And the angel of the Lord will guide thee on thy way and show thee the place where thou shalt lay the body of Adam, which is in fact the centre of the earth. There the four quarters of the earth come together; for when God created the world, his power went before him like the wind, from all the four quarters, and in the centre his power stood still. There will salvation take place for Adam and all his descendants. This secret was transmitted by Adam to all generations."

The secret that Adam passed on to all generations, so that only one person at a time ever knew it, clearly refers to Adam's grave and the salvation to be expected from it. The resemblance to our Grail legend is striking. As Joseph of Arimathea and his descendants guarded the Grail vessel—which signified the grave of Christ—so did Melchizedek guard Adam's grave. Just as the location of the Grail is not known, neither is Adam's grave known. No one may be told where it is to be found, and Melchizedek is said to be dead so that no search can be made for him. Thus, although the story of the Grail must manifestly be a description or explanation of the Trinity, beneath this is concealed

[29] *The Book of the Cave of Treasures*, ed. Budge, p. 123; or *Die Schatzhöhle*, edited and translated into German by C. Bezold.

the idea of a holy grave and its guardian and of a dead Anthropos-figure eagerly awaiting redemption. The old Grail King would correspond to the dead Adam[30] and, like the latter, would also have to await his turn for a new redeemer.

We must return to the problem of the secret tradition. In these two legends of Adam a central idea is that from the very beginning of creation a secret plan or disposition existed, which endured from Adam to Christ and which connected the figure of the primal Father of humanity with the latter. Consequently, if the emergence of a similar idea is indicated in the Grail legend it must surely be taken to mean that the plan of salvation continues beyond Christ, presumably to Perceval as the *tierz hom*, and to the realization of the Holy Spirit in the sense already indicated. Interestingly enough, the idea of a secret tradition is also to be found in alchemy. There, likewise, it has its origins in the Oriental legends about Adam[31] and hands down its secret knowledge as that of Enoch-Metatron-Hermes (Idris), of the Agathodaimon (Seth) and of Adam. It is probable that there is even a parallel underlying tradition, especially among the (Shiite) Sabean Arabs and the Druses.

A secret tradition of this kind is clearly hinted at in the Latin alchemical text of an Arab author, Calid. In his work *The Three Precious Words* he writes: "And these are three valuable words, concealed and revealed at the same time, given not for the perverse nor for the godless, neither for unbelievers, but for the believers and the poor, from the first to the last men."[32] By "these," Calid understands the alchemical secret of the preparation of the philosopher's stone through the transmutation of the four elements and of the four qualities of the substance through the influence of the planets. In the *Aurora consurgens*, which also took up this idea from Calid, it is clearly combined with the

[30] In the poem *Diú Krône* (see p. 328) the King says to the finder of the Grail: "We only seem to be alive, in reality we are dead."

[31] Cf. D. Chwolsohn, *Die Ssabier und der Ssabismus*, especially Vol. II, pp. 26*ff*; and among other works, R. Reitzenstein, *Poimandres*, p. 173; and A. Montgomery, *Aramaic Incantation Texts from Nippur*, Vol. III, p. 123. This book was called to our attention by Rivkah Schärf-Kluger.

[32] *Liber trium verborum*, p. 228.

realization of a brotherhood of men in the spirit of the Holy Ghost. The text concludes with a paraphrase of the Song of Solomon in which the *coniunctio* of the opposites is celebrated. The pair build three tents or huts for themselves and "their sons," tents in which God dwells by the side of man. This, however, is considered to be the three-fold fruit of the alchemical work, "which [Calid] saith to be three precious words, wherein is hidden all the science, which is to be given to the pious, that is to the poor, from the first man even unto the last." [33]

The secret "precious words" to be handed on are here concerned with the alchemical secret of the "work," which is seen in this text as a *continuing incarnation of the divine in man.* At the same time, it is the becoming visible of the Second Adam, sunk in the scattered elements, an incorruptible god-man who confers the Kingdom of Heaven on his "sons," i.e. on those who bestir themselves over the alchemical work. The tradition of the Ethiopian *Book of Adam and Eve,* according to which God gives Adam, among other things, a golden wand for the lighting of his cave—the gold in this connection representing the sign of the Kingdom—could easily be related, not only psychologically but also historically, to the previously mentioned alchemical ideas. Golden wands are mentioned, in the same sense, by the alchemists.[34] But the "Kingdom" is the treasure in the field or the pearl of great price, i.e. the hidden predisposition to wholeness which slumbers in the depths of the unconscious of each person—a hidden treasure that calls to those who are meant to find it.

[33] Von Franz, *Aurora Consurgens*, p. 149.

[34] In the *Symbola Aureae Mensae*, p. 72, for instance, the alchemist Michael Maier, referring to Vincent de Beauvais, says of John the Baptist: "who makes gold from rods and gems from stones."

CHAPTER XVIII

The Figure of Adam

A MEANINGFUL FEATURE of the legend of Adam is that his grave is on Golgotha, in the centre of the world. As early as Ezekiel we read (Ezekiel 5:5): "Thus saith the Lord God; This is Jerusalem: I have set it in the midst of the nations and countries that are round about her." According to Judaic tradition, Jerusalem was situated in the centre of the land of Israel, the Sanctuary was in the centre of Jerusalem, the Hall of the Temple was in the centre of the Sanctuary, the Ark of the Covenant was in the centre of the Hall and before the Ark lay the foundation stone of the world; for it was said that the world was established from that centre.[1] According to another legend Adam was created in the centre of the earth, in Jerusalem, on the site where later the Cross was to be erected.[2] In the *Christliche Adamsbuch*[3] it is written: "And angels carried Adam's body forth and buried it in the centre part of the earth, in Jerusalem, on the same spot where God was to be crucified." Obviously, the Christian legends also preserved these ideas. A memorial to this belief, still found today in the Church of the Holy Sepulchre in Jerusalem, is the so-called *omphalos*, i.e. navel of the earth. This is an upright pillar of marble, about two feet high, topped by a flattened cupola surrounded by wickerwork, said to denote the centre of the world.[4]

1 According to W. H. Roscher, *Omphalos.*

2 Wallis Budge, *The Syrian Cave of Treasures*, p. 53; or C. Bezold, *op. cit.*, p. 27.

3 A. Dillmann, *Corpus Adame angeli susceperunt et portantes sepelierunt in medio loco terrae, in Jerusalem, eo loco ubi Deum crucifixerunt.*

4 Baedecker, *Palästina*, 7, 39. Cf. A. Jeremias, *Handbuch der altorientalischen Geisteskultur*; and A. Haucks, *Realencyclopaedia für Theologie und Kirche*, article

The centre of the world accordingly is where Adam was created, where he lies buried and where Christ is to be crucified. Christ's sepulchre also certainly belongs to this region. The ancients understood this concretely; in later times it was taken to indicate that Christ and his work of redemption were at the centre of the world. This view, however, also has a profound psychological meaning, namely that the centre of the human soul is the place where "the power of God, flowing together from the four quarters, stands still," i.e. where the opposites are united, where the hidden treasure lies buried and from whence salvation emanates.

Even though it is nowhere clearly stated, it can be assumed that the Grail Castle, in so far as it is thought of as a kind of heavenly Jerusalem, also represents a centre of this kind, especially since the Grail is itself closely connected with Golgotha. It is the same realm referred to in Chinese texts as the "yellow castle" or the "heavenly heart" and that sometimes also possesses a corresponding character in the mandalas drawn by Western people today.[5] In his exhaustive work,[6] in which he cites a vast amount of archaeological and literary material, L. J. Ringbom shows that the Grail Castle, in addition to portraying the idea of the "heavenly Jerusalem," is also connected with the mystical idea of a king's grave, an otherworldly or paradisal garden and a mysterious world centre, and that it exhibits markedly mandala-like qualities.[7] This idea of an "otherworldly" Jerusalem, which it was more important to win even than the earthly one, also played a considerable part in the fantasies of the Crusaders,[8] especially among the lower classes;

on "Palästina," p. 562. In Delphi, too, there was an Omphalos sacred to Zeus, which marked the mean between the Eastern and Western hemispheres. Cf. Roscher, *op. cit.*

[5] Jung, Commentary on "The Secret of the Golden Flower," in *Alchemical Studies*, par. 33.

[6] *Ibid.*, Plate A10.

[7] *Graltempel und Paradies*. It does not seem to be proven that all these motifs can be historically traced back to Iran; far more likely, it is a question of the same archetype that underwent various transformations.

[8] Cf. P. Alphandéry and A. Dupront, *Le chretiénté et l'idée de la Croisade*, especially Vol. I.

it is clearly a projection of the Self as an inner centre, extending far beyond the ego, which expresses wholeness and harmony and from which radiate healing, integrating influences.[9] According to the legends, Adam is buried in the centre of this mystical spot, and even if the author of our work was hardly conscious of these elements or of their significance, yet he clearly regards his Joseph as an analogue to Adam. The prison where Joseph has to spend forty-two years is located under the earth and is therefore also a type of grave, and Joseph is an Adam in need of redemption. Like Adam and the ailing Grail King, he is an image of the man in need of salvation and not of the sinner only, but of the original image or original being concealed or buried in man, whose captivity and redemption formed the content of the Anthropos doctrine of late antiquity. This conception, which found its specific formulation in Gnosticism, is not just a heretical idea but is based on a fundamental feeling that can also become an immediate experience in the souls of present-day men and women.

It is therefore not surprising that the figures of the old and the renewed Adam should also play an important part in alchemy.[10] Adam appears there as a synonym for the transformed substance and for Mercurius, and is described as androgynous in order to symbolize the mysterious antithetical nature of the arcane material.[11] The alchemists even went so far as to equate their Adam with the figure of their King, whether old or in need of regeneration. A poem by Basilius Valentinus describes him as sitting in a bath, uniting with Venus! In other texts he is characterized as the "exalted man," as the "inner, invisible man" dwelling within us. His descent into the bath or his state of concealment in the grave of matter symbolizes an unconscious condition, the incarnation of the Self, so to speak, alternatively that process through which it will be reborn, i.e. will change

[9] Concerning the meaning of mandala symbolism, cf. Jung, "A Study in the Process of Individuation," in *Archetypes and the Collective Unconscious*, pars. 525*ff*.

[10] Cf. *Mysterium Coniunctionis*, pars. 544*ff*.

[11] For example, cf. *ibid.*, par. 547.

over into a renewed power of experience.[12] Like Christ, in the texts already quoted (Chapter 5), Adam, in the alchemistic versions, is struck in the heart by arrows of love.[13] In the alchemical *coniunctio* he is united with his own inner opposite, Eve. The alchemists projected their transformative substance on to him because, according to the Bible, he was created by God out of clay. This clay they interpreted as a kind of *massa confusa* or "chaos" out of which everything could be made.[14] Through the four stages of the process,or through separation into the four elements,the original chaos then achieves order and inner unity and a new Adam, in whom the four elements have become indestructibly one, comes into being in the stone. The numerous attributes which the alchemists ascribe to their Adam, such as four- and eight-foldness, roundness, microcosmic nature, and the four elements of which he consists, clearly indicate this aspect of Adam as the Self[15] and form a complete parallel to the ideas in *The Syrian Cave of Treasures*. Jung has already stressed these parallels in *Mysterium Coniunctionis*; the reader is referred to his explanations.[16] The four-foldness which appears so abundantly in the symbolism of Adam is concerned, as Jung explains, with the structures of consciousness (the four functions) and indicates the essentially *psychic* nature of the Adam symbol. He is the psyche *par excellence*. He does not, however, represent only the psyche but, equally, the Self and is therefore "a visualization of the 'irrepresentable' Godhead." [17] Taking Adam in this sense, as the god-image appearing in the soul, explains the infinitely rich development of the fantasy about his grave, as it is transmitted in *The Syrian Cave of Treasures* and related texts, and also the influx of these images into the Grail legend. If Adam represents the image of God manifesting in the human soul, this also corroborates the previously mentioned interpretation of the two Grail Kings in need of redemption. The older, only appar-

[12] *Ibid.*, par. 552. Cf. also *Psychology and Alchemy*, par. 410.

[13] Cf. *Psychology and Alchemy*, Fig. 131, and *Mysterium Coniunctionis*, par. 493.

[14] *Ibid.*, par. 433 and note 22.

[15] Cf. *Mysterium Coniunctionis*, par. 558.

[16] *Ibid.* [17] *Ibid.*

ently living Grail King corresponds to the "Old Adam" and thus to the image of the Old Testament god, since he was made in the image of Jahweh. The wounded king on the other hand corresponds, as already explained, to Christ as the "Second Adam." Likewise, the alchemical Adam is depicted as wounded with the arrows of love by a feminine figure.[18] And finally Perceval, too, is a renewed and later form of this same Adam, the *tierz hom* who redeems Christ, the Adam Secundus. But while the "Old Adam" sinned once, by eating the fruit of the Tree of Knowledge, Perceval first sinned by *not* asking the decisive question; not until he asked it did he expiate Adam's old guilt by a new deed, so to speak. This agrees with a modified religious point of view according to which the achievement of consciousness is no longer felt to be an offence, but, on the contrary, the highest task of man.

This same idea—that a more differentiated consciousness based on an individual relation to God is necessary—also seems to be expressed in the continuation of the legend where the Grail takes on a kind of judicial function. After Joseph has been freed by the Emperor Vespasian and has converted him, he is baptized and leaves with his family to preach Christianity. Oppressed by famine, Joseph remembers that Christ had said to him that he should turn for guidance to the "Three Powers." To obtain the answer to his question, Joseph must set up a square table, place the Grail in the centre with the fish caught by Brons beside it and then summon his companions together. The sinners will then be revealed. The *grant sénéfiance* (act of great significance) that he has to perform is therefore the symbolic enactment of the Last Supper; just as on that occasion the traitor Judas was rejected, so here the guilty will be known by the fact that they cannot find places at the table nor perceive the effect of grace emanating from the Grail. In so far as it discriminates between the virtuous and the wicked, the Grail exercises Christ's office of Judge. In order that Joseph may be entrusted with the Grail he is also granted its judicial function. The Grail therefore acts like an exteriorized or projected

[18] *Ibid.*, par. 493.

conscience.[19] Whenever he entrusts counsel of the Grail, Joseph will hear the voice of the Holy Spirit in his heart; this means that this power of discrimination is no longer outside but is now manifesting itself from within him.

Although the author does not speak of it, perhaps because he simply was not conscious of it, he has nevertheless established a connection here that makes this achievement of Joseph's appear relevant to Christ's work of redemption. Adam and Eve sinned in that, transgressing God's commandment, they ate of the Tree of the Knowledge of Good and Evil. "And the serpent said unto the woman, Ye shall not surely die: For God doth know that in the day ye eat thereof, then your eyes shall be opened, and ye shall be as gods, knowing good and evil" (Genesis 3:4–5). When, with his own hands, Christ explicitly entrusted the Grail to Joseph, he also granted him the same indwelling divine privilege of the power of discrimination and thereby annulled Adam's sin. This was remitted in the sense that Joseph acquired with the Grail the knowledge of good and evil and therewith the possibility of making amends for Adam's lapse, for with this knowledge he had also to take the corresponding responsibility upon himself. Had Adam and Eve been prepared for the coveted consciousness and had they acknowledged their guilt—instead of saying plaintively, "The woman whom thou gavest to be with me, she gave me of the tree, and I did eat" (Genesis 3:12) and "The serpent beguiled me, and I did eat (3:13)"—then the story of salvation might perhaps have taken another course.

This modified conception of evil and the demand for greater consciousness raise a problem that, having undergone various alterations, runs through all the Grail legends. The greater power of discrimination which distinguishes the Christian era leads first of all to a conflict which calls for a solution that in its turn resolves the suspension of life which was a condition of the conflict—and this solution is expected from the Holy Spirit, the

[19] Objects that carry out this function are also frequently found in fairy-tales. The Irish legend of Badurn's vessel, mentioned earlier (Chapter 7), which shattered when a lie was told, is a good example. In Heinrich von dem Thuerlin's *Diû Krône* there appear a cup and a glove which act in the same way.

Comforter. The latter, however, speaks to Joseph from the Grail vessel and guides him through every hardship in an individual manner. Looked at in this way it is all the more astounding that the Grail realm should have fallen into a state of obscurity and affliction and to be in need of redemption while awaiting Perceval's question. In this situation, the guiding voice of God that emanates from the Grail appears either to be no longer effective or, more probably, to be no longer understood by men. This brings us to a problem closely connected with the one that so occupied de Boron, namely the enigma of a fourth principle related to and amplifying the Trinity.

CHAPTER XIX

The Trinity: The Problem of the Fourth

THAT THE HIGHEST psychological value, the image of God, is experienced in triadic or trinitarian form is only in partial accord with the average natural psychic structure. It is to be accounted for by special circumstances.[1] In general, the natural symbol of wholeness and the god-image consists of a quaternity that has its analogy in the four functions of the individual.[2] On closer inspection, the Christian symbol of wholeness is only seemingly a three-fold one, for its opponent is the Devil as the fourth. The latter is the essentially substantial counterpart of Christ, and although theologians seek to minimize his reality through the theory of the *privatio boni*, he cannot, in the last resort, be separated from the nature of the Godhead; he forms the shadow of God in all its sinister reality.[3] "It is difficult," says Jung, "to make out in what relation he stands to the Trinity. As the adversary of Christ, he would have to take up an equivalent counterposition and be, like him, a 'son of God.' But that would lead straight back to certain Gnostic views according to which the devil, as Satanaël, is God's first son, Christ being the second. A further logical inference would be the abolition of the Trinity formula and its replacement by a quaternity."[4] We actually find a point of departure for this view in de Boron's version of the Grail where the fourth is, admittedly, not the Devil but the Grail. When Joseph wishes to

[1] With this cf. Jung, "A Psychological Approach to the Dogma of the Trinity," in *Psychology and Religion*, pars. 169*ff.*

[2] *Ibid.*, pars. 245*ff.*

[3] Cf. *ibid.*, pars. 248*f*; and Rivkah Schärf-Kluger, *Satan in the Old Testament*, pp. 153*ff*; also Jung, "Answer to Job," in *Psychology and Religion*, par. 579.

[4] *Psychology and Religion*, par. 249.

use the Grail as an oracular symbol for the first time, the voice of Christ tells him that when he requires counsel he should call on the Three Powers that are One and on the Holy Woman who bore the Son. Then he will hear the voice of the Holy Spirit in his heart. This means nothing less than that the Grail really forms a quaternity in which the blood contained within it signifies the Three Persons of the one Godhead, and the vessel can be compared to the Mother of God,[5] as in the Victorian hymn:

> *Salve, Mater Salvatoris,*
> *Vas electum, vas honoris,*
> *Vas caelestis gratiae.*

Something resembling a quaternary god-symbol is evident in the medieval representations of the Coronation of the Virgin;[6] and the dogma of the Assumption gives even more weight to this idea. Precisely because Mary is taken up to heaven *with her body*, an element of reality, i.e. matter, pertaining to space and time, is brought in to join the purely spiritual Trinity.[7] According to traditional views, however, matter is subject to the "Lord of this world," and the world-corrupting element of evil thereby approaches the luminous Trinity via the feminine principle. As Jung says:

> One can explain that matter was originally pure, or at least capable of purity, but this does not do away with the fact that matter represents the *concreteness* of God's thoughts and is, therefore, the very thing that makes individuation possible, with all its consequences. The adversary is, quite logically, conceived to be the soul of matter, because they both constitute a point of resistance without which the relative autonomy of individual existence would be simply unthinkable.

[5] This idea was also rendered pictorially in medieval art. Thus, in the Musée de Cluny in Paris there is a figure of Mary which can be opened and which contains within itself God the Father, Christ and the Holy Ghost. (*In gremio matris sedet sapientia patris.*)

[6] Cf. *Psychology and Religion*, pars. 251–52 and par. 122.

[7] Cf. *ibid.*, par. 251.

The will to be different and contrary is characteristic of the devil, just as disobedience was the hallmark of original sin.[8]

If we think in non-trinitarian terms, the logic of the following schema seems inescapable:

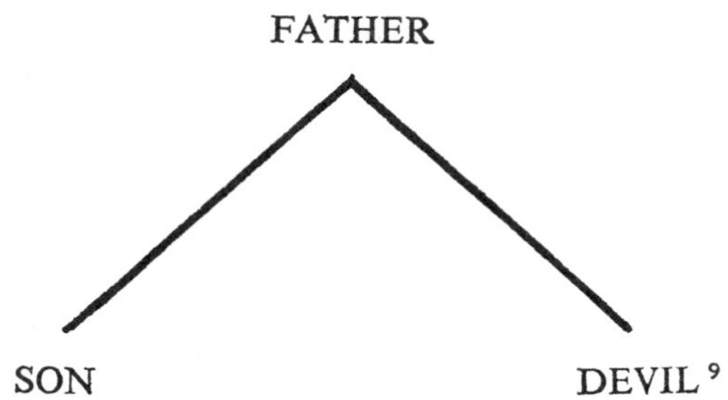

Hence it follows that the idea of an Antichrist emerged so early and continued to gain in importance during the Middle Ages since, as we have seen, the Christian age is completely governed by the idea of an absolute antithesis. In the light of such a concept, the Holy Spirit then becomes the Fourth which restores the original unity of the Father on a higher level.

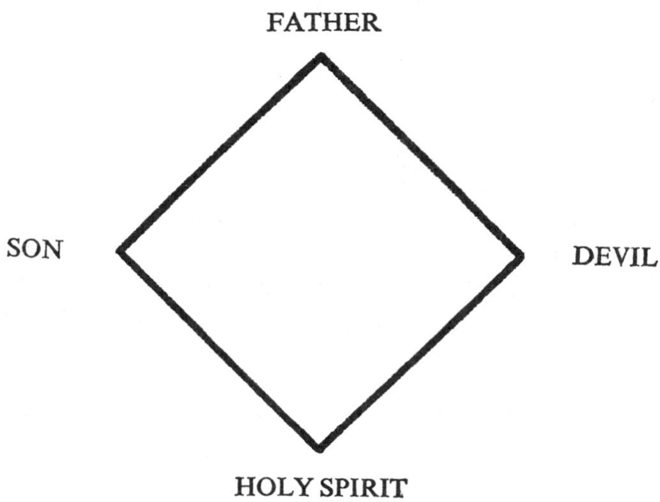

[8] *Ibid.*, par. 252.

[9] *Ibid.*, par. 256.

> Despite the fact that he is potentially redeemed, the Christian is given over to moral suffering, and in his suffering he needs the Comforter, the Paraclete. He cannot overcome the conflict on his own resources; after all, he didn't invent it. He has to rely on divine comfort and mediation, that is to say on the spontaneous revelation of that spirit, which does not obey man's will but comes and goes as *it* wills. . . . The Holy Ghost is a Comforter like the Father, a mute, eternal, unfathomable One in whom God's love and God's terribleness come together in wordless union. . . . Looked at from a quaternary standpoint, the Holy Ghost is a reconciliation of opposites and hence the answer to the suffering in the Godhead which Christ personifies.[10]

In the Grail legend, the wounded Grail King is the symbol of man suffering from the Christian conflict, but Perceval, as the *tierz hom*, would be the man elected to the vessel of the Holy Spirit which brings reconciliation. This election, however, cannot occur without an understanding of the divine reality of evil; in the story it is *this* step which, because it runs so counter to the traditional Christian view, is revealed time and again as the true problem. The figure of Lucifer therefore embodies the Grail King's invisible opponent as well as the figures of Perceval's adversaries; and finally Perceval must even undergo a struggle with the Devil himself; that is, the confrontation with this basic problem is unavoidable.

Even when the quaternary schema is arranged as overleaf with the Grail vessel (as substitute for the Mother of God) rather than the Devil added to the Trinity as the Fourth (for which the above quoted passage from the legend gives occasion), this does not dispose of the problem of evil. For, like the body of Mary, the Grail is something individual and material and thus also attracts the problem of evil to itself, because it too reaches down into the reality of earthly humanity.

This is the reason for the *siège périlleux* (the dangerous seat) at the table of the Grail brotherhood, a seat which acquires a

[10] *Ibid.*, par. 260.

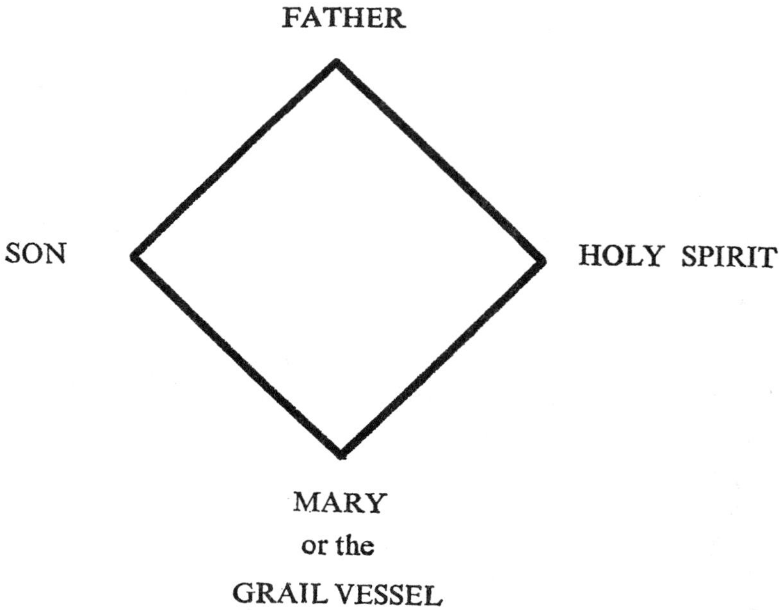

special significance towards the end of the story. It is said in the beginning of the legend that tables will have to be set up so that Christ may be sacrificed on them, because he was sitting at table when he knew that Judas should betray him. Almost more emphasis is here laid on the moment of betrayal than on the crucifixion and Christ's own death. Here, the *siège périlleux* is placed between Joseph, who takes the place of Christ at the table, and his brother-in-law Brons, the future Grail King, who sits beside him; it represents the empty place vacated by Judas when Christ said that he would be betrayed. The idea of an ultimate judgment is therefore already linked with the Last Supper where Judas, as the traitor, could no longer endure to sit at the table. Just as he had to leave it, so sinners can find no room at the Grail table. Whether or not it was customary to imagine Judas as sitting next to Christ, it was at any rate thought to be so in this case. The resultant vacant place might, and could, be taken by no one except the predestined and most virtuous man who should one day find the Grail. It is a remarkable fact that the discoverer of the Grail—who in his attribute of the redeemer is to some extent a reappearance of Christ or, as the *tierz hom*, represents an incarnation of the Holy Spirit[11]—should have to occupy just precisely Judas' seat. Judas accordingly appears here as the accompanying counterpart to Christ, whose place is later taken over by the Grail hero.[12] Looked at from the point of view of the above quoted reflections, this astounding motif nevertheless becomes more comprehensible. Evidently, Perceval has been chosen to reunite the too widely sundered opposites of good and evil with the help of the Holy Spirit and the Grail. But in reality this intuition reached far beyond the medieval intellectual horizon; the problem therefore remained in the realm of vague hints, achieving no real formulation. Like the Grail King's invisible opponent, it hovers around in the background, without gaining any clear definition. The motif of the Grail becoming invisible and being finally carried away into the Beyond is probably also connected with this unsolved problem.

At the conclusion of the story, the Grail is handed over to Joseph's brother-in-law Brons, who departs for the West, for Britain, to preach Christianity. There in Avalon, "where the sun goes down," he must await his grandson and eventual successor. According to Geoffrey of Monmouth, the mortally wounded King Arthur was carried to Insula Avallonis, the Island of Apples (or of the Avallo), to be restored to health by the nine sisters skilled in healing and magic who dwelt there, one of whom was the famous Morgana.[13] This apple island is analogous to the Isles of the Blest of antiquity, where golden apples were tended by divine maidens, and to the Celtic "Land of the Living," likewise situated in the West. The concept of an Elysium of this kind also continued into Christian times. In the legend of the voyage of Bran the Blessed, widely distributed in

[11] Cf. Bodo Mergell, *Der Gral in Wolframs Parsifal*, p. 114.

[12] Cf. the antithetical representation of Christ and Judas in the illustration facing p. 321.

[13] Concerning Morgana, see Holmes and Klenke, *Chrétien, Troyes and the Grail*, pp. 33–34. According to Giraldus she was a sister of Arthur whom the minstrels had represented as a *dea phantastica*.

the Middle Ages and later, this Irish saint, during his journey to the *Terra repromissionis*, the Promised Land, also comes to an island, equally in the West and planted with apple trees. This apple orchard signifies the second Paradise, the goal and salvation that have to be rediscovered after the loss of the first Paradise through the instrumentality of an apple tree.

As late as the sixteenth century, the Isle of Bran the Blessed, as it was later called, still constituted the great chimera, especially of Spanish seafarers. The belief was that it should be sought for south of the Canary Islands; yet it was equally said of it that it could not be found if it was looked for and for this reason it was also described as "the undiscovered island of Bran the Blessed." [14] During the period of the efflorescence of the Grail legend, Avalon was identified with Glastonbury, whose British name, *Ynis vitrin*, was interpreted as the Island of Glass. This explanation probably originated, however, in the efforts of the monks of the cloister to appropriate an interesting tradition to themselves, in conformity with the fashion of the age.[15]

[14] A. Jubinal, *Le Légende Latine de S. Brandaines*, according to an eleventh-century MS. Cf. also Marx, *La Légende Arthurienne*, p. 85, and the literature cited there.

[15] They thus laid claim to Joseph of Arimathea because it was maintained that he had landed at Glastonbury-Avalon and there founded the first British Church. His grave, an empty sarcophagus to be sure, is shown to this day in the local church. A work that appeared in 1937, *St. Joseph of Arimathea at Glastonbury*, by the Rev. L. M. Lewis, Vicar of Glastonbury, speaks of a tradition according to which Joseph first came as a dealer in metals to the tin, copper and lead bearing coasts of Britain, and which suggested that it was even possible that Christ had accompanied his uncle, Joseph, on the journey, since it was not known where he had lived between his twelfth and thirtieth years. Joseph was further said to have brought the Virgin Mary—"in whose Assumption only a very few believe"—to Glastonbury, where she died and was buried in St. Mary's Chapel. F. Lot calls Glastonbury a "workshop of falsifications" (E. Faral, *La Légende Arthurienne*, Vol. II, p. 404). The monks of Glastonbury also came under suspicion of having stolen the relics of Joseph of Arimathea from the cloister of Moyenmoutier in Lorraine, to which they had been brought by Fortunat, Patriarch of Grado—anything to enhance the fame of their monastery. The same purpose was equally served when, after a fire in the year 1190, the grave of King Arthur and Queen Guinevere was also discovered in Glastonbury! It simply had to be there that he was brought after Avalon, and Avalon must indeed be identical with Glastonbury.

The island in the West refers, therefore, not only to Britain but also to an otherworldly land.[16] (The reader is reminded that in the discussion of Chrétien's *Perceval* the Grail Castle was considered as being in the hereafter.) In the *Perlesvaus* it is called Eden, *Chastel de la Joie* (Castle of Joy) or *Chastel des Ames* (Castle of Souls), all designations of Paradise. Thus, the Grail moves into the other world. On consideration, it seems curious that the Grail should have been brought to the West for the express purpose of introducing Christianity into Britain; curious, because it is scarcely compatible with the missionary purpose of Brons and his companions that the Grail should sink into the other world, into obscurity. A very difficult passage in our story may have some connection with this. The divine voice that commands the Grail to be handed over to Brons and Brons be sent to the West adds, "*et illeuc en avant sera la mesprison*" ("and for that he will be disgraced")[17] or, according to another manuscript, "*la prison sor lui*" ("prison for him"). It is possible, even probable, that this is an error on the part of the author or of the person who wrote the prose version, since in the verse composition it states quite clearly and unequivocally that

Qu'il le gart des or en avant;
N'i mespreigne ne tant ne quant,
Toute la mesproison seroit
Seur lui, et chier le comparroit.

He must guard it from this time on
And must not hold it in disesteem,
Or scorn and disgrace will fall upon him
And he will have to pay for it dearly.[18]

In our version, when the Grail is handed over to Brons it seems as if both of them fall into disrepute or into captivity, marking

[16] For example, cf. Marx, *op. cit.*, p. 85.

[17] *Mesprison* means "offence," "insulting treatment," "contempt," or "disgrace."

[18] Robert de Boron, *Le Roman de l'Histoire dou Graal*, ed. Nitze; and also verses 3339*ff*.

the beginning of the state of concealment or burial of the Grail and its guardian.

It seems not unlikely that this removal of the Grail is related to the fact that it constellates the problem of the Fourth within the Trinity and the question of the nature of evil. But the age was not yet ripe for this enigma. Consciously, de Boron wished only to make the Christian doctrine more comprehensible to the simple understanding of the laity, but thoughts and questions that were not quite in accord with the teachings of orthodoxy arose within him, clearly unintentionally. However, an archetypal symbol broke through into the area of this unanswered question, destined, at any rate figuratively, to solve the problem of the Three and the Four. This symbol is the figure of Merlin which already in Chrétien's version stands so curiously in the background, its role never fully made clear. But before going more closely into the meaning of this figure, the contents of de Boron's Continuation called "Merlin" may be summarized briefly.

CHAPTER XX

The Figure of Merlin

"MERLIN," THE SECOND half of Robert de Boron's work, does not, as might be expected, give any account of Brons' voyage to the West or of his and his companions' fate or of the activities connected with their mission. Rather, with a leap in time and space, it transplants us immediately to Britain, the goal of their journey, at the time of the fifth-century Saxon invasions under Hengist and Horsa which brought much distress to the land. According to Geoffrey of Monmouth, Arthur's father Uther Pendragon, whose counsellor Merlin was, had come to the throne at that time. This gives an idea of the period in which the story is set. The historicity of the characters and events, however, is not definitely proved. Rather, the figure of Merlin appears to have been introduced into the literature by Geoffrey,[1] who tells us that at the behest of Bishop Alexander of Lincoln, he translated a manuscript, *The Prophecies of Merlin*, from the Breton into Latin (*circa* 1134) and later incorporated it into his *Historia*. Still later, around 1148, he was also supposed to have written a *Vita Merlini* and to have dedicated it to Archbishop Robert of York.[2] Geoffrey writes that he was urged by his contemporaries, and especially by the Bishop of Lincoln, to publish Merlin's prophecies because they were being much talked about.[3] There is

[1] Faral, *La Légende Arthurienne*, Vol. II.

[2] According to J. J. Parry, "The Vita Merlini," this text has only been attributed to Geoffrey but was not his own work.

[3] Faral, *op. cit.*, Vol. II, p. 39: "Nondum autem ad hunc locum historiae [ch. 109] perveneram, cum, de Merlino divulgato rumore, compellebant me undique contemporanei mei ipsius prophetias edere, maxime autem Alexander Lincolnensis episcopus."

no evidence, however, that either Merlin or his prophecies, which suggest the biblical prophets and the Sibylline Books, were known before that time; neither is Geoffrey's authorship clearly proved. The Welsh texts, in which Merlin is spoken of as Myrddhin, are all of a later date; moreover it has not been established that there ever was a bard of that name.[4] But, through Geoffrey's or Pseudo-Geoffrey's writing, Merlin became known as a British seer and prophet, with a fame and a reputation far beyond that country. Even before Geoffrey, a similar figure appears in the anonymous *Historia Britonum* (seventh to ninth centuries), who was known not as Merlin but as Ambrosius and who was thought to be descended from a Roman who had settled in Britain. This was the foundation for the belief that there were two Merlins, one Ambrosius Merlinus, the other Merlinus Sylvester. The figure of Merlin was romantically developed in the Breton songs and stories of that time; particularly well known is the tale of his love for the fairy Vivien (Niviene or Viviane), although it plays no part in our legend.[5] In de Boron, he possesses to some extent the characteristics imparted to him by Geoffrey, together with sundry retouchings or additions for the purpose of introducing him into the Grail legend and of using him as a unifying link in the transition from paganism to Christianity. A totally different meaning, however, unexpectedly attached itself to him.

With his gifts of clairvoyance and prophecy and his magic powers, Merlin far excelled the general run of humanity and—like the hermit who counselled Perceval—embodied in many respects the archetype of the Wise Old Man, i.e. of the spirit, except that he was far closer to nature than was the hermit; he was, rather, a pagan nature being, so that he could be related to

[4] See *ibid.*, pp. 39*ff*; and Zumthor, *Merlin le Prophète*. Cf. also Loomis, *Arthurian Literature*, pp. 20*ff*. Cf. also A. O. H. Jarman, *The Legend of Merlin*. According to Jarman, *op. cit.*, p. 21, it was Geoffrey who built up the Merlin legend, using the figure of Suibne, the Welsh Myrddhin and the Scottish Lailoken. The latter would be the oldest figure of a *gelt* or "wild man of the woods." Jarman also maintains that Geoffrey's material was transmitted to Robert de Boron through the *Roman de Brut*.

[5] Concerning this aspect, see the article by H. Zimmer, "Merlin."

the nixies, dwarfs and elves and is thus in reality a far more primitive figure than de Boron's "Devil's son," to whom his attributed role of the Antichrist does not really do justice. Since Geoffrey, the author of the *Vita Merlini*, probably served either directly or indirectly as de Boron's source, the latter must have been acquainted with this nature-spirit aspect of the prophet. Also, it is certainly not accidental that he should select this character to prepare the ground for the arrival of the Grail in Britain, for as we know, its removal to that country also signified the introduction of Christianity there. Allegedly, Merlin came from Wales, from Carmarthen or Caer Myrddhin—the town or castle of Merlin, which is said to be named for him. So through his place of origin, he is well suited to serve as the connecting link between the Grail, with its Oriental origins, and Britain, its place of destination. In a special sense he is a representative of that heathen Britain to which Christianity was to be brought, along with the Grail.[6] The story is set in a time when England was not yet fully Christianized;[7] Merlin even says that until then there had been no Christian kings in the land. Looked at from this point of view Merlin can be seen as an incarnation of the as yet unchristianized England and its barbarous customs. In so far as it embraces Christianity, however, his nature has much in common with the process of the adoption of Christianity by the West, discussed earlier. Over and above that, he anticipates a far more intensive development of the Christian symbols.

It has been asserted that Merlin is a purely literary creation, not based on any historical reality whatever.[8] This makes it all

[6] To be sure, Christianity is thought to have come very early to the Britons, probably via Gaul or directly from the East. It cannot, however, be traced historically before the fourth century. In any event a British Church was already in existence, which was represented at the Synod of Arles in 314 by the Bishops of York, London and Caerleon in Wales. The Saxons who overran the country from the fifth to the seventh centuries were so hated by the Britons that they refused to preach the Gospel to the invaders. About the year 590 Pope Gregory the Great sent Augustine (later the first Archbishop of Canterbury) to convert the Anglo-Saxons, whose king, Ethelbert, was baptized in 597.

[7] In *La Queste del Saint Graal*, ed. Pauphilet, p. 4, the year 454 is mentioned.

[8] Cf. Zumthor, *op. cit.*, pp. 41–42.

the more surprising that he should suddenly have achieved tremendous fame and been responsible for such a vast amount of literature. When something of this kind occurs, it is obvious, from the psychological point of view, that it is a case of the breakthrough of an archetypal image which represents an intensively constellated psychic content. As we shall see, this figure of Merlin is not a little bound up with the previously discussed problem of evil and with the question of the Fourth which could restore totality to the Trinity. But first we will turn to the story of Merlin as told by Robert de Boron.[9]

The text which follows "Joseph of Arimathea" begins: "The Enemy was extremely wroth when Christ broke open the gates of hell and released Adam and Eve." With these words, a connection is once more established with the Gospel of Nicodemus, the second part of which recounts Christ's descent into hell.

The devils deliberate among themselves as to how they can once again entice men back to hell. They conclude that since the greatest harm inflicted on them by the prophets was caused by their references to the coming Redeemer and their exhortations to repentance, they will nullify Christ's work by sending a prophet up from hell. One of the devils, the only one to possess the ability to take on human form and to become a father, is chosen to carry out the plan. He is to beget a son to be the counterpart of the Son of God. A pure young girl is selected to be the mother and the ground is prepared for the projected scheme through the misfortunes which overwhelm her family. The Evil One waits a long time for an opportunity, but then one evening, when the maiden forgets her father confessor's advice never to be in her room without a light, because light is hated by the Devil, he succeeds in creeping in to her during the night and accomplishing his purpose.

The following morning she realizes something has happened, and since she can discover no one in the room it becomes clear to her that she has been deceived by the Devil. In despair she goes to confession. The priest, later to be known as Blaise, makes

[9] "*Merlin*," *Roman en Prose du XIIIe siècle*, published by Paris and Ulrich; and Nitze, *L'Estoire dou Roman dou Saint Graal*, Appendix.

the Sign of the Cross over her, sprinkles her with holy water, which he also gives her to drink, and as a penance imposes a rule of lifelong chastity on her. Thus—to his great fury—the Devil's power is broken.

When her condition becomes known the girl is put in prison. In due course the Devil's child is born; he is baptized and named Merlin, after his mother's father. Eighteen months later, when his mother is to be condemned to death, the small Merlin causes general amazement by speaking and assuring his mother that she will not have to die on his account. During the trial he appears on her behalf and causes embarrassment by saying that the judge does not know *his* father either, which, because it turns out to be true, leads to the girl's acquittal. Thus, early on it is apparent that Merlin sees further and knows more than others. He has, in fact, received a two-fold heritage: from his pure mother the gift of foreseeing the future and from his devilish father a knowledge of the past. After a time Merlin informs his mother and Blaise[10] that he will soon have to leave them because he is being sought by some people who have promised to bring his blood to their master. He will go with these people, but he will not permit them to kill him. Before his departure, however, Blaise is to write down what he, Merlin, reveals to him. This is the story of Joseph of Arimathea, of the holy vessel and of his own birth. Blaise must go where the Grail people are to be found and diligently write his book. "None the less," says Merlin, "it will achieve no recognition since thou art no apostle. The apostles write nothing concerning Our Lord that they have not seen or heard for themselves; thou too must write nothing about me except what thou hast heard from me. *And because I am dark and always will be, let the book also be dark and mysterious in those places where I will not show myself.* Later it will have to be joined on to the book of Joseph of Arimathea and the two together will make a fine volume. The two will become one, except that I am not able to utter the secret words that Christ said to Joseph—it would even be wrong to do so."

[10] Probably a form of Bleho Bleheris.

We now learn the purpose for which Merlin is being sought. Vertigiers or Vortigern, King of Britain, who has achieved to this dignity illegally by seizing the kingship after having the rightful heirs murdered, sees his position threatened and tries to have an impregnable tower built. The walls of this tower, however, keep collapsing for no apparent reason. Finally the astrologers and wise men who have been summoned read in the stars that the blood of a fatherless boy will have to be mixed in with the mortar. Messengers are sent out to search for such a boy and think they have found him in Merlin when they hear another boy, at play, calling to him that he has no father. On condition that he not be slain, Merlin declares himself willing to go to Vertigiers and tell him why the tower keeps falling down. Led to the site, in the presence of the wise men and astrologers, he reveals to the King that *there is a large quantity of water under the foundation of the tower and beneath it two dragons, one white, one red.* The dragons, oppressed by the weight of the stone, are forced into movement, with the result that the walls collapse. The king has excavations made; the dragons are found and, as Merlin has likewise predicted, they immediately begin fighting each other, the white killing the red. According to the explanation given by Merlin, the red dragon signifies Vertigiers, the white one the rightful heirs, the two brothers Pendragon and Uther who will shortly join battle against him. In the battle Vertigiers is defeated. Pendragon becomes king first, being succeeded after his early death by Uther who takes the name of Uther Pendragon and appoints Merlin his permanent counsellor. The latter accepts the honour but reserves the right to absent himself from time to time; however, he assures the king this should cause him no worry. This characteristic places Merlin in his setting alongside the well-known figures of Melusines, undines and swan knights and maidens, all of whom contain in themselves the mystery of semi-human nature beings. Henceforth, he stands beside the King in word and deed, sees into the hearts of everyone, has cognizance of all coming events and knows how each should be dealt with. On his advice and by means of his magic power the colossal monoliths of Stone-

Kerunnus with stag antlers. The bowl of Gundestrup

The senex Mercurius (corresponding to Merlin) as mediator between the King and his son, from Lambspringk, 'Figurae et emblemata'

henge are brought over from Ireland to be a memorial to those who have fallen in the battle of Salisbury.[11]

The connection with our story is established in Merlin's revelation to the King of the mystery of the two holy tables. At the same time, he explains that he owes his knowledge of the past to his demonic nature but that Christ has endowed him with the gift of foreseeing the future. "Thereby the devils have lost me and I will never act according to their purpose." On the contrary, he pledges himself to Christ; he says to the King, "Thou must believe that Our Lord came down to earth to save mankind and that he sat at meal and said to the apostles, 'One among you shall betray me.'" He tells the King about Christ, about Joseph of Arimathea and his companions, about the Grail, the table and the empty place, and calls on him to set up the third, specifically round, table in the name of the Trinity. "These three tables signify the three powers of the Trinity. If thou doest this then will great wellbeing both of body and soul accrue to thee, and things will come to pass in thy time over which thou wilt be much amazed. I assure thee, a thing will come to pass about which the whole world will speak. If thou believest me, this wilt thou do and have cause for nothing but rejoicing."

The King expresses agreement with the words, "I would not that Our Lord should be deprived on my account," and entrusts Merlin with the setting up of the table. The latter selects Carduel in Wales for the purpose and summons the people thither at Whitsuntide. Fifty knights are singled out to take their places at the table, upon which the King commands a meal to be served. An empty place appears at this round table, too, and Merlin proclaims that it will first be occupied in the time of Uther's successor by a knight, as yet unborn, who will have found the Grail. Whereupon Merlin takes his leave of the

[11] This power is characterized as spiritual in the passage in which the stones are brought and set up: "Erexit illos circa sepulturas ingenuimque virtuti praevalere comprobavit" ("He set them up round the graves and thus proved that the spirit can achieve more than strength"), Geoffrey of Monmouth, *Historia*, Ch. 130; E. Faral, *La Légende Arthurienne*, Vol. III, p. 215.

Round Table, which he now wishes to avoid, for, as he says, "Those who are gathered together here must believe what they see happen and I would not that they should think that I had brought it about."

During the celebration of the festival in commemoration of the founding of the Round Table, the King falls in love with the beautiful Ygerne, the wife of the Duke of Tintagel, but she offers him scant encouragement. Uther goes for help to Merlin who, allowing free rein to his devilish side, enables the King, by means of his skill in effecting transformation, to approach the object of his desire in the form of her husband. Arthur is the result of this romantic episode. As a reward for his help, Merlin demands that the boy be handed over to him, a feature frequently encountered in fairy-tales. He gives the newborn child into the care of a couple, and he is brought up with their son Key, who is of the same age. The story ends with the coronation of Arthur who has meanwhile grown into a youth. King Uther dies without an heir and leaves the land rulerless. Merlin is consulted and counsels waiting patiently until Christmas, when God will show him who is to be chosen. On Christmas morning, a block of stone with an anvil in which a sword is embedded appears before the church. An inscription announces that God has chosen as the King whoever may be able to draw the sword out of the stone. All of the knights try, without success. By chance the young Arthur passes by and pulls it out. When his feat becomes known, he has to make the attempt a second time, in the presence of the assembled people. Again he succeeds, but the barons, taking him for the son of his foster father, are not pleased to be getting a King of such humble origins and therefore decide to wait until Easter on the off chance that another candidate might appear. When no one else comes forward the coronation is set for Whitsuntide. Until that time Arthur is to be further tested. He is found to be liberal and sagacious; nothing more stands in the way of the coronation. The ceremony takes place on Whitsunday Eve. "When this was concluded and the people were leaving the church after Mass, the stone with the anvil was found to have disappeared, no one knew whither . . .

Thus Arthur became King and ruled long in freedom over the land of Logres."

With this event, the story of Merlin comes to an end and that of Perceval begins. In essentials de Boron's "Perceval" agrees with Chrétien's version, and the few divergent features have already been discussed.

The figure of Merlin, on the other hand, is so diverse and presents so many aspects that it will be worth our while to consider a few of them more closely from the psychological point of view.

Merlin stands in the background of King Arthur's Round Table as a mysterious spiritual power. At first glance, his dual or multiple aspect and his knavish and clownish characteristics lend him a Mephistophelian quality, but his knowledge of the past and future betoken a greater degree of consciousness than is possessed by Arthur and his knights who are, indeed, remarkably unconscious and unthinking. It is due to this greater consciousness that Merlin, like the Grail, functions as a form of projected conscience, in that he exposes the mistakes and crimes of the people. As the prophet of hell put into the world by the Devil he is, moreover, clearly distinguishable as the Antichrist. In this role, the already often stressed motif of Judas is taken up once more but without the betrayal reaching the point of consummation, for the power of good is shown to be stronger than evil and thanks to his mother's virtue, Merlin's devilish inheritance cannot work itself out. This negative trait appears most clearly in his magic power and in his enjoyment of playing tricks on others and fooling them. But for the most part, neither of these traits has a destructive character, except in the case of Ygerne, whose spouse is a victim of the attempt made on his life, as was Uriah of old when, in similar circumstances, King David rid himself of Bathsheba's husband. *As the Antichrist, Merlin would expand the Trinity into a quaternity.* It is part of the essential quality of the quaternary number, considered as a psychic symbol, that the fourth does not just follow the three as one more unit but that, according to the saying of Maria Prophetissa, ". . . out of the third comes the one as the fourth."[12] This

[12] With this cf. *Psychology and Alchemy*, par. 26.

means that *in the fourth a new dimension is introduced* in which the original one, the totality, manifests itself afresh while comprising the three in unity.[13] So that, in the final analysis, Merlin is not simply the Antichrist which is joined to the Trinity as the Fourth but is also an incarnation of the primal Father God in whom the Father, Son and Holy Spirit are embodied. This new dimension is the human and natural one that appears to signify a realization of the divine which has penetrated more deeply into our world.

[13] It is not possible to discuss this highly significant matter within the limits of this work. The reader is referred to Jung, "Synchronicity: An Acausal Connecting Principle", in *The Structure and Dynamics of the Psyche*, pars. 816*ff.*

CHAPTER XXI

Merlin as Medicine Man and Prophet

THE REMARKABLE story in which the young Merlin discloses that a pair of fighting dragons—one red and one white—are responsible for the collapse of King Vertigier's tower is to be found in Geoffrey of Monmouth as well as in Robert de Boron. Psychologically it is Merlin who points out a problem of the opposites, which has become unconscious again, a problem of which the people of the time certainly knew nothing, but by which they none the less felt themselves to be undermined.

The red and white dragons play an important part as a motif of alchemical symbolism, where they also portray the psychic problem of the opposites. Bernard of Treviso, the fifteenth-century Italian alchemist, depicts the problem in the following parable.[1] He goes into an orchard, the place of the "chymical" transformation, and there finds a castle "in which lived two dragons, the one red and heavy of cadaver,[2] the other white and without wings. They came together and embraced each other in the heat of the sun, as it is in Aries. They played together until the conjoined dragons disappeared and both jointly changed into black ravens. The ravens then moistened each other until they became white, until the sun entered Leo; until, therefore, the raven that had become white had become red as blood in the latter, in the heat, and in this work was transformed into a conjunction."

It is possible that the legend of Merlin was known to the Count of Treviso and that he incorporated it into his system of

[1] *Des Bernardi Grafen von der Marck und Tarvis Chymische Schriften*, trans. into German by Joachim Tanck, pp. 293*ff*.

[2] Body.

alchemical ideas. Depicting the opposites as dragons indicates that the split is constellated far down below, in the world of instinct, and that there is as yet no sort of relationship.

According to the alchemistic point of view, however, these opposites should be united, since red and white are the colours of the bridegroom and bride who come together in the "chymical wedding." Something is therefore separated which in nature should be united; and it is Merlin who draws men's attention to this faulty situation. This suggests that he is the one who can bring the unconscious problem of opposites up into consciousness and in this way might act as a "lightbringer" for men. But, according to Geoffrey's *Vita Merlini*,[3] he withdraws into the forest, away from human society, because he has gone mad from suffering as the result of a battle between the Scots and Britons (Merlin was a Briton). In this battle, three brothers of the Briton chief—perhaps of Merlin's own chief—were killed. In the forest, Merlin leads the life of a wild animal, and when by chance he is discovered, the emissaries of his sister Ganieda have to soothe him with song and lyre before they can prevail upon him to return to the world of men. At the sight of a crowd of people, his madness breaks out anew. He is released and is once more free to return to the forest. There he wishes to remain and even consents to his wife Gwendolina taking another husband, though not without intimating that he will be present on the wedding day with a very exceptional gift. A few days after he reads in the stars that Gwendolina is about to remarry, he appears before the house of the newly wedded couple, riding a stag and driving a pack-deer before him. He calls to Gwendolina, who is much amused at the spectacle. But when her bridegroom appears at the window, Merlin wrenches off the stag's horns and throws them at the head of his rival, whose skull is shattered. He then flees back to the forest on his stag. Crossing a stream, he loses his balance and falls into the water. He is fished out by his sister's servants and delivered to her.

Once again he is captured and in his yearning for the forest

[3] According to Faral, *La Légende Arthurienne*, Vol. III.

loses all joy in life. There is no alternative for his captor but to give in to his longing and release him. However, he allows his sister to provide him with a few comforts. She builds him a house in the forest, with seventy windows and doors, where he can devote himself to his astronomical observations. With her servants, Ganieda settles herself a little way off in order to dwell near him. During the summer, Merlin lives in the open; when the winter cold sets in and he can find nothing to eat, he returns to his observatory where, fortified by his sister with food and drink, "he explores the stars and sings about future happenings."[4] Later he teaches her to prophesy and extols her as his equal.

It is noteworthy that while Merlin reveals the unconscious conflict symbolized by the two dragons, yet he is unable to endure the senseless strife of men among themselves; in a deeper sense these two motifs belong together. It is the unconsciousness concerning the inner problem of the opposites that leads to war and hinders the royal wedding of the white and red. Merlin, who certainly knows this, despairs of the stupidity of men who are unable to see it.

In the way in which from then on he lives in the forest with his sister, hidden far away not only from others but from his wife as well, dedicating himself to the observation of the stars and to prophecy, he appears to have taken on more than a little of the nature of the Druid priest and Celtic bard. Furthermore, he resembles the general type of primitive medicine man and

[4] Faral, *op. cit.*, pp. 323–24:

> Cumque venire hiems rigidis hirsuta procellis,
> Quae nemus et terras fructu spoliabat ab omni,
> Deficeretque sibi pluviis instantibus esca,
> Tristis et esuriens dictam veniebat ad aulam:
> Illic multotiens aderat regina dapesque
> Et potum pariter fratri gavisa ferebat,
> Qui, postquam variis sese recreverat escis
> Mox assurgebat, complaudebatque sorori.
> Deinde domum perargrans ad sidera respiciebat,
> Talia dum caneret, quae tunc ventura sciebat.

Cf. also Parry, "Vita Merlini," pp. 36*ff.*

priestly personality.[5] The shaman and the medicine man and the analogous figure, the Celtic Druid, embody, as it were, the type of religious man who, in complete independence and solitude, opens up a direct and personal approach to the collective unconscious for himself and tries to live the predictions of his guardian spirit, i.e. of his unconscious. The result is that he becomes a source of spiritual life for his surroundings. As Mircea Eliade has shown,[6] states of temporary insanity are often an attribute of the shaman and medicine man. More especially, the disturbance of psychic balance which characterizes the early stages and the initiation of novices is frequently accompanied by a plunge into water; this also happens to Merlin.[7] The Eskimoes, however, differentiate between this form of disturbance and psychic illness when the shaman himself seeks out the cure for his own suffering, whereas the ordinary sufferer from mental illness does not do this. In fact, a spring gushes up beside the raving Merlin, by whose waters he is healed and is later enabled to heal others. His madness therefore should be looked upon as an initiation by means of which he comes into closer contact with the otherworldly powers. As a result of his cure, he pledges himself, as many shamans do, to an isolated forest existence in the service of the divine. Parallels to Merlin's life are to be found not only among primitive peoples but also in the Judaeo-Christian and Islamic traditions, where it is especially the life of the prophet Elijah which, in its legendary formulation, exhibits close similarities to that of Merlin.[8]

[5] In *Shamanism*, pp. 25*ff*, Mircea Eliade has shown that this kind of priest-medicine man corresponds to a type that is spread over the whole world and that the aspects and phases of development of his personality correspond, as Jung has shown, to the process of individuation.

[6] *Ibid.*

[7] It was only after the publication of the German edition of this book that the author (M.-L. v. F.) discovered with great pleasure that Brigit Beneŝ had found connections with shamanism in the legend of Buile Suibne (*Zeitschrift für keltische Philologie*). As the Irish parallel to Merlin, Suibne, together with Lailoken and Myrddhin (also analogous to Merlin), has many connections with shamanism (p. 313). Suibne is associated with the stag: "These are my stags, from glen to glen."

[8] Cf. "Elie le Prophète," in *Etudes Carmélitaines*, Vol. II, and especially Jung's introduction to the same, pp. 15*ff*.

Helen Adolf was the first to draw attention to this parallel:

> Elijah, among the Jews, is the "prophet" καιτ'ἐζοχήν; his prophecy even goes on in the Bird's Nest, where the "effigies are woven of all the nations who band together against Israel." Merlin, too, is a *devins* and in his farewell speech says that in the *esplumoir* "*je profetiserai tou que nostre Sire commandera.*"
>
> Elijah did not die, but was translated to Heaven . . . It is the same with Merlin: "*Lor dist que il ne poroit morir devant le finement del siecle.*"
>
> Elijah records the deeds of men and the chronicles of the world, as do Merlin and Blaise.
>
> Elijah is shown in close connection with the Messiah ben David . . . and with the Messiah ben Joseph (or Ephraim), who will be slain by the Antichrist, but resuscitated by Elijah. This reminds us of Merlin, who, after the fateful battle where Arthur is grievously wounded, goes into his *esplumoir*, expecting the time when Arthur (who thus represents both Messiah ben David and Messiah ben Joseph) will return from Avalon.

Among other similarities, Adolf remarks that:

> It is Merlin who points out to Perceval the road that leads to the house of the Fisher King. He seems to know all about the Grail. According to Jewish tradition, all lore, especially all secret lore, emanates from Elijah. He is also credited with having founded the Cabala. "What Moses was to the Torah, Elijah was to the Cabala."
>
> There seems to be ample evidence in favour of our argument that there is a connection between Merlin, the seer, and Elijah, the prophet. We shall be still more inclined to grant such a possibility, if we take into consideration that a contact between Jewish tradition and Arthurian romance already existed. I refer to the legend of Solomon and Asmodeus, which is said to have inspired parts of Merlin's own history.
>
> Of course, the legend of Solomon was a favourite of the Middle Ages and had spread all over Europe. But Elijah shared the privilege of being a hero in Jewish as well as Christian tradition. . . . Moreover, we are able to show that

there was a connection between Asmodeus and Elijah, so that by the very fact that Merlin borrowed from Asmodeus, he also stepped into the shoes of the prophet.[9]

It is possible that the cleric Helyes, who according to legend recorded Merlin's prophecies, was in reality Elijah.[10] In the legend Elijah appears as the religious prophetic personality who also has the rascally and even somewhat demonic traits which so often characterize the typical heathen medicine man and which are also so clearly displayed by Merlin. Thus, Elijah goes so far as to murder a man; he changes himself into an hetaera in order to rescue a pious rabbi; and he plays repeated pranks on men by wandering around on earth, unrecognized, with Khidr. In such connections as these he becomes a personification of the trickster archetype[11] whose function, among others, is to compensate the disposition to rigidity in the collective consciousness and to keep open the approaches to the irrational depths and to the riches of the instinctual and archetypal world.[12] A prophet such as Elijah is not, however, merely an example of an individuated personality but, as Jung explains[13] and as is even indicated by his name, he is also a human personification of Yahweh, i.e. of God. In the legend he is identified with the Metatron, the figure known in the *Pistis Sophia* as the "little Yahweh." [14] Thus, his image represents an aspect of the highest God, inasmuch as the process of individuation, when seen from the "other"—the archetypal—side, actually depicts a process of the incarnation of the divine.[15] In later times Enoch, Elijah and John the Baptist were equated with the Metatron. In the *Pistis Sophia*

[9] See "The Esplumoir Merlin," *Speculum* XXI, pp. 173*ff*, and the further literature there mentioned.

[10] Cf. Zumthor, *op. cit.*, p. 198.

[11] Cf. Paul Radin, *The Trickster*, with commentaries by Karl Kerenyi and C. G. Jung.

[12] Cf. *ibid.*, especially pp. 210–11.

[13] "Elie le Prophète," pp. 15*ff*.

[14] Concerning the Metatron as the "little Yahweh," cf. H. Bietenhard, *Die himmlische Welt in Urchristentum und Spätjudentum*, especially p. 157.

[15] Cf. Jung, "Transformation Symbolism in the Mass," in *Psychology and Religion*, par. 427.

Jesus says: "I found Elizabeth, the mother of John the Baptizer, before she had conceived him, and I sowed into her a power which I had received from the little Iaō [Yahweh], the Good, who is in the Midst, that he might be able to make ready my way. . . . So the power of the little Iaō, who is in the Midst, and the soul of the Prophet Elias, they were bound into the body of John the Baptizer."[16] They represent the "completed man" and the Ancient of Days.[17] Like John the Baptist, Elijah (Elias) is unusually hirsute, as if the animal were still extremely prominent in him. This same remarkable hairiness is exhibited once again by Merlin. Our story tells us that Merlin inherited his outer appearance from his father and that those present at his birth were horrified by his hairy body. He is further characterized as being close to the animal in that he always returns to the forest—for which reason he is known as Merlinus Sylvester—and that he appears as the shepherd of wild animals. This latter trait is particularly in evidence in the *Vita Merlini*[18] in which Geoffrey goes so far as to compare him directly with Orpheus.[19]

He lives in his forest observatory with three trusted companions (a quaternity group): his pupil, the bard Thelgessin or Taliesin; his sister Ganieda; and a former sufferer from mental illness who has been cured by drinking from the healing fountain that springs up beside Merlin's house.[20]

Merlin's laugh is especially well known; it is the result of his more profound knowledge of invisible connections. For instance, he laughs aloud when he sees a poor, tattered man sitting down, or when he sees a youth buying himself a pair of shoes. The reasons are that the poor man is unknowingly seated on a buried treasure, while the young man is fated to die the following day.[21] Merlin's loneliness is understandable. His all-embrac-

[16] *Pistis Sophia*, pp. 9–10; Bietenhard, *op. cit.*, p. 157.

[17] Cf. Charles Allyn Williams, "Oriental Affinities of the Legends of the Hairy Anchorite." Williams also cites the parallel figure of Elias.

[18] According to Faral, *op. cit.*, Vol. III.

[19] Cf. Zumthor, *op. cit.*, p. 43. Another parallel would be Enkidu in the epic of Gilgamesh; see Williams, *op. cit.*

[20] *Ibid.*, p. 40. The madman had become insane because he had eaten the poisoned fruit of one of Merlin's deserted loves.

[21] Cf. *ibid.*, p. 42; further examples are to be found on p. 41.

ing knowledge, which grants him insight into the unconscious connective processes, isolates him from ordinary people, to whom his reactions must appear nonsensical. For this reason, he remains in the forest in a state of voluntarily chosen poverty and renunciation of love and refuses to let himself be drawn back into the world by glittering temptations. For, as he says, "Nothing would please me that could take me away from here, from my Calidon, which in my opinion is always pleasing."[22] Calidon is an oak grove in which he lives and which suggests Wotan.[23] In this grove he serves God only, and to the man cured of mental illness he utters the significant words: "Now must thou go hesitantly forward to thy confrontation with God, who gave thee back to thyself, and now mayest thou remain with me, in order, again in obedience to God, to redeem the days of which insanity robbed thee."[24] Taliesin likewise renounces his scientific avocations in order to be able to follow his teacher, and Ganieda, Merlin's sister, gives up her love affair so that they can live together as a quartet. Finally, at a great age and famous for his holiness and surrounded by a circle of spiritual pupils, Merlin retires from all society and withdraws into eternal silence.[25]

The decisive factor in Merlin's forest life appears to have been his absolute surrender or *religio*, i.e. his painstaking attentiveness

[22] Verses 1237–38. Cf. Zumthor, *op. cit.*, p. 40.

[23] Verse 1239, *ibid.*, p. 43:

> Tunc Merlinus ait: tibi nunc cunctanter eundum
> est in agone Dei qui te tibi reddidit et nunc
> mecum maneas, ut quos tibi surrepiebat
> vis verunca, dies iterum reparare labores
> obsequio Domini. . . .

(Parry, op. cit., p. 113) ("Then Merlin said: You must now continue in the service of God who restored you as you now see yourself [lit.: to yourself], you who for so many years lived in the desert like a wild beast, going about without a sense of shame. Now that you have recovered your reason, do not shun the bushes or the green glades which you inhabited while you were mad, but stay with me that you may strive to make up in the service of God for the days that the force of madness took from you. . . ."—Verse 139, Canto XA, 2014, i).

[24] Verses 1449*ff*, *ibid.*, p. 44.

[25] *Ibid.*, p. 45.

to the divine, through which he incarnated something of its knowledge and mystery within himself. The living reality of the unconscious was thereby enabled to manifest itself through him. It is as if a part of the unconscious, the προσφυὴς ψυχή (additional unconscious psyche) of man, that unites with the animal world and with cosmic nature,[26] fears the clutches of consciousness and can live only when man to some extent voluntarily surrenders collective adaptation and the superiority of consciousness and his own free personal will, so that he can offer a possibility of life to that more archaic and at the same time more prospective part of himself. Under this condition such an act of surrender grants him presentiments of the future that reach far beyond the present moment, just as, for example, the motifs of the Grail legend reach out beyond the Middle Ages into our time, and will perhaps reach even further. Merlin thus becomes the legend-entwined image of the whole man, the *homo quadratus* or *homo altus* of alchemy, in which the ordinary man has become one with the wholeness that transcends him. His renunciation of the judgments of a self-assured, one-sided consciousness and of self-willed emphasis cause him to appear at times as the *jocosus*, the fool who not infrequently meets with strange mishaps, such as the plunge into the water after his vengeance on his adversary. These curious ineptitudes on Merlin's part call to mind Jung's comments on the archetypal trickster: "The trickster is a primitive 'cosmic' being of *divine-animal* nature, on the one hand superior to man because of his superhuman qualities, and on the other hand inferior to him because of his unreason and unconsciousness. He is no match for the animals either, because of his extraordinary clumsiness and lack of instinct. These defects are the marks of his *human* nature, which is not so well adapted to the environment as the animal's but, instead, has prospects of a much higher development of consciousness based on a considerable eagerness to learn, as is duly emphasized in the myth."[27] The archetype of the trickster therefore always appears as a healing figure when collective consciousness is in

[26] Concerning this idea, cf. *Aion*, pars. 269*ff*.

[27] *Archetypes and the Collective Unconscious*, par. 473.

danger of stiffening obstinately into one-sidedness. Again and again he holds open the approaches to the divine-animal substrata of the psyche, and this was obviously also Merlin's task in medieval culture.

The observation of the stars, to which he devotes his declining years, is likewise significant. We know from Caesar that the Celtic Druids observed the stars,[28] and in this respect Merlin embodies this type of medicine man or priest. At that time, the heavenly bodies were still the great messengers of fate and the future. Their astrological—i.e. symbolic—groupings enabled the projections of the collective unconscious to be perceived, and in them may be read the secular "constellations" of the archetypes, thus extensively foreshadowing our cultural history and spiritual destiny.[29] Through this curious life in his forest observatory, Merlin is, as it were, merged in the *unus mundus*, in union with the origins of all cosmic and psychic being, the unity of which is most clearly foreshadowed in the phenomenon of synchronicity, of which the astrological coincidences are indeed also a part.[30] By observing it, the understanding sometimes touches briefly on the "absolute knowledge" of the unconscious and is thereby filled with presentiments that stretch far beyond every conscious reflection and are capable of anticipating future possibilities of human development—which is exactly what constitutes the nature of prophecy.

[28] *De bello Gallico*, VI, 18.

[29] Cf. *Aion*, especially par. 128, and, also by Jung, "Flying Saucers, a Modern Myth," in *Civilization in Transition*.

[30] Cf. Jung, *Mysterium Coniunctionis*, par. 662, and "Synchronicity: An Acausal Connecting Principle," in *The Structure and Dynamics of the Psyche*, *passim*.

CHAPTER XXII

Merlin and the Alchemical Mercurius

A PRODIGIOUS LITERARY output elaborating the figure of Merlin from many points of view was soon grafted on to the Merlin legend. "Prophecies of Merlin" also began to appear, which more or less prepared the way for the political and ecclesiastical conflicts of the age.[1] The flood of this literature mounted higher and higher during the following centuries, appearing in Brittany, Spain and Italy.[2] The followers of Joachim of Floris published the ideas of their teacher concerning the coming of the Antichrist (whom they saw in the Emperor Frederick II, 1194–1250) under the title *Verba Merlini*,[3] and a Venetian Joachinist published a further work entitled *Les Prophéties de Merlin*.[4] This work, which is orthodox in its doctrine, contains some very forceful criticism of abuses within the Church. In Italy these works were followed by political writings which went in for every possible tendentious theme, so that the Church eventually reached the conclusion that such productions dealing with Merlin were dangerous. The Council of Trent (1545–1563) placed the *Merlini Angli liber obscurarum praedictionum* (*Book of Dark Predictions by the English Merlin*) on the Index of Prohibited Books;[5] after this the tide of literature on the subject subsided on the Continent.

When a figure, in itself highly fantastic, is suddenly on everyone's lips to such an extent, it is natural to assume that it corresponds to an intensively constellated content of the collective

[1] Cf. Zumthor, *Merlin le Prophète*, pp. 55*ff*; and San Marte, *Die Sagen von Merlin*.

[2] Cf. Zumthor, *op. cit.*, pp. 97*ff*.

[3] *Ibid.*, p. 100.

[4] *Ibid.*, pp. 101–2.

[5] *Ibid.*, p. 113.

unconscious, and it might be expected that parallel manifestations would be discernible. In point of fact, the efflorescence of the Merlin literature coincided in time with that of Occidental alchemy, and in the latter we find a personification of the arcane substance, which bears a striking resemblance to Merlin, namely the alchemical Mercurius. In alchemistic literature, Mercurius personifies the *prima materia* and in him the ancient god of revelation was not only kept alive but also enriched with numerous amplifications. The doctrine of the godlike Anthropos of late antiquity survived, not exactly *expressis verbis* but disguised under a thousand forms, in the speculations of the alchemists concerning the *materia*. Jung has brought the most important aspects together in his essay on "The Spirit Mercurius,"[6] to which we must refer since it is impossible to describe the manifold aspects of this figure in a few lines. A concealed nature god,[7] and personification of the *lumen naturae*,[8] the alchemical Mercurius is at the same time an embodiment of the great inner man, the Self, which displays features complementary to the ecclesiastical figure of Christ.[9] He is the guide and counsellor of those who in solitude prepare themselves to seek the immediate experience of the divine. *It is remarkable how many features Merlin and the Mercurius of the alchemists have in common.* Both are capable of infinite transformations. Both are compared, now with Christ, now with the Antichrist.[10] Both serve as analogues for the inspiring breath of the Holy Spirit,[11] or are derided as false prophets. Both have the nature of the trickster, both are hidden away, both are the mysterious agent behind the transformation of the "King"[12] and are connected with the gods of love.[13] Both are associated with Saturn,[14] and both engender or themselves fall victim to insanity.[15] Finally, both represent the mystery of a "divine vessel"[16] which serves as the object of men's search. Both are connected with the

[6] In *Alchemical Studies*, pars. 239–303.

[7] *Ibid.*, p. 112 and 135–36.

[8] *Ibid.*, p. 99.

[9] *Ibid.*, pp. 87 and 135–36.

[10] *Ibid.*, pp. 103, 105 and 111.

[11] Cf. *ibid.*, p. 99.

[12] *Ibid.*, pp. 119*ff.*

[13] *Ibid.*, pp. 102 and 115–16.

[14] *Ibid.*, pp. 116–17.

[15] *Ibid.*, pp. 116*ff.*

[16] *Ibid.*, p. 102.

experience of the divine in nature or in the unconscious. Two songs of Taliesin, who as already mentioned was looked upon as the pupil and companion of Merlin,[17] extol this spirit:

> I have been in many shapes before I attained a congenial form.
> I have been a narrow blade of a sword;
> I have been a drop in the air;
> I have been a shining star;
> I have been a word in the book;
> I have been a book in the beginning;
> I have been a light in a lantern a year and a half;
> I have been a bridge for passing over threescore rivers;
> I have journeyed as an eagle;
> I have been a boat on the sea;
> I have been a director in battle;
> I have been a sword in the hand;
> I have been a shield in fight;
> I have been a string of a harp;
> I have been enchanted for a year in the foam of water;
> there is nothing in which I have not been.[18]

In an Irish counterpart to this song, from *The Book of Cecan* and *The Book of Ballymote*, Taliesin says:

> I am the wind that blows upon the sea;
> I am the ocean wave;
> I am the murmur of the surges;
> I am seven battalions;
> I am a strong bull;
> I am an eagle on a rock;
> I am a ray of the sun;
> I am the most beautiful of herbs;

[17] There was even one work called *A Dialogue between Merlin and Taliesin.*

[18] Cf. "The Book of Taliesin," according to C. Squire, *Celtic Myths and Legends*; or S. Skene, *Four Ancient Books of Wales*, Vol. I, p. 276. These literary references were very kindly supplied by P. Wolff. Concerning the question of dates, cf. Nitze, *Perlesvaus*, p. 154.

I am a courageous wild boar;
I am a salmon in the water;
I am a lake upon the plain;
I am a cunning artist;
I am a gigantic, sword-wielding champion;
I can shift my shape like a god.[19]

In these utterances, Taliesin describes himself as a kind of cosmic spiritual being, creative and divine and capable of self-transformation. At the same time, he suggests the figure of Mercurius who is frequently described by the adepts as just such a spirit, also capable of transforming himself. One text calls him "the spirit of the world become body within the earth." [20] He is also a wind or *pneuma* and the water of the sea,[21] he incarnates in the eagle and other animals,[22] as well as in the sunbeam.[23] The alchemist Avicenna says of him: "He is the spirit of the Lord which fills the whole world and in the beginning swam upon the waters. They call him also the spirit of Truth, which is hidden from the world."[24] We are forcefully reminded of Merlin who was accustomed to telling the truth and who lived hidden away from the world. Mercurius likewise is cunning and duplex (double); one text says of him that "he runs around the earth and enjoys equally the company of the good and the wicked." [25] He is an embodiment of the original man,[26] a figure that unites Christ, the light half of the symbol of the Self, with its dark half, the Antichrist, in *one* being.[27] If we think of Merlin as a parallel to Mercurius it becomes understandable that de Boron should describe him as the Antichrist and then conversely depict him once more as a servant of Christ.

[19] Cf. Squire, *op. cit.*; and Arbois de Jubainville, *Cycle Mythologique*. These references were also provided by Herr Wolff.

[20] Cf. the whole of "The Spirit Mercurius," in *Alchemical Studies*, especially par. 261.

[21] Cf. *ibid.*, pars. 265 and 261, where Mercurius is described as *totus aereus et spiritualis*.

[22] Cf. Lambsprinck, *De Lapide Philosophico*.

[23] Cf. Senior, *De Alchemia*, pp. 9*ff*.

[24] *Alchemical Studies*, par. 263.

[25] *Ibid.*, par. 267. [26] *Ibid.*, par. 268. [27] *Ibid.*, par. 270.

Moreover, we are entitled to compare Merlin with the alchemical Mercurius since the alchemists themselves did so. Verses about a Merculinus are quoted in the *Rosarium philosophorum* (probably fifteenth century). The joining of the two names in this instance could have arisen out of a misreading of Mercurius, but even so it is no coincidence. In addition there is also another well-known alchemical writing, the *Allegoria Merlini*, which describes *the mystery of the murder and transformation of the king.*[28] Merlin stands equally behind Arthur and the Grail King as maker, guardian and counsellor of the King, as well as being in the background behind Perceval. Officially he is a helper, but he also possesses another side which comes to our attention in the description of the Saturnian man with the wooden leg. Like Merlin the latter is also an astronomer and magician, indeed of a rather more dangerous and uncanny aspect, and for this reason we have emphasized his role as the figure of the Grail King's opponent. The King himself has a "ghostlike" background.

Many scholars identify the Grail King with Bran (which would account for his name—Brons), a god-hero and king of the infernal regions of the Mabinogi,[29] and this aspect lingers behind the christianized figure. In the work known as the "Elucidation"[30] he is said to understand necromancy and to be a magician who can change form at will. In the *Queste del Saint Graal*[31] his suffering is caused by two snakes which curl around his neck (the same problem of the opposites as portrayed by the white and red dragons). In such guise he comes strikingly close to the nature of Merlin, i.e. he loses the characteristics of a collective principle of consciousness and (like the *sol niger* of alchemy) is assimilated to an archaic dual aspect of the Self symbol. He and his opponent are then identical, and both—the King as well as his invisible enemy—correspond in many respects to Merlin. The latter therefore unequivocally embodies an

[28] For a closer comparison see *Mysterium Coniunctionis*, par. 357.

[29] Cf. Marx, *La Légende Arthurienne*, pp. 68–69, 201 and 285; also Dorothy Kempe, *op. cit.*, p. xxi.

[30] Cf. *ibid.*, p. 185.

[31] *Ibid.*, p. 285.

enigmatic aspect of the Self, in which the opposites appear to be united. It is as if he raised the King to the throne as well as having prepared *and* brought about his downfall, i.e. as if he incarnated the dual aspect of the Self in which he is once more analogous to Mercurius. Because he lives with his sister, he can be compared with the well-known brother-sister pair of alchemy, a figure embodying the dual aspect of the arcane substance.

Jung's comprehensive statement about Mercurius may also be applied word for word to Merlin:

> He is both material and spiritual. [Merlin is a physical man, later a spirit which speaks from a grave.]
>
> He is the process by which the lower and material is transformed into the higher and spiritual, and vice versa. [As his opponent, Merlin pulls the Grail King down into *physis* and for his spiritualization sends Perceval up to Mount Doulourous.]
>
> He is the devil [as the Antichrist], a redeeming psychopomp, an evasive trickster, and God's reflection in physical nature.
>
> He is also the reflection of a mystical experience of the artifex that coincides with the *opus alchymicum*. As such, he represents on the one hand the self and on the other the individuation process and, because of the limitless number of his names, also the collective unconscious.[32]

It is amazing how such a figure of the Self emerges almost simultaneously as Mercurius in Occidental alchemy and as Merlin in the Grail legend. This indicates how profound the psychic need must already have been at that time for some such undivided personification of the incarnated Godhead that should heal the opposites of Christ-Antichrist.

Another of Merlin's aspects should be discussed here: his connection with the symbol of the stag. The stag appears in the curious episode in which Merlin punishes the unfaithfulness of

[32] *Alchemical Studies*, par. 284.

his wife. He rides to her on a stag and kills the enemy with a stag's antler which he hurls at him. This relation to the stag he also has in common with Mercurius who is often described in alchemical texts as the *cervus fugitivus* (fugitive stag).[33] It is possible, however, that a memory of the Celtic god Kerunnus—a god, according to Marx,[34] who underwent a transformation mystery—also survives in this stag symbol. Kerunnus is dismembered and cooked in a bowl (!) in order to arise again, rejuvenated, from the dead;[35] he therefore undergoes a truly alchemical transformation mystery. *In this Merlin would himself be the hidden content of the Grail.*[36]

In the third part of the de Boron trilogy, Merlin appears to Perceval as an aged man carrying a sickle round his neck and wearing high boots. He instructs Perceval to go to a tournament, and when Perceval asks him who he is he replies, "*Si fait, grand partie de ton afaire gist sor moi*" ("Yes, indeed, a large part of your affair rests with me"), and reminds him of his oath not to sleep twice under the same roof until he has found the Grail.[37] It is asserted here that Merlin is the mysterious instigator of Perceval's quest; *he* is charged with the hero's task, precisely because he represents the Self, the inner wholeness to which Perceval should attain through the quest of the Grail. Thus Merlin *is* the mystery of the Grail. The sickle which he carries round his neck equates him more or less with Saturn, whose role we have already discussed.

In other versions he appears as an old hermit,[38] sometimes

[33] Cf. p. 259 above. In the story of Grisandole, Merlin appears openly as a stag. Cf. Zumthor, *op. cit.*, pp. 197–98. Cf. also, Suibne's connection with the stag; see Beneŝ, p. 313.

[34] *Op. cit.*, p. 184.

[35] On the cup of Gundestrup. See also Marx, *op. cit.*, pp. 184–85. An unpublished manuscript by Margarete Riemschneider also suggests that behind the stag-god Kerunnus the secret of the Grail might be hidden. Information about this MS. was received too late to make use of it in the text of this volume, but thanks are due Mrs. Riemschneider for the opportunity of glancing at her exposition. Suibne also has some connection with the stag, which also plays a role in Brigit Beneŝ' *Schamanismus*, p. 315.

[36] Like the *pneuma* in the above-mentioned vessel of the Poimandres.

[37] Cf. Zumthor, *op. cit.*, pp. 162–63.

[38] *Vulgate Merlin.* Cf. Zumthor, *op. cit.*, p. 199.

clad in white,[39] the ghostly colour of the Celts,[40] sometimes as a woodcutter in the forest or, in the guise of an *ombre* (shadow), he encounters the hero on his path. Here it is worth while once more to examine Merlin's role in Chrétien's continuators.[41] There Merlin himself does not actually appear, but a woman riding a mule helps Perceval with advice and a magic ring. Later, it turns out that she is a daughter of Merlin, and when Perceval ties his horse to the pillar at Mount Doulourous she tells him that the pillar was erected by her father. Here the invisible Merlin works indirectly on Perceval through the figure of the anima. In this version it is as if the symbol of the Self were not personified independently behind the anima but only effected its purpose from its place of concealment behind the scenes. In de Boron, on the other hand, as also in his continuator, who discusses the Christian problem of the opposites far more earnestly, the figure of the being who heals the opposites comes unexpectedly into the picture and even becomes the dominating figure in his work. It seems, however, that yet another trace of Merlin may possibly be found in Chrétien's continuators, namely the red-robed woman who emerges from the water and sends Perceval out to bring back the stag's head.

This Red Star Woman, whose robe symbolically ascribes to her the power of enlightenment, turns out to be an heiress of the fairy Morgana, from whom she received the chessboard at which Perceval is checkmated by an invisible opponent. Might not this unseen chessplayer turn out to be "the hidden Merlin," with whom the woman lives (as Morgana had done)? In any event it is an archetypal motif in fairy-tales that before the hero can gain her love he must first separate the anima figure, whom he must win, from an invisible pagan spirit which he has first to overcome. In a Norwegian fairy-tale, "Der Kamerad," [42] a

[39] In the *Huth-Merlin*.

[40] Cf. A. C. L. Brown, "The Bleeding Lance," p. 43.

[41] According to the views of many scholars, the above-mentioned text was not written by Robert de Boron and was reciprocally influenced by Chrétien's continuators.

[42] F. van der Leyen and P. Zaunert, *Die Märchen der Weltliteratur*, pp. 25–26 (No. 7).

princess has nightly intercourse with a troll and together they kill all of her admirers, until the arrival of the hero who is able to vanquish the troll. In a North German parallel story,[43] the troll is an old man who lives in a mountain and serves before an altar on which lies a prickly fish. This ancient one must be defeated before the hero can marry the princess.

Here the "old man in the mountain" is certainly Wotan awaiting the moment of his return and in the meanwhile (because he is not acknowledged or taken seriously) taking possession of the man's unconscious soul, the anima, in a sinister form. The game of chess, however, points rather to Kerunnus who is often portrayed with a games board.[44] Like Wotan's runes, all these games served the purpose of a divinatory investigation of the will of the gods. In Merlin the older image of God is probably resuscitated, an image in which aspects of Wotan are mingled with those of the archetypally related Kerunnus, an image of inner wholeness which presses its still unfulfilled claims on man. Similar to the above-mentioned fairy-tales, Merlin—always assuming that it was he who stood behind the water nixie—likewise constellates a somewhat dangerous fate for the hero. The task of finding the stag's head, which the Red Star Woman sets Perceval, might perhaps be taken to mean that the stag represents the Merlin-Mercurius who haunts the anima like an invisible lover and whom Perceval must first overcome before he can win her. But in this case, why should the Grail Bearer suddenly intervene and delay Perceval's finding of the stag? Supposing, as we have suggested, that Merlin were the divine contents of the Grail vessel, we would then be faced with a duplication of the motif. The secret aim of both figures is to lead Perceval to the symbol of the Self, but the Grail Bearer is more inclined to set him on the path of *a further development of the Christian symbol*, while the water nixie would guide him towards *a return to the pagan nature spirit*—the latter not necessarily to be

[43] "The Bewitched Princess," in *Die deutschen Märchen seit Grimm*, the same edition, pp. 237–38.

[44] This is quoted from Margarete Riemenschneider's as yet unpublished manuscript. She compares Kerunnus with the Hittite Rundas, who was also a stag-god and a god of play.

interpreted as something of inferior value. In the final analysis both women are striving in the same direction.

In this connection Garsales, the White Knight, could be interpreted as a Christian ethical attitude opposed to the intentions of the second anima. Since Merlin has both a Christ and an Antichrist aspect, the problem posed was almost insolubly difficult for medieval man who was incapable of thinking in paradoxes.

In the story, the stag appears in duplicated form, for which the following diagram might be considered:

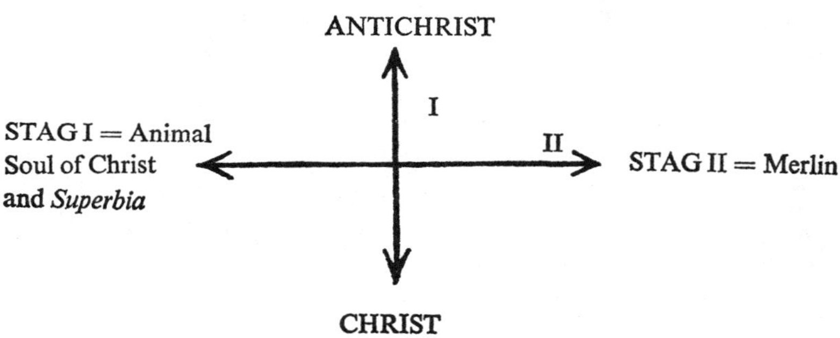

Inasmuch as he carries the animal components of the Christ symbol and, as the image of *superbia*, is impressed with devilish traits,[45] the first stag nailed to the tree is a central figure between the polar opposites of Christ and Antichrist. It is a *regressive* outer manifestation of the Redeemer, in which the light and dark sides *still* appear to be united. The second stag, pursued by Garsales, would be a progressive form of the manifestation, equivalent to Merlin, a saviour in whom the opposites appear closer together on a more conscious level. The axis of tension (Christ–Antichrist) illustrates the *moral* problem of good and evil, while the second axis (Stag I–Stag II) depicts the problem of the regression or progression of the life process and the danger of sinking back into the original pagan oneness instead of progressing to a renewed state of unity. It is not only the stag but

[45] Cf. above, p. 260.

also the figure of the anima which appears in duplicated form. This indicates an emotional uncertainty of outlook which it is obviously almost impossible to overcome at first. It does certainly require great breadth of consciousness and maturity of feeling in order to understand thoroughly a figure such as the alchemical Mercurius or the Merlin of the Grail legend. Until modern psychology uncovered the fundamental dual nature of man—the fact that he consists of a conscious and an unconscious personality, each of which compensates the other—such a realization was practically impossible; it was only with difficulty that the conscious mind was able to free itself from unequivocal single-track formulations. Furthermore, medieval man had still another task to accomplish, one which accorded with the upward striving so clearly revealed in the architecture of that age. He had risen from below, out of the darkness of unconsciousness and barbarism, and his problem was to overcome the purely natural condition in which primitive man is still held captive[46] and to assume a spiritual attitude. For this task the Christian doctrine provided not only the most complete expression but also offered help and guidance. Even today many people are still labouring over this problem; moreover, it is individually posed in every human life. Nevertheless, the problem for modern man is on the whole a different one, in so far as during the course of the centuries he has extensively identified himself with good, or with the spirit, and is therefore no longer below but above—or at least imagines himself to be above. It has therefore become necessary for him to retrace his steps to the dark instinctive side once more.

If the uniting of opposites into a synthesis was not possible in the Middle Ages, nevertheless, everything seems to point to the fact that our age is charged with the duty, if not of accomplishing this task then at least of taking it in hand.

The uncertainties of modern life will more and more compel people to concern themselves with their "other side," and it is

[46] The same condition is described in the myth of the Hopi American Indians, where the people at first live under the earth but, attracted by the light, take themselves ever higher up.

certainly not by chance that the findings of psychology are forging an instrument that can both show us the way and help us to accomplish the task. *The opening up of the unconscious* induces a broadening and deepening of consciousness which makes possible a new and better orientation, thus proving to be of invaluable assistance. Moreover, through the reanimation or inclusion of the archetypes—which are definitely not mere images but also *idées forces*, i.e. powers—it is precisely these powers which become available. In addition to knowledge and understanding, the influx of these forces into consciousness also makes it possible to bring about the required attitude which is necessary, as has already been explained at length, for the completion of the wholeness.

CHAPTER XXIII

Merlin's Solution of the Grail Problem

OF "PERCEVAL," the third part of Robert de Boron's (or his successor's) work, we will consider only the role of Merlin, since the rest of the action accords almost entirely with Chrétien and Wolfram von Eschenbach.[1] But unlike those versions, de Boron's "Perceval" begins not with the hero's youth but with Arthur's coronation, at that point where the "Merlin" section ends. Merlin appears during the coronation feast and is recommended to the King as counsellor. He tells Arthur about the three tables and prophesies that the King, like two British princes before him, will become King of France and Emperor of Rome. But first the Round Table must, through his efforts, achieve renown.

Whereupon the story of Joseph and the Grail is recounted once again. In addition, it is mentioned that Brons, the Fisher King, is now in one of the world's most beautiful spots—"*en ces îles d'Irlande*" ("in those isles of Ireland"). Things are going badly for him, however, for he has succumbed to a severe illness. Despite his great age, he will not be able to die until a knight of Arthur's Round Table succeeds in finding the court of the Fisher King. Should the knight then ask what purpose the Grail has served and is now serving, the sick King will straightway be healed and, after having imparted the secret words to the knight, will die. The spell under which Britain lies will consequently be broken.

The story now turns to Perceval's destiny. An event occurs at

[1] Hucher, *Perceval ou la Quête du Saint Graal, d'après le M. S. Didot*; and Weston, *The Legend of Sir Perceval.*

Arthur's court which has a special significance, since it reintroduces us to the problem of the *siége périlleux*. While lingering at the court, Perceval asks at the evening meal about the meaning of the empty place and begs permission to seat himself there, threatening departure should this be denied him. The King finally gives in to his importunities; but no sooner has Perceval settled himself than the stone seat splits with such a terrifying din that everyone present imagines the world is coming to an end. A great darkness falls and a voice reproves Arthur for having violated Merlin's commandment. "This Perceval," the voice says, "has undertaken the most hazardous enterprise that any man has yet ventured. From it the most arduous tasks will ensue, both for him and for all those of the Round Table." It is only because his father and grandfather (the Fisher Kings) found favour in the sight of God that Perceval was not swallowed up by the earth, as Moys had been when he wanted to sit in that place. The voice further informs them—as Merlin too had prophesied—that one of Arthur's knights is destined to find the Grail; whereupon the entire company prepares to set out in search of the Fisher King's dwelling. They take their departure and ride in company as far as the crossroads; there they separate so that each may seek the Grail on his own.

As we have seen, Merlin has already advised Arthur concerning the establishment of the Round Table; he has also mentioned the motif of Judas and has said that the empty seat, the *siège périlleux*, will be occupied for the first time by a knight who has found the Grail. By seating himself on it before accomplishing this deed, Perceval has disobeyed Merlin's command, as it were, and it is for this reason that the stone is sundered.

As is clear from the context, the empty place at the table, the dangerous seat reminiscent of Judas, symbolizes an unsolved problem, an unanswered question within the spiritual world of Christian chivalry. This unresolved question has to do with the problem of evil and of the betrayal of Christ. When Perceval sits in this seat he is *unwittingly* putting himself in the place of Judas, and this was obviously not intended. Even though he has to solve a problem related to the integration of evil, he was not meant to fall into its power unconsciously. Therefore, the stone seat splits under him, i.e. this occurrence is a miraculous portent which advises him of the fact that a split threatens the domain of the Christian knights of the Round Table, a split which can only be reconciled by the redemption of the Grail region. The sundered stone corresponds, so to speak, to the suffering Grail King[2] as a symbol of the Self in which the opposites are no longer united. *But it is Merlin who is cognizant of this task; it is he who has the new totality in mind and who tries to lead Perceval towards it.* In the "Perceval," after the hero has redeemed the Grail realm, there follows a very significant and peculiar epilogue[3] in which Merlin appears once more to impart the decisive information.

On this occasion Arthur is seated at the Round Table with his companions when a loud crash frightens them exceedingly. The stone which had split under Perceval is now joined together again. The assembled company does not know what this can mean, until Merlin appears and explains.

> "Know, Arthur, that in thy time the most sublime prophecy that was ever made has been fulfilled; for the Fisher King is healed, the spell under which Britain has languished is broken, and Perceval is become Lord of the Grail. From now on he will renounce chivalry and will surrender himself entirely to the grace of his Creator." When the King and his knights heard this they began to weep with one voice, and to pray God that He would bring it to a favourable conclusion.

The knights are distressed that the wonders and adventures have now come to an end. They feel superfluous; they consider that there is no point in remaining at Arthur's court; they would

[2] In so far—as we have sought to show above—as the Grail King is split, i.e. no longer able to hold the opposites together.

[3] As a separate story in expanded form it is known as "La Morte le Roi Artu," or "Mort Artu" for short, and forms the conclusion to the *Lancelot Grail* cycle. Cf. J. Frappier, *Etude sur le Mort le Roi Artu.* On the other hand, the material stems either from Geoffrey of Monmouth's *Historia* or from a French translation of the same. See Weston, *op. cit.*, Vol. II, Ch. 12. Cf. Faral, *La Légende Arthurienne*, Vol. III, pp. 274*ff*, where Arthur's withdrawal to Avalon is assigned to the year 542.

sooner go overseas and seek fresh fame. When Merlin's prophecy that Arthur is destined to become King of France and Emperor of Rome is recalled, preparations are made for a crusade to France, where Normandy, Brittany and other areas are to be conquered, in order subsequently to take the field against Rome. Arthur's nephew Mordred is named regent during the King's absence. On the march to Rome, news arrives that Mordred has seized power, as well as the Queen, for himself. This naturally occasions great consternation. The knights are ordered back to the fatherland, to punish the traitor Mordred, who has allied himself with the Saxons and is preparing a bloody reception for the returning forces. In long and terrible battles, every knight of the Round Table meets his death. Finally, Mordred also falls. Arthur, mortally wounded, is brought to Avalon,[4] where he is said to have been healed by his sister Morgana, who would appear to be one of the fairies of that island.

From the writer Blaise, to whom Merlin told it, Perceval now learns of the downfall of the Knights of the Round Table. This grieves him exceedingly, "for he had loved them much." Merlin appears in person at the Grail Castle to bid Perceval farewell, because it is God's will that henceforth he shall appear no more before people. However, he will not die until the end of the world, when everlasting joy will be his portion. He prepares for himself a concealed dwelling-place close to Perceval's house in the forest. "There will I live and prophesy whatever the Lord shall inspire in me, and all who see my abode will call it Merlin's *esplumeor*."[5] *The Grail legend also comes to an end with Merlin's disappearance.*

The meaning of the word *esplumeor*, a *hapax legomenon*, is uncertain. It may denote the magician's dwelling or that place where he lays aside his assumed form. According to another view, it might be taken to indicate someone who uses the pen. Jessie Weston[6] suggests that the word could signify a kind of

[4] Concerning Avalon cf. also Nitze, *Perlesvaus*, pp. 55–56.

[5] For this word cf. Zumthor, *Merlin le Prophète*, p. 166; and Helen Adolf, "The Esplumoir Merlin," p. 173.

[6] *The Legend of Sir Perceval*, Vol. II, Ch. 12, note 2.

bird cage in which falcons spent the moulting season; although this is nowhere attested to, the meaning would not fit too badly, in fact. In this connection, it might perhaps be construed to mean the place where Merlin moulted, i.e. underwent a transformation. A parallel to, if not the source of, the *esplumeor*, which strikes one as important, has been found by Helen Adolf in certain cabalistic literature.[7] This is the motif of the bird's nest in the Garden of Eden, into which the Messiah withdraws during the Last Judgment. The soul of the Messiah is there compared to a swallow in a nest.[8] The sheltering wings of the divinity, God's protective care for mankind, and the Shekinah also have a connection with this image. The bird's nest is therefore the "dwelling of God" in the cosmic tree. According to other texts, the new Messiah is there awaiting his time, reposing in Elijah's bosom.[9] Thus, Merlin's concealment resembles that of the Messiah and, like the latter, Merlin is expected to come again at the end of time. Merlin's essential seclusion, which he himself repeatedly emphasizes, could well be connected, psychologically speaking, with the fact that, as the *principium individuationis*, he portrays a mystery of the individual which cannot be realized collectively but which, pointing the way and bringing illumination, comes from time to time to the assistance of other solitary individuals. As we have seen, Merlin is also an incarnation of the *Deus absconditus* and is therefore just as unfathomable as the latter.

It is surprising that Perceval's discovery and possession of the Grail should have such a disastrous result as the abolition of the Round Table.[10] It is a feature peculiar to this form of the story that the Round Table is thought to be the third of the three tables which, taken together, represent the Trinity. The discoverer of the Grail, in this case Perceval, is the *tierz hom*, the third guardian of the Grail and therefore the representative of the Holy Spirit, whose era (according to Joachim of Floris) was awaited in the thirteenth century and in our story was expected

[7] "The Esplumoir Merlin," p. 173. [8] *Ibid.*, p. 176. [9] *Ibid.*, p. 182.

[10] It is only in de Boron's rendering that the "Mort Artu" is joined to the story of Perceval in this way.

to dawn with the finding of the Grail. How then does it make sense that the first result of this discovery is that this "third table," the Round Table, is abolished?

In the first place, as a more superficial explanation, it may be said that the dawning of a new age means at the same time the end of the previous one. The Round Table not only represented the coming era of the Holy Spirit but also the existing world of chivalry. This had reached its zenith, however, in the twelfth and thirteenth centuries, had even perhaps passed it, so that in the decline of the Round Table we can detect a premonition of the approaching end of the world of chivalry, a world which, with the coming of the Renaissance, had to give way to the bourgeois social order.

The fame and the ideal quality of the Round Table undoubtedly sprang from the union of the secular aspect with the spiritual—spiritual in so far as deeds of chivalry served a higher ethical goal. The same idea also underlay the orders of chivalry which were instituted at that time. The spiritual aspect of the Round Table can be seen in the way the knights made it their duty to search for the Grail. In our story this is very particularly emphasized by the fact that the Round Table was expressly established as the "third table."

At that time, Merlin had prophesied that the empty place at this table would at some future time be occupied by that best and most virtuous knight who should succeed in finding the Grail. Our author appears to have quite lost sight of this idea, for he does not return to it or explain why the prophecy was not fulfilled. Instead of occupying the *siège périlleux*, Perceval remains in the Grail Castle, renouncing chivalry in order to submit himself entirely to the grace of God ("*Il a pris a le cavalerié congié, et se volra desormais tenir a le grasse do son Creator*"). He thus becomes a holy man; in many versions he even deserts the Grail Castle in order to withdraw into the wilderness as an anchorite.

This solution would be an appropriate one for that time, although not in conformity with the tendencies outlined in the beginnings of the story which raised the expectation that Perceval would occupy the seat and take on the role of earthly representative of the Holy Spirit. Because he does not do this, the Round Table is to a certain extent deprived of the Spirit. No wonder, therefore, that the knights weep when they hear this; the inevitable result is the fatal drifting apart of the opposites of spirit and world, which became so evident just precisely in the Middle Ages. Because Perceval turns entirely to the spiritual, the Round Table now becomes altogether worldly. The Quest of the Grail, by which the world, i.e. chivalry, and the spirit, i.e. the life vowed to God, were to have been brought together, now loses its objective and in its place there appears a destructive striving after purely temporal power. The realm which Arthur wished to establish was neither that of the Grail nor of the Holy Spirit, but a material world dominion; a tendency we have already recognized as underlying Gauvain's restless wanderings.

It is a curious fact, moreover, that a literal Grail realm is mentioned only in the German versions of the legend. In the French versions the finder of the Grail is indeed a King, but he retires from the world, either into his castle or as a hermit in the wilderness, and dies, while the Grail itself is caught up into heaven.

It is only in Wolfram that the Grail King both administers an invisible, i.e. a spiritual, kingdom and is lord of an international brotherhood. The knights in Wolfram are called *templeise* (probably some sort of allusion to the Templars) and, as men raised to a certain degree of authority, they intervene in worldly affairs when necessary.[11] Feirefiz, Perceval's pagan half-brother who marries the Grail Bearer, is sent to India, there to establish just such another kingdom.

This brings us to a further point. It is not only the opposites of worldly versus spiritual matters that are moving apart but also those of the individual and the collective. The French Perceval not only renounces the world for religion but also surrenders collectivity in favour of individuality. An allusion to a phenomenon of the age may also be glimpsed here, namely the

[11] One example is Lohengrin. The Brotherhood of the Knights of the Grail or *Templeise* is suggestive of Arthur's Round Table, excepting that Arthur is not the Grail King.

emphasis on the individual, which likewise set in with the Renaissance and the increase in consciousness and to which the Reformation bears historical witness. In spite of Perceval's strange-seeming, virtuous, medieval monastic retirement, the fact that he has his cloister and his church, i.e. the Grail Castle, for himself, so to speak, could indicate an aspect of something which has come ever more into prominence since the Reformation: the idea of man's unmediated relation to God.

There is yet another aspect to be taken into account. As a "round thing" the Round Table expresses totality. The circle is indeed described as the most complete of all forms. In one passage in the *Queste del Saint Graal* it is stated that the Round Table signifies the roundness of the earth, the stars and the planets.[12] It is therefore also a totality which, moreover, is also expressed in the international character of its company. But at Arthur's Round Table a place is now empty, something is lacking for completeness.[13]

[12] Pauphilet, p. 76: "Après cele table fu la Table Reonde par le conseil Merlin, qui ne fu pas establie sanz grant sénéfiance, car en ce qu'ele est apelée Table Reonde est entendue la reondece del monde et la circonstance des planetes et les elemenz el firmament; et es circonstances dou firmament voit len les estoiles et mainte autre chose; dont len puet dire que en la Table Reonde est li monde senefiez a droit" ("Afterwards the Round Table was set up on Merlin's advice, and its establishment was not without significance, for it was called the Round Table to signify the roundness of the world. And the situation of the planets and the elements in the firmament, and in the circumstances of the firmament can be seen the stars and many other things; so that one could say that the world is rightly signified by the Round Table").

[13] A similar image of a round form from which something is missing appears in a vision of the Blessed Julienne, prioress of Mont-Cornillon near Liege (died 1258 in Namur). She saw the full moon in its brilliance, but a small section of its disk was missing. The vision appeared repeatedly until finally Julienne thought that possibly it contained some sort of mystery which she ought to understand. In answer to her prayers it was revealed to her that the moon represented the Church, but that the dark place in its disk showed that one feast was still missing from the yearly cycle, namely that of Corpus Christi, which should thenceforth be celebrated for increase of faith. The feast was actually introduced on the strength of this vision. From F. Browe, *Die Verehrung der Eucharistie im Mittelalter*, Ch. III. We would interpret this vision somewhat differently, rather in the sense of the empty place at Arthur's table which, as we know, represented the place vacated by Judas.

Perceval does not occupy this seat because, as a holy man far from the world, he is quite unable to do so. He could only have occupied it if in some way he had consciously taken upon himself the role of Judas, whose place it is, or if he had allied himself with the latter. As the opposite of Christ, the absolute Good, Judas incarnates the principle of Evil. It is not, however, a question of identifying with one of two mutually exclusive principles; what has to be redeemed is the hidden man, the Anthropos. In this Perceval does not succeed because, by choosing holiness instead of humanity, evil, as the opposite of good, is constellated anew. This is promptly manifested in the traitor Mordred,[14] again a kind of Judas who brings about the downfall of Arthur and his world—and his own ruin at the same time, to be sure. Wolfram finds a better, i.e. a more psychological, solution: in the end the reconciliation between Parzival and his heathen, black and white half-brother is achieved. The opposites are not so glaring here, of course, but are modified by the fact that Feirefiz is not evil, only pagan, and no enemy to the Grail.[15] It is obvious that only the bravest and noblest of all knights could occupy the *siège périlleux*, for it is an exceedingly arduous undertaking. Whoever might wish to achieve it would have to be capable of uniting good with evil into a whole. He would have to accomplish something similar to Christ's descent to earth to be born into human lowliness. The idea that the Son of God brings about the redemption of the world in this manner really shows that man, for his own part, should also do the same in order to redeem the as yet unredeemed "Adam"—man, that is, as he is really meant to be, the *true* man.

Expressed psychologically, this is the integration of the

[14] Interestingly enough, in a further formulation of the story of Merlin, belonging to the *Lancelot Grail* cycle, Mordred is said to be the son of Arthur and his half-sister Morgana. Morgana, as the wife of King Loth of Orkney, once visited Arthur's court, which resulted in a love affair between the two, who were ignorant of their relationship.

[15] In de Boron's version these opposites hardly appear, their presence is more implicit, i.e. good is in Christ and the Guardians of the Grail, evil in the sinners who were sent away and also, it might be suggested, in Judas and the *siège périlleux*.

shadow, as a result of which the gap in the circle is filled, its wholeness achieved. Judas' empty place—the void has a further numinous significance—is therefore extremely dangerous because anyone who occupies it thoughtlessly and without due authority is swallowed up by the earth. In other words, he who investigates evil all too easily becomes its victim.

Acceptance of the shadow naturally does not mean that special effort should be made to do evil; for the most part this will happen of its own accord. But it is important to recognize evil as such. This is by no means always easy, for the Devil seldom encounters us wearing horns and hooves or in the form of a dangerous serpent one would willingly avoid, but in a far more harmless, not to say seductive, aspect. Something considered to be particularly good is often secretly evil, in the same way that something basically good, or that leads to good, may at times appear to be evil. It is therefore impossible to characterize human behaviour either as always good or always bad. This relativization of the concept does not, however, imply an obliteration of the difference, for there exists in the human soul an inborn sense of right and wrong, whose verdict is incontestable. In our story, the Grail represents this court of justice, which could be described as the archetypal feeling or value judgment. That opposing tendencies are present in man is a fact of experience; formative and destructive forces are at work in him as they are in nature, to which he belongs.

The integration of the shadow consists in recognizing not only tendencies corresponding to conscious intentions or wishes but also those that are not in agreement or may even be in direct opposition.[16] At the other end of the scale, the identification with the light side implies an equally great danger. Whoever is caught in the sun's field of attraction and is drawn too close to it is burnt up. In this connection we are reminded of the apocryphal saying of Christ: "Who is near unto me is near unto the fire." For this reason the Grail, too, is dangerous and harms

[16] Concerning the psychological concept of the *shadow*, see *Psychology and Alchemy*, par. 36; Toni Wolff, *Einführung in die Grundlagen der komplexen Psychologie*, p. 108; and Jolande Jacobi, *The Psychology of C. G. Jung*, p. 109.

those who are not aware that they should keep the distance enjoined.[17]

It is significant that the Grail King, who should occupy Judas' seat, also sits in Christ's place, for Christ said to Joseph, "Sit thou in my place, as I sat during the meal." A certain identity or intimate connection therefore exists between the two seats; this is the reason they are placed side by side.

In our story, the medievally conditioned Perceval, who strives only upward, turns into an ideal figure or into one half of a pair of opposites and is unable to fill the empty place. The awaited Third Kingdom, that of the Holy Spirit, likewise remains an unfulfilled ideal. The reign of a thousand years, which should indeed be a reign of God upon earth, cannot be realized because of a renunciation of the world and of life. Perceval should not have taken himself into the seclusion of the Grail Castle; in order to remain in the picture, he should have brought the Grail to the Round Table, so that instead of the Spirit being divorced from the world, the world would have been impregnated by the Spirit.

[17] Cf. Hucher, *Le Saint Graal*, Vol. II, p. 307, where Nascien goes blind after looking inside the Grail vessel, and Pauphilet, *La Queste del Saint Graal*, pp. 255–56, where the same thing happens to Lancelot.

CHAPTER XXIV

The Disappearance of Merlin

IT IS TO some extent perhaps an expression of this unsolved problem of matter and spirit that Merlin, like Perceval, also withdraws from the world. As a creature of opposing origins, equipped with both divine and demonic qualities, he is indeed *the original man in need of redemption*—the archetype of the Anthropos. Either he disappears more and more into the wilderness of the forest or he allows himself, according to the Breton tales (not a part of the Grail cycle), to be bewitched by Vivien, the fairy who so captivates him by means of his own love-spell that he is unable to return to the human world.[1] This spell is an *enserrement* or *entombement* in a tower or a rock tomb, from which, as an invisible form, Merlin's spirit still often speaks to individual heroes.[2] Later, the word *esplumeor*, denoting his dwelling or his grave, was lost, and the only reference is to *Merlin's stone*, which heroes often come across in the course of great adventures.[3] The last that is heard of Merlin—when he vanishes under the fairy's spell—is the frightful, heart-rending cry with which he curses the woman and bewails his lot.[4]

In some of the variants of the story, Merlin's stone is later replaced by a tower in which are to be found the *Merveilles del Graal* (Wonders of the Grail), or by a bewitched bed which

[1] Cf. here Heinrich Zimmer's fine study, "Merlin." Zimmer evaluates Merlin's disappearance entirely positively, as a renunciation of worldly power and rationalism and as submission to the unconscious.

[2] Cf. Zumthor, *Merlin le Prophète*, pp. 218–19.

[3] Cf. *ibid.* Thus, in the "Lancelot," III, 275, we are told that Gauvain and his people "si vienent à une pierre qui a non li Perons Merlin" ("came to a stone which is a platform of Merlin"). In Girard d'Amiens this stone is called *Perron Merlin*, and in M. M. Bojardo, *Petron do Merlino*, pp. 220–21.

[4] Cf. Zumthor, *op. cit.*, p. 255.

inflicts madness.[5] According to the *Huth-Merlin* the bed is Balain's grave.[6] As a further wonder, Merlin builds in the sea a rotating island made of a metal wall and held fast by a magnet.[7] He is also supposed to have assembled the monoliths of Stonehenge.[8] Later he becomes the generalized archetypal image of the magician who fashions two metal dragons, erects copper ramparts around Carmarthen, invents seven league boots, and so on. The miraculous constructions, especially Stonehenge, the tower, the stone and the rotating island, are symbols of wholeness which closely resemble the stone and mandala symbolism in alchemy. The wonderful bed, reminiscent of the bed in Gauvain's adventures, once again stresses the identification of the wooden-legged man with Merlin.[9] The concept of a miraculous bed of this kind goes back to the legend of King Solomon who, according to the Song of Songs (3:7–8), possessed such a bed, which then became identified with his throne. According to late Jewish legends, whoever mounted this throne unlawfully would be wounded by a lion.[10] The throne is also described as a chariot or a *Minnebett* (bed of love). In alchemy[11] this bed is identified with the alchemical vessel and with the Bride of God; it symbolizes the place of unification, of the *unio mystica* with the divine, a place which is also surrounded by infinite danger, where he who lacks understanding falls victim to his drives and affects (the lion). As the constructor of the bed, Merlin is here identical with Solomon.[12]

It is of special importance that Merlin's grave in later versions is merged with the miraculous bed and the stone, or it is replaced by a house of glass into which Merlin disappears

[5] Cf. *ibid.*, pp. 218*ff.*

[6] *Ibid.*, p. 220.

[7] *Livre d'Arthur*, cited by Zumthor, p. 221.

[8] *Ibid.*, pp. 225*ff.*

[9] Probably copied from the Oriental legends of Solomon's throne or bed. Cf. Kampers, *op. cit.*, especially pp. 51*ff.*

[10] *Ibid.*, p. 25.

[11] *Aurora consurgens*, I, Ch. 12. See von Franz, *Aurora Consurgens*, pp. 227 and 378.

[12] Concerning the connection between the Grail and the legend of Solomon, cf. Kampers, *op. cit.*, pp. 38*ff.*

forever.[13] The house of glass bears a close resemblance to the Celtic legend of the revolving glass island, the island with four horns, which represents a land of the dead or of ghosts.

These later formulations confirm what we have already inferred in relation to the amply interpreted writings of Chrétien and de Boron. Merlin is the content of the Grail vessel (which is also a grace) or the spirit of the Grail stone. He is—in the language of the alchemists—the "spirit" of the stone, i.e. the Mercurius or, in psychological terms, the *principium individuationis*. Merlin's voice can be heard coming out of the stone which he has erected; this is the alchemical stone itself and *Perceval's real quest is to find it.* In the final analysis, therefore, Perceval and Merlin are one; although it is the seeking Christian man who is embodied in Perceval, while in Merlin it is a pagan impulse inciting to the search which at the same time is also the goal. The fact that Perceval and Merlin are not fully amalgamated is due to the relative incompatibility of the Christian spirit with that of alchemy, since in Christ, God became man by His own will, whereas the philosopher's stone is evolved into a new light-bringer through human intention and skill.[14] "In the former case," says Jung, "the miracle of man's salvation is accomplished by God; in the latter, the salvation or transfiguration of the universe is brought about by the mind of man—'Deo concedente,' as the authors never fail to add. In the one case man confesses 'I under God,' in the other he asserts 'God under me.' Man takes the place of the Creator. Medieval alchemy prepared the way for the greatest intervention in the divine world order that man has ever attempted: alchemy was the dawn of the scientific age, when the daemon of the scientific spirit compelled the forces of nature to serve man to an extent that had never been known before."[15] It is the demonism of this spirit which destined Merlin for the role of Antichrist. He did not take on this role, however, because he withdrew from the world and its power politics and resolved to serve only God

[13] Cf. Zumthor, *op. cit.*, p. 257.
[14] Cf. Jung, *Alchemical Studies*, pars. 163–64.
[15] *Ibid.*, par. 163.

in his "Calidon." In the *Huth-Merlin* he says, "*Je voel mieus m'ame sauver que la terre!*" ("I would rather save my soul than [possess] the earth!")[16] Man's power drive and his *superbia* are what make the scientific spirit dangerous; in itself, if it remained in *obsequio Domini*, it would be a light-bringer and a perpetuator of Christ's work of redemption. The ninth-century legend of Alexander says of the stone that it heals the lust for worldly power. Alexander finds a stone at the entrance to Paradise and hears the words: "If you would learn to know its nature and power, then leave all ambition far behind." Merlin has found this stone or has himself turned into it—for which reason he renounces the world.

In the later formulations of his character Merlin's renunciation of all worldly power expresses itself not merely by living withdrawn in the forest as an anchorite but also by surrendering, willingly/unwillingly, to the opposing power principle, the force of Eros. The reference here is to the curious motif in the Breton stories wherein Merlin, at the end of his life, is lulled to sleep by the magic he himself has taught to a fairy and, through the action of a spell, is confined for all time in a rock grave or a stone. In the *Vita Merlini* the fairy Morgana is a sister of Arthur and one of the nine fairies of the *Insula Pomorum* (Island of Apples—Avalon).[17] She is an evil sorceress who destroys her lover, something like Circe in the *Odyssey*. In the *Lancelot*[18] she creates a *Val sans Retour* (Valley of No Return) in which she confines her lovers. According to the Vulgate Merlin,she is called a *boine clergesse* (good clergywoman) and has a special understanding of astronomy and necromancy. She has been taught the latter by Merlin himself, for he is passionately in love with her[19] and has fallen completely into her power. She then turns the art against him.

The legends which centre round Merlin are resolved through one of two extreme solutions; according to some versions (Geoffrey of Monmouth and Robert de Boron) Merlin completely renounces the realm of Venus, while in others he falls

[16] *Huth-Merlin*, I, pp. 158–59, quoted Zumthor, *op. cit.*, p. 208.
[17] Zumthor, p. 238. [18] Quoted, *ibid.* [19] *Ibid.*, pp. 238–40.

into the fairy's power for all time. This latter figure is also called *la Dame du Lac* (the Lady of the Lake) or Morgana, a name which most authorities trace back to the Celtic water goddess Muirgen. The red-robed nixie in Chrétien's continuators also appears to be an analogous figure and has actually inherited her magic chessboard from Morgana.[20] In many versions, the fairy casts her spell over Merlin because she wishes to preserve her virginity—the same motif we have seen when Merlin's mother remained chaste even while falling into the power of the demonic incubus. In these versions, Merlin accordingly succumbs to a figure resembling his mother. Indeed, it is always a question of the same personification of the mother-anima-image in different forms.[21] In alchemy this figure has also been equated with Mercurius, who even appears there as "most chaste virgin." [22] Merlin and his fairy are personifications, as it were, of the one Mercurius in his masculine and feminine forms.[23] This may be why, in one version, the fairy lures Merlin into a cave in which lies an embalmed pair of lovers, representing his own double, so to speak. The fairy is also related to Aphrodite the foam-born[24] and to Venus, because at a later date her magic realm was compared with the Venusberg.[25] Her Breton sister is traced back to Diana, while Muirgen seems, rather, to be related to the Celtic Epona. Obviously, it is always a case of the same archetype, in connection with which the fairy receives now more positive, now more negative traits.[26] The negative evaluation of the sprite's union with Merlin is connected with the Christian prejudice towards the realm of Eros, from which it follows that the masculine and feminine are able to oppose each

[20] Cf. Marx, *La Légende Arthurienne*, p. 87.

[21] Concerning the anima as the derivative of the mother imago, cf. *Aion*, pars. 20*ff.*

[22] "The Spirit Mercurius," in *Alchemical Studies*, par. 273.

[23] J. Loth even thinks that this fairy was also a masculine Celtic deity.

[24] *Paracelsica*, p. 166.

[25] Venus appears in the funerary vessel in Christian Rosencrantz' *Chymical Wedding*.

[26] Concerning the problem of the anima in the Middle Ages, cf. also Antoinette Fierz-Monnier's outstanding dissertation, "Initiation und Wandlung."

other only in a battle for power; this induces intellectual suppression of Eros on the part of the masculine, imprisoning possessiveness on the part of the feminine. Love, in the broadest sense of the word, is missing. This prejudice was also conducive, in the later literature, to Merlin's inclusion in anti-feminist writings and his portrayal as the victim of an evil woman.[27] But even so, the final episode of Merlin's disappearance cannot be evaluated as unqualifiedly negative. Heinrich Zimmer puts it very beautifully:

> The wish-dream of virtue and good sense—to unravel the terrors and tangles of the thread of the world and to weave perfection into a carpet of ideal pattern— . . . cannot enter the mind of the wise Merlin, who sees the future ages unrolling like the present before his seer's eye. He gives his power of understanding pure unreason into the tenderly bewitching fingers . . . of Vivien's knowledge. In so far as Merlin knowingly surrenders himself to Vivien's bewitchment, to enchantment through the arts of enticement, knowing what he is handing over to her bit by bit . . . he raises himself to the calm untroubled heights of an Indian god, who withdraws unconcerned from the world into the stillness of the Self.[28]

We are reminded of Merlin's disappearance by yet another example from the realm of Oriental culture. Before his death, Lao-tse, so runs the legend, retired into the Western Mountain with a woman dancer. And yet—what a difference! Whereas Lao-tse gives no impression of being unfree or of languishing under a spell, Merlin's vanishing is an ill-starred and tragic destiny. Lao-tse's philosophy was an instrument of consciousness and functioned as a protection against being overwhelmed by the anima, whereas Merlin has only magical and necromantic knowledge which the fairy is able to steal from him. Far-reaching as is Western man's understanding of the outer world which surrounds him, it is balanced by a correspondingly

[27] Concerning this matter, cf. Zumthor, *op. cit., passim.*

[28] "Merlin," pp. 150–52.

infantile and primitive comprehension of the problems of anima and shadow and of the nature of the psyche in general. In the Middle Ages, this knowledge had not outgrown astrological and alchemical ideas, and it remained for Jung's psychology to discover the psychic contents relating to it. It also requires an unusual spiritual and ethical consciousness if this knowledge is not to fall back into the hands of the anima and regress into magic. It is common knowledge that, after his death, Lao-tse's learning deteriorated, in Taoism, into magic pure and simple. Modern psychology will undoubtedly have to contend with the same problem.

The figure of the Melusine also reappears in alchemy, especially in Paracelsus, where she dwells in human blood or "in an underwater Paradise" and appears as a phantom or, according to Gerhard Dorn, as a *visio in mente apparens* (vision appearing in the mind).[29] Like the Mercurial serpent, she possesses the capacity to cure diseases and to change her shape.[30] According to the Paracelsian Dorn she "must return to the watery realm."[31] The anima equally induces illusions and every possible aberration, for which reason the adept must confront her with wisdom and a capacity for discrimination. Jung says: "She [the Melusine] should no longer dance before the adept with alluring gestures, but must become what she was from the beginning: a part of his wholeness."[32] "The apparent contradiction between the rejection of the *gesta Melosines*[33] and the assimilation of the anima is due to the fact that the *gesta* occur in a state of anima possession, for which reason they must be prevented. The anima is thereby forced into the inner world, where she functions as the medium between the ego and the unconscious."[34]

It is interesting to consider how Wolfram von Eschenbach, the somewhat later and probably most important formulator of the Grail legend, has modified the motif of Merlin. His Merlin figure is the magician Clinschor, beside whom the *surziere* (sorceress) Cundrie steps boldly into the foreground; both are

[29] Cf. *Alchemical Studies*, pars. 179–80, and especially par. 214.
[30] *Ibid.*, par. 218. [31] *Ibid.*, par. 223. [32] *Ibid.*
[33] The deeds of the Melusine. [34] *Ibid.*, par. 223, note 15.

pronouncedly pagan figures. Clinschor is a eunuch who was castrated in the course of a love affair, after which he devoted himself solely to magic. He exhibits obvious connections with the figure of Solomon, with emphasis on the ill-omened aspect. In addition to this, however, Wolfram has included the well-known love affair of King Solomon and the Queen of Sheba (as elaborated in Oriental and Ethiopian[35] traditions) in his description of the relationship between Perceval's father, Gahmuret, and Belakane, from which the black and white Fierefiz is born. As for leaning towards the higher cultural tradition of the East, Wolfram succeeds in humanizing the relationship between the non-Christian wise man and the fairy; according to later traditions the Queen of Sheba belonged to the spirit world.[36] In Fierefiz, therefore, the light Christian and dark pagan spirits succeed in coming together on the human level. According to Max Wehrli,[37] the Orient signifies everything that has become unconscious. Like Prester John, Fierefiz's son is later the founder of a Christian Grail realm in India. Fierefiz and Parzival marry respectively the Grail Bearer, Repanse de Schoye, and Condwiramurs, one of her companions, thus bringing about a marriage *quaternio*, the significance of which, in relation to wholeness, has already been extensively discussed. On the other hand, Clinschor and Cundrie disappear. They, indeed, represent that "heathen" remnant of the figures of King Solomon and the Queen of Sheba which is incapable of assimilation. In Wolfram, the German spirit has been united with the cultural values of the Orient in an uncommonly fruitful manner, and it would seem as if it were possible to

[35] Cf. Kampers, *op. cit.*, p. 33; and Helen Adolf, "New Light on Oriental Sources of Wolfram's Parzival." Dr. Adolf derives Belekane from Makeda, the Ethiopian name of the Queen of Sheba. For the legend itself, cf. M. Griaule, "La légende illustrée de la Reine de Saba," and C. Bezold, "Kebra Nagast." See further, Enno Littmann, *The Legend of the Queen of Sheba*. Cf. W. Staude, "Die äethiopische Legende von der Königin v. Saba und die Parzival Erzälung des Wolfram von Eschenbach." To this should be added that in alchemistic literature the Queen of Sheba is called Bilqîs, which suggests a direct connection of name between her and Belekane.

[36] For examples see Kampers, *op. cit.*, pp. 33, 49, 67, 69 and 111.

[37] *Op. cit.*, p. 35.

humanize, i.e. to integrate, a more considerable part of the figure of Merlin through this detour connected with the assimilation of the East. Wolfram definitely possesses a "wisdom" (his connection with alchemy) which is lacking in the other formulators of the material, for it was the symbolic traditions of alchemy, whose value can scarcely be overestimated, which probably enabled him to assimilate the unconscious contents that had in part remained pagan. Thus he managed, as he tells us, "not to forswear God"[38] but, nevertheless, "to maintain the world."[39] In alchemy, he found that philosophical wisdom which makes possible the perilous middle way between a too great splitting off of the anima and the unconscious as a whole, and a dissolution into it. This implies a spiritual modesty which does not assert more than it knows[40] and which guards against precipitate judgments and seeks, *in obsequio Domini*, to

[38] Cf. B. Mockenhaupt, *Die Frömmigkeit im Parzival Wolfram von Eschenbach*, pp. 25*ff*. Cf. also F. Ranke, "La portée symbolique du Graal chez Wolfram von Eschenbach," pp. 226–27.

[39] Max Wehrli, "Wolfram von Eschenbach," says about this: "It would thus be incorrect only to interpret Parzival from above, as a mere exemplification of Christian doctrine. It is, indeed, in the nature of the art of courtly romance, and of romance as a class of literature in general, to undertake the adventure of emancipation and to press it forward into regions which are not restricted by dogma, and which, in any case, were not open to the pre-courtly sacred poetry of redemption. It is played out within a completely individual mythology, which looks as if it were in competition with the Christian mythos, and in spite of its analogies to the latter with its Oriental elements (alchemistic and astrological, among others), is not absolutely Christian in the strictest sense. There is food for thought in the fact that the knowledge of the most exalted mystery, the knowledge of the Grail, is attributed to Flegetanis, who on his father's side is a pagan, on his mother's a Jew and a descendant of Solomon. . . . However much this mythology of romance is brought into connection with the Christian teaching, it yet seeks—figuratively—to develop its own inherent natural understanding, and above all to make its own individual conquests in the realm of an expanded spiritual doctrine." Nevertheless, it is too little stressed in Wolfram that the anima problem is now only partly in evidence, and that (like Merlin and Vivien) Clinschor and Cundrie disappear, i.e. cannot be integrated.

[40] S. Singer calls Wolfram's work the Canticle of Doubt. But "doubt" is meant here in the modern sense of the world, and not as Wolfram himself uses *zwîvel*; for the latter meaning, cf. Peter Wapnewski, "Wolframs Parzival," p. 116. With this cf. Wehrli, *op. cit.*, p. 37.

grope after the meaning of the complications, problems and final goals laid down by life and the unconscious.

In the conclusion of his romance, Wolfram was able to bring the symbol of wholeness—as represented by the Grail stone and the marriage *quaternio*—closer to the consciousness of his age. This emerging symbol is also to be found in those other writers whom we have discussed; for after Merlin's disappearance, a stone, from out of which his spirit speaks, remains, as also does the Round Table. His legacy therefore is a symbol of the Self. But for all that it is only now that those premonitory intimations of the unconscious which are incarnated in the figure of Merlin —namely the task of the realization of the Self—are appearing, to penetrate into the consciousness of our own age. The image of the "third table," which Merlin commanded Arthur to construct and which had to be round like the world, strikes one as containing this idea of wholeness particularly clearly. It is a highly significant thought that just this most remote of goals, the Self, is expressed by the very oldest and simplest of archetypal images—the circle.[41] If we see it not only as a static image of wholeness but pursue the simile further, then it is also found to contain the following more profound meaning: as the sphere of the earth and its orbit are held in their course by the operation of two opposing forces, so the path of mortal man is also determined by similar powers. As a result of the dual effect of these forces, the circle, and roundness generally, first come into being. This narrow path between the opposites, which must be adhered to with the greatest constancy, because every deviation places the goal in question, is the way to the realization of the Self.

[41] Concerning this symbol of the "round thing," which is emerging so pressingly in our own time, cf. Jung, "Flying Saucers: A Modern Myth," in *Civilization in Transition.*

THE END

Bibliography

AACHEN, ALBERT VON. *Geschichte des ersten Kreuzzuges.* Jena, 1923.

ADELMANNUS. "De veritate corporis et sanguinis Christi." 1060.

ADOLF, HELEN. "The Esplumoir Merlin," *Speculum*, XXI (1946).

—— "New Light on Oriental Sources of Wolfram's Parzival." *Publications of the Modern Language Association of America*, Vol. 42 (1947).

—— *Visio Pacis, Holy City and Grail.* Pennsylvania State University, 1960.

ADSON, ABBOTT OF MOUTIER-EN-DER. "Epistola ad Gerbergam reginam, de ortu et tempore Antichristi." See SACKUR.

ALBERTUS MAGNUS. See *Theatrum chemicum.*

"Allegoriae sapientum . . . supra librum Turbae."
See *Theatrum chemicum.*

ALPHANDÉRY, P. and DUPRONT, A. *La chrétienté et l'idée de la Croisade.* Paris, 1959.

ANDERSON, FLAVIA. *The Ancient Secret.* London, 1953.

ANITCHKOF, E. "Le Graal et les Rites Eucharistiques." *Romania*, Vol. 55 (1929).

—— *Joachim de Flore et les Milieux courtois.* (Collezione Meridionale Editrice) Rome, 1931.

APULEIUS. *The Metamorphoses or The Golden Ass.*

ARNOLD, I. (ed.). *Le Roman de Brut de D. Wace.* 2 vols., Paris, 1938–40s

ARTIS AURIFERAE *quam chemiam vocant* . . . Basel, 1593. 2 vols. *Content. quoted in this volume:*

Volume I
(Aurora consurgens, quae dicitur Aurea hora [pp. 185–247]
Maria Prophetissa: Practica . . . [pp. 319–24]
Calid: Liber trium verborum [pp. 352–61]
Tractatulus Avicennae [pp. 405–37]

AUGUSTINE, SAINT. In *Evangelium Johannis Tractatus.*

"Aurelia occulta philosophorum." See *Theatrum chemicum.*
"*Aurora consurgens.*" See ARTIS AURIFERAE.
AVICENNA. "De arte Alchemia." See ARTIS AURIFERAE.
BÄCHTOLD-STÄUBLI, B. (ed.). *Handwörterbuch des deutschen Aberglaubens.* Berlin/Leipzig, 1936.
BAEDEKER. *Palästina.*
BALE, J. *Illustrium maioris Britanniae scriptorum summarium.* Ipswich, 1548. See also MIGNE, *Pat. Lat.*
BARTSCH, K. (ed.). *Parzival* by Wolfram von Eschenbach. Leipzig, 1927–29.
BAYNES, CHARLOTTE. *A Coptic Gnostic Treatise.* Cambridge, 1933.
BENES, BRIGIT. *Spuren von Schamanismus in der Sage von Buile Suibne.* Zeitschrift für keltische Philologie, 1961.
BENOIST, JEAN. *Histoire des Albigeois et des Vaudois.* Paris, 1691. 2 vols.
BERNARD OF TREVISO. See *Theatrum chemicum* and TANCK.
Bernardi Grafen von der Marck und Tarvis Chymische Schriften. See TANCK.
BERNHEIMER, R. *Wild Men in the Middle Ages.* Cambridge, Mass., 1952.
BERTHELOT, MARCELIN. *Collection des anciens alchèmistres grecs.* Paris, 1887–88. 3 vols.
BEYERLE, K. "Das liturgische Leben der Reichenau." In *Die Kultur der Abtei Reichenau.* Munich, 1925.
BEZOLD, C. "Kebra Nagast." *Abh. der Phil.-hist. Klasse der Bayr. Akad. der Wiss., 23, 2.* Munich, 1905.
—— (ed.). *Die Schatzhöhle.* Munich, 1883–86.
BEZZOLA, R. "Guillaume IX et les origines de l'amour courtois." *Romania*, Vol. 66.
—— *Les origines et la fonction dc la littérature courtoise en Occident.* Paris, 1944.
—— *Le sens de l'Aventure et de l'Amour.* Paris, 1947.
Bibliographical Bulletin of the International Arthurian Society. Paris.
Bibliotheca chemica curiosa. See MANGETUS.
BIETENHARD, H. *Die himmlische Welt in Urchristentum und Spätjudentum.* Tübingen, 1951.
BIRCH-HIRSCHFELD, B. A. *Die Sage vom Graal.* Leipzig, 1877.
BLACK ELK. *Black Elk Speaks.* Ed. Neihardt. Lincoln, 1961.
BOGDANOW, FANNI. *The Romance of the Grail.* Manchester University Press, 1966.
BOLTE, J. and POLIVKA, G. *Anmerkungen zu den Kinder- und Hausmärchen der Brüder Grimm.* 1913*ff.* 5 vols.
BONNET, H. *Reallexikon der ägyptischen Religionsgeschichte.* Berlin, 1952.

Book of Adam and Eve. See MALAN.

Book of the Cave of Treasures. See BUDGE.

BORON, ROBERT DE. *Roman de l'Estoire dou Graal* ("Josef d'Arimathie," "Merlin," "Perceval"). See MICHEL; FURNIVAL; HUCHER; NITZE.

BOUCHÉ-LECLERQ, AUGUSTE. *L'Astrologie grecque.* Paris, 1899.

BOUSSET, W. *Der Antichrist.* Göttingen, 1845.

BRAUN, J. *Liturgischen Handlexikon.*

BREUGLE, RICHARD L. *King Arthur of Britain.* New York, 1964.

BROWE, P. *Die Verehrung der Eucharistie im Mittelalter.* Munich, 1933.

BROWN, A. C. L. "The Bleeding Lance." *Publications of the Modern Language Association of America,* Vol. XXV (1910); New Series, Vol. XVIII.

—— *The Origin of the Grail Legend.* Cambridge (Mass.), 1943.

BROWN, D. A. *Bibliography of Critical Arthurian Literature.*

BRUCE, J. D. *The Evolution of Arthurian Romance from the Beginnings down to the Year 1300.* Johns Hopkins Press, Baltimore, 1923; 2nd edition, Göttingen and Baltimore, 1928.

BRUGGER, E. "L'Enserrement Merlin." *Zeitschrift für französische Sprache und Literatur,* Vol. 29.

—— "Die Nodons-Nuadu Hypothese als Erklärung des Namens des Fischerkönigs". *Romance Philology,* IX (1956).

BRUNEL, CLOVIS. "Les 'hanches' du Rois Pêcheur." *Romania,* LXXXI.

BUDGE, WALLIS. *The Book of the Cave of Treasures.* London, 1927.

—— *The Life and Exploits of Alexander the Great, being a series of translations of the Ethiopic histories of Alexander by the Pseudo-Callistenes and other writers.* London, 1896.

BURDACH, K. "Der Graal." *Forschungen zur Kirchen- und Geistesgeschichte,* Vol. 14. Stuttgart, 1938.

BÜTTNER, H. (ed.). *Meister Eckeharts Schriften und Predigten.* Jena, 1909.

CAESAR, JULIUS. *De Bello Gallico.*

CAESARIUS OF HEISTERBACH. *Dialogus miraculorum.* See STRANGE.

CALDWELL, R. A. "Wace's *Roman de Brut* and the variant version of Geoffrey of Monmouth's *Historia regum Britanniae.*" *Speculum,* 1956.

CALID. *Liber trium verborum.* See ARTIS AURIFERAE.

CAMBRENSIS, GIRALDUS. *Itinerarium Cambriae or Itinerary through Wales.* Everyman's Library.

CAMPBELL, C. A. *Die Tempelritter.* Stuttgart, no date.

CAMPBELL, J. F. *Popular Tales of the West Highlands.* Edinburgh, 1862.

CAMPION, J. and HOLTHAUSEN, F. (eds.). *Sir Perceval of Gales*. Alt- und Mittelenglische Texte, Vol. 5. Heidelberg, 1913.

CAPPELLANUS, ANDREAS. *De amore libri tres*. Ed. E. Trojel. Copenhagen, 1892; English version, see PARRY.

CHRÉTIEN DE TROYES. *Li Contes del Graal*. See HILKA.

Christliche Adamsbuch. See DILLMANN.

CHWOLSOHN, D. *Die Ssabier und der Ssabismus*. St. Petersburg, 1856. 2 vols.

CODEX ASHMOLE. 1420. Fol. 26, the Bodleian Library, Oxford.

COLLUM, C. C. "Die schöpferische Muttergöttin." In *Eranos-Jahrbuch*. Zurich, 1938.

CONNELLY, MARC. *The Green Pastures*. New York, 1930.

CORBEIENSIS, S. PASCHASII RADBERTI ABBATIS. *Lib. de corpore et Sanguine Domini*. See MIGNE, *Pat. Lat.*

DEINERT W. *Ritter und Kosmos im Parzival*. Munich, 1960.

DIBELIUS, M. "Die Isisweihe des Apuleius und verwandte Initiationsriten." *Bitzungsber. der Heidelberger Akad. der Wiss., Phil.-hist. Klasse*, 1917.

Didot-Perceval. See ROACH.

DIELS, H. *Fragmente der Vorsokratiker*. 6th edition, 1951.

DIEZ. *Etymologisches Wörterbuch der romanischen Sprachen*. 5th edition. Bonn, 1887.

DILLMANN, A. (ed.). *Christliches Adamsbuch*.

DÖLGER, F. J. *Ichthys*. 1910. 2 vols.

DORN, GERHARD. "Philosophia chemica." See *Theatrum chemicum*.

—— "Speculativae philosophiae . . ." See *Theatrum chemicum*.

—— "De transmutationibus metallorum" See *Theatrum chemicum*.

DUPRONT, A. "La Chrétienté et l'idée de la Croissade." Paris, 1954.

ECKHART, MEISTER. *Schriften*. Ed. H. Büttner. Jena. 1934.

EGINHARD. *Vie de Charlemagne*. "Les classiques de l'historie de France." Paris, 1923.

EISLER, R. *Orpheus—the Fisher*. London, 1921.

ELIADE, MIRCEA. *Shamanism*. New York, 1964.

—— "La vertu créatrice du Mythe." In *Eranos-Jahrbuch*, XXV. Zurich, 1965.

Elucidation. See THOMPSON.

"L'Estoire del Saint Graal." See *Lancelot Grail*.

"L'Estoire de Merlin." See *Lancelot Grail*.

EVANS, S. *The High History of the Holy Grail*. London, 1903.

EVOLA, J. *Il Mistero del Graal*. Fribourg i. Br. and Bari, 1937.

FARAL, E. *La Légende Arthurienne*. Paris, 1929. 2 vols.

—— *Recherches sur les sources latines des Contes et Romans courtois du moyen-âge*. Ancienne Librarie Honoré Champion. Paris, 1913.

FIERZ-DAVID, LINDA. *The Dream of Poliphilo*. New York, 1950.

FIERZ-MONNIER, ANTOINETTE. "Initiation und Wandlung." Berne, 1951.

FORDHAM, MICHAEL. *Children as Individuals*. London and New York, 1970.

FOURQUET, J. *Wolfram d'Eschenbach et le Conte del Graal*. Paris, 1938.

FOX, J. C. "Marie de France". *English Historical Review*, XXV.

FRANZ, MARIE-LOUISE VON (ed.). *Aurora Consurgens: A Document Attributed to Thomas Aquinas on the Problem of Opposites in Alchemy*. Translated by R. F. C. HULL and A. S. B. GLOVER. New York, 1966.

FRAPPIER, J. *Etude sur la Mort le Roi Artu*. Paris, 1936.

FRAZER, SIR JAMES. *The Golden Bough*. London, 1911–15. 12 vols.

FROBENIUS, LEO. *Erythräa, Länder und Zeiten des heiligen Königsmordes*. Berlin, 1931.

FURNIVALL, F. (ed.). *Seynt Graal or the Sank Ryal* (Robert de Boron). London, 1861–63.

GASTER, MOSES. "The Legend of the Grail." In *Studies and Texts*. London, 1925–28.

GEOFFREY OF MONMOUTH. *Historia regum Britanniae*. See HAMMER; GRISCOM.

GLASER, O. *Skythenkörige als Wächter des heiligen Goldes*. Archiv für Religionswissenschaft, Vol. 34, 3/4.

GOSSEN, C. "Zur etymologischen Deutung des Grals." *Vox Romanica*, Vol. XVIII, 2.

Grand Saint Graal. See *Lancelot Grail*.

GRIAULE, M. "La Légende illustrée de la Reine de Saba." In *Documents*, 9th year of publication, No. I. Paris, 1930.

GRIFFITH, R. H. *Sir Perceval of Galles*. Chicago, 1911.

GRISCOM, ACTON (ed.). *Historia regum Britanniae* (Geoffrey of Monmouth). London, 1929.

GRIMM. *Fairy Tales*.

GUBERNATIS, A. DE. *Die Thiere in der indogermanischen Mythologie*. Leipzig, 1874.

HAGEN, P. *Der Graal*. Strasburg, 1900.

HAIGHT, ELIZABETH. *The Life of Alexander of Macedon*. New York, 1955.

HAMMER, J. DE. *Mémoire sur deux coffrets gnostiques du moyen âge*. Paris, 1832.

HAMMER, JAKOB (ed.). *Historia regum Britanniae* (Geoffrey of Monmouth). 1951.

Handwörterbuch des deutschen Aberglaubens. See BÄCHTOLD-STÄUBLI.

HARDING, M. ESTHER. *The Way of All Women.* Revised edition, New York, 1970.

HASTINGS, J. *Encyclopaedia of Religion and Ethics.* Edinburgh, 1921.

HAUER, J. W. *Der Yoga als Heilsweg.* Stuttgart, 1932.

HAUCKS, A. *Realencyclopaedie für Theologie und Kirche.* Leipzig, 1877–88.

HEISTERBACH, CAESARIUS VON. See STRANGE.

HELINANDUS. *Chronicle. c.* 1204.

HERODOTUS. *Historiae.*

HERTZ, W. *Die Sage von Parzival und dem Graal.* Breslau, 1882.

HILKA, ALFONS (ed.). *Der altfranzösische Alexanderroman.* Halle, 1920. (Includes LEO's *Historia de Préliis.*)

—— (ed.). *Der Percevalroman von Chrétien von Troyes* (*Li Contes del Graal*). Halle, 1932.

HIPPOLYTUS. *The Refutation of all Heresies.* 1911.

HOFER, SAINT. *Chrétien de Troyes Leben und Werken.* Graz, 1954.

HOLMES, URBAN T. and KLENKE, AMELIA. *Chrétien de Troyes and the Grail.* University of North Carolina Press, 1959.

HOMER. *The Odyssey.*

HONORIUS OF AUTUN. *Elucidarium.* In MIGNE, *Pat. Lat.*

—— *Gemma Animae.* In MIGNE, *Pat. Lat.*

HOPFNER, T. (ed.). *Über Isis und Osiris* (Plutarch). Prague, 1940.

HUCHER, E. (ed.). *Perceval ou la Quête du Saint Graal, d'après le M.S. Didot.* Le Mans, 1878.

—— (ed.). *Le Saint Graal, ou Josef d'Arimathie: Première Branche des Romans de la Table Ronde* (Robert de Boron). Le Mans, 1874–78.

HURWITZ, S. *Die Gestalt des sterbenden Messias.* Zurich, 1958.

Huth-Merlin. See PARIS & ULRICH.

IRENAEUS, SAINT. *Adversus* (or *Contra*) *haereses libri quinque.* See MIGNE, *Pat. Lat.*

ISELIN, L. E. *Der morgenländische Ursprung der Graalslegende.* Halle, 1909.

Iter ad Paradisum der Alexandersaga. Ed. J. Zacher. Königsberg, 1859.

JACOBI, JOLANDE. *The Psychology of C. G. Jung.* London, 1942; New York, 1943.

JARMAN, A. O. H. *The Legend of Merlin.* University of Wales Press, 1960.

JEREMIAS, A. *Handbuch der altorientalischen Geisteskultur.* Leipzig, 1913.

"Josef d'Arimathie." See BORON.

JOUBAINVILLE, ARBOIS DE. *The Irish Mythological Cycle and Celtic Mythology*. London, 1903.

JUBINAL, A. *La Légende Latine de S. Brandaines*. Paris, 1836.

JUNG, CARL GUSTAV. *The Collected Works of C. G. Jung*. London, New York and Princeton, especially the following:

Aion. Vol. 9 (2). 1959.
Alchemical Studies. Vol. 13. 1967.
The Archetypes and the Collective Unconscious. Vol. 9 (1). 1959.
The Development of Personality. Vol. 17. 1954.
Mysterium Coniunctionis. Vol. 14. 1963.
The Practice of Psychotherapy. Vol. 16. 1954.
Psychology and Alchemy. Vol. 12. 1953.
Psychology and Religion. Vol. 11. 1958.
Structure and Dynamics of the Psyche. Vol. 8. 1960.
Symbols of Transformation. Vol. 5. 1956.
Two Essays on Analytical Psychology. Vol. 7. 1953.

—— *Kindertraumseminar*, 1938–1939. Zurich, privately printed.

—— *Psychological Types*. London and New York, 1923.

—— See also KERENYI.

JUNG, EMMA. *Animus and Anima*. New York, 1957.

JUNK, V. "Graalsage und Graalsdichtung des Mittelalters." *Sitzungsber. der Kais. Acad. der Wiss. Wien, Phil. -hist. Klasse*, Vol. 168. 1911.

KAHANE, HENRY and RENÉE. "Proto-Perceval und Proto-Parzival." *Zeitschrift für romanische Philologie*, Vol. 79, 3/4. Tübingen, 1963.

—— "Wolframs Gral und Wolframs Kyot." *Zeitschrift für deutsches Altertum und Literatur*, Vol. 89. 1959.

KAMPERS, F. *Das Lichtland der Seelen und der heilige Gral*. Cologne, 1916.

KEMPE, DOROTHY. *The Legend of the Holy Grail*. London, 1905; reprinted 1934.

KERENYI, KARL. "Seele und Griechentum." Seminar at the Psychotechnischen Institut, Zurich, 1943–44.

KERENYI, KARL and JUNG, C. G. *An Introduction to a Science of Mythology* (British Title), London, 1950; *Essays on a Science of Mythology* (American title), New York, 1949.

KLENKE, AMELIA. "Liturgy and Allegory in Chrétien's Perceval." *University of California Studies in the Romance Languages*. 1951

—— "The Spiritual Ascent of Perceval." *Studies in Philology*, LII.

—— See also HOLMES.

KLUGE, F. *Etymologisches Wörterbuch der deutschen Sprache.* Berlin, 1957.

KÖHLER, ERICH. "Die drei Blutstropfen ins Schnee." *Germanisch-romanische Monatschrift,* Vol. 40. 1959.

—— *Ideal und Wirklichkeit in oler höfischen Epik.* Tübingen, 1956.

—— *Trobador Lyrik und Höfischer Roman.* Berlin, 1962.

KOLB, HERBERT. *Munsalvaesche: Studien zum Kyotproblem.* Munich, 1964.

KROPP, A. *Ausgewählte koptische Zaubertexte.* Brussels, 1931.

LAMBSPRINCK. *De Lapide Philosophico.* Frankfurt, 1652. See also MUSAEUM HERMETICUM.

Lancelot Grail ("L'Estoire del Saint Graal," "L'Estoire de Merlin," "Li Livres de Lancelot," "La Queste del Saint Graal" and "Le Morte Artu"). See SOMMER.

LANGFORS, A. (ed.). *Histoire de l'Abbaye de Fécamp.* Annales Academiae Scientiarum Fennicae, Vol. XXII. Helsinki, 1928.

Légendes bretonnes. Paris, 1912.

LEISEGANG, HANS. *Die Gnosis.* 2nd edition. Jena.

—— "The Mystery of the Serpent." In *The Mysteries,* Vol. 2 of the Papers from the Eranos Yearbooks. Edited by JOSEPH CAMPBELL. New York, 1955.

LEJEUNE, RITA. "La date du Graal de Chrétien de Troyes." Le Moyen-Age, LX.

LEO. *Historia de Préliis.* See HILKA.

LEWIS, L. M. *Joseph of Arimathea at Glastonbury.* 1937.

LEYEN, F. VAN DER and ZAUNERT, P. (eds.). *Die Märchen in der Weltliteratur.* Jena.

"Liber Alphidii." See CODEX ASHMOLE.

"Liber Platonis quartorum." See *Theatrum chemicum.*

LINCY, LE ROUX DE. *Essai sur l'Abbaye de Fécamp.* Rouen, 1840.

——. *Livre des Légendes.* Paris, 1836.

LINKER, R. W. *The Story of the Grail* (Li Contes del Graal). Chapel Hill, 1952.

"Li Livres de Lancelot." See *Lancelot Grail.*

Litterature des XII et XIII Siècle. Paris, 1956.

LITTMANN, ENNO. *The Legend of the Queen of Sheba.* Bibliotheca Abessinica, Vol. 1. Leiden, 1904.

LOCKE, F. W. *The Quest of the Holy Grail.* University of California Press, 1960.

LODS, JEANNE. *Les Lais de Marie de France.* Paris, 1959.

LOOMIS, ROGER SHERMAN (ed.). *Arthurian Literature in the Middle Ages.* Oxford, 1959.

—— *Arthurian Tradition and Chrétien de Troyes.* New York, 1949.

—— *Celtic Myth. and Arthurian Romance.* New York, 1949.

—— "The Grail in the Perceval Saga." *Germanic Review*, XXXIX. March, 1964.

LOSCH, F. *Balder und der weisse Hirsch.* 1892.

LOT-BORODINE, M. "Le conte del Graal." *Romania*, LXXVIII.

LOT, S. "Nouvelles Etudes sur la Provenance du cycle Arthurian." *Romania*, XXVIII, 1899, p. 321.

LUC, B. "Le Graal pyrénéen." *Archives de Mont Segur et du Saint Graal.* Published under the direction of F. W. Wheeler.

LÜERS, GRETE. *Die Sprache der deutschen Mystik des Mittelalters.* Munich, 1926.

Mabinogion, The. See RHYS.

MACCULLOCH, JOHN ARNOTT. *The Religion of the Ancient Celts.* Edinburgh, 1911.

MACDONALD, A. J. *Berengar and the Reform of Sacramental Doctrine.* London and New York, 1930.

MAGNIEN, W. *Les Mystères d'Eleusis.* Paris, 1950.

MAIER, MICHAEL. *Symbola Aureae Mensae.* Frankfurt, 1614.

MALAN, S. C. (trans.). *The Book of Adam and Eve.* London, 1882.

MALORY, SIR THOMAS. *Le Morte d'Arthur.* Ed. J. Rhys, Everyman's Library. See also VINAVER.

MALOU, J. B. *Du culte du Saint Sang de Jésus-Christ et de la rélique de ce Sang qui est conservée a Bruges.* Bruges, 1927.

MANESSIER. See ROACH.

MANGETUS, JOHANNES JACOBUS (ed.). *Bibliotheca chemica curiosa, seu Rerum ad alchemiam pertinentium thesaurus instructissimus. . . .* Geneva, 1702. 2 vols. *Contents referred to in this volume:*

Volume I

Hermes Trismegistus: Tractatus aureus de lapidis physici secreto [pp. 400–45]

Turba philosophorum [pp. 445–65; another version, pp. 480–94]

Allegoriae sapientum supra librum Turbae philosophorum XXIX distinctiones [pp. 467–79]

Volume II

Rosarium philosophorum [pp. 87–119]

MARIE DE FRANCE. See LODS; WARNKE.

MARX, JEAN. "Le Cortège du Château des Merveilles." *Etudes celtiques*, IX (1960).

—— *La Légende Arthurienne et le Graal.* Paris, 1952.

—— *Medium Aevum*, XXIII.

MERGELL, BODO. *Der Gral in Wolframs Parsifal.* Halle, 1952.

"Merlin." See BORON.

MEYER, E. H. *Die Mythologie der Germanen.* Strassburg, 1903.

MICHA, ALEXANDRE. *La Tradition Manuscrite des Romans de Chrétien de Troyes.* Paris, 1939.

MICHEL, FRANCISQUE (ed.). *Le Roman du Saint Graal* (Robert de Boron). Bordeaux, 1841.

MIGNE, JACQUES PAUL (ed.). *Patrologia Latina.* Paris, 1844–64. 221 vols.

MOCKENHAUPT, B. *Die Frömmigkeit im Parzival Wolfram von Eschenbachs.* Bonn, 1942.

Modern Language Quarterly. Seattle, Univ. of Washington Press.

MONTGOMERY, A. *Aramaic Incantation Texts from Nippur.* University of Pennsylvania Press, 1913.

"Le Mort Artu." See *Lancelot Grail.*

MUSAEUM HERMETICUM *reformatum et amplificatum . . . continens tractatus chimicos XXI praestantissimos. . . .* Frankfurt, 1678. *Contents referred to in this volume:*

[Hermes Trismegistus:] Tractatus aureus de lapide philosophorum [pp. 1–52]

Lambspringk: De lapide philosophico figurae et emblemata [pp. 337–72]

MUSTARD, HELEN M. and PASSAGE, CHARLES E. (eds. and trans.). *Parzival.* New York, 1961.

MYLIUS, JOHANN DANIEL. *Philosophia reformata.* Frankfurt, 1622.

NELLI, R. (ed.). *Lumière du Graal.* Paris, 1951.

NENNIUS. *Historia Britonum.* See WINDISCH.

NEUMANN, ERICH. *The Great Mother.* New York, 1953.

—— *The Origins and History of Consciousness.* New York, 1954.

NEWSTEAD, HELAINE. *Bran the Blessed in Arthurian Romance.* New York, 1939.

NINCK, MARTIN. *Wodan und germanischer Schikalsglaube.* Jena, 1935.

NITZE, W. A. "The Bleeding Lance and Philip of Flanders." *Speculum*, 1946.

—— "The Fisher King and the Grail in Retrospect." *Romance Philology*, VI.

—— "The Fisher King in the Grail Romances." *P.M.L.*, XXIV, 1909.

—— "Messire Robert de Boron, Enquiry and Summary." *Speculum*, April, 1953.

—— *Perceval and the Legend of the Holy Grail.*

—— (ed.). *Perlesvaus*. 1937.

—— (ed.) *Le Roman de l'Estoire dou Saint Graal* (Robert de Boron). Les Classiques français de moyen-âge. Ancienne Librarie Honoré Champion. Paris, 1927.

—— "The *Siège Périlleux* and the *Lia Fail* or Stone of Destiny." *Speculum*, 1956.

NITZE, W. A. and JENKINS, T. ATKINSON (eds.). *Le haut livre du Graal, Perlesvaus*. University of Chicago Press, 1932.

NUTT, A. T. *The Legends of the Holy Grail.* London, 1902.

—— *Studies on the Legend of the Holy Grail.* London, 1888.

ORIGEN. *De Principiis*. In MIGNE, *Patrologiae Latina.*

O'SHARKEY, EITHNE. "The Maimed King in Arthurian Romance." *Etudes celtiques*, VIII, fasc. 2 (1959).

OTTO, RUDOLF. *The Idea of the Holy*. Translated by JOHN W. HARVEY. Oxford, 1926.

PALGEN, R. *Der Stein der Weisen: Quellenstudien zum Parzival.* Breslau, 1922.

PARIS, G. and ULRICH, J. (eds.). "*Merlin*," *Roman en prose du XIIIe siècle* (*Huth-Merlin*). For the Société des anciens Textes français. Paris, 1886.

—— (eds.) *Trois Versions rimées de l'Evangile de Nicodème*. Société des anciens textes français, vol. for 1885.

PARRY, J. J. *The Art of Courtly Love.* Columbia University Press, 1941.

—— "The Vita Merlini." *Studies in Language and Literature*, August 1925, No. 3. University of Illinois.

PAUPHILET, A. (ed.). *La Queste del Saint Graal.* Les classiques français du moyen âge. Paris, 1923.

—— "Au Sujet du Graal." *Romania*, LXVI (1940–41).

PEEBLES, ROSE JEFFRIES. "The Legend of Longinus in Ecclesiastical Tradition and in English Literature and Its Connection with the Grail." Bryn Mawr College Monographs, Vol. IX. Baltimore, 1911.

"Perceval." See BORON.

"Peredur." See *The Mabinogion.*

Perlesvaus. See NITZE & JENKINS.

Petit Saint Graal. See BORON.

Pistis Sophia. Edited and translated by G. R. S. Mead. London, 1955.

PLATO. *The Collected Dialogues of Plato.* Edited by Edith Hamilton and Huntington Cairns. New York, 1961.

"Platonis Liber quartorum." See *Theatrum chemicum.*

PLESSNER, M. "Hermes Trismegistus and Arabian Science." *Studia Islamica*, II (1945).

PLUTARCH. See HOPFNER.

POKORNY, J. *Der Graal in Irland und die mythischen Grundlagen de Graalsage.* Mitt. der Anthropolog. Gesellschaft. Vienna, 1918.

PONSOYE, P. *L'Islam et le Graal.* Paris, 1957.

POPE, A. U. "Persia and the Holy Grail." *The Literary Review*, I (1957).

POTVIN, C. (ed.). *Wauchier de Denain.*

"Practica Mariae." See *Artis auriferae.*

PROCLUS. *Commentaries on the Timaeus of Plato.* Translated by Thomas Taylor. London, 1820. 2 vols.

PROSPER OF AQUITAINE. *De Promissione, et praedicatione Dei.*

PRZYLUSKI, J. "Ursprung und Entwicklung des Kultes der Muttergöttin." In *Eranos-Jahrbuch 1938.* Zurich.

PSEUDO-CALLISTENES. See BUDGE.

PSEUDO-WAUCHIER. See ROACH.

"La Queste del Saint Graal." See *Lancelot Grail.*

Queste del Saint Graal. See PAUPHILET.

RADIN, PAUL. *The Trickster.* Commentaries by Karl Kerenyi and C. G. Jung. London, 1956.

RAHN, O. *Der Kreuzzug gegen der Graal.* Fribourg, 1933.

RANKE, F. "La portée symbolique du Graal chez Wolfram von Eschenbach." In *Lumière du Graal.* See NELLI.

—— "Zur Symbolik des Grals bei Wolfram von Eschenbach." *Trivium*, IV.

REITZENSTEIN, RICHARD. *Poimandres.* Leipzig, 1904.

Die Religion in Geschichte und Gegenwart. Tübingen, 1910.

REUSNER, HEIRONYMUS. *Pandora: Das ist, die edelst Gab Gottes, oder der Werte und heilsame Stein der Weysen.* Basel, 1588.

RHYS, J. *The Arthurian Legend.* Oxford, 1891.

—— *Celtic Folklore.*

—— (ed.). *The Mabinogion.* Translated by Lady Charlotte Guest. Everyman's Library.

—— (ed.). *Sir Thomas Malory's "Le Morte d'Arthur."* See MALORY.

RICHSTÄTTER, K. *Die Hertz-Jesu-Verehrung des deutschen Mittelaters.* 2nd edition. Munich, 1924.

RINGBOM, L. J. *Graltempel und Paradies.* Stockholm, 1951.

RIPLEY. *Opera omnia chemica.* Cassel, 1649.

ROACH, W. (ed.). *The Continuations to the Old French Perceval by Chrétien de Troyes* (Pseudo-Wauchier, Wauchier de Denain and Manessier). University of Pennsylvania Press, 1949.

—— (ed.). *The Didot-Perceval According to the MSS of Modena and Paris.* University of Pennsylvania Press, 1941.

ROCHAT, A. *Über einen bisher unbekannten Percheval li Galois.* Zurich, 1855.

ROLLESTON, T. W. *Myths and Legends of the Celtic Race.* London, 1911,

ROQUES, MARIO. *Le Graal de Chrétien et la Demoiselle du Graal.* Geneva and Lille, 1955.

—— *Studies in Philology*, XLIV.

Rosarium philosophorum. See MANGETUS.

ROSCHER, W. H. *Lexicon der griechschen und römischen Mythologie.* 1884–1937.

—— *Omphalos*, Vol. 29. Abh. der Phil. -hist. Klasse der Kgl. sächs. Akad. der Wiss. Leipzig, 1913.

RUSKA, JULIUS (ed.). *Tabula smaragdina.* Heidelberg, 1926.

—— (ed.). *Turba philosophorum.* Quellen und Studien zur Geschichte der Naturwissenschaften und der Medizin, I. Berlin, 1931

SACKUR, E. (ed.). *Sibyllinische Texte und Forschungen.* Halle, 1898.

SANDKÜHLER, K. *Die Geschichte des hl. Graal.* Stuttgart, 1958.

SAN MARTE. *Die Sagen von Merlin.* Halle, 1853.

SCHÄRF-KLUGER, RIVKAH. *Satan in the Old Testament.* Northwestern University Press, 1968.

SCHARFENBERG, ALBRECHT VON. *Jüngere Titurel.* 1270.

SCHEFTELOWITZ, J. "Das Fischsymbol in Judentum und Christentum". *Archiv für Religionswissenschaft*, Vol. 14 (1911).

SCHOLL, G. R. F. (ed.). *Diû Krône.* 1852.

SCHROEDER, L. VON. "Die Wurzeln der Sage vom heiligen Graal". *Sitzungsberichte der Kais. Akad. der Wiss. Phil. -hist. Klasse*, Vol. 166. Vienna, 1910.

SCHWIETERING, J. *Mystik und höfische Dichtung im Hochmittelalter.* Tübingen, 1962.

SCOTT, W. *Heremetica.* 4 vols. Oxford, 1924.

SÉCHELLES, D. DE. *L'Origine du Gral.* Saint Priene.

Secret of the Golden Flower. Translated by Cary F. Baynes, with commentaries by Richard Wilhelm and C. G. Jung, London and New York, 1931; new edition, 1962.

SENIOR. *De Alchemia.* 1566.

SINGER, S. *Wolfram und der Gral.* Bern, 1939.

SINNER, J. R. VON. "Catalogus Codicum MSS. Bibliothecae Bernensis." *Bernae,* Vol. II (1770).

SKENE, W. F. *Four Ancient Books on Wales.* Edinburgh, 1868.

SOMMER, H. O. *The Vulgate Version of the Arthurian Romances* (the *Lancelot Grail*). Washington, 1908–16.

SOUVESTRE, E. *Le Foyer Breton.* 1845.

"Speculativa philosophia." See *Theatrum chemicum.*

STAERK, W. *Über den Ursprung der Graalslegende.* Tübingen and Leipzig, 1903.

STAPEL, W. (ed.). *Parzival* by Wolfram von Eschenbach. Munich, 1950.

STAUDE, W. "Die äethiopische Legende von der Königin von Saba und die Parzival Erzählung des Wolfram von Eschenbach." *Archiv für Völkerunde,* XII. Vienna, 1957.

STEIN, W. J. *Weltgeschichte im Lichte des heiligen Graal.* Vienna, undated.

STERZENBACH, T. *Ursprung und Entwicklung der Sage vom heiligen Gral.* Münster/Westphalia, 1908.

ST. HOFER. *Chrétien von Troyes Leben und Wirken.*

STRANGE, J. (ed.). *Dialogus Miraculorum* by Caesarius von Heisterbach. Cologne, 1851.

SUHTSHEK, F. VON. "Herrn W. von Eschenbachs Reimbereitung oder Pârsiwalnâms." *Klio,* 1932.

—— "Die iranischen Quellen in Wolframs Parsifal." *Zeitschrift der Deutschen Morgenl. Gesellschaft,* Vol. 82 (1926) and Vol. 83 (1930).

—— "Wolfram von Eschenbachs Pârsivalnâmâ-Übersetzung." *Forschung und Fortschritt,* VII (1931).

Syrische Schatzhöhle. Ed. C. Bezold. Munich, 1886.

Talmud Sanhedrin. "Der babylonische Talmud." *Hebr. u. deutsche,* Vol. 7. Berlin, 1842.

TANCK, JOACHIM (trans.). *Des Bernardi Grafen von der Marck und Tarvis Chymische Schriften.* Nuremberg, 1746.

THEATRUM CHEMICUM, *praecipuos selectorum auctorum tractatus . . . continens.* Ursellis, 1602. 3 vols. Vol. IV, Strasbourg, 1613; Vol. V. Argentorati, 1622; Vol. VI, Argentorati, 1661. *Contents quoted in this volume:*

Volume I
Dorn: Speculativae philosophiae, gradus septem vel decem continens [pp. 255–310]
Dorn: Philosophia chemica. . . . [pp. 472–517]
Dorn: Congeries Paracelsicae chemicae de transmutationibus metallorum [pp. 557–646]
Bernard of Treviso: Liber de alchemia [pp. 773–803]

Volume II
Albertus Magnus: Super arborem Aristotelis [pp. 524–27]

Volume IV
[Beatus] Aurelia occulta [pp. 462–512]

Volume V
Turba philosophorum [pp. 1–57]
Allegoriae sapientum . . . supra librum Turbae [pp. 64–100]
Liber Platonis quartorum . . . [pp. 114–208]

THOMPSON, A. W. *The Elucidation: A Prologue to the Conte del Graal.* New York, 1931.

THUERLIN, HEINRICH VON DEM. *Diû Krône.* See SCHOLL.

TISCHENDORF, W. C. VON. *Evangelia Apocrypha.* Leipzig, 1876.

"Tractatus aureus Hermetis." See *Musaeum Hermeticum.*

TREVELYAN, G. M. *History of England.* London, 1926.

"Turba philosophorum." See MANGETUS, RUSKA and *Theatrum chemicum.*

VERGIL. *Aeneid.*

VINAVER, E. (ed.). *The Works of Sir Thomas Malory.* Oxford, 1947. 3 vols.

VINCENT DE BEAUVAIS. *Speculum historiale.* 1624.

—— *Speculum naturale.* See MIGNE.

"Vita Merlini." See PARRY.

VITALIS, ORDERICUS. *Histoire de la Normandie.* Ed. by M. GUIZOT. Caen, 1826.

WACE, D. *Le roman de brut.* Paris, 1939. See also ARNOLD; CALDWELL.

WACE, D. and LAYAMON. *Arthurian Chronicles.* London, 1937.

WAITE, A. E. *The Holy Grail; its Legends and Symbolism.* London, 1933.

WALDBERG, E. (pub.). *Deux Versions inédites de la Légende de l'Antéchrist en Vers Français de XIIIe Siècle.* Skrifter Utgivna av Kungl. Humanistiska Vetenskapssamfundet I Lund (Acta Reg. Societatis Humaniorum Litterarum Ludensis), Vol. XIV.

WAPNEWSKI, PETER. "Wolframs Parzival." *Studien zur Religiosität und Form.* Heidelberg, 1955.

WARNKE, M. (ed.). *Lais de Marie de France.* Oxford, 1944.

WAUCHIER DE DENAIN. See POTVIN; ROACH.

WECHSSLER, E. *Die Sage vom heiligen Gral.* Halle, 1898.

WEHRLI, MAX. "Wolfram von Eschenbach." *Der Deutschunterricht,* V (1954).

WEISMANN, H. *Das Alexandergedicht des XII Jahrhunderts vom Pfaffen Lamprecht.* Frankfurt, 1850.

WESSELOFSKY, A. VON. *Zur Frage uber die Heimat der Legende vom heiligen Graal.* Archiv für slawische Philologie, XXIII, 1901.

WESTON, JESSIE L. *From Ritual to Romance.* Cambridge University Press, 1920.

—— *The Legend of Sir Perceval.* London, 1909.

—— *The Quest of the Holy Grail.* London, 1913.

WILCKE, W. F. *Geschichte des Tempelherrenmordens.* Leipzig, 1826.

WILLIAMS, CHARLES and LEWIS, C. S. *Arthurian Torso.* Oxford, 1969.

WILLIAMS, CHARLES ALLYN. "Oriental Affinities of the Legends of the Hairy Anchorite." *University of Illinois Studies,* No. 2 (May 1925).

WILLIAMS, MARY. "Some Aspects of the Grail Procession." *Folklore,* LXXI (1960).

WILLIAMS, R. (ed.) *Y Saint Graal.*

WILSON, HARRY B. "Apocryphal Gospels and the Arthurian Romance." *Zeitschrift für roman. Philologie,* 75 (1959).

—— "The Grail King in Wolfram's Parzival." *Modern Language Review,* LV, 4, 1960.

WINDISCH, E. "Das Keltische Brittanien bis zu König Arthur." *Abh. der Phil. -hist. Klasse der Kgl. sächs. Gesellsch. der Wiss.,* Vol. XXIX, No. VI. Leipzig, 1912.

WOLFF, TONI. "Einführung in die Grundlagen der Komplexen Psychologie." In *Die Kulturelle Bedeutung des Komplexen Psychologie.* Zurich, 1935.

WOLFRAM VON ESCHENBACH. *Parzival.* See BARTSCH; MUSTARD & PASSAGE.

WOLFS, WERNER. "Der Vogel Phoenix und der Graal." *Studien der deutschen Philologie des Mittelalters,* 1950.

WUNDERLICH, EVA. "Die Bedeutung der roten Farbe im Kultus der Griechen und Römer." In *Religionsgeschichtliche Versuche und Vorabeiten.* Giessen, 1925.

Y Saint Graal. See WILLIAMS, R.

ZACHER, J. *Pseudokallisthenes.* Halle, 1867.

ZARNCKE, F. "Der Graaltempel." *Abh. der Phil. -hist. Klasse der Kgl. sächs, Gesellsch. der Wiss.*, Vol. XVII. Leipzig, 1879.

—— "Der Priester Johannes." *Abh. der Phil. -hist . . . der Wiss.*, Vol. XVII. Leipzig, 1879.

ZIMMER, HEINRICH. "Merlin." *Corona*, IX, 2 (1939). Munich and Berlin.

—— *Der Weg zum Selbst.* Zurich, 1954.

ZUMTHOR, P. *Merlin le Prophète.* Lausanne, 1943.

Index

Other Titles from Sigo Press

The Unholy Bible *by June Singer*
$24.95 cloth, $12.95 paper

Emotional Child Abuse *by Joel Covitz*
$17.95 cloth, $10.95 paper

Longing for Paradise *by Mario Jacoby*
$21.95, $12.95 paper

The Psychology of C. G. Jung, Vol. I *by C. A. Meier*
$25.50 cloth,

Puer Aeternus *by Marie-Louise von Franz*
$17.95 cloth. $10.95 paper

Dreambody *by Arnold Mindell*
$17.95 cloth, $11.95 paper

Encounters with the Soul *by Barbara Hannah*
$17.00 cloth, $10.50 paper

Dreams of a Woman *by Sheila Moon*
$17.95 cloth, $11.95 paper

Images of the Self *by Estelle L. Weinrib*
$17.95 cloth, $12.95 paper

Sandplay *by Dora M. Kalff*
$12.95 paper

Death of a Woman *by Jane Hollister Wheelwright*
$12.95 cloth

You may purchase Sigo Press titles from your local bookseller or, if unavailable, directly from Sigo Press at 77 North Washington Street, Room 201, Boston, MA 02114.